Skill, Technology and Enlightenment:
On Practical Philosophy

ARTIFICIAL INTELLIGENCE AND SOCIETY

Series Editor: KARAMJIT S. GILL

Bo Göranzon (Ed.)

Skill, Technology and Enlightenment:
On Practical Philosophy

Springer-Verlag
London Berlin Heidelberg New York
Paris Tokyo Hong Kong
Barcelona Budapest

Bo Göranzon
Mathematician and Researcher, Swedish Center for Working Life,
Box 5606, S-11486, Sweden

Cover illustration by Lennart Mörk

ISBN-13:978-3-540-19920-5   e-ISBN-13:978-1-4471-3001-7
DOI: 10.1007/978-1-4471-3001-7

British Library Cataloguing in Publication Data
A catalogue record for this book is available from the British Library

Library of Congress Cataloging-in-Publication Data
A catalog record for this book is available from the Library of Congress

Typeset from author's disc by Editburo, Lewes, East Sussex, England

69/3830-543210 Printed on acid-free paper

Preface

This book has one of its main starting points in the international conference on *Skill and Technology: On Diderot, Education and the Third Culture*, held in Stockholm in September 1993. This conference brought together 100 researchers and artists in the fields of technology, philosophy, the history of ideas, divinity, literature, economics, chemical physics, the creative and performing arts etc. The three opening addresses to this conference, by Lars Löfgren, Artistic and Managing Director, the Royal Dramatic Theatre, Stockholm, Janne Carlsson, Vice Chancellor of the Royal Institute of Technology, Stockholm, and Anders L. Johansson, Director of the Swedish Institute for Worklife Research, Stockholm, are reproduced after this preface.

The book has another starting point in the Dialogue Seminar held at the Royal Dramatic Theatre in Stockholm by the Swedish Institute for Worklife Research and the Royal Institute of Technology, Stockholm. Over the past five years workshops related to the Dialogue Seminar have been held in Norwich, Stockholm, Bodø, Cambridge, Innsbruck, Moscow, Paris and London. One of the workshops took as its theme *Beyond All Certainty*, a dramatization of the meeting between Alan Turing and Ludwig Wittgenstein, their destinies and their respective views of knowledge. The play, written by Bo Göranzon and Anders Karlqvist and performed by the Great Escape Theatre Company, the University of East Anglia, Norwich, has been played to audiences in Stockholm, Norwich, Cambridge and Bodø, with the performances being followed by workshops. The results of the work on *Beyond All Certainty* are presented in Section IV of this book.

The contours of the Skill and Technology research field and a multitude of issues that require thorough investigation are presented in this and the five preceding books in this series. They are:

(i) *Knowledge, Skill and Artificial Intelligence* (eds. Bo Göranzon and Ingela Josefson, Springer-Verlag, 1988)
(ii) *Artificial Intelligence, Culture and Language: On Education and Work* (eds. Bo Göranzon and Magnus Florin, Springer-Verlag, 1990)
(iii) *Dialogue and Technology: Art and Knowledge* (eds. Bo Göranzon and Magnus Florin, Springer-Verlag, 1991)

(iv) *Skill and Education: Reflection and Experience* (eds. Bo Göranzon and Magnus Florin, Springer-Verlag, 1992)
(v) Bo Göranzon: *The Practical Intellect: Computers and Skills* (Springer Verlag & UNESCO, Paris, 1992).

A description of the research field and the contents of these six books are to be found in the last section and the appendix of this book.

The Swedish Work Environment Fund has given financial support to this research and development.

Many people have made important contributions and given their personal support to developing the research field of Skill and Technology. They include Professor Albert Danielsson, Industrial Economics and Organization, the Royal Institute of Technology, Stockholm; Professor Kjell S. Johannessen, the Institute of Philosophy, University of Bergen; Professor Tore Nordenstam, Institute of Philosophy, University of Bergen; Ingela Josefson, Assistant Professor, the Swedish Institute for Worklife Research, Stockholm; Magnus Florin, Dramaturgist, and Lennart Mörk, scenographer and artist, the Royal Dramatic Theatre, Stockholm; Professor Allan Janik, Brenner Archive, Innsbruck University; Professor Stephen Toulmin, The Center for Multiethnic and Transnational Studies, University of Southern California, Los Angeles; Jon Cook, Director, Centre for Creative and Performing Arts, University of East Anglia, Norwich; Professor Richard Ennals, Kingston Business School, Kingston University; Rolf Hughes, author and researcher, Centre for Creative and Performing Arts, University of East Anglia, Norwich; Lars Kleberg, Assistant Professor, Counsellor for Cultural Affairs, The Swedish Embassy, Moscow; Mr. Peter Gullers, photographer, Uppsala, Sweden; Jan Erik Degerblad, Doctor of Technology, The Swedish Work Environment Fund; Jan Unenge, Assistant Professor, Department of Mathematics, University of Jönköping; Bengt Molander, Assistant Professor, Department of Philosophy, Gothenburg University. It is a privilege to work with such professional people.

I had the opportunity to take the post of Visiting Fellow at Clare Hall College, Cambridge University from September 1992 to June 1993. During this time I worked on the shape of this book. I am very grateful to Professor Nicholas Lash, Faculty of Divinity, Cambridge University, and Göran Prinz-Påhlson, author and researcher, Cambridge, for their excellent support.

I would like to pay special tribute to Jon Cook for his contribution to the shaping of this book and to Rolf Hughes for his excellent summaries of chapters. Struan Robertson has shown a notable ability to stimulate progress in the final stages of the book, and had overall responsibility for the English translations.

The contributors to this book represent a wide variety of thinking in this field, and their individual styles of writing also vary. They have, for example, chosen to express the third person singular as "he, she" or even "s/he". To avoid making extensive changes and unnecessary distinctions the chapters are published with the authors' usage unchanged. Similarly, the preferences of individual authors as to notes or references have also been followed.

Stockholm   *Bo Göranzon*
August 1994

Addresses

Address by Janne Carlsson, Vice-Chancellor, the Royal Institute of Technology, Stockholm

In the introduction to the program for this seminar Bo Göranzon asks, "Why Diderot?" Why should a seminar on culture and technology centre round Diderot? In his introduction, Bo gives a rational explanation, which I need not repeat here.

What Bo does not mention is that there is a natural connection between Diderot and the earlier Dialogue seminar dealing with the remarkable Swedish instrument builder, Georg Bolin.

Diderot was – in addition to everything else – an expert on musical instruments and acoustics. He himself wrote the articles on instruments in the French Encyclopedia. He is famous for his ability to describe instruments, not only their technical details, but also their timbre.

I represent the Royal Institute of Technology, KTH, founded in 1827, i.e., 33 years after the École Polytechnique in Paris. Why are we, a technical university, here at the Royal Dramatic Theatre? Well, the main reason is Professor Bo Göranzon, his Dialogue Seminars, and his program on Skill and Technology.

At KTH we try to awaken awareness in our students of their future role and their responsibility for the development of our society. We also encourage them to study the humanities, and our teachers to include non-technical aspects – humanistic, social, ecological – in their courses.

Creating an educational program of this kind requires us to have faculty members who are truly involved in and committed to the idea of broadening the curriculum in the humanistic direction. We have these people in, for instance – and I should perhaps say mainly – the group of Professor Danielsson and Professor Göranzon. We appreciate your work very much.

We at KTH should be devoted to these ideas. Since the 1870s our logotype has included the motto "Vetenskap och konst" (Science and Art). It is a constant reminder to us not to forget non-technical aspects in our daily actions.

Diderot gave me an association to Georg Bolin. I am sure that most of us make another association as well. We connect Diderot with Jean le Rond d'Alembert, the other great name behind the French Encyclopedia, which was published from 1750 to 1780.

D'Alembert was a mathematician, philosopher and natural scientist. His well-known principle of mechanics has played an important role in the development of mechanics and the related parts of the engineering sciences.

His main philosophical thesis was that all our knowledge is based on experience. This – I understand – is a central idea behind the work of the "Skill and Technology" group.

Perhaps it would be an interesting endeavor for the "Skill and Technology" group to reflect upon the relations and the cooperation between the two editors of the French Encyclopedia, one representing science, the other art: the two cultures. Could that possibly be a topic for a future seminar?

But first we have an interesting Diderot seminar to look forward to. On behalf of KTH I welcome you all, and extend a special welcome to our friends from abroad.

Address by Lars Löfgren, Artistic and Managing Director, the Royal Dramatic Theatre, Stockholm

In almost ten years of dynamic encounters between art and the world of work, dialogue as a reflection on experience has grown to become an international event at the Royal Dramatic Theatre in Stockholm. Denis Diderot, the encyclopaedist, saw the work of the actor as a model for knowledge in action. But in the theatre we know that the performance only evolves and becomes material through the participation of the audience; first when the portrayals of the actors are seen by an audience, then through the influence of the language and, last but not least, through the audience's personal insights into the parts, the empathy which in turn creates experience and involvement. In this way, the audience influences the actors' interpretation of their parts, and thus becomes both a prerequisite for, and a part of, the performance itself. The reflection of experience is always essential if work is to produce good results. "A good painting is never produced other than by a master who has done a great deal of reflecting, meditation and work. Drawing a good sketch requires talent, and talent cannot be acquired. However, time, patience and work confer the ability to achieve excellence, and this ability can be acquired," writes Diderot. But there must be someone who sees and experiences the excellence of the accomplishment. Without "you" there is no "I", either at work or in private life. Dialogue is a precondition for the very existence of society.

Address by Anders L. Johansson, Assistant Professor, Director of the Swedish Institute for Worklife Research

It is my belief that this conference will give us not only the opportunity to meet eminent scientists from other countries, it will give us the opportunity to highlight one of the most important dilemmas in our modern society: the growing gap between democracy and the wishes of the people on the one hand, and the logic of science, technology and modern technocracy on the other.

From the perspective of Skill and Technology we are able to identify different groups in our society: those who, by virtue of their work and professions, are committed and take an active part in progress and development, and those who are marginalized and only passive parties to this process.

As I see it, the study of this technology and science-based tension between democracy and technocracy is of outstanding importance.

As a consequence of this dilemma there is a growing risk that we will underestimate and even ignore practical skill and ordinary worklife experience. And we have clearly come a long way since then!

It is my hope that this conference will mark a new chapter, a new starting point in research in:
- skill and technology
- democracy and technology, and
- the use of language.

I am convinced that our institute, together with the Royal Institute of Technology and such eminent researchers as Stephen Toulmin, Allan Janik, Bo Göranzon and Ingela Josefson to mention just a few, will, as the result of this conference, have the capacity to develop important research programs.

In short, I am confident that this will be a productive meeting and a conference of great importance for forthcoming research on skill and technology.

Contents

SECTION VII. Epilogue

Contributors

Christopher Bigsby
Director, Professor, Arthur Miller Centre, University of East Anglia, Norwich, NR4 7TJ, UK

Peter Brödner
Dr.-Ing, Head of Production Systems Dept, Institut Arbeit und Technik, Florastrasse 26-28, D-45879, Gelsenkirchen, Germany

Janne Carlsson
Vice Chancellor, Professor, Royal Institute of Technology, S-10044 Stockholm, Sweden

Jon Cook
Director, Centre for Creative and Performing Arts, University of East Anglia, Norwich, NR4 7TJ, UK

Albert Danielsson
Professor, Department of Industrial Economics and Management, Royal Institute of Technology, S-10044 Stockholm, Sweden

Richard Davies
Actor, Researcher, The Centre for Applied Research in Education, University of East Anglia, Norwich, NR4 7TJ, UK

Richard Ennals
Professor, Kingston Business School, Kingston University, Kingston Hill, Kingston upon Thames, KT2 7LB, UK

Magnus Florin
Dramaturgist, The Royal Dramatic Theatre, Box 5037, S-10241 Stockholm, Sweden

Bo Göranzon
Doctor of Technology, Swedish Institute for Worklife Research, Box 5606, S-11486 Stockholm; Adjunct Professor, Skill and Technology, Royal Institute of Technology, S-10044 Stockholm, Sweden

Lars Gustafsson
Author, Adjunct Professor, Department of Philosophy, Austin University, 2312 Tower Drive, Austin, TX 78703, USA

Paul Henry
President, Collège International de Philosophie, 20 Avenue des Gobelins, 750 05 Paris, France

Marian Hobson
Professor of French, Queen Mary and Westfield College, London, and 21 Church Lane, Trumpington, Cambridge, CB2 2LA

Rolf Hughes
Author and Researcher, Centre for Creative and Performing Arts, University of East Anglia, Norwich, NR4 7TJ, UK

Jon Hyde
Director, Great Escape Theatre Company, 34 Trinity Street, Norwich, NR2 3BE, UK

Allan Janik
Professor, Brenner Archive, Innsbruck University, A-6020 Innsbruck, Austria

Anders L. Johansson
Director, Assistant Professor, Swedish Institute for Worklife Research, Box 5606, S-11486 Stockholm, Sweden

Ingela Josefson
Doctor, Linguist, Swedish Institute for Worklife Research, Box 5606, S-11486 Stockholm, Sweden

Erland Josephson
Author, Actor, Royal Dramatic Theatre, Box 5037, S-10241 Stockholm, Sweden

Anders Karlqvist
Professor, Department of Architecture, Royal Institute of Technology, S-10044 Stockholm, Sweden

Lars Kleberg
Assistant Professor, Culture Counsellor, Swedish Embassy, Ulitsja Mosfilmovskaya 60, 119 590 Moscow, Russia.

Nicolas Lash
Professor, Faculty of Divinity, Cambridge University, St John's Street, Cambridge, CB2 1TW, UK

Lars Löfgren
Artistic and Managing Director, The Royal Dramatic Theatre, Box 5037, S-10241 Stockholm, Sweden

Jon Monk
Professor, Faculty of Technology, The Open University, Walton Hall, Milton Keynes, MK7 6AA, UK

Igor Naletov
Professor, The Institute of Philosophy, Academy of Science, Moscow, Russia

Tore Nordenstam
Professor, Department of Philosophy, University of Bergen, Sydenyplass 9, N-5000 Bergen, Norway

Dag Prawitz
Professor, Department of Philosophy, University of Stockholm, Skeppargatan 4, S-11452 Stockholm

Göran Printz-Påhlson
Author, Clare Hall College, Cambridge University, Cambridge, CB3 9AL, UK

Michael Robinson
Professor, School of Languages and European Studies, University of East Anglia, Norwich, NR4 7TJ, UK

E.S. Shaffer, Reader, Department of English and American Studies, University of East Anglia, Norwich, NR4 7TJ, UK

Solveig Schult Eriksen
Professor, Institute of Romance and Classical Studies, University of Oslo, Postboks 1007, Blindern, N-0315 Oslo 3, Norway

Kate Startin
Systems Consultants, 15 Lark Rise, Martlesham Heath, Ipswich, Suffolk, IP5 7SA, UK

Thomas Tempte
Master Cabinet Maker, Stjalkhammars G a Skola, S-59098 Edsbruk, Sweden

Stephen Toulmin
Professor of Philosophy, The Centre for Multiethnic and Transnational Studies, University of Southern California, Los Angeles, CA 90089-7724, USA

Jan Unenge
Assistant Professor, Mathematics, University of Jönköping, Trånghallavägen 25, S-56400 Bankerud, Sweden

Fedor Valach
Professor, Slovak Technical University, Faculty of Chemical Technology, Department of Chemical Physics, Radlinskeho 9, 812 37 Bratislava, Slovakia

Georg Henrik von Wright
Professor of Philosophy, Skepparegatan 4, SF-00150 Helsinki, Finland

Summaries
Rolf Hughes

Section I. Introduction

Chapter 1. Introduction
Jon Cook and Bo Göranzon

Section II. On Practical Philosophy

Chapter 2. The Practical Intellect and Master-Apprenticeship
Thomas Tempte

An account is given of the author's apprenticeship with experienced and highly-skilled carpenters. The author searched for a history of implements and an all-embracing thesis, a universal philosophy. In Diderot's *Encyclopaedia* he discovered detailed documentation on the tools of his day and sketches depicting craftsmen at work, a vision of an overall framework of handicraft production. The differences involved in operating the Egyptian lathe and the Diderot lathe are explained, providing an illustration of how the skills necessary for mastership are transmitted. Questions from apprentices and journeymen are valuable aids to reflection, prompting the craftsman to reconsider techniques, methods, materials and history.

In the second part of the chapter, the author reflects on the relationship between theory and practice. Practitioners of a skill are often called upon to illustrate, or *endorse*, the ideas of the theorists. Contempt for and/or skepticism towards practical work is rooted in traditions going back several thousands of years. Yet dialogue between theory and practice creates energy. A practical intellect – evident in the workshop, studio, or farm – cannot be described with scientific exactitude, but may be a combination of emotional energy and intellectual analysis. Theory is usually associated with power and practice with action. Yet any attempt to exercise the one without the other is itself impractical. For both theoretical and practical reasons, it is important to recover the lessons and methods of the past.

Chapter 3. From Montaigne to Diderot: Pascal, Jansenism and the Dialectics of Inner Theater
Allan Janik

In learning philosophy, students learn typically to read dialogues according to the Platonic model of dialogue, which inculcates a particular mode of reading and understanding. Yet the skills we must master in order to appreciate Plato can prevent us from grasping Diderot's philosophical depth. *Rameau's Nephew* realizes an important element in the Platonic programme, the moment of self-discovery, by conceiving dialogue as inner theatre. The author argues that Montaigne taught Diderot what it means both to read and write dialogically, the rhetoric of dialogue, as it were, whereas Pascal (himself indebted to Montaigne and to Plato, principally through his Christian counterpart, St. Augustin, another author of dialogues) taught him its logic. In his *Conversation with Monsieur de Saci*, an important work for establishing the logic of *Rameau's Nephew*, Pascal laid out his procedure for dealing with conflicting wisdom. He 'stages' an encounter between the opposed views of Epictetus and Montaigne and thereby sets the reader spiritually in motion. In his presentation of an alternative perspective in the form of an antinomy, Pascal paves the way from Montaigne to Diderot by supplying the latter with a 'dia-logical' strategy for structuring the confrontation between the philosopher and the parasite in *Rameau's Nephew*. Both Pascal's dia-logic and his Jansenist values, moral and rhetorical, mark a crucial stage in the development of inner theatre from Montaigne to Diderot.

The author considers the Jansenist literary critique of the values of Baroque absolute monarchy in Racine's drama, specifically *Bérénice*, and LaRochefoucauld's aphoristic transformation of Montaigne's 'method' in his *Maximes* as stages on the way to Diderot's inner theatre. The *Maximes* are dialogical in the sense that the relationship between their style and content creates paradoxes which provoke critical reflection on the part of the reader. They are therefore an important contribution to practical philosophy. Thematic parallels in LaRochefoucauld's maxims and Diderot's *Rameau's Nephew* are discussed. Montaigne and Pascal are contrasted as practical philosophers. For Montaigne, the aim of practical philosophy was to induce reflection upon experience using *examples* as a means for conveying practical wisdom and for illustrating how things can go wrong when we appraise a situation wrongly. Practical wisdom is a facility for the 'appraisal' of situations, and the *essay* is the appropriate form for testing the validity of our judgements. With Pascal, on the other hand, practical philosophy becomes an existential prolegomenon to a change of perspectives about the value of the things of this world. It is essentially a religious phenomenon with a *binary* structure; as such, dialogue, a medium for comparing the relative merits of contrary perspectives, and aphorism, a method for making us look again at the things we take for granted, are its proper vehicles.

In developing a logical strategy capable of juxtaposing conflicting views in such a way that both tension and complementarity become apparent in a third perspective, Pascal provided a 'logic' for inner theatre which Diderot could employ in a secularized form to mould a type of philosophical dialogue which did not sacrifice conversation to dialectics or vice versa as is so often the case in the Platonic dialogues.

Chapter 4. Imaginary Confessions

Stephen Toulmin

Dramatic script.

Chapter 5. *Rameau's Nephew:* Dialogue as *Gesamtkunstwerk* for Enlightenment

Allan Janik

Rationalists from Carnap and the Vienna Circle to Habermas and Critical Theory have taught us to conceive Enlightenment as progress resulting from the cultivation of a critical, scientific attitude to life as well as the technical implementation of the results of scientific inquiry in society. Yet the technocratic, 'progressive' concept of Enlightenment was by no means the only way of conceiving what it meant to be 'enlightened' in the eighteenth century. David Hume's dictum 'reason is and ought to be the slave of the passions' indicates a concern – similar to that expressed by Diderot in *Rameau's Nephew* – with the ways in which human nature *limits* our capacity for 'improvement' according to a consciously developed plan. Before considering how we might improve ourselves, in other words, we need to have an accurate picture of what we actually are. Freud's psychotherapy presupposes a similar picture of rationality, but the concept of Enlightenment that informs his therapeutic practice is linked to a highly speculative theory, the meta-psychological structure of the so-called Oedipus Complex. We need an account of a philosophical route from the rationalistic (i.e. Carnap–Habermas) view of Enlightenment to the one we find in Hume, Freud and Diderot which will show us the way toward understanding the relationship between Diderot's philosophical strategy and his artistic tactics.

The author contends that Plato's Allegory of the Cave is one way of mapping that route. Plato's allegory has become the classical account of the liberation of society from the bonds of convention on the basis of science. However, his recourse to *mythos* to communicate his insights – i.e. telling a story whose point hearers must establish for themselves – brings Plato closer to Diderot than he is either to Carnap or Habermas in his presentation of what is involved in being 'enlightened'. The literary form incorporates the cognitive content of his message into an aesthetic experience designed to provide a deeper, more coherent alternative to the everyday picture of the world.

For Diderot, unlike Plato, the most serious aspect of the problem of appearance and reality concerns not simply ignorance but *hypocrisy* within the Cave. Before Enlightenment in the conventional Platonic sense is possible it will be necessary to lay bare the social dynamics within the Cave (i.e. to ask the question how hypocrisy itself is at all possible) – an investigation that will ultimately require a drastic revision of the respective roles of theory and example, word and gesture, in human experience. The protagonists in *Rameau's Nephew* – *moi*, the personification of Neo-Stoic values such as they were understood circa 1760, and *lui*, the *epitome* of Plato's contented Cave dweller who yet incorporates everything sensual that the puritanical Allegory of the Cave enjoins us to eschew – allow Diderot to explore a value that the secular Enlightenment adopted from its Augustinian Christian (i.e. Jansenist) sources, namely sincerity and its opposite hypocrisy. *Lui*'s 'naturalness', for example, consists precisely in his conversational forthrightness with *moi*; he presents himself in the terms of a paradoxically 'sincere' insincerity. Moreover, in accepting the primacy of pleasure over logic, and acknowledging a role for *consistent inconsistency* in life, Diderot defends the consequences of hedonism through the character of *lui* and thereby responds to the Platonic view that *virtue* is the only real happiness.

The author discusses the *form* of *Rameau's Nephew* as a dynamic counterpoint to (or parody of) Plato's flight from the body to the soul; just as a musical form might overcome Platonic dualism by reconciling sensual beauty with rigorous intellectual structure, so Diderot's dialogue can show us a certain bodily 'logic' incapable of abstract analysis behind the nephew's antics.

A further distinction between Plato and Diderot is made on the subject of skill; skill acquisition, for Plato, involves a form of propositional knowledge (i.e. a matter of learning true propositions), whereas for Diderot it is rather a matter of mastering certain specific techniques. In *Rameau's Nephew*, as elsewhere in Diderot, we have a profound epistemological rehabilitation of the notion of practical skill as true knowledge. Traditional philosophy, by concentrating on the perfect world of logical truths, has entirely ignored the ways that the world, or the Cave, functions; in epistemological terms, knowledge has been severed from learning. Diderot juxtaposes two conflicting conceptions of the relationship between words and knowledge, the representational and the mimetic, allowing the tension between them to illuminate one another in a manner reminiscent of Pascal's ways of dealing with the complimentary truths and falsities of Stoicism and Skepticism.

Diderot's philosophical artistry creates a *Gesamtkunstwerk* in two related but distinct senses. First, he pays no attention to traditional boundaries between genres.

Dialogue and narrative, fact and fiction, the elegant and the grotesque interweave continually. His descriptions attempt to capture spontaneous gesture and therefore aspire to the condition of music and dance. Secondly, the reader is drawn into the dialogue and encouraged to reflect on the disquieting encounter with *lui*, which may be an encounter with the *lui* within ourselves. Diderot's artistry reveals how easily we deceive ourselves by becoming attached to inaccurate self-images.

Rameau's Nephew is ironic in the paradoxical Platonic sense that it makes something great seem small for the sake of letting its actual greatness emerge 'dialectically', rather than in the Wagnerian opposition between the monumental and the pathetic. Diderot prefigures both Strindberg's exploitation of ambiguity in *Miss Julie* as well as the 'transcendental irony' of Offenbach and Georg Trakl's ironic 'deconstructions' of the Symbolist's poetical dream world. His insistence that 'the important point is that you and I should be, and that we should be you and I', anticipates Feuerbach and Kierkegaard and, ultimately, the twentieth century philosophy of dialogue in Ferdinand Ebner and Martin Buber.

Chapter 6. Morals in the "Theatre of the World"

Solveig Schult Ulriksen

This paper is essentially a response to Allan Janik's reading of *Rameau's Nephew* as a confrontation with and challenge to Platonic thought. The author acknowledges the influence of Socrates and Plato, Diogenes and Seneca on the development of Diderot's thought. In the *Encyclopédie* article 'Cynique' Diderot approves as a sign of 'good judgement' the Cynics' reaction against Platonic idealism, their leaving the realm of sublime hypotheses for 'the study of morals (*moeurs*) and the practice of virtue'. The Socratic and the Cynic function are both at work in the dialogue *Rameau's Nephew*, represented not by the philosopher-Moi but by the anti-philosopher-Lui, whose shameless frankness unmasks hypocrisy and vice and thereby allows, in the words of Allan Janik, the 'enlightener to be enlightened'.

The author cites Jacques Chouillet's analysis of the relationship between the two characters in *Rameau's Nephew*, suggesting a continuous negotiation of power, an alternation between complicity and critique of each other's positions. The text is discussed in terms of its relation to the 'genre' of Menippean satire, a literature which thrives on the ruins of philosophy.

Noting the centrality of the theatre motif in *Rameau's Nephew*, the author suggests that the metaphor of universal theatre – the ancient topos of *theatrum mundi* – informs the inherent theatricality of nearly all of Diderot's writings with their imaginative staging of encounter and conflict. The protean figure of *lui* reveals the true nature of the world as an enormous theatre, where everyone takes 'positions' in the social masquerade; he forces the philosopher-spectator (and reader) to participate in the drama by revealing his own fragmented self.

The moral debate between the philosopher and the parasite is left unresolved. The moral values mocked by the Nephew are re-established by what are generically the weapons of satire: laughter and indignation. The confusion of ethics and aesthetics is denounced and priority given to ethics, while the Nephew himself reintroduces ethical norm in the dialogue with his appeal for justice.

Chapter 7. The Traditions of Dialogue and the Future of Philosophy

Igor Naletov

Philosophical thought in Russia has passed through Marxism, Stalinism and post-Stalinism, and now seeks a way forward from political, economic and spiritual deadlock, which are manifest in the stereotypes of isolationism and the Russian mania for creating systems. Marxism proclaimed the annihilation of a universal philosophical system through the revolutionary critical practice of dialectics, which in turn became the only scientific and universal philosophical system capable of delivering self-emancipation. Dialectics was premised upon the possibility of achieving absolute truth and therefore could not oppose the creation of systems *per se*. Philosophy may be deconstructed into specialist (or special interest) categories, or may retain its claims to be a unified and universal system of thought. The availability of differing philosophical positions has led to some confusion; can materialism be combined with idealism, determinism with indeterminism, freedom with moral responsibility? The apparent chaos arising from a radical eclecticism makes a return to a monological style of thinking appealing with its stable solutions to fundamental problems.

In the philosophy of Diderot, dialogue incorporates the complexity and the limits of scientific disciplines and different systems of belief. In depicting mutually dependent contradictions (between spirit and nature, nature and education, freedom and necessity, motion and stasis), Diderot's dialectical way of thinking expressed an almost absolute flexibility, a philosophy of uncertainty opposed to the creation of systems. Diderot manages to capture a sense of thought *in motion*. His knowledge is not explicit but latent in the structure of the dialogues themselves. Definition is achieved through the play of oppositions, a strategy tolerated by neither Hegel nor Marx. Diderot's philosophy, unlike that of Marx or Engels, was premised on paradox and contradiction. In Diderot's works, opposites are equal.

An open philosophy implies not an endless series of possibilities, but a particular set of alternatives. Freedom of choice should not be a conclusion, but a fundamental prerequisite of philosophy.

Chapter 8. Comments

Lars Kleberg

SECTION III. Acting as a Model for Skill

Chapter 9. We Must Safeguard the Freedoms of Our Craft

Erland Josephson

How does one describe an actor's knowledge or skill? The author recalls being taken through his lines by Sir John Gielgud during the making of Peter Greenaway's film of *The Tempest*; by paying close attention to the rhythm and phrasing of the lines, an awareness arose of a tradition, a form of knowledge that had been developed and refined over hundreds of years. The signs which separated phrase and sentence were not Shakespeare's, they were the actors'; their placement an expression of the actors' experience, of their recommendations and their practice. They reflected hard-won knowledge, a battle with phrasing, with feelings and insight, technique and clarity, with characterization and with contact with the audience. Gielgud was in turn passing on his knowledge and experience of this tradition.

An actor learns by example, by experience, practice, and innovations which uncover new and usable forms of knowledge. An actor's knowledge, furthermore, is *embodied*; it exists in the actor's senses, expressions, gestures, and in the grain of the voice. Internal processes are retained through a sensual memory. Experience is passed on through practical teaching rather than theoretical formulations. An actor organizes his intelligence in a different way to other people – his intelligence is restless and hungry, its main objective not confirmation, but new experience – and his knowledge and experience are subjected to constant interrogation by inquiring audiences.

Part of an actor's knowledge comes from exposure to, or dialogue with, successive audiences; knowledge is refined as much by its expression as by its formulation. The actor must abandon his supposedly humble position as 'interpreter', as a vehicle for other people's ideas. It is the actor who provides the substitute experience and who makes it tangible, understandable and relevant to audiences. The actor constructs a platform from both the known and the contradictory, and from here he has the opportunity to create new attitudes in a matter of a few hours. This must be safe-guarded, the freedom of the actor's craft.

Chapter 10. Some Reflections on Diderot's Paradox

Lars Gustafsson

Diderot is convinced that there is a great chain of being connecting all phenomena, but he is opposed to the idea that anyone should know its different links. Creativity for Diderot is to know where a field of knowledge comes to an end; knowledge is also a knowledge of limits. Diderot's thought reveals a great deal of internal coher-ence and consequence to a modern readership, but is expressed in fragmentary and paradoxical terms. At the core of his philosophical method is curiosity, or the capaci-ty for being surprised.

Diderot's paradox may be formulated in different ways according to the interests of the reader; the psychologist might say that the most convincing way to represent an emotion theatrically is to do so in an emotionally detached way; the student of Nature might express Diderot's result by arguing that imitation of Nature cannot be carried out with natural means; and the person interested in the logical foundations of semantics might say that the act of representation always has to be different from the thing being represented. Diderot himself explores the paradox from different perspectives; psychologically, as a distinction between *sense* and *sensibility*, as a 'logi-cal' interpretation, and as a formulation in terms of Nature and its limits. Logical, empirical and psychological considerations therefore form a strange unity of para-doxes in the essay, most obviously under the aesthetic concept of *expression*. An actor's *skill* will determine the expressiveness of a performance. Such skill, for Diderot, is connected with a certain detached state of mind, requiring more sense than sensitivity, or intellectual rather than emotional faculties. What we experience in a performance is 'expressivity' itself rather than the transmission or transposition of the actor/performer's emotions; we respond to a skill (or a set of skills) rather than an emotional substance. Does it follow that all expressions which are equally skilful are of equal importance? If so, Diderot's paradox seems to question an entire hierarchy of values, a hierarchy based on distinctions such as 'important' and 'unim-portant', 'representative' and 'non-representative'. Discussing the oscillation between the derived and the literal meaning of the word 'express', the author draws parallels between Diderot's paradox and deconstructivist modern discourse. It is above all Diderot's fascination with the empty spots in our knowledge which consti-tutes his originality as an Enlightenment philosopher.

Chapter 11. The Actor as Paradigm?

Christopher Bigsby

As metaphor, as symbol and as fact the theatre has been seen not merely as a mirror to our psychological and social nature but as a key to those transformations which are the essence of private and public truth. Historically, however, acting, and its related terms, has had a pejorative meaning, associated with feigning, dissembling, and thus insincerity. The author discusses the distinction between sincerity and seeming – a distinction crucial to Diderot – and suggests that the actor, rather than manufacturing deceit, effects a redirection, or refocusing, of those tactics and social representations which are the stuff of daily intercourse.

The theatre is a *sensual* medium; the body is recuperated so that abstract speech is rooted in physical being, the categories, the systems, the social and psychological roles in which we otherwise place our faith are destabilized by the embodied skills of the actor before us.

It is one of the skills of the actor to draw on levels of being and sensibility otherwise proscribed or denied by custom or acculturation, to cross boundaries, deny the permanence of meaning, the fixity of language, the precision and singularity of interpretation. *Noh* theatre supplies the terms *Riken no ken* ('outside view') and *Gaken* ('inside view' – i.e. the performer's own view); the actor needs both, to see his performance from within and without simultaneously. An actor's skills should be invisible, subsumed in the task they facilitate. Training in traditional Japanese theatre consists of learning prescribed forms of expression and physical and vocal techniques. The aim of training is to enable the actor to perform an action without worrying how to do it, and thereby to arrive at a freedom of communication. The skill is not to be aware of the skill, which moves from the level of learned procedure to apparently instinctive behaviour.

When does one cease to act? The author suggests that the dichotomy between authenticity and performance is a false one. Rather than associate acting with deceit or the absence of individuality, one might see it as an integral part of social and moral existence, having to do with plenitude and possibility, with transformation and empathy, with performatic skills which have become so intuitive that they are indistinguishable from intuition itself. Acting therefore presents an alternative possibility. The theatre is *the* dialogic form; it does not mirror or mimic social action. It is the thing itself. The actor is polyvocal, various, and thus a denial of the monologic culture in which a singular text is interpreted in a singular way by a priesthood of initiates. In the theatre all meaning is subject to change and interpretation is available to all.

The actor recuperates the world night after night and makes it strange for us. New meanings are reborn through repetition. The actor resists the deceptive perfection of an inert language, denies fetishisation, the unyielding and unalterable perfection of the object represented to us in its unchanging coherence. The skills of the actor are the skills of all; the greater fear is not that we may all be actors, observed in our actions, given meaning by an audience, but that we live our lives unobserved and our actions and decisions are accordingly drained of significance and purpose.

Chapter 12. Actors and Acting

Michael Robinson

This chapter explores the nature of the actor's skill using a collage of quotations in order to establish a number of reference points for a consideration of what it is an actor actually does and to suggest some of the disturbing paradoxes to which his figure gives rise.

As pointed out in the previous chapter, hostility to the theatre has been, historically, widespread. The theatre questions established notions of fixity, continuity, stability, and coherence. The actor is transgressive not only because his ambivalent, equivocal, multiple, carnivalesque nature on stage has the ability to confound all sexual, social or political distinction and discrimination; the element of transgression already exists as a possibility in the encounter which the theatre sets up between the exciting, strange, and on occasion aggressive energy of the actor and the audience. The author explores other instances of anti-theatrical prejudice; the significance of parallels between acting and prostitution, acting and femininity, acting as a surrogate existence for the actor's supposed absence of personality, and the actor as a proliferating and unnatural multiplication of signs, an identity that circulates, that is not fixed, and which associates in a promiscuous violation of identity with crowds.

Rather than discuss the real or metaphorical consonance of theatre and life, the author suggests we emulate Diderot in considering the different forms of knowledge and skill employed by the actor in researching, establishing, and defining a role before presenting it to the public.

The actor finds a bodily emotion for each feeling, s/he works through physical actions that express psychological realities. The actor's body is normally the primary theatrical sign, the repository of the role which is acquired and stored in the performer's muscular memory. S/he is at once artist and instrument; philosophy in the theatre unfolds itself as 'a thinking of the body' (Bert O States). The actor's instinct, intuition and intellect provide a focus for his/her work on a dramatic text. Intuition here may be associated with 'organized reasoning', a kind of tacit knowledge that we have internalized into a system for understanding and acting in the world, and which may be applied to the situations with which the actor is confronted in the dramatic text. Skill, dexterity, physical and vocal training, and a knowledge of tradition may all be essential aspects of training, but one should add the notion of 'emotional memory', as defined by Stanislavski, and the account of the actor's corporeal memory in Diderot's *The Paradox of Acting*. The actor, as both Diderot and Stanislavski were aware, is a master of physical actions in which the imaginative world of the text is realized in constant dialectical play with the world of real experience, but cannot be mistaken for that world, except as a social activity in which actors and audience are mutually engaged.

The author cites two differing accounts of actors preparing for a role – Stanislavski's intuitive discovery of appropriate correlations in life and Henry Irving's 'natural, yet highly artificial' stage presence.

The words spoken by the actor started originally as an impulse for expression, and are hence part of a complex, fluid, multivocal process; the words of a text may imply a body and its shape and movements, a voice and its articulations and inflections, but only in production do these words assume theatrical meaning, firstly through the intervention of the actors and a director, and secondly through the decoding of the complex processes of verbal and non-verbal communication by an audience.

Chapter 13. Comments

Bo Göranzon

SECTION IV. Alan Turing and Ludwig Wittgenstein – A Meeting of Different Traditions of Knowledge

Chapter 14. *Beyond All Certainty*

Bo Göranzon and Anders Karlqvist

Dramatic script.

Chapter 15. Thoughts on Acting and the Play *Beyond All Certainty*

Richard Davies and Jon Hyde

A combination of written and tape recorded reflections from the *Great Escape Theatre Company* on rehearsing and performing the play *Beyond All Certainty*.

Chapter 16. The Legacy of Turing–On the Limits of the Calculable

Anders Karlqvist

How much can we learn about *pi*? In most practical contexts it would be enough to say that π is 3.14, which is an approximate value of an irrational number. If the statement 'the number π exists' is a true statement, how, in the absence of a computer with sufficient calculating ability, can we verify the statement 'the 10^{100} decimal in π is 3'? The truth or falsehood of this statement is hidden from us for all time, but most of us would be prepared to accept the statement as either true *or* false, blaming practical circumstances for our lack of absolute certainty rather than pointing out that mathematics is in itself an incomplete science.

Furthermore, if we test the statement 'the decimal sequence of π contains an infinite number of threes', there is no algorithm we can use to determine whether the statement is true or false. What then do we mean by the terms true or false? Can we formulate meaningful mathematical statements that are neither one nor the other?

The chapter surveys the life and legacy of Alan Turing. The author explains the importance and the operation of the Turing machine, which is capable of carrying out all mathematical calculations and gave the idea of mathematical computation an exact and generally-applicable content. The Turing machine also allows us to question whether or not we can acquire knowledge of the physical and biological world by using *computations* as a tool – to dream, alongside Leibniz, of a rational universe accessible to mathematical calculations.

The desire for the *formalization* of mathematical arguments, expressed by Hilbert, Russell, and Frege among others, is a further manifestation of this dream. If mathematics could be shown conclusively to be *consistent*, i.e. free from internal contradictions, and *complete*, i.e. that *every* meaningful mathematical statement could be proved to be either true or false, then from a series of given primitive concepts and axioms, a mechanical application of the rules of logic would produce every possible mathematical proposition. The dream of the perfection of mathematics, however, was punctured both by Wittgenstein and by the Czech mathematician Gödel. In physics, similarly, the theory of relativity and quantum mechanics replaced the mechanistic and deterministic world designed by Newton with a world based on probability calculations, creating in the process an unbridgeable gap between objective reality and our capacity to acquire knowledge about that reality. The unlimited capacity of reason proved to be a chimera, even when confined to its own specialist area of mathematics.

The author discusses the role of paradox in human reason and thinking. Russell's attempt to eradicate the possibility of mathematical contradictions in *Principia Mathematica* is undermined by Gödel's deployment of paradox to demonstrate that in every formal system there are true statements that cannot be proved. For Wittgenstein, on the other hand, paradoxes and contradictions were uninteresting. There are no mathematical truths to discover, he argued; proof simply means establishing the meaning of certain symbols.

Gödel's propositions may be reformulated by constructing a statement within the mathematical system which is self-referencing and contradictory in the same way as Epimenides' paradox. Self-referencing systems have an important role in encouraging us to escape the framework of rational linear thinking. One may speculate about whether or not self-reference is an important feature of complicated systems in nature, and, if so, whether calculability has a limited scope in acquiring knowledge about such systems.

Turing's universal calculating machine allowed the concepts of calculation, algorithm and programme to be given a precise content. The concepts agree with what we today call computer software: they are executed mechanically in a sequence according to given instructions, and without external interference. All variations of hardware and programming languages may be traced to the primitive design of the

Turing machine, with its zeros and ones on a paper ribbon. Zeros and ones may be regarded as the basic building blocks of mathematical calculations.

A computer may be described in terms of the number of building-blocks – 'bits' – that are needed. The complexity of a programme may be measured by the length of the sequence of zeros and ones. Theories may be perceived as algorithms capable of reproducing observations and extending this body of observation, i.e. predicting. Observations of *random* phenomena have no theory in this sense. Prediction becomes impossible. Chaitin's development of Gödel's results using a computer and a self-referring paradox are discussed in this context.

'True or false', the author concludes, are blunt criteria for scientific understanding. In the transfer of mathematical knowledge a vague form of communication may be an advantage in making the essence of an idea comprehensible. The mind's ability to intuitively understand the point of an argument before one has, with the help of the laws of logic, established it is correct, offers us a deeper idea about understanding and one which is difficult to capture in the artificial intelligence that the computer represents. Can we compare human consciousness with a Turing machine? To deter-mine whether or not an algorithm is applicable requires insight rather than another algorithm. A Gödelian argument leads inevitably to the conclusion that human con-sciousness is not capable of formalizing its mathematical intuition.

The computer, with its sophisticated and highly efficient capacity for calculation, may take us closer to the border country of thinking, but never through it. We see the mirror image of these limits in arithmetic. The theory of numbers cannot answer all the true statements about itself. Logic does not permit this. We cannot think about thinking with anything other than our own thoughts. We cannot study our brain with anything other than our own brain, even if our instruments and calculating machines can sharpen our sight and speed up our calculations. We must therefore continue to live with our great mystery: to remain a mystery to ourselves.

Chapter 17. "Nothing is Hidden"

Georg Henrik von Wright

Wittgenstein discovered some of the inherent imperfections in formalized logical and mathematical systems and therefore plays an important part in connection with 'the legacy of Turing'. In all systems with an abundance of structures there are propositions that are 'unverifiable' – one cannot establish, within the system, whether they can be proved or not. The significance of these results may be gauged by placing the discoveries of Turing and Gödel against the background of what the author terms 'the classical world picture of European science'.

At the beginning of this century Hilbert's tenet that there are no questions in math-ematics whose answers are in theory inaccessible to thought, was overturned by Turing and Gödel three decades later. Hilbert's 'comprehensive' perception of math-ematics derived from Leibniz's vision of a 'calculus ratiocinator' formalized in a 'characteristica universalis'. The ideal science of this classical picture of the world was physics, premised on the notion that there are laws which strictly govern all events (and calculated reason is therefore able to resolve all mathematical problems).

Shortly before the emergence of Gödel and Turing, the deterministic world picture of physics had been undermined by a series of breakthroughs in quantum physics. The discoveries of Geisenberg and others led to a 'fundamental crisis' in physics which may be seen as a parallel to the situation in logic and mathematics after Gödel. The author suggests we adopt an 'intra-science' and an 'extra-science' perspective on discoveries which overturn previous theoretical assumptions. The 'intra-science' perspective celebrates new advances as scientific advances, while the 'extra-science' view sees science as a 'conception of the world' and its effects on 'general paths of thought', its 'paradigmatic' influence as a model for thinking, among other things, about man and his societies. The author proposes a sober appraisal of theoretical innovation from both an 'intra-science' and an 'extra-science' perspective (a dual perspective adopted by Wittgenstein), and assesses the significance of Gödel, Turing and Wittgenstein's discoveries within these terms.

Chapter 18. Turing and Wittgenstein – Two Perceptions of Reality

Dag Prawitz

Turing's contribution to philosophy may be summarized within the following themes:

(i) Turing's definition of an abstract general computer i.e. what we now call a *Turing machine*

(ii) Turing's theory that everything which is computable may be computed with a Turing machine, and

(iii) Turing's ideas about an artificial intelligence and its criterion summarized in what is commonly called the *Turing test*.

Turing's philosophical legacy, according to this summary, could contain three main assets: the *Turing machine*, the *Turing thesis* and the *Turing test*.

The Turing Machine

The *Turing machine* represents Turing's main contribution to logic. Calculators – human, mechanical and electronic – seem very different in terms of their hardware but very similar in terms of their functional ability, or software. With the assistance of simple, abstract operations, Turing succeeded in providing a description of a calculator, or family of calculators, which in terms of functional ability correspond to all known calculators. The so-called universal Turing machine is capable of imitating any Turing machine when it is fed with a code number for that machine. Turing even designed a single abstract machine which can match all known calculators and thereby opened up the possibility of Gödelerian self-referentiality.

Turing's Thesis

In contrast to the Turing machine, which is a contribution to logic and mathematics, Turing's thesis is a contribution of a logical-philosophical character. The thesis is that the intuitive concept of the calculable and the concept of the determinable can be defined, or explicated, with the help of Turing machines; something is calculable or determinable only if it can be calculated or determined by a Turing machine, and this explication or definition, Turing argues, corresponds to our intuitive concepts of calculability or determinability. Philosophical explications of provable, definable, measurable or knowable concepts have failed to match Turing's thesis in terms of precision, simplicity and inherent plausibility.

The Turing Test

The Turing test is in the nature of a provocative, philosophical speculation. Turing suggested a criterion for establishing whether or not an artificial 'calculator', a computer, possessed intelligence. If the computer functioned in a manner indistinguishable from human intelligence – if it were able to process and produce a text from a person communicating in writing from an adjoining room, for example – then one might ascribe to the artificial intelligence human attributes such as consciousness.

One might object to Turing's thesis on the basis that humans have abilities which are in theory impossible to get a machine to carry out, and, even if a machine could successfully imitate man's external behaviour, there would still be a crucial difference between man and machine. Human thought includes certain types of experience which involve internal processes not readily translatable into the codes of external behaviour that a machine might understand.

The author discusses the meeting between Turing and Wittgenstein, with reference to the play *Beyond All Certainty*. The confrontation is compared to the meeting between Turing and Churchill, a conflict between a scientific and non-scientific mind.

Wittgenstein's view that in mathematics we are dealing with inventions rather than discoveries could be termed 'extreme conventionalism'. Mathematical proof should be seen as a decision we take to use the relevant concepts in a certain way; by calling something proof we make it proof, and this, according to Wittgenstein, is a choice, a decision we make. It is through our practice that we give importance to our symbols. Every new proof is only a new convention; it becomes an agreement by being accepted and thereafter used by us. In this sense Wittgenstein is an extreme conventionalist, in contrast to the realism or so-called mathematical Platonism advocated by Gödel.

The meeting between Turing and Wittgenstein illustrates one of the most important and topical issues in philosophical theory, namely the conflict between realism or Platonism on the one hand, and different forms of anti-realism – such as idealism, conventionalism, constructivism – on the other. The difficulty in finding a reasonable position between those of Wittgenstein and Turing is the difficulty of both respecting the objective validity of a mathematical proof, which means that we are not at liberty to prove what we want, and simultaneously freeing ourselves from the notion of an already-stated and independent mathematical reality, which mathematical proof does no more than uncover. It is this philosophical balancing act that the meeting between Turing and Wittgenstein challenges us to perform.

Chapter 19. Carved in Stone or Carried by the Wind?

Stephen Toulmin

In discussing the ambiguous phrase 'Beyond all Certainty', the author indicates that Wittgenstein sought not to teach us that we can arrive at *no* kind of certainty, but that philosophers have deceived us, by pretending that formally based geometrical Certainty alone has any intellectual relevance. Wittgenstein directs us beyond an inappropriately *formal* Certainty – decontextual logical necessity – toward an appropriately *pragmatic* Certainty, a well grounded contextual certitude. With the demise of Cartesian 'foundationalist' epistemology, the illusion that Certainty is a formal feature of human knowledge, exemplified in the logical coherence of *texts*, is replaced by the rediscovery of another Certainty, one which emerges as a pragmatic feature of our knowledge, in particular situations and within particular modes of *praxis*.

The Cartesians have historically confused two kinds of Skepticism: the Pyrrhonism of, for example, Montaigne's *Apologie de Raimond Sebond*, as taught by Sextus Empiricus in antiquity, and the method of Systematic Doubt developed in Descartes *Méditations* and *Discours*, which rejects all claims to 'knowledge' for which no Euclidean foundation is available. According to Descartes, we must deny any proposition that we cannot prove. For classical skeptics, by contrast, *denying* truths that go beyond the reach of experience is as misguided as *asserting* them. The late 20th century escape from Cartesianism frees us from a dogmatism exemplified as well in misplaced *denials* as in misplaced *assertions*. Abandoning Foundationalism thus leads us into Pragmatism, which is to be understood as a move from theory-based to practice-based philosophy. Any appeal to 'theory' now has to be accepted as a kind of Practice.

Twentieth century philosophy has seen a transition from Propositions to

Utterances (or 'language games', 'speech acts', 'illocutionary performances' etc.); this has accompanied a redirection of attention from Formal Logic towards the rehabilitation of Rhetoric, a shift, in other words, from the logical question 'How do propositions *cohere?*' to the pragmatic question, 'How are utterances *put to use?*' The Philosophers' traditional Dream, to arrive at Truths that can be 'carved in stone', must remain a dream. What 'meaning' do functional, situated, timely *utterances* retain, once we replace them by functionless, desituated and timeless *propositions*?

Against this background, the rationalist question of certainty was a distraction from serious issues of *practice*. Narratives re-emerge of a sort that pre-dated Descartes. Language Use, Pragmatism, and Narrative become a central feature of any possible advances in Philosophy today. The author compares a clinical, casuistical approach in medical ethics to the formal theories of Bioethics in order to contrast the practical basis of diagnosis and treatment with the dream of moral standards *carved in stone*. The *meanings* that concepts, beliefs, judgements and utterances have in situations are embedded in the situations. They are *praxis* based, not *text* based; and whatever *certainty* physicians' judgements may have is not a formal result of formal deductive inference, but a pragmatic outcome of mature experience.

Chapter 20. Experiment, Science, Literature

Göran Printz-Påhlson

Diderot argued that the observation of nature, thought and experiment were our principal means for extending and deepening scientific enquiry; 'Observation collects the facts, thought combines them, and experiment verifies the result of the combination.' Rousseau, in contrast, posited a qualified and practicable primitivism in place of the sciences which 'generate idleness' and are themselves 'the effect of idleness'.

Diderot's tripartite division of scientific principles still seems valid in our thoroughly technologized society. Although thought is often redefined as 'consciousness', the pursuit of truth continues to be regarded as a function of theory and observation. The internal relationship of these two concepts has been variously interpreted, according to the current understanding of a third, more instrumental or operational concept: that of 'experiment'. The author discusses three occasions where the analogy of 'experiment' has been applied with different bias to innovations in literature: Goethe's *Wilhelm Meister's Apprenticeship*, Wordsworth's 'advertisement' and subsequent Preface to the 1798 and 1800 editions of the *Lyrical Ballads*, and Zola's naturalist manifesto *Le roman expérimental*. The (so-called) humanist is opposed not to a culture of science, but to the all-embracing claims of reductionism, which include the belief that 'science' as a unified viewpoint can provide an objective picture of everything in terms that are translatable into a final vocabulary. Experimental knowledge, as Diderot knew, is tentative, heuristic, enquiring, and opposed to reductionism in all its forms.

Chapter 21. Scientific "Fact-Fictions"

E. S. Shaffer

In *The Postmodern Condition* Jean-François Lyotard proclaimed the end of 'grand narratives', particularly those of the Enlightenment premised on notions of reason, progress, and the liberty of humankind. In his more recent book, *The Inhuman*, Lyotard underscores this, exhorting us to abandon the narrative of 'the emancipation of humanity'. He predicts the Death of the Sun as a 'fact' projected into the future. Post-modernism will be followed, Lyotard tells us, by 'post-solar thought', a 'fact' which will put a stop to the religions, myths, aesthetics, and grand narratives of death that modern thought has dealt in.

The author invites us to reflect upon what sort of fact this is, comparing the so-called scientific facts of Stephen Hawking's *A Brief History of Time* and the *Encyclopaedia Britannica* to the deliberately menacing quality of Lyotard's statement of 'fact' that the sun will perish in precisely 4.5 million years. This kind of 'fact' is the subject of recent 'science fiction' and the author cites a number of apocalyptic scenarios, or scientific hypotheses, posited in the near future by J.G. Ballard. Ballard himself has claimed that the literature that will survive as the fiction of our time is 'science fiction (or, in the term employed by Darko Suvin, 'speculative fiction'), while reworkings of more traditional material will sink without trace. These fictions lay claim to public attention and credence, and command it, in a way nothing clearly labelled 'fiction' can.

The author compares the 'factual' scenario posited in Lyotard's *The Inhuman* to one of Ballard's 'fictional' ones in his *Myths of the Near Future*. Both centre on a diseased sun, and display the symptoms of human time-disease. Both are seeking a new version of time that will make it possible to stave off extinction – or at least consciousness of extinction. In comparing these scenarios, the author suggests, it becomes evident that we are dealing not with theoretical systems (though often there is a putative theoretical matrix), nor with scientific facts (though some scientific facts are incorporated) but with a cluster of metaphors. That they are drawn from science does not make them any less metaphorical.

Contemporary scientific fact-fictions display the attraction between different spheres of discourse expressed in or effected by the deceptive similarity of concepts, the overlapping of terms, analogy, or poetic metaphors. They are more prone to erase the distinctions between discourses than to observe them.

Literary critics tends to celebrate the capacity of fiction to fictionalize fact and factualize fiction. The author suggests, however, that the new scientific fact-fictions, which dominate discourse of all kinds, deserve closer critical scrutiny. If the public is subjected to the rhetorical use of these scientific fact-fictions by pundits claiming scientific status for their diagnoses and nostrums, it can hardly be expected to make accurate distinctions and informed policy decisions.

Chapter 22. Comments

Rolf Hughes

SECTION V. Education and the Information Society

Chapter 23. Some Enigma Variations: A Selection of Dialogues Prompted by Turing's Work

Jon Monk

A dialogue between 'me' and 'myself' concerning Alan Turing.

Chapter 24. The Two Cultures in Engineering

Peter Brödner

Engineering, historically, has been premised on two incompatible basic assumptions on the nature of humans and the function of technology, on the way of seeing the world, and on the human's being in the world:

(i)   the 'closed world' paradigm suggests that all real-world phenomena, the properties and relations of its objects, can theoretically be transformed by human cognition into objectified, explicitly stated, propositional knowledge. Human cognition and this kind of knowledge would then represent the real-world phenomena so completely that they could be modelled, explained and simulated in all aspects, and therefore reproduced by smart machines.

(ii) the 'open development' paradigm contests the completeness of explicit, conceptual, and propositional knowledge. It assumes the primary existence of practical experience, a body of tacit knowledge grown with a person's acting in the world. Human interaction with the environment unfolds a dialectic of form and process through which practical experience is partly formalized and objectified as language, tools or machines (form), the use of which, in turn, produces new experience (process) as a basis for further objectification.

The paper reflects on these two paradigms with specific focus on production engineering. The productivity of manufacture, the author argues, depends to a large extent on the usability and learnability of the (computer) artefacts used and the skills developed through work. The design and use of artefacts and their effectiveness, in turn, relate back to the basic question of how humans and machines are viewed. Developing an adequate model of humans, therefore, forms a necessary basis for the design of usable systems.

In order to produce the achievements of common sense that symbol manipulating machines have so far failed to simulate, an adequate conception of the human being is necessary. The author suggests that recent findings about biological and cultural evolution (Bateson, Maturana and Varela) and about human acting (Holzkamp, Volpert) provide useful insights in this respect.

A cognitive action or cognition emerges if a human develops appropriate behaviour in a context; all primary experience that humans gain from their cognitive actions is first of all implicit, internal (or embodied) knowledge private to the acting person ('tacit knowledge'). Intelligence can thus be defined as a person's ability to actively appropriate parts of the environment by producing a functional internal representation of his or her actions through which the environment is restructured at the same time ('structural coupling'). Consequently, meaning must be realized in the acting itself.

The conceptual understanding and theoretical knowledge being developed by interfering with the surrounding world and by symbolically interacting with their fellow creatures (constituting the social system) can then be objectified as tools or as language. Tools and machines, like concepts, represent 'coagulated experience' – they incorporate objectified, explicit knowledge (knowledge of how they work and knowledge of how to work with them) – or 'implemented theory'. It is the bodily experience and the embodied tacit knowledge that forms the core of human skill, expertise, and competence. Gathering experience through the use of artefacts, exploring their functions and meaning, and adapting to new situations or new ways of using them, this is what constitutes its abundance and ingenuity.

The chapter discusses the limitations and problems of knowledge based systems when attempting to represent or objectify the vague conceptions and the mostly implicit background knowledge of the experts into facts and rules. Instead of imitating human abilities and trying to replace them by machine artefacts, they should be productively combined with the performance of appropriately designed machines.

Among the unique human abilities, the sensory perception discriminating holistic patterns, distinguishing differences and similarities, learning and inferring from experience, making fine judgements, coping with unforeseen events and acting in a goal-oriented fashion without relying on rules are the most important. Work and technology must be designed so that these abilities can be maintained and developed through work. The chapter offers guidelines for design to support this and describes two prototype systems being developed at the Institute of Work and Technology which have been designed in accordance with these basic assumptions and guidelines.

Chapter 25. A Confrontation between Different Traditions of Knowledge. An Example from Working Life

Ingela Josefson

The chapter presents a conflict between nursing as a 'scientific' discipline and nursing taught and learned on the foundation of practice. Which form of knowledge shall constitute the core in the education and training of nurses? Should the main emphasis be placed upon theory or practice?

Two nurses are quoted with different opinions about theory and practice in nursing. *Karin* claims that theories are needed in nursing 'to understand what we do as nurses'. The younger nurses tend to have a more profound theoretical education than the older nurses. She gives an example of a problem on the ward being tackled by two young nurses. A different attitude to nursing knowledge is described by *Ingrid*. She recalls how a group of childminders, themselves middle-aged women with children of their own, forfeited their practical knowledge of child-rearing when they entered an educational situation. Trust in expert knowledge, she concludes, deprives people of their common sense in certain situations.

As an example of our high estimation of theoretical knowledge at the expense of practical knowledge, the author points out that recent educational policy has transferred former practical education in nursing and nursery school teaching to the universities and their traditions of knowledge. This may be an attempt to give status to an under-valued profession like nursing, and is premised upon the assumption that theories improve quality in nursing, yet the specific problems in nursing for which theories would be useful need to be identified. The education and training of nurses at universities have contributed to a separation between practice and theories in nursing; although universities may be good at teaching medical theoretical knowledge, which is an important basis for professional knowledge in nursing, there is no tradition for conveying the practical knowledge needed in clinical work.

Practical knowledge manifests itself in the ability to take care of a sick person according to her unique circumstances. Theoretical knowledge aims at teaching the student to perceive similarities. In *Philosophical Investigations* Wittgenstein questions how judgements are made and learned, and what it means to discern differences. His reflections on teaching and learning focus attention on apprenticeship; one may learn to discern by observing how more experienced people manage difficult situations. Wittgenstein's later philosophy provides perspectives for reflection on the complicated relationship between general rules and the concrete perception of the unique case. The rules may work as guidelines but the priority should lie in considering the unique case. Reflection on the salient feature of each unique case creates a foundation for developing the interdependence between practical and theoretical knowledge. Examples in this kind of knowledge formation provide a basis for reflection.

Sophocles' *Antigone* presents two different worlds of values; the conflict between the civic obligation to obey the ruler and the obligation of love towards the family. For doctors the tragedy served as a model for reflection upon different conflicts of value in their practical medical work; among research students, on the other hand, their disciplinary background seemed to determine what they saw in the play.

The author raises two questions at the end of the chapter:What happens in a society when practical knowledge is made abstract? How should the universities meet the demand for the nursing profession to become more 'scientific'? One way would be to reject education and training in these fields. Another would be to widen the traditions of knowledge at the universities. There are traditions in philosophy and literature which might make substantial contributions to the development of practical knowledge.

Chapter 26. Engineering, Culture and Competence

Richard Ennals

The focus of this chapter is on engineering skills, their cultural context, and the extent to which they can be sustained and developed through an approach to education and training which is based on competence. It is argued that a broader approach is required, one which gives due attention to the tacit knowledge of the skilled worker and the culture of working life.

The author discusses recent government policy in the United Kingdom aimed at increasing the emphasis on competence based qualifications as opposed to traditional academic modes of study and assessment. The conventional assumption has been that engineers are concerned with making things, and that the age of manufacturing has passed. Very few British politicians have a background in engineering, science or technology. In a free market economy, where cutting costs is a primary objective, there is a reluctance to fund professionals and their professional bodies for protracted periods of study when employees can be contracted on a casual basis.

The typical graduate engineer today is not directly engaged in the manufacturing process; his/her products instead tend to be designs or reports, formulations in language and symbols that are comprehended and used by the managers who constitute their audience. This suggests that the engineer must develop expertise in a complex process of knowledge representation and mediation. Engineers are actors in the world of business, organizations and politics, and need access to insights from the humanities and philosophy, from acting and the social sciences, much of which is best achieved through practice and reflection. Wittgenstein was an aeronautical engineer by profession, and drew on a background of practical experience, skill and reflection when discussing examples of language games with a physical aspect. He brought together the different symbolic worlds between which the engineer has to mediate.

Computer technology permits us to end such arbitrary divisions of labour as the false distinction between work by hand and by brain; the same engineer can both think and produce products. Yet computing systems have blurred understanding of skills and are incapable of considering questions of reliability, safety, and acceptability, for which, as Jon Monk has argued, experience, tradition, experiment and theory are required.

The so-called 'Third Culture' rejects the over-rigid demarcation between arts and social sciences on the one hand, and natural sciences and technology on the other. Science and technology are viewed in a cultural context; people, rather than technology, are assumed to be at the centre of systems. Technological systems are regarded as implementations of ideologies, and are to be treated with similar caution: systems are based on models of reality, often with arbitrary approaches to quantification, and can never be relied on as substitutes for human judgement.

Engineers need to play a central role in this 'Third Culture', but this will require changes in the current educational and political system. Narrow vocationalism is destructive of a common culture, and serves only the interests of a ruling elite, typically drawn from a background in the Arts.

The author provides examples of common classes of concern across professions and disciplines; the skilled actor, for example, can manipulate his audience as an engineer can modify his system, and playing an active role in a real-time set of events, dispels views of the adequacy of pre-packaged solutions. The actor has to engage in implicit dialogue with his audience as the engineer does with his client, often working with inadequate material. Engineers are often called upon to write consultancy reports on the working of particular systems, or to compare and contrast alternative solutions to specified problems; they are, in effect, critics for part of their work. Engineers and critics share many characteristics in regards the study and manipulation of their systems or cultural products, but they have little social discourse. Extending the dialogue between the professions makes for change, mobility, and the revival of productive skill.

Chapter 27. Engineering Training with a Human Face: The I-Program at the Royal Institute of Technology, Stockholm

Albert Danielsson

This chapter details some of the aims and principles behind the I-Program at the Royal Institute of Technology, Stockholm.

If engineers are to participate successfully in managing both the design and implementation of technical applications, they will need the ability to make integrated assessments. Skills in the technical and natural sciences are essential for these integrated assessments; without such skills there is a risk that the assessments will miss the point and be as one-sided as a pure and simple economic calculation without any real content – with the emphasis on form rather than on content.

Technical applications must be designed and implemented in stages. As a rule each stage should be dealt with by people who are well-qualified in their area. But an assessment of the entire chain requires an overall view of its parts and, above all, and understanding of the whole. The skill brought to bear must cover natural sciences-technology-economics as a chain and as a whole.

Engineers with different educational backgrounds often get different jobs, involving different tasks and areas of responsibility, and gain therefore different practical experience. The even greater differences in views, skills, work tasks etc. between engineers on the one hand and economists on the other are a constant source of misunderstandings and poor co-operation. Wittgenstein has taught us that concepts arise from the particular practical experience of their users. Concepts, language, and thus whole areas of skills are also related to occupational training and experience. To communicate effectively one must become familiar with the conditions that obtain in several parts of the whole – or with the ways that knowledge is portrayed in these different areas of skill.

Aside from acquiring basic technical knowledge and an understanding of those parts of the natural and social sciences that apply to the technology to be used, knowledge is needed of the situation in which the technology is to be applied, and this must also include the way the situation has developed.

The objective of the training course at the Institute of Technology is defined as giving knowledge and understanding of Technology-Economics-Leadership. It encompasses both the parts and the whole. Training must contain examples of technical applications. To understand and manage a composite operation we must consider both the parts and the whole as well as the environment and context in which this whole is set.

In a course of training, content and structure are related to each other in often complex ways. Some subjects will need laboratory work to be understood and learned, while others (for example co-operation with and the management of other people) require experience if they are to be meaningful. Where there is a lack of experience (including common experience) new ideas cannot be based on an existing common language; they cannot be *said*, they must be *shown*. If new scientific findings have to be *shown* to be accepted, good teaching methods for a training course in this area must be based on *showing* the content. One way of showing is to provide examples, cases, reference equipment etc.

The author cites two aims of education that are related to the design of a course:
- The ability to solve problems of varying complexity.
- The ability to formulate problems.

The selection of subjects and methods for a course establishes from the outset a hierarchy of significance, and shapes our perception of what a problem is and how it should be defined. What is sometimes referred to as the right to formulate problems is one of the most important ways of exercising influence. The most important factor in a course of education is the way in which it relates to the world.

The author argues that a training course needs to be based on a thoroughly-prepared and well-informed assessment introduced at the training stage through the way in which the different parts of the operation are dealt with and presented, and the sequence in which they are presented. It is important that the actual determination of what a problem is remains a constant part of this approach.

Chapter 28. The Systems Analysis Skill

Kate Startin

This chapter presents a study of different types of software development communities. The study aims to look at what practitioners actually do and the way they reflect on it, rather than what theorists say they do. It is assumed that the relationship between theory and practice is problematic. The two communities are accordingly described in terms of the personal histories of those involved, how they organize themselves and communicate with each other, and how they conceive of knowledge. It is observed that the differences between the communities are systematic, in that one of the communities values the technical skill, while the other values the communication skill. The key concept *application* is described for each community, and the consequences in their differing development practice. The role of communicability is emphasized as a unifying factor in the differing conceptions of the term 'application'. The claim is made for the greater competence and communicability in the systems analysis work of the low-tech community.

A preliminary study of the work involved in systems analysis is presented, and an attempt made to begin to name some of the tacit knowledge being used. Some reasons are given about why the knowledge seems to be localized in one of the communities described, and suggestions made as to how it might be shared with the other one.

Some suggestions are made about the possibility of deconstructing the process by which suitable computer applications are unconsciously recognized by systems analysts.

Lastly, the author's personal experience as an analyst is presented as an example of the sort of background that systems analysts may have. The study itself is the result of reflection on the author's long experience in the software industry. It seeks to understand a significant anomaly – that familiarity with the accepted theory does not coincide with the best practice.

Chapter 29. Comments

Jon Cook

SECTION VI. On Diderot, Analogy and Mathematics

Chapter 30. Diderot, Implicit Knowledge and Architecture: The Experience of Analogy

Marian Hobson

This chapter suggests that Diderot's digressive practice may be deeply related to his notion of analogy acquired by 'an infinity of successive observations whose memory is effaced, and whose effect remains'. Diderot is developing a notion of analogy which moves beyond the vague to become precisely what links experience in a synthesis, an analogy which will both regulate the artist's treatment of the beautiful and anchor it to notions of the objective and of the functionally dynamic.

The author discusses the last two chapters of *Essais sur la peinture* [Essays on Painting] in which Diderot considers the size of Saint Peter's in Rome, which is said to be so perfectly proportioned that it does not seem as big as it is. The word 'proportion' translates the Greek 'analogon' and the notion fundamental to both is that of ratio. Is it better to make a building seem bigger or smaller than it is? The problem Diderot proposes (in, typically, a chiasmus) is that of an overall harmony which impedes general effect, versus a defect in harmony which makes the whole seem extraordinary and imposing.

The problem of illusion of size in architecture may be compared with the respective value of proportion and line, or colour and illusion in painting. Diderot argues that in the same way as architecture has been impoverished by a concern for modules, when it should only recognize 'the infinite variety of conventions' (i.e. social function), so the same concern for proportion in figure painting has erased the concern for the characteristic, the traits that individualize and particularize, the traits that show 'the habitual functions'. Yet, Diderot asks, is not such a view of art relative? Does the phrase 'the infinite variety of conventions' indicate that there would be no common rule to such an art, merely a fitting to circumstance?

Michael Angelo created the most beautiful possible form for Saint Peter's dome. When it was measured by the French mathematician La Hire he found that its outline was the curve of greatest resistance. Michael Angelo, Diderot notes, was inspired by the experience of the play of dynamic forces in everyday life. It is the notion of function which enables Diderot to link the beautiful to the true and the good; the form which is the most economical and strong for a certain purpose will be the one instinctively felt as 'right' in both moral and aesthetic senses.

The author traces the connections between themes which are linked twice in Diderot's writings: tiny experiences; in the case of architecture, physio-dynamic experiences of space within which one is moving; then the problem of taste, and its relation to factors like social organization which may seem to make it dependent on human convention; then the question of proportion, and whether it is numerical and stable, or whether it varies according to the same factors as taste.

Citing responses to the basilica from the seventeenth to the eighteenth century – different accounts of the 'progression of surprise' its perfect proportions produced in the visitor – the author provides a historical context for the question of illusion in space and, the question which interested Diderot, that of the nature of proportion. Diderot's contact with architects in the 1760s and his thinking about proportion give a depth and a physiological content to the static formal idea of proportion, enabling him to move towards a more dynamic conception of sensation traces and memory. 'Rapport', the author suggests, moves from proportion to analogy, so that it can be linked with epistemology, with our organization of experience; in this way it will point to Kant's concept of 'analogies of experience' in the *Critique of Pure Reason*.

The chapter traces discussions about classic and gothic architecture which provided an important context for Diderot working on his own aesthetics. Perronet, for example, claimed that Soufflot's dome, which is not resting on pillars but carried by a system of side buttressing, had achieved an elegant and economical mean between gothic and classic construction. Moreover, he claims, the edifices are constructed 'in imitation of the structure of animals', an analogy which makes of the gothic cathedral a dynamic complex of thrusts and counter thrusts, and suggests that he has been applying such principles to considering living animals' distribution of weight. Engineering and architecture thus become linked to human perception of spatial appearance. What is now at stake is not objective and static proportion, perceived merely by the eyes, but an illusion created by the eyes exploring and translating what they see into internal sensation, and sense of dynamic counterpoise. Beauty becomes linked to a relating of the internal sensations together by analogy, a possibility we acquire from instinct and experience, so that the view of an object or a building leads us to a complex sense of function united in form, to a harmonious unification of little sensations of push and thrust, to a relation constituted by feeling the active forces of strain and counterstrain in a building.

Kant's conception of the analogies of experience is that we necessarily link our perceptions dynamically in relation to time, to temporal determination. The analogies are part of the deep and mysterious way we connect together what we perceive, not logical but analogical.

Both Diderot and Kant reflect on the interconnectedness of experience. In Diderot's writings on aesthetics, the question of connection is both an intellectual and a practical problem; his writing explores the connections as the mind does when it perceives the beautiful, and in both cases what is going on is a working by analogy.

Chapter 31. On Mathematics at the Time of the Enlightenment, and Related Topics

Paul Henry

The Enlightenment was a period of doubt and pessimism in the future of mathematics shared by almost all the leading mathematicians and philosophers of the time. Philosophers even exploited such doubts for philosophical ends and reinforced them rather than trying to dissipate them. Condillac posited a *langue des calculs* – an artificial language, a perfect one, devoid of the ambiguities and indeterminations of ordinary languages, a language in which the correspondence between words and simple facts would be kept. He takes the object and method of mathematics as a model of a perfect language and not as a model of knowledge. His *langue des calculs* is close to Leibniz's symbolic artificial language, but the *caracteristica universalis* is intended as a method, a *filum Ariadnes* to guide our thought to the discovery of truths. Leibniz's main concern is that thought can mislead itself and get lost. Condillac's main concern is that languages put a screen between us and nature, between us and facts. We find in Condillac the idea of a pre-linguistic, factual knowledge, or of a knowledge made independent from languages even when it is expressed through the *langue des calculs*. His metaphysics is not a primary science or philosophy; like the *langue des calculs*, it presupposes the scientific facts and provides order only to what has already been established as scientific facts. Condillac does not repudiate mathematical knowledge, but believes it needs to be taken back to its source which is the sensation.

Diderot's critique of mathematics is far more radical. He does not believe in the usefulness of such a language as the *langue des calculs*, although he does rely upon the observations made by contemporary scientists, particularly in his *Éléments de physiologie*. For Diderot too, the philosopher must start with the facts established by the scientists and discuss not scientific observations, but the doctrine or theory in which they are embedded. Diderot's *Éléments de physiologie* are very illustrative of his conception of the task of the philosopher, and of what he calls 'experimental philosophy' as well, by which he intends to indicate the importance of relying upon the practice of professionals in any field. The task of the philosopher, according to Diderot, starts with the practical activities of scientists, artists, or craftsmen. Making scientific observations – or mathematical calculations – is as practical an activity as that of the actor on stage or the craftsman making an armchair. The philosopher defends general issues, brings them into contact with the knowledge of the professional and thereby refines or confirms them.

For Diderot, mathematics is a combination of signs which are by themselves devoid of any meaning; mathematics can be, therefore, a purely formal, conventional, and arbitrary language. He opposes the belief that the only good method for acquiring knowledge is the *more geometrico* method – the idea that the whole of knowledge can and should be rebuilt starting with clear, distinct and unquestionable truths from which all the rest should be deduced. It is the Cartesian method which he contests. The author compares Diderot and Spinoza on this point, and argues that Diderot's conception of knowledge was more accessible, more 'democratic' and practically useful. Knowledge for Diderot is not homogeneous but heterogeneous, and there is no legitimate hierarchy between different types of knowledge. Furthermore, there is no standpoint from which we can hope to gather, even in a purely formal way, the whole of knowledge.

The author next discusses the impact of Karl Friedrich Gauss's *Disquisitiones arithmeticæ*, and compares d'Alembert and Lagrange's attempts to re-establish methodological rigor in mathematics to those of Gauss and Cauchy. Gauss is not satisfied with the fact that the use of complex numbers has never introduced contradictions. This is the basis of his criticism of the demonstrations of the fundamental theorem of algebra proposed by Euler, d'Alembert, Lagrange and others. Gauss demands that we identify 'an adequate substratum'. As for complex numbers, he finds this substratum in the orientation of space. He praises Kant for having criticized Leibniz's attempt to reduce space to a pure phenomenal relation between substance, and for seeing in asymmetry the proof of the absolute character of spatial positions. But he criticizes Kant's view that the orientation of space is a form of our intuition. For Gauss, space has an absolute existence, an existence independent of our intuition. The object of geometry for Gauss is the 'true nature of space', about which, he acknowledges, we know almost nothing. Since Gauss needed geometry as a foundation for algebra, he grounds the whole of mathematics upon knowledge which he believes to be beyond the reach of human reason and experience.

Although we cannot claim that Enlightenment philosophy has directly influenced mathematics, the criticism of mathematics as a model for knowledge by leading Enlightenment philosophers such as Diderot clearly marks a historical development. The Enlightenment brought about a radical challenge to the classical conception of knowledge and understanding. Thus Gauss's conception of a mathematical knowledge based on what we know almost nothing about owes a debt to the Enlightenment critique of the classical conception of knowledge. Furthermore, Diderot's materialism, aligned to his conception of knowledge, seems to be linked to what Gauss put into practice, that which protected him from Kant's idealism and opened new ways for mathematics.

Chapter 32. Interdisciplinary Scope

Fedor Valach

The trend to predict new facts is evident in the present development of natural sciences. In 1900 David Hilbert formulated twenty three mathematical problems, the sixth of which was the axiomatization of physics, which should substantially simplify the tasks of physicists by permitting all statements to be developed through a finite number of axioms. Yet the project has so far failed; even the development of non-causality in relativistic and quantum physics has been unable to create such a closed model and has, instead, opened many new problems. In this context, Diderot's struggle to create a definite model of knowledge appropriate for mathematics may be the main reason for his opposition to the mathematicians of his age.

Gauss's concept of tacit knowledge linked mathematics to physics in a truly interdisciplinary manner. The natural sciences are usually foremost in connecting trends between different disciplines. Yet the concept of 'discovery' in mathematics should be distinguished from that as applied to the natural sciences. The first type of discovery only fills certain gaps in grammar. A conclusion in any natural science is usually connected with a *hypothesis* and uses several sources of evidence. An interdisciplinary knowledge emerges from the sources belonging to various disciplines. Citing Wittgenstein's criticism of Russell's concept of implication, the author argues that the *interdisciplinary method* can be developed by considering the role of *experience*. If experience can verify a statement in any natural science, the concept of hypothesis should lose its meaning. The *postulative formulation* of any interdisciplinary science should be adequate.

Experimental physics has proved the existence of rational numbers. In physics the 'vanishing' quantities of mathematical analysis have not lost their dimension. The author claims that the problem formulated by Gauss as the 'true nature of space' (Euclidean and non-Euclidean space) will be solved by experimental and theoretical physics. The fact that Gauss was not satisfied with the non-contradiction as a proof may have its roots in his highly developed *physical* thinking. This might also explain his criticism of demonstrations of the fundamental theorem of algebra.

Although pure mathematics may be interesting only if it can be proved, a mathematical theory becomes scientifically proved if it can be used as a model in a natural science.

Diderot's contacts with architects and engineers reveal his fascination with geometrical proportions. The author raises the question of geometrical symmetry in nature by asking why growing crystals keep their symmetry class. Symmetry fulfills an important role in art and engineering. It can normally be divided into translational symmetry and local symmetry. The former means repetition, for example the periodical repetition of tones in music. The latter is the equivalence of properties within the finite space. Experience repeated many times can lead through deformations of material objects to the forms of various kinds of symmetries. The geometrical invariants in symmetrical objects, so called symmetry elements, have the properties of algebraic units (groups and sub-groups). It seems that such connections between proportions in the architecture of Saint Peter's basilica and abstract algebra fascinated Diderot.

Chapter 33. Mathematics, Professional Knowledge and Technology: The Role of Mathematics in Society

Jan Unenge

This chapter considers the role of mathematics in society. Mathematics was 'born' of the need to be able to state numbers and carry out some arithmetical operations with these numbers. The ability to 'count' then became part of man's essential basic knowledge. Mathematics subsequently developed both as a tool in economics and trade, in astrology, to calculate areas of land etc., and, with scientists like Descartes, Newton and Leibniz in the 1600s, as a science governed by abstract principles.

In school, the value – and status – of mathematics has not been questioned until recent times. There has been a change in the way mathematical knowledge and skills are generally viewed. More and more people are talking about 'different kinds' of mathematics; situation mathematics, for example, and ethno-mathematics, and it is generally agreed that we need a day-to-day mathematics, separate from the academic discipline. This 'new' kind of mathematics must be rooted in the structure of everyday life instead of the internal structure of mathematics itself. It must be a part of public education, and be perceived as an important part of human knowledge and general cultural training. Thus it must in some sense return from what are to many people the specialized symbols of mathematics to a more everyday language.

One of the changed roles for mathematics in today's society is the increase in the use of mathematical models. Mathematical algorithms have become an important aid to such models. A number of research projects related to the teaching of mathematics have focused on algorithms as rule-following. 'Algorithmatization' – the learning and application of an algorithm regardless of the appropriateness of the task's context – has been identified as a serious risk in mathematics teaching.

Solving a mathematical problem may be said to have three phases:

(a) Choosing a strategy.
(b) Carrying out one or more calculations.
(c) Reflecting on the result of the calculation.

In the first phase the problem is interpreted, the formula, mathematical model and algorithm are selected, as is the kind of mathematical calculation. In the second phase, the calculations are done and the equation is solved. In the third phase the result is assessed and an attempt may be made to verify it, for example by a feasibility assessment. The author discusses the implications for professional knowledge of the use of computers in tackling these distinct phases and cites some of the findings of the 'Alternative Teaching Paths in Mathematics' research project (the ALM project). These include the discovery that pupils using pocket calculators can solve problems that they would not normally be given until they were much older, and can solve a problem that they do not understand at all – by finding a method for phase (b) without having understood phase . They are nor equipped, therefore, to reflect on the answer – i.e. to complete phase (c). This risk is not exclusive to any particular occupation or occupational group. What are the consequences of the fact that when using these tools one can evidently produce an answer to a problem that one de facto does not understand and cannot solve? Should professional knowledge not include the skill of assessing the feasibility of the answers we get from pocket calculators or computers? What kind of training is needed at different levels of professional life to allow the use of pocket calculators, computers and other aids to reflect professional knowledge?

In school mathematics phase (b) dominates because traditional textbooks and teaching concentrate mainly on the answer to the problem. The situation is quite different in the world of work (and in daily life). There is often no – or only one – right answer, and the wrong answer may have financial or other, dangerous repercussions. The ability to perform pen and paper calculations appears to be disappearing. One cannot immediately use the pocket calculator in a curriculum which has not been planned with this tool in mind; there must be a clear and non-artificial way of justifying the use of this aid. There is a clear need to overhaul both the content and objectives of courses. By analogy, the same kind of analysis is essential if these tools are introduced at work. However, when the pocket calculator is introduced outside the school, it is introduced into a real world where phases (a) and (c) are embedded in professional knowledge and when the calculator may sometimes be a technical aid in performing phase (b). Experience from the world of work, in other words, may provide the background to improved professional knowledge. This may also guide us in finding ways to describe what is meant by using the pocket calculator and computer *effectively and with judgement*, and may additionally indicate *what* mathematical knowledge is required.

To problematize this by studying working life is an important aim of the research into professional knowledge and technology. It is a question of breaking down the theory of knowledge, of reflection, into two parts; the first part is interpreting a result and reflecting on this interpretation, the second is to have such a distance on the 'tool' – the computer/pocket calculator – that one no longer blindly trusts the results it produces.

The mathematical knowledge requirements of different professions need to be analyzed. It is likely that a common core of mathematical requirements exists in several occupations; when we identify that core we can provide the proper education in mathematics for occupational training and working life and thereby raise the level of professional knowledge.

Chapter 34. Comments

Magnus Florin

SECTION VII. Epilogue

Chapter 35. Diderot and Dialogue: Reflections on the Stockholm Conference

Nicholas Lash

This chapter offers summary reflections on issues raised during the Stockholm Conference on Skill and Technology and in the present volume. The remarks are grouped under five headings: acting, the wisdom of grandparents, rules and reasoning, the end of Enlightenment, and the future of dialogue.

Chapter 36. Themes and Possibilities

Bo Göranzon

Section I:
Introduction

Chapter 1

Introduction

Jon Cook and Bo Göranzon

This book is organized in a way that responds to different kinds of reading. It brings together pieces of differing provenance and disciplinary perspective. A reader might take it up as a contribution to the study of Diderot, or because it offers a reflection on the nature of acting, or because of what it has to say about the history of ideas and traditions of knowledge, or, again, because of the commentary it offers on the nature of mathematics, or on the relation between the arts and the sciences, or on the future of professional education. The heterogeneity of the book's contents is obvious enough and is matched by the various identities of its contributors: mathematicians write alongside literary critics and philosophers; actors, physicists and engineers present arguments and commentary on topics as diverse as learning how to play a part on a stage, Hilbert's twenty-three mathematical problems, and the working cultures of the computer industry. Although this heterogeneity is not accidental, it is clear that it does not correspond to any established disciplinary paradigm whether in computing studies, the history of ideas, or literary criticism. Yet what is in this book would answer to the interests of people involved in any of these disciplines. In this sense the book invites a 'loose' encyclopaedic reading. Each chapter or section can be taken as the equivalent to an entry in an encyclopaedia and read in its own right, or it can form the starting point for a process of cross-referencing which makes use of the comments at the end of each section as a guide. According to this way of reading, the book has a structure of a network which the reader can assemble in a number of different ways.

Yet the work that follows this introduction is not put together at random. The section, 'On Practical Philosophy', establishes a series of contexts for understanding a key phrase in the book's title. Its opening chapter states a central issue which runs through the whole book, the relation between theory and practice, and, although the arguments that follow do not propose a solution to the various ethical and intellectual problems that group around the relation between the two, they do share a common emphasis: practice is not justified by theory; if anything, the opposite is the case. Nor, by the same token, is theoretical knowledge taken as superior to the understanding and judgements embodied in practice. The chapters that go to make up the opening section of the book explore the historical and epistemological consequences of an emphasis on practical philosophy. Through these the importance of an idea of theatre emerges: by way of a metaphor for the

activity of thinking and writing as a staging of encounters between traditions and perspectives which cannot be resolved by a single theory; as
a means of stressing the dialogic nature of thinking in practice, and as a
crucial way of understanding the form of Diderot's thought. It is here
that we find the elements of an alternative account of enlightenment to
those which are based on a belief in the triumph of reason and axiomatic
knowledge.

The next section of the book, 'Acting as a Model for Skill', takes up and
develops this emphasis upon theatre. The concern in the opening section
with the discovery of a philosophical tradition is replaced by a focus on a
particular activity and what it means to be skilled in an activity. This provides a more detailed exemplification of the importance given to learning
by example within the tradition of practical philosophy. Diderot again
emerges as a central figure in his account of the essentially paradoxical
nature of the skilled actor, at once immersed in and detached from the role
being played, a line of thinking which finds its equivalent in the Noh theatre's emphasis on the importance of an actor having simultaneously an
inside and an outside view of a performance. The cultivation of these skills
cannot occur through learning a theory but are developed in contact with
skilled practitioners and in a continuing experience of and reflection on
practice.

While all the pieces in this section are about the nature of acting in the
theatre, they are also presented as a model for understanding what it means
to be skilled. And this brings out another dimension of what is intended by
practical philosophy: its concern with an epistemology of skill, with the particular kinds of knowing and judgement that seem to be typical of someone
who is skilled at what they do.

The concern with the dialogue between different traditions of knowledge
and the theatre as a practice and a metaphor is evident in the next section of
the book, Alan Turing and Ludwig Wittgenstein – a Meeting of Different
Traditions of Knowledge. The section begins with a play script and with the
actors' comments on producing the play. This continues the reflection on
the nature of acting from the preceding section. But it brings out another
important feature of the book: it contains examples of what it advocates.
The publication of the play Beyond All Certainty in this volume marks a further point in the evolution of a text which has developed through a number
of performances in different places, including the cities of Stockholm,
Norwich and Cambridge. Rather than choosing to write an essay or commentary on the disagreement between Wittgenstein and Turing, the two
authors of the play stage a dialogue between them which brings out the
implications of that disagreement for other aspects of Wittgenstein's and
Turing's thought and for what was lived in that thought. A similar impulse
lies behind the Imaginary Confessions that form a part of the section, On
Practical Philosophy. This is another text that has evolved through performance. It uses dramatic presentation as a counterpoint to the more analytical and retrospective accounts of philosophical thought that surround it, at
once inventing in a new form one of the oldest genres of philosophical writing, The Lives of the Philosophers, and presenting the history of reason as a
history of passion, suffering and comedy. Some Enigma Variations, which

opens the section on Education and the Information Society, continues these experiments in dramatic form and dialogue. This piece itself forms a bridge between the discussions of the legacy of Turing and Wittgenstein and the reflections on practical and theoretical education which are the main concerns of Section V.

This reflexive structure does not simply mean that a book which contains essays about the theatre and acting also includes the script of a play. One of the main arguments of the book is that knowledge is internally related to its mode of presentation, and, as a corollary, that there are important kinds of knowledge that cannot be presented in explicit and axiomatic form. It is part of the practical nature of practical philosophy to respect and acknowledge this fact, but also to explore the substantial questions it raises about the relation between different modes of knowledge formation and representation. This is why the book's emphasis on dialogue is central to its intellectual concerns. *Beyond All Certainty* is a play about a dialogue between two major figures in the intellectual culture of the west. But it is also, at another level, a dialogue between dramatic form and mathematical argument, between the cultures of science and the arts. The pieces collected in Section IV take up this dialogue in different ways, including the essays which turn to the question of the relation between science and literature.

Dialogue does not automatically imply consensus. The account of Turing's work in *Some Enigma Variations* does not simply confirm the view of Turing developed in *Beyond All Certainty*. This is one example in a book that is traced through with dialogues about Diderot, Wittgenstein, Turing, the history of mathematics, epistemology, the nature of learning and education. Each separate section of the book is intended to open up new perspectives on issues raised in the other sections. The argument about the education of skilled practitioners which opens the book is taken up again in Section V, Education and the Information Society, but in a way which alludes to some of the intervening statements on drama, mathematics, and the epistemology of skill. Sophocles's *Antigone* is cited as a major example in the education of doctors. Engineers can learn how to do their work by reflecting on the skills of actors, and so on. Apart from these particular points of connection, Section V takes up the argument about the theory and practice which informs the whole book, but this time in relation to institutional questions about professional education and training.

Diderot was a mathematician of some ability. Julian Coolidge, in his "Mathematics of Great Amateurs" (Oxford, 1949) includes Diderot among his elected sixteen and thus places him in a class with Leonardo da Vinci, Albrecht Dürer, John Napier and Blaise Pascal. Diderot was genuinely interested in mathematics, especially in their applications. Coolidge concludes by saying, "I cannot leave Diderot without expressing my admiration for his really stimulating mathematical work when his other interests were so large and varied.

Section VI, On Diderot, Analogy and Mathematics, re-engages with Diderot's work in a way that explores his thinking about one example of a skilled practice, architecture, and its philosophical and aesthetic implications. Another topic in this section is a discussion of the reason for Diderot's criticisms of mathematics.

Why Diderot?

Why should a thinker two hundred years dead be put at the center of the current dialogue on culture and technology? It is by no means easy to comprehend why the thinking of Denis Diderot, so long neglected in discussions of the theory of science, should figure prominently in debates on technology and society at the present time.

Yet international interest in Diderot's conception of knowledge is increasing. For example, in a book entitled *Bright Air, Brilliant Fire, On the Matter of the Mind* (1992) one of the world's foremost brain scientists, Gerard Edelman asserts that biology is the key to understanding the brain and argues against the currently fashionable view of the brain as a computer. In setting the problems of his book Edelman refers to Diderot's play *Le Rêve de D'Alembert* as predicting the research of human consciousness.

Another example: the science faculty of the University of Paris has recently decided to officially rename itself Université de Paris Denis Diderot as of October 1993.

These are two small signs of the Diderot renaissance that is now taking place. Also, new editions of Diderot's writings appear frequently and interest in both his ideas and his unique mode of presenting them is abundant.

Still, this fact hardly answers the question why Diderot is the focus of a major international conference on Skill and Technology in Stockholm, September 1993. The answer is rather that Diderot brings together all the issues that have imposed themselves on Swedish scholars engaged in researching and investigating the concept of skill. Diderot poses provocative questions, more so than even Ludwig Wittgenstein (who was, and still is, essential as regards the epistemology of skill) about the respective functions of art and science in the process of Enlightenment, tacit knowledge and the value of work, questions that have arisen from the 1980s project "Skill and Technology", which culminated in the international conference "Culture, Language and Artificial Intelligence" held in 1988 at the Royal Dramatic Theatre.

Moreover, Diderot had a conviction that dialogue and dialogue alone is the appropriate medium for reflection on the things which we know, up to the moment when we are asked about them (i.e., tacit knowledge); this concept of Diderot's is analogous to the position that the Dialogue Seminar at the Royal Dramatic Theatre has reached independently.

It was therefore natural that Diderot should become the next topic of discussion in our continuous research of skill and technology. In 1989 a group of scholars and writers from Austria, England, France and Sweden met in Paris to map out the aspect of Diderot's thinking which could help us illuminate the formation of skill and knowledge. Since then, a series of seminars in Stockholm, Innsbruck, Moscow, Norwich and London have explored the possibilities offered by Diderot in helping us with the problems of developing a perspective on technology and society, the limits of Enlightenment, the relation between cultural criticism and the epistemology of practical knowledge, tacit knowledge and a non-elitist conception of expertise, the role of the arts as a basis for reflection etc.

Education and the Third Culture: Literature and Science

The international conference in Stockholm, September 1993 is (among other things) a part of a process of building a curriculum for an international graduate programme in the area of culture, skill and technology, a process that has been under way since 1989. The main feature of the thinking that has so far gone into developing the curriculum are outlined in a series of books published by Springer-Verlag: this includes a recent publication of a volume of papers on Skill and Education.

The Third Culture, as conceived beyond established distinctions between science and the humanities, is essentially an educational project, aimed at re-drawing the boundaries between academic disciplines, at re-evaluating intellectual hierarchies, at developing an educational practice at an advanced level which will not be short-circuited by divisions between vocational practice and academic thinking.

The curriculum for the graduate programme has developed a number of distinct principles:

(a) thinking through "dédoublement" the ability to think in a perspectively or dramatically dialogue-oriented way. This calls for a capacity to recognize the paradoxical nature of knowledge, to be able to act in a context of uncertainty; to recognize the value inherent in the sudden transformation of one point of view by another. We possess many example of this thinking, including the plays of Shakespeare and works by Diderot, as well as the philosophy of Wittgenstein. The question is whether we can make a new productive use of these examples, something transcending the routine recycling of their greatness within the framework of academic culture.

(b) The accumulation of a number of productive examples or case studies which students can use as a reference point for future thinking.

(c) Clear transitions from one kind of level of work to another in a context where students will be able to reflect.

(d) Bridging the gap between education and practical work, between "pure" and "applied" knowledge.

(e) The ability to think across disciplinary boundaries.

The Stockholm Conference provided an opportunity to apply and assess these principles: the problem is not simply to reflect on existing contexts but to attempt the invention of new contexts.

Section II:
On Practical Philosophy

Chapter 2

The Practical Intellect and Master-Apprenticeship

Thomas Tempte

Part I

In 1968 I was accepted at Professor Carl Malmsten's studio workshop for cabinet-making in Stockholm. I had behind me five years' working experience and, naturally, thought that I had grasped the fundamentals of the furniture-making trade. For three of those years I had been apprenticed to a very fine factory which specialized in the construction of railway wagons with elegantly-appointed interiors. I was fascinated and entranced by the work, and each day was a new, exciting experience. The trade, it seemed, was one of immense complexity. At this particular workshop there were about 100 carpenters, all very skilled men – and a few who were very skilled indeed. Many of them continued to work after retirement and had many years of work experience behind them. In the years before they settled down some had spent time in Paris or in the wood-industrial district of Berlin (a complex of workshops, timberyards and industrial research institutes), or at the big factories in Chicago in the 1920s. Many had mastership proficiency, some having at some point worked on their own account. These men were treated with great respect by the master-carpenter.

The Second World War had sounded the death-knell of handicrafts in Europe, which were now in rapid decline. The older men talked about this with a mixture of matter-of-factness and regret. The aim and aspiration of these men were to make a thing of excellence and endurance. I observed the easy way in which they worked, the lightness of touch, the concentration – and I saw the results. My youthful, optimistic mind reacted strongly against the madness of doing away with this method of production, a method which seemed to be so utterly sane and sensible, and so enjoyable.

I began to be aware of – and drawn towards – vast fields of knowledge, though nothing visibly confirmed their existence. The wholesome past was something to be utilized and practiced. There were signs of its existence everywhere: fragments of old tools, a template hanging on the wall – made on the basis of an altogether different premise than our own. I was struck by the fact that the design of an old relic quite clearly bespoke the purpose for which it was intended, and was not made of, say, a synthetic material, as is now the case. I began quizzing the older craftsmen: Why this? Why that? My interest in their knowledge and skills pleased them, but they were anxious about my future. "You've got a head on you lad, this is no place for you! In 20 years' time, the carpentry trade will be a thing of the past". No, no! I objected. And then they went on telling me things.

Stubbornly I persisted in my search for further knowledge, beyond their lucid descriptions of the trade. Somewhere (I thought), there must surely exist an all-embracing thesis, a universal philosophy. I had no idea of what I was looking for. When I came to Stockholm I began combing the museums, but found nothing about the history of implements. The museum staff knew nothing about tools either. Then, in 1966, quite by chance, I acquired a *Festschrift* on the history of the Order of Joiners and Carpenters. Ah, so there had been an Order of Carpenters. When? How did it function? Why had it been dissolved? Oh, it was a Guild. But wasn't that a reactionary organization – what! (I couldn't believe my eyes) – had their function also been to safeguard the ancient secrets of the craft and to preserve the quality of the work? And finally, a few pictures: an early 16th century plane from Nuremburg with chased-iron and ivory details. A carpenter's bench with marquetry work. This was something I recognized – from Kalmar Castle (in southern Sweden) where I had been fascinated by the intarsia panelling in the bedchamber of the mad King Erik XIV; the walls, ceiling and floor had all been inlaid by carpenters from Augsburg. In 1966 I went up to the Nordic Museum in Stockholm and asked if they knew of any useful book for a carpenter, containing descriptions of the old handicraft methods and techniques. In the 1960s "the past" could be 1920 or 1880. But now it was beginning to dawn on me that "the past" could also be the 16th century. Well, they said, we have a book about handicrafts from the 1930s. This I knew of. And a bit further back in time we have Roubo? ... and also Diderot, of course, – Aha? – "Yes, it is very comprehensive..." Oh yes? – The illustrations are published in separate volumes. Perhaps we should start with the section on carpentry ... I was dumbfounded – there were bold wooden designs carved on tool after tool.

Quite suddenly I was inundated by history. And it was systematic. But I wasn't! I was seized by confusion. What were these tools used for? Those planes all look alike. Why are they all included in the picture? What kind of a tool is this? But look there, a small hand. That must be some kind of molding tool. That little hand placed so aptly there so ... (to show how the tool was held) ... page after page. I was bowled over. It was as I had always sensed. The past had contained something worthwhile after all. Someone called Denis Diderot had seen fit to document the passing moment. What beautiful tools he had depicted and what sophisticated work had been carried out by those now long dead and forgotten, Those drawings are better than photographs – they actually show the objects to advantage. What an odd carpenter's bench, how big it is! Can it be real? Small sketches of craftsmen, like beetles crawling over the benches. And quite suddenly a realistic portrait of two carpenters sawing out pieces of veneer.

My hunch had been confirmed. Handicraft is a wiser method of production and the progression of human knowledge and skill is not necessarily vertical. Some work of an earlier age is in fact superior, and made with the simplest of tools. I began perusing all the structures made by man. I strolled around the town, reflecting on the age of buildings and the methods of construction. Which kind of roof-truss? Which were stone-built? The 17th century Riddarhuset, House of the Nobility, and the Royal Palace from the 18th century. Had cranes been used in the work? How was the work organized? The gap between theory and practice widened into a bottomless chasm. The old carpenters had advised me to go on studying. Well that is just what I was doing now.

Was Diderot intellectual or intelligent? Are they the same thing? I looked up the word "intellectual": someone who understands, it said. A lawyer, perhaps, could be intellectual, or was he intelligent? Was a carpenter intelligent ...? Well of course. Perhaps intellectual too? Yes, well in that case he couldn't remain in the trade, could he? Could one be intellectual in different ways? Intellectual, as in a person who tries to understand, someone who asks questions, the answers to which create new questions. An intelligent person is "quick to grasp"; he comprehends, but does he understand? If he continues to ask questions, then perhaps he isn't intelligent after all. He asks himself or he asks others. One day – when one has reached a certain age, comprehension or understanding will dawn, and one will live in the light of this knowledge. Maybe that's what's meant by being "intellectual".

Having been a maker of furniture for 34 years, I know when I don't understand. I have left behind the youthful passion to understand, to know, to be in control .... Practical working experience in the trade seems to run in 7 year cycles. These reflect the old "craft cycles". Way back, in ancient Ur in Sumer the craftsman's training and acquisition of skills followed the same cyclic rhythm. In my case, it was only in the 4th seven-year cycle that I have been able to create furniture as I want it. After 28 years, that is. After a seven-year apprenticeship, one made one's "Apprentice's piece", after which one became a journeyman for a further 7 years, and then one made one's "Masterpiece".

My vision of an overall framework of handicraft production had been confirmed, for example, by Mr. Diderot. I found that the best tools from pre-industrial times were based on an altogether different concept. The efficiency of the machines derived from means other than strength, working upon the material in many subtle ways.

I had already made a number of replicas of old implements, and this time I wanted to make an actual artefact that had been made with such tools. So having decided to make a reconstruction of the small, white-painted cedarwood chair that had belonged to Tutankhamun, I then set about constructing the world's oldest lathe. Soon after this I decided also to reconstruct the simple wooden lathe from Diderot's Encyclopaedia. I made them at the same time, alternating between the two. Ostensibly different, I realized afterwards that they represented the initial and final versions of a particular technical concept. They both work with a rocking movement, and they have many features in common. The twin-angled spindles are based on a traditional concept that is now lost to us. The twin-angled spindle has survived for 6000 years. With his encyclopaedic survey of handicraft, Diderot marks the end of the epoch of manual production. But before that, the Renaissance has already ushered in the new era. In Germany, water power is being harnessed and placed in the service of the mining industry. In Holland, land is being reclaimed from the sea by the construction of dykes and with the aid of wind-driven mills to pump out the water. In Augsburg, in the 14th century, the water of the river Lech is diverted through the city, providing power for the machines. At the beginning of the 15th century, the city water-tower is filled by means of a plunger-pump plant. Here too is built an elaborate multi-bladed fine-toothed framesaw mill for the production of precision sawn veneer. Which will, eventually, be used to produce the elaborate cabinets that will become a hallmark of the city for centuries to come. In Augsburg, which is controlled by the Protestant Burgher class, resides the Catholic emperor Maximillian of Hapsburg; it is the seat of the rich and powerful Fugger family. The Mozart family are prominent cabinet-makers here. This is where the Silk Route ends and the Hanseatic League begins, it is the gateway to Northern Europe; in Augsburg, the Middle Ages end and the Modern Age begins. It is here that Luther defends his doctrine and where the Reformation is initiated. And so the city of Augsburg endures, with its well-preserved workshops, historical monuments and archives, until, centuries later, it is razed to the ground by allied bombing raids during the Second World War.

In Egypt, iron was not discovered until about three centuries BC. The only known metals were copper and bronze, and flintstone was the stone most commonly quarried. Egyptian tools, in comparison to those depicted in Diderot's Encyclopaedia, appear primitive. A large number of implements have been preserved but they do not show a great deal of specialization. About a dozen different types of cutting chisels, five or six different types of saws. The hatchets are of a similar design, with some slight variation in size. The most common tool seems to have been a copper hatchet (adze). Seeing this and thinking of the work that the Egyptians have left behind, one has to admit that a sophisticated technology is not the obvious prerequisite for an excellent result. The artistry of their furniture-making is, in many ways, unsurpassed, both as regards expression and technique. Anyone who has stood in front of the mighty pyramids in Giza has felt their powerful impact; the massive stone-blocks and the soaring, straight lines of their outer wall facing. It is pointless to recount their height in figures. They are visible over a large part of the city of Cairo, and stand like mysterious mountains in the sunset. Enigmatic and incomprehensible, they have stood there for 40 centuries. The entire plateau on which the Cheops pyramid stands was levelled and smoothed using a small copper adze. To have organized and executed such a gigantic feat man must have developed other sides of himself than those we use today. To us the implements are not even primitive; rather they are rudimentary, to say the least. And yet look at the results!

Incidentally, it is of interest to know that the finds from the Great Pyramid have hitherto been insignificant. Last summer German archaeologists, with the help of a small robot equipped with a video camera, succeeded in discovering a narrow passageway within the pyramid leading up to a small copper-hinged door. Perhaps the Pharaoh of the Cheops Pyramid has managed to safeguard his secrets from the curious gaze of posterity for 4,000 years. What would an Encyclopaedia in the Egyptian kingdom 4,500 years ago have looked like, I wonder? What does Diderot capture in his? The oldest lathe in the world is actually the oldest known depiction of a lathe. It is from a relief in the tomb of the High Priest Petosiris. It is a two-man lathe and requires a good deal of mutual understanding between the operators. Fourteen years ago I demonstrated the two lathes in Sigtuna, not far from Stockholm. I was assisted by my apprentice and journeyman. The young apprentice, Ebba Siodahl, was required to split pieces of wood for turning from a tree stump. Since then nearly two cycles-of-learning have turned and Ebba has acquired a proficiency of her own. Today she is a qualified and experienced architect, and has outgrown me by far. Our forthcoming demonstration of a lathe may serve as an illustration of how the skills necessary for mastership are transmitted. At the Egyptian lathe she provides assistance, chiefly in the form of intelligent muscle power. At the Diderot lathe she is herself the master-craftsman, after having first observed and served.

Perhaps my most stimulating period was the time I had both an apprentice and a journeyman working with me. They quizzed me about techniques, methods and materials, history, and approaches. I really had to cross-examine myself, search my memory, consult old notes. Or look things up in books and think out new solutions. Their questions awoke new insights in me, and sometimes even questions of my own would receive an answer. One of the questions they asked was simply: "What exactly is hand-icraft?" After that one I was in a turmoil for several days! And I'm still wrestling with the answer. The Egyptian lathe is supposed to be in an Egyptian carpenter's workshop. It is in the company of a carpenter's block, a few saws and the ingenious folding chair, sella curulis, which was attributed foremost to a Commanding General.

Part II

Some reflections on cross-contacts between theory and practice

I have on several occasions, been invited to speak at conferences like this one. And as one of the few producing practitioners at such gatherings, I have often been given a favorable reception! On a few occasions I have encountered outbursts of enthusiasm similar to those accorded a professional entertainer. This is very flattering, but above all puzzling.

The things I speak about are derived from my own personal experience, work that I have actually done with my own hands. What about you academicians? Are you interested in first-hand knowledge? Or do you perhaps practice it yourselves? More often than not, the practitioners have had to illustrate the ideas of the theorists – endorse them, so to speak. From time to time, the artisan or craftsman is elevated to the status of a medium. This is short-sighted and something of an ill-turn.

It often strikes me that the academic world is rigid and ungenerous. Creativity is not exactly a resounding success, and originality is usually thwarted or opposed, rather as it is among my own colleagues. But we do not try to deny it.

Here, I would like to say that such a stringent critique is not directed at the present audience. You are here because you are, more or less, open to such ideas – but nevertheless. Such pitfalls are everywhere – yes, even where we least expect. Gnothi seavton. (Know Thyself.)

I do, of course, strongly believe that our entire culture is rapidly distancing itself from practical work, and a personal contact with natural materials. All the raw materials that we use come out of this planet which sustains us. Therefore it is not enough to know how to tackle a problem, or to understand how we function when we work – we also have to know just how much we can extract from material resources and the consequences of our taking; regrowth and recycling. This is a paradigm for handicraft in a global perspective. Some years ago a philosopher said to me: we shall have to return to handicraft because it is the only logical way to go. It is, presumably, as simple as that. Contempt for and/or skepticism about practical work is deeply rooted in traditions going back several thousand years. This is what an Egyptian scribe writes to his son, three thousand six hundred years ago: "The stamper of floors is in his clay in his lifetime – among the living. The clay makes him uncleaner than rope and leather thongs until he has burnt his clay. His clothes are stiff from plaster and his loincloth is in rags. His breath as it goes out is hot, even when fresh air blows into his nostrils. He treads the clay with his feet and is hurt. The rooms of his house are filthy and the floors in disrepair ....

But when the scribe is in office at the Palace there shall not be found there any misery or vileness, and he shall not fall into disgrace. For he has understanding for other people. Behold – there is not anything superior to books, as there is not anything superior to water". A dialogue between theory and practice creates energy. A monologue or one-sided imbibing of one of them creates stagnation. Perhaps I am naive, but I believe in the power of this dialogue to create the conditions for improvement, and to arrive at a greater understanding. I have found that it works. I have been asked many times to give lectures, or to teach with compendium and slides. But that is exactly what I do not have to offer. Come and visit me instead at my workshop, look around my woodyard and storeroom. Or come out with me into the forest, and I'll show you the trees that can be felled for different purposes. At this point, interest usually wanes, a sure sign that the practitioner's knowledge is of no great value. Of course there are many explanations for this – but, there it is. To me it would be unthinkable to leave my profession as yet and travel around, talking, TALKING about it. One day perhaps, when age has taken its toll, and I'm old and decrepit ....

The practical intellectualism is to be found in the workshop, in the studio, on the farm. It can hardly be described with scientific exactitude, but it can be sought in the magnetic field between our emotions, which create energy, and our intellect, which is capable of analysis. When these are in harmony we become enabled to shape the new.

Many people consider my criticism of the academic world to be aggressive and vengeful. This is a misconception. I am merely pointing to the paradoxical division between theory and practice. Nobody has ever been able to give me a satisfactory explanation for the sense in it. But theory is usually linked with power, and practice with action. To act without thinking or to give instructions that are impossible to carry out seems to me to be impractical.

I am a practitioner who has also had the opportunity to move on the fringes of the theoretical world. My gratitude to art experts in museums, archives and institutions in Sweden, England, and Germany knows no bounds. They have maintained and preserved the cultural heritage with great wisdom and foresight. In France and Italy I have met with both arrogance and indifference. Which is surprising, considering that they have produced what is perhaps the greatest fine art in the world, but also the legacy of Rome, a slave-maintained society. In Northern Europe work was not seen as a curse, nor were practical matters considered shameful. Work was a divine gift – of necessity burdensome – but a gift nonetheless. For the past 10 years I really haven't been able to give much thought to these IDEAS, which have, of course broadened and matured during this time. I have, however, persevered in my decision to stand when I work. But I do assure you: there is no dialogue between theory and practice! Sometimes a theorist acquires the intellect of a practitioner and vice versa. Diderot understood the significance of his commitment and succeeded in creating favorable working conditions. but Diderot's ideas were (also) forgotten for several centuries. His activities were an intrinsic part of that which led up to the French Revolution.

I have pondered a lot about why the past speaks so strongly to me. It is not nostalgia, nor is it an escape from the intrusive present. From the age of seven I lived with my maternal grandparents, both of whom had led active lives, and been politically committed from their youth. They were extremely interested in history; both written and orally transmitted. To them, history was a living entity and they would often speak about people from two generations back in such a natural way as to bring the past vividly before me. The fact that I am not alienated from the past must surely explain why I never doubt that "nothing is buried in time". My grandparents came from a background of precision instrument makers; clocks and the like. Work was an inevitability, and the basis for everything. They embraced socialist values, in the belief that Socialism would create justice and dignity for all. Work, love and culture (in the sense of cultivation) "The Cause of Work is the Hope of the World". The past has given us the present.

Tolerance and humility were the ideals, even if difficult to live up to. These values I suppose, opened my mind to the circumstances and conditions of my first apprenticeship and later led me to feel such strong loyalty towards the manual side of work. I am led more by a strong emotional intuition than by the rationality of French Enlightenment. I have learnt more and more to trust that intuition.

Translated by Angela E-Adegren

From Montaigne to Diderot: Pascal, Jansenism and the Dialectics of Inner Theater
Allan Janik

Coming from Plato's dialogues to *Rameau's Nephew* can be compared with emerging from bright sunlight into complete darkness, if it is allowed to use an analogy from Plato himself, inasmuch as our first impression of Diderot after Plato will assuredly be one of incompetence, superficiality, chaos and confusion. After Plato, *Rameau's Nephew*, for all its amusing social criticism, will almost certainly strike the reader as formally structureless, thematically trivial and philosophically pointless. Even in comparison with an early Platonic dialogue such as the *Euthyphro*, which reaches no conclusion, Diderot's dialogue seems to the student raised on Plato to suffer under the comparison. At least in the case of the early dialogues there is a philosophical point to their inconclusiveness. Thus Euthyphro's failure to provide anything more than examples of what it is to be pious, without being able to explain why they are indeed examples of the same phenomenon, allegedly shows us that he cannot be said to *know* what piety is. From this admission of ignorance readers should, presumably, learn that they must look outside of the world of everyday experience to the world of forms to discover the universal and necessary characteristics of piety. To know that you do not know something is, paradoxically, to know something very important, as every student of Plato learns. But this is precisely what frustrates the student of Plato, i.e., the *typical* philosopher, in approaching *Rameau's Nephew*. Turning the last page of Diderot's dialogue where the cleverly amusing parasite and the slightly-sobered *philosophe* go their separate ways is a puzzling and frustrating experience because there is simply nothing philosophical there to grasp onto – or so it seems.

In fact, our typical philosopher has been accustomed to the relative illumination of candlelight and must learn to appreciate bright sunlight in approaching Diderot. In learning philosophy, students learn typically to read dialogues in the way Plato wrote his. This is not always as advantageous as it seems; for what we learn in coming to appreciate the strategy and structure of Plato's early, so-called "elenctic", dialogues[1] is a particular mode of reading and understanding dialogues, which is certainly a necessary element in any sound philosophical education. However, not all philosophical dialogues are Platonic dialogues,[2] so the skills we have mastered in learning to appreciate Plato are not universally applicable; moreover, they can actually prevent us from grasping Diderot's philosophical depth. We can see why this might be so if we consider the reactions of a student who had not yet found initiation into the Platonic way of thinking when she was required to explain what happens in Book I of the *Republic* (which has the form of the early dialogues[3]). Having summarized what was said in the encounter between Socrates and Thrasymachus, she asserted boldly, "Socrates wins the argument because Plato wrote the dialogue!".[4] It is a philosophy teacher's nightmare to confront such a view; nevertheless, we ignore it at our peril; for, apart from being a typical Philistine reaction to Plato, it contains an important truth about Plato's dialogues: to the skeptical they have a way of appearing mighty contrived. In fact, Plato seldom succeeds in writing genuine dialogues, if one understands by that term *conversations*, in which *two opposed points of view* with respect to a certain matter are articulated and defended *à outrance*. Either the conversation seems genuine and the dialectics artificial (as in the early dialogues) or the dialectics engulf and annihilate conversation (as in the later dialogues). Above all, if it is Plato's intention to bring us to *self-knowledge* in the elenctic dialogues he is less than successful inasmuch as we often feel coerced into taking his side (the sad part about my student's attitude to the encounter between Socrates and Thrasymachus is that *Republic* I, along with the *Gorgias*, is one of Plato's more successful efforts at combining dialogue with dialectics; unfortunately, not everyone is capable of the concentration that reading such philosophical literature demands!). In any case, on this view of the matter Plato's dialogues are not conducive to thinking for ourselves – and his way of writing dialogues shows it.

As soon as one begins to take seriously questions about the significance of dialogue as a form for airing both sides of a debate with a view to letting readers form their own opinions, *Rameau's Nephew* takes on entirely new dimensions. Diderot's literary brilliance and philosophical depth combine, not to create an alternative to Plato's concept of dialogue, but to realize an important element in the Platonic program, the moment of self-discovery, by conceiving dialogue as inner theater. Just as Montaigne is the key to understanding the philosophical origins of inner theater as prose strategy for developing a critical stance with respect to received ideas and opinions, Pascal, who learned no less from Plato (principally through his Christian counterpart St. Augustin, another author of dialogues) than Montaigne, is the key to understanding the "logic" – or better, the dia-logic – of Diderot's inner theater. And so we finally come to the point of this discussion: just as Montaigne's notion of "conferring" showed Diderot the way to reading as a mode of self-discovery through critical confrontation with a text, Pascal showed him the logical structure that the text must have to draw the reader into dialogue with it. Briefly, we could put the point as follows: if Montaigne taught Diderot what it was to read dialogically as well as certain stylistic elements of writing dialogically, the *rhetoric* of dialogue, as it were, Pascal (himself profoundly, and, as we shall see, in more ways than he was himself prepared to admit, indebted to Montaigne) taught him its *logic*.

Dialogue enters philosophy with Plato partly in response to the problem that, with respect to many crucial issues, there is not only no consensus of opinion among the learned; in fact the wise seem often to contradict one another. In Plato's day a book collecting contradictions in the opinions of the learned, the *Dissoi Logoi* or *Twofold Opinions*, was widely discussed.[6] Later in the early medieval period similar problems arose with respect to reconciling the truth of various contradictory statements about the style and substance of true belief found in assertions or "sentences" the Church fathers.[7] The eminently dialogical Scholastic method of question and answer, which enables us even today to read theological disputations otherwise dry as dust with fascination, was formed to deal with similar problems of reconciling a superfluity of conflicting wisdoms. In both cases the strategy is essentially the same: to eliminate ambiguities, to eliminate outright inconsistencies and, above all, to develop a more general and thus more comprehensive theory in whose terms what is really true on both sides of the conflict can be subsumed and the apparent conflict thereby reconciled. Such reconciliation at a higher level is necessary for Plato and the Scholastics because they are deeply committed to the notion that "truth is one", i.e., the idea that all true propositions form a consistent whole in a way that, say, Montaigne as an anti-systematic practical philosopher is not compelled to be. Pascal's method, his dialectic as I shall call it, is an "existentialist", Augustinian version, of this recognized philosophical gambit.

Pascal's dialectic is at once made possible and necessary by the fact that Descartes and Jansenism stand between him and Montaigne making absolute claims to certainty and with respect to values respectively. Pascal, like the early Wittgenstein, was convinced that in real life we never want a mathematical answer to our problems; but also like the early Wittgenstein he was convinced that only mathematics leads us to knowledge.[8] For both Pascal and Wittgenstein the *point* is the same scientific and existential problems are entirely different spheres of human experience. Pascal's strategy (from which the early Wittgenstein could profitably have learned) is to show that "objective" and "subjective" certainty, the mind and the "heart" or emotions stand in a paradoxical, one might even say an antinomic, relation to one another. Thus Pascal opposes the method of geometrical proof, which is compelling in the abstract and general sphere of theoretical knowledge (*esprit de géométrie*), to rhetoric, which seeks these nuances of argumentation that will be "intuitively" compelling for a particular person in a particular situation (*esprit de finesse*). Both have a crucial role to play in human experience: human beings cannot dispense with either, but the two ways of thinking and acting are absolutely incompatible with one another. In the juxtaposition of the two, then, a sort antinomy arises. The matter is further complicated by the fact that justification in the sphere of the mathematical may be wholly general but it can never be absolute; for we can always ask for a justification of the method and terms of justification of the mathematical method itself and so forth *ad infinitum*. On the other hand, nothing is more actual in my experience than my own emotions; yet, these emotions can lay no claim on objectivity. Nor can "I" myself; for I am nothing more than my desires, fears loves and hates. Objectively that very "I", which is the absolute center of my being is nothing more than those loves, hates and fears as David Hume would later emphasize. Pascal's solution to his antinomy is to insist that neither objective nor subjective claims to knowledge have the total character that they make for themselves. The partial character of both the subjective and objective sides of our experience points to the fact that the "foundations" of our experience lie outside of it.

The ultimate "foundation" for knowledge, as for life itself, is faith, i.e., the admission that the finite cannot reach the infinite, i.e., the nothingness of my own being, my "Self", provides the crucial clue to the way beyond doubt. This is the core of Pascal's thought.[9] Our concern here is with his *method* of procedure as it illuminates the "argument" of Diderot's dialogue; later we shall take a look at what Jansenism contributed to the substance of Diderot's thought in *Rameau's Nephew*.

Fortunately for us, a clear account of the origins of Pascal's method has survived in the form of a conversation which was recorded between the newly-converted Pascal and one of his spiritual directors, Monsieur de Saci, at Port Royal. In his "Conversation with M. de Saci"[10] Pascal laid out his mode of procedure for dealing with conflicting wisdoms. This short work, which has in fact been a key to the formidable task of establishing the intended order in the *Pensées*, will turn out to be our key for establishing the logic of *Rameau's Nephew*. The dramatis personae of the conversation are the newly converted Pascal and Monsieur de Saci, a figure renown for his piety and learning. Pascal impressed Saci with his brilliance and a grasp of Christian wisdom, which was so profound that Pascal seemed to know the whole teaching of the Fathers of the Church without having read them. Saci was renowned for his ability to gear his conversation to the interests of his visitors. So the conversation with Pascal had to be about philosophy. Saci's question to Pascal was: which philosophers had he read with most profit? Pascal responded with a paean to Epictetus and Montaigne but which, nevertheless, elaborated their achievements as showing us the limits of worldly wisdom.

Pascal admires Epictetus as the philosopher, who understands duty as rooted in reverence for divine order and justice perhaps best among pagans. He finds Epictetus's stress upon the notion that God provides us with the means to discharge our obligations and to live contentedly in conformity with Nature by pursuing a virtuous life wholly admirable. Similarly, he admires the Stoic's admonition to suffer the most unpleasant tribulation, even to face death, in silent resignation. Further, Pascal praises the way Epictetus encourages us to accept our fate in the way that actors accept roles that they have not chosen in the theater, i.e., with a view to playing them "naturally" and pleasingly. Moreover, the emphasis in Epictetus upon the personal, inward, character of moral resolve impresses Pascal profoundly. True, there are certain problems such as the Stoic admonition to suicide when we can no longer fulfill the duties of our station but in general Epictetus provides us with an admirable account of the life of reason as it would have been had mankind not "fallen" into sin.

However, if Epictetus provides us an account of the glory of reason without revelation, Montaigne, the skeptic, shows us the other side of the coin, i.e., the poverty of reason without revelation. He is not an Academic skeptic, who insists that we cannot know anything, but a Pyrrhonist who admonishes us to reflect upon just what it is that we can *really* be said to know. He reminds us that there is a difference between mere opinion and genuine knowledge, that the more we consider the matter the less we can be said to know in the strict sense. Thus, Montaigne's merit consists in reminding us how often we flatter ourselves by thinking that we know something with certainty when in fact it is merely a matter of personal prejudice rather than justified belief. Skepticism is for him, then, a method for attaining intellectual equilibrium amidst the temptation to go overboard by committing ourselves to any and all modish ways of thinking. Montaigne's critical scrutiny of received opinions, then, shows us clearly that reason is full of contradictory opinions and thus the vanity of thinking that we can simply adopt the views of even the most distinguished thinkers without being deceived. In short, in Pascal's view Montaigne establishes that we are not to find certainty in this world, that, if we are to find it at all, we must seek it elsewhere. At this point Pascal reminds us that God and truth are one and the same: certitude, or lack of it, with respect to the one will also apply to the other. Yet, the distance between the finite and the infinite is an infinite distance, so there is no particular reason why we should expect to know God or truth with absolute certainty. Our knowledge of these matters can only be a matter of faith. In order to make the case for skepticism with respect to all forms of worldly wisdom complete, Montaigne further shows us that we only know that words like "soul", "body", "movement", "time", "space" and the like have the same meaning a-posteriori, i.e., that people who use them generally understand one another; we have no assurance that there is an a-priori certainty in the matter of meaning. Even the axioms of geometry, i.e., the basis of all proof are themselves unproved. In short, Montaigne's skepticism teaches us that pure thinking is little better than dreaming and in so-doing he teaches us to be humble with respect to what the intellect, unaided by the light of faith, can know.

M. Saci seemed not to be particularly impressed by Pascal's defense of the importance of philosophical acumen and quoted St. Augustine, the ultimate authority for the Jansenists, to that effect. This provoked Pascal to defend Montaigne's significance alongside Epictetus for Christian thought as providing a sort of dialectical *præambula fidei*.

Pascal argues that Stoicism and Skepticism are the only two possibilities for reason divorced from faith. Stoicism, ignorant of the fallen character of the human condition optimistically treats of human nature as healthy, i.e., as it might have been before The Fall. Thus, Stoics assume that reason alone can fathom the order in the universe to the point of understanding the nature of duty. Skeptics, on the other hand, ignoring the Fall, take human nature to be more impotent than it actually is. The latter fall into what amounts to a sin of despair; whereas the former fall into what amounts to a sin of presumption. Both see aspects of the human condition with complete clarity; however, both fallaciously assume that they see the whole when they only have a partial perspective. Reason without faith develops schizophrenically. Skeptics take the fallen condition of the human race for an ultimate truth and conclude that it is forever condemned to its present state of ignorance; whereas Stoics see only the grandeur of uncorrupted nature with its ability to control its own destiny. The one ultimately becomes a sort of spiritual laxity; whereas the other falls into an equally opprobrious pride. Only the Gospel is capable to reconciling these two opposites at a higher level, namely, that of living faith. Once we know from Revelation that the key to understanding the human condition is the notion that Christ, the God-man, died for our sins, we can understand why merely rational perspectives have to be partial. Conversely, since we are, despite our faith, still mere mortals and, as such, must understand the infinite through the finite, the philosophical antinomy that Stoicism and Skepticism present has a theological significance: in contrast to the Stoic, the Christian approaches virtue, as Kierkegaard would later emphasize,[11] without gritting his teeth; in contrast to the Skeptic, the Christian can doubt without falling into despair, i.e., because faith allows him to believe things he does not understand. In short, knowledge of what is alive and what is dead in reason helps faith to distinguish itself from its counterfeits. Thus, a perfect morality has room for both duty and human imperfection because it is based upon love, which prevents it from falling prey to pride or laxity. Thus, the Gospel reconciles what remains paradoxically irreconcilable to reason unaided by faith.

It is important to emphasize here that Pascal is not speaking about faith as a mere matter of intellectual assent. For him, as a Jansenist, faith is principally a God centered, as opposed to a worldly, *way of living*. So it is not merely a matter of simply slipping comfortably from one perspective to another but a matter of re-orienting our corrupted *will*. In short, we can appreciate the true aspects of Stoicism and Skepticism only when we learn to live in a truly Christian way. Here we seem to be a long way from *Rameau's Nephew* but in truth that is only on a superficial view of the matter. Pascal's goal in leading us to faith by "staging" an encounter with the opposed views of Epictetus and Montaigne has been one of setting us spiritually in motion, of combatting our moral lethargy. Epictetus, Pascal tells us, should shake up the lazy, who seek repose in material things by showing them that they are blind to spiritual reality and slaves to their own materialism. Montaigne is no less indispensable in jolting us out of the comfortable security, either of conventional wisdom or of science. Moreover, Pascal insists that Epictetus and Montaigne need to be read together because Epictetus alone shakes us out of our laziness only to replace it with pride; whereas Montaigne is "absolutely pernicious" for those who are at all inclined to impiety or vice. Read together, evil is opposed to evil, not for the sake of producing virtue, but in order to disturb us in our vice. The principle is clear: the most dangerous evil in spiritual life is complacency or conformism; therefore, whatever challenges our intellectual inertia has already got us half way to the truth. As such Pascal's strategy would seem much closer to Montaigne than Epictetus, who drily and directly tells us what morality is all about; while Montaigne induces us to think about the matter, albeit in a structured and disciplined way, for ourselves.[12] It is Pascal's peculiar way of setting us into motion by presenting us with an alternative in the form of an antinomy that paves the way from Montaigne to Diderot by a dia-logic for inner theater. Montaigne taught us to conceive our "inner" life as a debate or critical dialogue; Pascal, who has clearly learned a great deal about "inner theater" from Montaigne, now seeks to teach us how we can reconcile similarly conflicting but actually complimentary positions on morality by a change of perspective, whereby the complimentarity is preserved and the conflict eliminated by the more comprehensive point of view. Pascal's aim was, of course, nothing less than facilitating a "change of heart" or religious conversion. If his text functioned as it should, its dia-logic ought to change, not simply his reader's way of thinking, but his whole way of living. By living a genuinely Christian life devoted to simplicity in all matters of taste and good works, rather than theological speculation, in matters religious we ultimately achieve the Stoic ideal of conformity with Nature without falling into presumptuous Stoic pride or skeptical despair.

Diderot's "argument" in *Rameau's Nephew*, while more modest in its scope, incorporates a very similar strategy: the reader should be drawn into the confrontation between the *philosophe* and the parasite in such a way that he should be led (indirectly in a skillfully-crafted narrative packed with dialectical twists and turns) to reconsider his own opinions about the relationship between ethics and social mores, art and Enlightenment, on the basis of thinking his way through conflicting but (in fact) complementary positions. The very tension between the juxtaposed alternative positions should be so artfully conveyed that the reader's mind, like Rameau's nephew himself, must dance to encompass and thereby transcend it. The substance of that discussion turns upon Diderot's parasite's efforts to show that what we conventionally understand as good and evil is virtually the opposite of what we take to be good and evil in practice, i.e., of *what we like to do*. Diderot's literary *tour de force* comes as he draws the reader into the dialogue by making him re-think the experience of *moi*, the narrator, *as he encounters the scurrilously profound mimicry of the parasite*. In effect Diderot's literary craft has been devoted to producing a text whose ending actually transpires in the mind of the reader.

My claim till now has been that Pascal represents a crucial nodal point in the development of inner theater from Montaigne to Diderot, supplying him with a "dia-logical" strategy for structuring the confrontation between *philosophe* and parasite in *Rameau's Nephew*, which could itself be construed along Pascalian lines as a confrontation between a most genteel Stoic and a charmingly ruthless Skeptic. In Diderot as in Pascal the conflicting positions are in fact complimentary and somehow inadequate in their complementarity: the parasite for all his cunning needs respectable, industrious people to sponge off; whereas the values that the *philosophe* stands for have meaning only inasmuch as they define themselves against the values of the parasite, i.e., he must define the "good" that he represents against an "evil" that he is not .... In order to complete our picture of the transition from Montaigne to Diderot via Pascal it will be necessary to examine the transformation (i.e., *Strukturwandel*) in thinking about the values of the genteel Stoic, the *honnête homme*, that took place between Montaigne and Diderot. This involves examining how the Jansenist revolt against the Baroque conception of the world and society transformed practical philosophy into, what for want of a better word, I shall call "moralism". To understand Jansenism's significance we should reflect upon the ways in which the differences between Montaigne and Pascal reflect intellectual as well as socio-political developments in French society.

Montaigne's world was that of the Northern Renaissance, i.e., a Renaissance culture deeply imbued with the spirit of the philosophical and political conflicts of the Reformation. Montaigne and Justus Lipsius were convinced that a return to the teachings of Stoic practical philosophy was the key to restoring order and stability, "constancy", to a chaotic world.[13] Oversimplifying vastly: Lipsius provided a Roman model for the re-organization of society based upon a strict system of controls which stipulated absolute *resignation* in matters public for the individual; whereas Montaigne supplied a technique for re-organizing the inner life, the life of the mind designed to make the rigorous social discipline Lipsius required bearable by exploiting the "inner" freedom that Baroque absolutism permitted in the cultivation of the critical imagination or "inner theater".[14] While the former issued in the Baroque conception of "enlightened" absolutism; the latter proved to be more than its intellectual counterpart, the ideal of the *libertin* i.e., an "inner" strategy for coping with the Baroque demand for strict outer, i.e., public, conformity to authority in all matters, especially religion. Although the Renaissance had subscribed to the time-honored principle, "cuius regio, eius religio", it was with little enthusiasm. Nevertheless, the religious conflicts in France and the Netherlands in the course of the six-teenth century became so intense and intractable that a return to the Roman ideal of religion as a principle of religious consolidation seemed the only possible means to stave off total chaos in public life. So it is probably not entirely accidental that the Cartesian method for arriving at absolute cer-tainty in all matters scientific and the revival of (Stoic!) speculative or theo-retical philosophy was coterminous with the establishment of religious orthodoxy as a political principle. Thus, the rigorous separation of "inner" and "outer" characteristic of Neo-Stoicism doubtless did much to explain why Cartesian dualism, itself little more than a revival of Augustinian dual-ism, would have been a plausible, indeed, desirable ontological position. If this is right, then we do well to see Descartes not as contradicting Montaigne's skepticism but as complimenting his Stoicism and that of Lipsius by providing it with ontological foundations – something which helps to explain why Descartes could so blithely dismiss the whole subject of ethics in recommending conformity in all matters ethical and religious. In any case, both the revival of speculative philosophy and the political demand for religious conformity certainly contributed to Pascal's way of conceiving the search for truth as having essentially to do with a way of thinking about dealing with conflicting *systems*, rather than assertions or examples as in Montaigne, in a way that would hardly have occurred to Montaigne. Be that as it may, Neo-Stoicism stipulated a social and political ideal for the aristocratic intelligentsia, which was to fill the crucial role of public administration in the "rationalized" Baroque state, the honnête homme or honorable man. It must be emphasized that this was a code of conduct whereby an educated elite (whose other distinguishing characteris-tic was its medium of communication, the Latin language) defined itself in relation to the uneducated "rabble", which constituted the vast majority of the populace.[15] Lipsius's account of the state marked one political end point of the Renaissance inasmuch as he insisted upon complete conformity to the religious beliefs of the ruler as the cornerstone of a stable society and thus demanded an end to the religious pluralism that the Hermetic philosophy of the Renaissance made possible.[16] While Montaigne, true to his Neo-Stoic commitments, conformed externally and condemned all forms of non-con-formity unequivocally, his conception of inner life as essentially free and critical, as "inner theater", proved totally subversive for the Baroque order that he welcomed so heartily: his concern, indeed fascination with the body and its functions would prove especially subversive to Cartesianism by sug-gesting that the body somehow "thinks" independently of the (Cartesian) mind. Be that as it may, Jansenism was a violent reaction against the vacuousness of the Baroque ideal as it was realized in seventeenth century France.

Three sorts of objections could be raised to the version of practical philosophy that Lipsius created with the invention of Christian Stoicism as it became institutionalized in the absolute monarchies of 17th century Europe. First, its justification was principally on the basis of socio-political necessity and not philosophical merit. Secondly, it was a wholly dogmatic conception of the state and politics, leaving little room for argument and discussion. In the jargon of Kant's philosophy political philosophy was entirely based upon heteronomy, i.e., the will of the ruler, and for that reason could be criticized as irrational.[17] Finally, how Christian was all of this? This latter question was provoked by dissenting sects such as the Puritans in England and the Jansenists in France. Two features of this story are particularly important for the development of practical philosophy from Montaigne to Diderot: first, the dissenters took the worldliness of the Baroque for anti-Christian because it denied the infinite distance between fallen man and God's perfection; secondly, the notion that man's self-love all but totally deludes us individually and collectively with respect to our own motivation. In their commitment to these ideas radical Christian dissenters paved the way for the Enlightenment and to *Rameau's Nephew*. It remains to see how that could have been possible by considering the Jansenist literary critique of the values of Baroque absolute monarchy in Racine's theater and LaRochefoucauld's aphoristic transformation of Montaigne's "method" in his *Maximes* as stages on the way to Diderot's inner theater.

We can begin by considering why the sort of Jansenist theology that Pascal represented required presentation in dramatic form. It is a premiss of Jansenism that the Fall renders mankind too egocentric to pay attention to the moral demands that reason makes upon rational creatures. For the Jansenist we become rational only through a "change of heart", i.e., through transforming our way of living such that we bring it into conformity with the Word of God as pronounced by Jesus Christ. The problem is: how do we ever get into a position to "hear" the Word of God in our "fallen" condition, which by its very nature entails closedness to the Divine Word? The answer to this question involves *showing* us as Kierkegaard would later in *Either/Or*, how our very egocentric desires indirectly and confusedly lead us the way to God, paradoxically, inasmuch as without God they are self-destructive. The task of Racine's drama is to show us the "wretchedness of man without God" in elegantly moving examples of self-destructive vanity.

At this point it will be worthwhile to reflect upon some of the principal differences between Montaigne's near contemporary, Shakespeare, and Racine as Pascal's Jansenist dramatist counterpart. Aesthetically, the most striking difference is Racine's strict adherence to the classical unities of space, time and action. Socially, the reason for this difference is particularly important for our story: Racine was writing in a Baroque context; while Shakespeare was still very much part of the Renaissance. Racine was writing for the educated elite at the court of Louis XIV; whereas Shakespeare was writing for a socially mixed public, i.e., one which included the "rabble" (reflected in figures like Falstaff, Bardolph and Pistol in *Henry V*, whose attention he was obliged keep (the main social distinction between England

and the Continent having a bearing upon culture is the hard and fast Baroque distinction between cultivated elite and "rabble" was never made in English society). Whereas courtesy (literally) *demanded* close attention to the play in the case of Racine's audience, and, therefore permitted him to build up his play almost in the manner of an argument systematically and uninterruptedly; Shakespeare's audience needed to be entertained as well as edified: he could never risk the chance of boring any element of his very heterogeneous audience. Stylistically, Racine represents a vast simplification and purification of language with respect to Shakespeare in which all forms of ornamentation and ambiguity such as allusion, conceit, metaphor and the like are rigorously banished from theatrical language in favor of elegantly simple direct statement. Thematically, we find neither comedies nor "problem" plays nor histories in Racine's oeuvre, only courtly tragedies: at first secular ones, later religious ones. Moreover, Shakespeare's tragedies very much follow Montaigne's chief pedagogical principle: to wit, that we learn most from examples of suffering resulting from bad judgment. For Racine, writing as a Jansenist critic of the Baroque, tragedy is rooted, not merely in bad judgment but in a sinful egocentrism pervading all secular modes of thinking, what Ferdinand Ebner would later term *Traum vom Geist*, that could only be transcended by a change of heart, i.e., a complete conversion of one's way of life. I shall concentrate on one of Racine's plays alone, *Bérénice* to illustrate Racine's Jansenist critique of Baroque monarchy.

Bérénice is the story of how, upon being proclaimed the new Roman Emperor, Titus banishes Queen Bérénice of Palestine, the woman he has loved for five years, and, indeed, loves still. He justifies his decision to banish her, and effectively his love itself, on the grounds that Romans do not accept to be governed by royalty. The Roman imperial theme itself is a clear indication that the work belongs to the Baroque (Lipsius's Baroque practical philosophy was entirely modeled on Seneca's Rome). In fact, Racine's bitter, elegantly understated, irony in the work begins by attacking the hypocrisy that the Roman Empire was not an hereditary monarchy. But that is only the beginning. One startling feature of *Bérénice* is that nothing much happens in the play. We are given a pellucid picture of Bérénice's absolute devotion to Titus, of his love for her, of his resolve to banish her and finally of her banishment and bitter disillusionment. Throughout the values of Baroque absolutism centering around "constancy" are satirized with mountingly bitter irony. In the Neo-Stoic scheme of things the ruler justified his claim to absolute power on the basis of his practical wisdom. Neo-Stoicism sought to institutionalize practical wisdom by creating a system of royal advisers and ministers, who would have absolute freedom to criticize royal opinions at the price of absolute loyalty (which took the form of a complete rejection of tyrannicide – cf. Shakespeare's *Julius Caesar*). The mark of practical wisdom, as we have seen, is "constancy" or steadfastness. This is what Racine so powerfully satirizes in his play; for the constancy (a word that occurs throughout the play) is anything but the mark of wisdom; rather, it is the mark of Titus's inflexibility in making what Racine clearly takes to be an inhuman decision. The office of Emperor becomes an end in itself – something which is all the more ironic inasmuch as Titus does not seem to be particularly power hungry, or even particularly egoistic. Constant devotion to his station and its duties simply necessitates that he banish the woman that he loves for the good of the state as a true Stoic ruler should. There is further subtle irony in the fact that almost every mentioning of this theme is coupled with a reference to the fact that the Roman people, i.e., the "rabble" in Neo-Stoic terms, would never tolerate having a queen rule them. So there is a certain intimation that Titus's actual motivation, be it conscious or not, has more to do with fear of the people than it does with dedication to the state. Although it is "Rome" that will not tolerate a queen, it is clear right from the start Titus has the court in his pocket, so who else can "Rome" be but the "rabble"? It seems, then, that in practice the ruler's practical wisdom is dictated, not from a "divine" insight into practical affairs, as the Stoic idea would have it, but from the mob below. It is not respect for fate in the form of divine providence that motivates the ruler to maintain his honor and perform his duties but fear. In any case, there is no sense in which Titus can be said to exercise autonomy. His will is subject to a higher one but its is hardly a wiser one. In his own eyes he really is at the mercy of fate. There is no reason to doubt his declarations of love for Bérénice or that he would become a coward in his own eyes were he to succumb to his love for her. And it is precisely the sincerity[18] of his love for Bérénice which makes him as much a tragic hero as her. It is less important for our purposes to identify Titus's motivation once and for all than to see that the value system to which he subscribes is something that nobody in his right mind would choose to institutionalize. His conception of himself and of his duty produces an absurd, inverted world in which sincerity, i.e., public affirmation of one's own inmost thoughts and feelings, is forbidden. Furthermore, the tragedy in this world consists precisely in the fact that it is a world devoid of dialogue. In *Bérénice* Titus and Bérénice scarcely speak to one another. Titus's sense of himself, i.e., of "his station and its duties", and his concomitant resolve to be Emperor so dehumanizes his personal world that it becomes a world of tragic monologues, from which genuine communication is absent.

But what does all this have to do with Pascal, let alone with Diderot? For the answer to this question we must consider the Jansenist conception of the world of fallen man.[19] That world is an inverted world, a world *wholly* without constancy as Pascal insists, in which all love is self-love. In it things mean the opposite of that which they seem to mean. LaRochefoucauld's *Maximes* provides us with a scathing Jansenist analysis of man's misery without faith and the perversion of values in that world. LaRochefoucauld's motto is a succinct expression of both his perspective on social values and his pithy way of provoking reflection upon them: "our virtues are most frequently only our vices in disguise".[20] Moreover, LaRochefoucauld's aphorisms aim at focussing our attention upon the ways in which the virtue of the *honnête homme*, what conventionally passes itself off as respectability or decency, is in fact anything but that. The relation between genuine wisdom, conventionality and mediocrity becomes a crucial question in this context. In fact, we have a Jansenist assault upon the Neo-Stoic value system and thus the Baroque world order from the perspective of Augustinian Christianity.

LaRochefoucauld's very choice of medium is a critical development of the Stoic practical philosopher's employment of pithy "sentences" from ancient authors encapsulating received wisdom. The difference is that

LaRochefoucauld transforms his "sentences" into scathing barbs which provoke self-reflection. We know that these aphorisms were highly polished
and written in the simplest possible language with a view to avoiding all
ambiguity. The comparisons, symmetries and asymmetries they contain
should provoke reflection on our values and motivations, i.e., on our very
identities, with a view to showing us how vanity inclines us to see ourselves
in a better light than we ought to. The structure of the *Maximes* is, then, dialogical to the extent that the relationship between style and content produces kind of *chiaroscuro* effect in the reader, provoking reflection on the
state of his own soul, i.e., upon their meaning for *him*. LaRochefoucauld's
frontispiece for the 1665 edition of the *Maximes* alludes to this: a putto per-
sonifying the love of truth dear to Augustinians, and thus to all Jansenists,
has removed the mask of impassivity (i.e., "constancy") from the bust of the
Stoic philosophical hero Seneca, beneath which is a fragment of a citation
from Horace (later to be the motto for Nietzsche's critique of Wagner)
"ridentem dicere verum Quid vetat?": "why couldn't we speak a hard truth
laughing?". Augustine had pronounced the principle "love correctly and do
what you will",[21] namely, that it is not what we do but *how we do it* that ultimately confers moral significance upon our actions. LaRochefoucauld seeks
to provoke us into reflection upon the difference between the appearance
and the reality of love as the first crucial step towards a "change of heart".

Here the Platonic concern with the real, i.e., transcendental self, which is
"at home" only in the World of Forms, the realm of real moral values, as
opposed to the egoism the our sensuality leads us into, became transformed
in Augustine's hands into concern with the distinction between apparent
self-love or vanity and the real self-love in which we lose our self to God.
The Jansenist read this truth in conjunction with the old moral principle,
corruptio optimi pessimi est, and came to the conclusion that the state of fallen
man is one in which self-love has replaced love of God and our neighbor.[22]
So LaRochefoucauld could write, "self-love is the biggest flattery of all"(2);
at once identifying the major theme in the *Maximes*, clearly echoing Pascal's
notion that wisdom begins with the realization that the self is detestable[23]
and implicitly criticizing the official Neo-Stoic values system according to
which flattery was taken to be an evil that one must be on the lookout for *in
others*. LaRochefoucauld, thus, wants to turn the tables upon the Stoics and
simultaneously reiterate an *Augustinian* admonition to "know thyself", i.e.,
to be on guard above all against that sort of vanity which makes us want to
see ourselves as better than we really are. Although the means is different
the goal is similar to that which Freud would later claim for psychoanalysis.
This is of, course, exactly the Stoic tendency to pride which Pascal condemned to M. de Saci. LaRochefoucauld further jibes at Stoic wisdom, "the
clemency of the princes is often only a political means for winning the affec-
tion of the populace"(15). Vanity, laziness and fear play as much a role in
the exercise of clemency as nobility, he insists. Similarly, "the constancy of
the sages is only a way of confining their agitation in their heart"(20).
Writing with more sting and less pathos than Nietzsche two centuries later,
LaRochefoucauld ruthlessly sought to turn the tables on the Stoics. One of
the fabled Stoic paradoxes was that all good actions are equally good and all
evil actions are equally evil. Now LaRochefoucauld was suggesting that it is
often hardly possible to distinguish between the two when we take a hard

look at the matter: "if we judge love by most of its effects, it looks more like hate than friendship" (72). Another paradox emphasizes how our actions often have the opposite effects from our intentions: "the desire to appear clever often prevents one from becoming so" (109). These maxims are an important contribution to practical philosophy inasmuch as they help us to reflect, i.e., to cultivate our critical faculty in distinguishing, say, genuine humility from mere submissiveness and genuine generosity from mere ostentation. Moreover, LaRochefoucauld's examples make is clear that it is often impossible to discern unambiguously whether an action should be considered virtuous or vicious, sincere or affected. Furthermore, he insists that the agent is often in no better position than anyone else to understand the nature of his actions: "if there is a pure love free of mixture with our other emotions, that is something hidden deep in our hearts and we do not even pay attention to it ourselves"(69).

LaRochefoucauld paves the way to *Rameau's Nephew* inasmuch as he *relativizes* the meanings of actions and intentions. However, the hidden God that gives these aphorisms a Christian meaning never enters the text, so it is relatively easy to make a transition from Jansenism to a sort of secular cynicism with respect to values. Indeed, as soon as he is read out of the context of Jansenism he is sure to be interpreted as a *libertin* of exactly the cynical sort that Rameau's nephew turns out to be. And, indeed, LaRochefoucauld has been often read this way. There are such a striking number of themes in the *Maximes* which later turn up in *Rameau's Nephew* that it is hardly possible for the similarities to be coincidence. Moreover, the dynamic quality of LaRochefoucauld's prose is no less reminiscent of Diderot.

Let us briefly consider some of the themes of LaRochefoucauld that pave the way to *Rameau's Nephew*: (I paraphrase) genuine sincerity is rare; what usually passes for it is merely dissimulation for the sake of winning the confidence of others (62), intelligence is always the dupe of the heart (102; c. Hume: reason is the slave of the passions); the only good copies are those that make fun of bad originals (133); there are people whose whole merit consists in being usefully foolish (156); there are countless actions which appear absurd but are wise and sound (163); hypocrisy is the homage that vice renders to virtue (218); all professionals posture to make an impression; society is an ensemble of postures (257); (in an almost Kierkegaardian vein) weakness is more opposed to virtue than vice (445); there are bad qualities which makes great talents (468). Two other maxims are particularly important for Diderot, so I cite them exactly: "Madness follows us our whole life long. If somebody should appear wise, its only because his follies are proportioned to his time and his destiny" (207); "Who lives without madness isn't as smart as he thinks" (209). So, it should be clear that it is not only Pascal's dia-logic but his Jansenist values, both moral and rhetorical, which mark a crucial stage in the development of inner theater from Montaigne to Diderot.

In conclusion it will do well, first, to reflect upon the transformation of practical philosophy that has taken place at the hands of Pascal and the Jansenists and, second, upon how Pascal and Jansenism contributed to the substance and logic of *Rameau's Nephew*. We can begin by contrasting Montaigne and Pascal as practical philosophers. For Montaigne the aim of practical philosophy was to induce reflection upon experience on the basis of *examples* of a moving character. For Montaigne examples could be the vehicle for conveying practical wisdom inasmuch as they were examples of how things can go wrong when we appraise a situation wrongly. Because practical wisdom is a facility for the "appraisal" of situations, it is fitting that the *essay*, a word etymologically related to the word *assay*, meaning to assess ore for its precious metal content, is the appropriate form for testing the mettle of our judgments. Moreover, the point of practical philosophy is to strengthen our capacity to make judgments in widely different circumstances with consistency, not the formal consistency of the logician, but the "constancy" so prized by the Stoics. Montaigne's method could be described as an open-textured casuistry inasmuch as it was a casuistry without fixed principles in terms of which we should develop the capacity to distinguish rules and their exceptions. Its premiss is that what can be a sound, wise course of behavior in one situation can be foolhardy and destructive in another. Thus experience becomes knowledge, i.e., a stabilized disposition to size up situations, in a kind of Munchausenesque reflection upon examples of how things go disastrously wrong. For Pascal, on the other hand, practical wisdom is also a sort of constancy in judgment but it is 1) *moral and religious* in nature and 2) a matter of *perspective* rather than *judgment*. Like Montaigne, Pascal conceives of practical philosophy as a set of exercises in constructing sound judgment. However, he considers that this is not a matter of learning to develop cognitive skill (in Aristotelian terms, "intellectual virtue") but a matter of training the will to turn away from egocentrism (in Aristotelian terms moral virtue"). All the lessons of Montaigne are useless without a "change of heart". Thus Pascal's philosophizing, like the aphorisms of LaRochefoucauld and the theater of Racine, are vehicles for setting us into motion in that direction, i.e., for inducing us to reflect upon our own vanity and the ways in which it leads us to self-deception. Since what is required is a subjective, religious experience, all the philosophy can hope to do is to set us to thinking about who and what we really are. Briefly, it must eschew theory completely and in its place cajole us by means of provoking, surprising and finally edifying us to the point that we are prepared to make an act of the will. Thus with Pascal practical philosophy becomes an existential prolegomenon to a change of perspectives about the value of the things of this world. It is essentially a religious phenomenon with a *binary* structure. As such dialogue as a medium for comparing the relative merits of contrary perspectives and aphorism as a method for making us take a "second look" at the things we take for granted are its proper vehicles. Practical wisdom comes to have a moralistic and religious overtone, which permits of easy detachment from epistemology and to a great extent from philosophy itself. Though the actual conflict would take three centuries to materialize directly the scene has been set for a titanic struggle between a secular "scientific" philosophy, such as that advocated by the Vienna Circle and the "existentialism" of a Kierkegaard, an Ebner or a Heidegger. It would take an analytic philosopher as deeply religious as Pascal to detach practical philosophy from religious thought and to establish epistemological credentials of practical reasoning by rescuing practical thought from religious perspectivism. I refer, of course, to the later Wittgenstein. But that is another story.

To summarize: Jansenism, paradoxically, in the course of demanding a return to an absolute Christian faith so relativized the moral significance of all actions that the sort of transvaluation of values that *lui* suggests became possible. Furthermore, the need to create the possibility of existential choice of the Christian life as the only certain path in an uncertain world i.e., for understanding how only faith reconciles in practice the paradoxes and antinomies of the conflict of received wisdoms, necessitated developing a logical strategy capable of bring conflicting views powerfully and movingly into juxtaposition in such a way that both tension and complementarity would become apparent in terms of a third perspective. It was Pascal's great achievement to develop such a strategy (building heavily upon Montaigne). In doing so he provided a "logic" for inner theater which Diderot could employ in a secularized form to mould a type of philosophical dialogue which did not sacrifice conversation to dialectics or vice versa as is so often the case in the Platonic dialogues. In fact, the foolish wisdom of Rameau's incorrigible nephew is already present implicitly in the Jansenist dialectics of inner theater.[24]

Notes

1 For the now standard view that Plato's "elenctic" dialogues represent his first efforts at philosophizing see Gilbert Ryle's unconventional but nevertheless unconventionally stimulating, *Plato's Progress* (Cambridge: Cambridge University Press), 120 et passim.

2 We forget at our peril that philosophers as different as Francesco Patrizi, Galileo, George Berkeley and David Hume wrote dialogues.

3 See Ryle, *op. cit.*, 48-49

4 This in fact occurred in my Plato class at Wellesley College in the Fall of 1977.

5 One could ask here: must this be the case, i.e., could they do the job better than Plato did or is the "message", i.e., theory of Forms incompatible with true dialogue, i.e., open exchange of opinion?

6 On the *Dissoi Logoi* see Ryle, *op. cit.* 115-117.

7 On the tradition of commenting upon the "sentences" of the Fathers, which Peter Lombard had collected in his book of that name, see Josef Pieper, *"Scholastik"* (München: Kösel, 1960), 130-132.

8 G.H. von Wright was the first to suggest this comparison in his "Biographical Sketch" in Norman Malcolm, *Ludwig Wittgenstein: A Memoir* (London: Oxford University Press, 1958), 21. Despite the mountain of literature produced annually by the Wittgenstein industry no one has to date explored this connection in any depth.

9 This account of Pascal is much indebted to Alban Krailsheimer's *Pascal* (Oxford, Oxford University Press, 1980).

10 Pascal, *Entretien avec M. de Saci, Oeuvres complètes* ed. Jacques Chevalier (Paris: Gallimard, 1954), 560-574.

11 Parallels between Pascal and Kierkegaard abound. The similarities between Pascal's "Wager" and Kierkegaard's "leap of faith", for example, are often drawn in the literature on Kierkegaard. The methodological similarities between Pascal's dialectic and Kierkegaard's in *Either/Or* are less often mentioned; yet the skeptical sensualist seducer and the moralistic Judge

William have a great deal in common with Montaigne and Epictetus as Pascal presents them. Kierkegaard's dialectic, to be sure, does not put these positions on an equal footing as Pascal does. On reason why this parallel has not been recognized has to do with the erroneous projection of Kierkegaard's three stages on life's way into the argument of *Either/Or*. I am indebted to Lars-Henrik Schmidt for information about the relationship between Pascal and Kierkegaard.

12 If this is right, and, if *Rameau's Nephew* does indeed owe as much to Pascal and Montaigne as I have suggested, then the conflict between *moi* and *lui* in Diderot's dialogue, as well as much in the conflicts between their respective successors, is in fact a conflict between two types of Stoicism, one conceiving philosophy theoretically as science, and the other conceiving in a more literary manner as an unsystematizable practical wisdom. Should this turn out to be the case a good deal of thinking about the development of philosophy from the Renaissance to the present stands in need of revision; for the very concept of philosophy currently employed in academic circles will turn out to be radically defective.

13 On Montaigne and Lipsius as representatives of Neo-Stoicism see my essay, "Montaigne: dialog som inre teater" *Dialoger* 21 (Stockholm, 1992), 22-33.

14 My account of the "Baroque" ethos is based upon Gerhard Östreich, *Geist und Gestalt des frühmodernen Staats* (Berlin: Duncker & Humblot, 1969) and *Strukturprobleme der Neuzeit* (Duncker & Humblot), 1980.

15 On Lipsius's view the function of the police was to keep the "rabble" in line, cf. Östreich, "Justus Lipsius als Theoretiker des neuzeitlichen Machtstaats", *Historische Zeitschrift* 192 (1961), 54.

16 It is not that such tolerance was necessary within the framework of Hermeticism, but that is was a possible alternative basis for a political order in which sectarianism would not have political implications as, for example, the Habsburg Emperor Rudolf II seems to have thought; cf. R.J.W. Evans, *Rudolf II and His World* (Oxford: Clarendon Press, 1984), 94 et passim.

17 This is what gives Kantianism the claim to being a "critical" philosophy and it explains why Kantianism was forbidden as subversive in a Baroque state like the Habsburg monarchy during the Metternich era; cf. Werner Sauer, *Österreichische Philosophie zwischen Aufklärung und Restauration* ("Studien zur Österreichischen Philosophie, Bd. 2; Amsterdam: Rodopi, 1982), passim.

18 Sincerity was emerging as principal "value" at this time; cf. L. Trilling's brilliant *Sincerity and Authenticity* (Cambridge, Mass.: Harvard University Press, 1971). It must be emphasized, as Trilling rightly does, that Shakespeare is one of the pioneers of the English tradition of "plain-speaking" as the closing lines of his greatest work, *King Lear* clearly indicate: to be able to "speak what we feel, not what we ought to say!" would be somehow to have the weight of this "sad time" lifted from us. For all their differences, Shakespeare and Racine are at least in this respect similar. Thus there is a profound sense in which Shakespeare is a precursor of Racine. The latter is not mentioned by Trilling – something, which I take to be a major gap in his work.

19 A Jansenist conception of the world: Lucien Goldmann has taken pains to distinguish the radical, world-denying Jansenism of Barcos and St Cyran from the more worldly, philosophically rationalist version of Arnauld. See his path-breaking, if not entirely reliable, *Le dieu caché: étude sur la vision tragique dans les Pensées de Pascal et dans le theatre de Racine* (Paris: Gallimard, 1959), 158. I am much indebted to Goldmann for my understanding of Jansenism. It is he that emphasizes that there is no genuine dialogue in *Bérénice, ibid.*, 372. Moreover, Goldmann insists that monologue is the only adequate expression for tragic humanity, *ibid.*, 76; i.e., humanity without God. For Goldmann, following Lukács, the *Pensées* are solitary dialogues, *ibid.*, 77.

20 LaRochefoucauld, *Réflexions ou sentences et maximes morales* (Paris: Gallimard, 1976). I shall cite LaRochefoucauld maxims by number from this edition. The preface by Jean Lafond, one of the leading French authorities on 16th and 17th century rhetoric is very helpful in approaching

this important thinker. The translation is my own. Important stylistic features pertaining to the "tactics" employed in the *Maximes* are analyzed by Pierre Lerat, "Le distinguo dans les *Maximes* de LaRochefoucauld" and Jean-Pierre Beaujot, "le travail de la définition dans quelques maximes de LaRochefoucauld", *Les formes brèves de la prose et le discours discontinu (xvie-xviie siècles)*, ed. Jean Lafond (Paris: Vrin, 1984), 90-99.

21 Delige, et quod vis fac, St. Augustine, In *Johann. ad Parthos.* VII, 8, *Patrologia latina*, ed. Migne XXXV, col. 2033. For an overview of the impact of St. Augustine's impact on modern thought including such figures as Pascal and Kierkegaard see Erich Przywara, "St. Augustine and the Modern World", *St. Augustine: His Age, Life, and Thought* (New York: Meridian, 1950), 251-286.

22 Jansenists were pragmatic, anti-mystical Christians, who emphasized that Christian belief was no better than the actions which embodied it; cf. Krailsheimer, *op.cit.*, 6.

23 Le *moi* est haisable, Pascal, *Pensées, Oeuvres Complètes*, no. 136.

24 Pascal appears to have had the idea that we are all continually talking to ourselves in a kind of day-dreaming and thereby conditioning ourselves to believe what we want to believe. For this reason "change of heart" seems to imply a sort of silence in the "inner theater". This would also seem to be the case in Ferdinand Ebner, who was profoundly influenced by Pascal.

Chapter 4

Imaginary Confessions

Stephen Toulmin

Introduction

S.E.T. enters as S.E.T.

Good Evening – When Bosse asked me to be responsible for this part of our Diderot Seminar, discussing the relations between Science and the Humanities on the lines of my book *Cosmopolis*, I was afraid it would be boring, both to you as audience, and to me as author. People always ask authors to speak about things that excited them 5 or 10 years ago, though meantime their heads have moved on. If I am here today, that is because I had second thoughts – that I had an idea about the relation of the Natural Sciences to the Humanities that goes well beyond that book.

The idea was this. Most of us are taught to think differently about the people who produce stratospheric intellectual creations – scientific theories or abstract philosophy – from those who produce novels, music, pictures, poems, and the rest. Thomas Aquinas is presented to us in different terms from François Villon, Descartes differently from Rabelais, Newton from Shakespeare, Einstein from Picasso.

In a poet or dramatist, personal oddity is legitimate topics of interest. Villon is hanged as a criminal, Shakespeare is on bad terms with his wife, a painter is eccentric or paranoid, self deceived or dyslexic. These things are relevant to their work because they show us their "humanity". How different it is in science and philosophy! Aquinas and Descartes, Newton and Einstein, are held out as interesting, not for their humanity – let alone their oddity – but as pure embodiments of Rationality. What is Great about them is (on this view) what each of them contributed to the Onward March of Rational Theory.

* * *

This is not just a literary convention or a scholastic tradition: it is something many historians insist on. The article on Descartes and his philosophy in the standard French Encyclopedia begins:

For a life of Descartes, almost all you need is two dates and two places: his birth on March 31 1596, at La Haye in Touraine, and his death at Stockholm on February 11 1650. His life is, above all, that of an esprit [an intellect]. His true life story is the history of his thoughts: the outward events of his existence are of interest only for the light they may throw on the inner events of his genius.

It is as though Descartes' whole intellectual development – his invention of a new Method, for example – was a purely rational process: the working out of a logical thesis hard wired in Descartes' esprit at birth.

Yet there is something strange and questionable about this contrast between the two kinds of creative people – scientists and philosophers on the one hand, artists and writers on the other. What is it? Let me recall a fallacy familiar, long ago, to medieval scholars: the "Fat Oxen" fallacy. Too often (scholars noted) we talk as though a man who drives Fat Oxen must himself be a Fat Man; or, for instance, as though the people who produce rational theories – in science or philosophy – must themselves be people of uncommon rationality.

Speaking generally, our reply must, of course, be "Obviously not"; but we need to go a bit further. May not looking at the personal oddities of philosophers or scientists also help us to improve our understanding of their ideas? Instead of philosophy being a Timeless Discourse between pure intellects – detached from "outward events" and personal oddities – may we not see it as embodied in a procession of highly idiosyncratic individuals, who attack the problems of their times in ways as complex, rich and personal as any poet or novelist, painter or composer.

One 20th century example: Gerald Holton, at Harvard, has written about the life and ideas of Albert Einstein. Early on, he was puzzled by two individual features of Einstein's methods of thought – what Ludvik Fleck would call his Denkstil. More than most of his colleagues, Einstein was happy with explanations in physics, only if he could visualize them, as embodying geometrical symmetries, or other kinds of spatial order. In his General Theory of Relativity, for example, he developed new ways of representing physical phenomena, by showing symmetries and other such spatial features in those phenomena.

The other distinctive thing about Albert Einstein is, at a glance, wholly personal. All his life, he found it hard to handle literary language of any sophistication. Until his death, Einstein's command of English never went far beyond Ogden and Richards' "Basic English": his reputation as a Sage was not unconnected with the apparent naiveté of his utterances. ("If we want Peace, we must Love One Another.") He failed the last year's examination at Gymnasium, and finished high school only by repeating the year at a Pestalozzi school, where the balance was shifted away from literary, toward practical skills.

Were these two idiosyncracies quite separate? Or are they connected? Working with Erik Erikson, the psychobiographer of Gandhi and Luther, Holton saw that they were, after all, less separate than we might assume. Dyslexic children – Erikson pointed out – resort to visual thinking where normal children employ verbal thinking; so Einstein's visual Denkstil may have been one more product of his lack of verbal skills.

Is that all? Something more needs to be said. Look at Einstein's place in the history of physics, and we find that his taste for "symmetries" and so on left an enduring mark on physical theory. In particle physics today, patterns of symmetry and antisymmetry help to fix the nature of the game; so some central aspects of contemporary physics seem to be byproducts of oddities in Einstein's psychological profile. Yet who, before Holton and Erikson, supposed that the history of 20th century physics had been indebted to Einstein's dyslexia?

This evening, I shall go back to the years from 1590 to 1725. Let me reintroduce you to four people, all of whom had the opportunity and good fortune to play striking parts in European thought. All four had individual – not to say, peculiar – personalities. Did this oddity affect their work or achievement? It is for you to decide. I will just try to give you a picture of the World through their eyes, and their preoccupations: both the public preoccupations they shared with others in their time, and personal ones that were theirs alone.

For this purpose, I take a lesson from a book written in the 1820s by the English author, Walter Savage Landor, who devised a genre he called "imaginary conversations." (Lucian did something similar in Antiquity.) Landor took figures from different periods of history, put them together, and asked what they would have talked about. Here I give you something analogous: not dialogues but monologues – not imaginary conversations but imaginary confessions.

I show each of my characters looking backward, at the end of his life. As in a drowning man, his earlier years unfold before him, and display hidden links he can present explicitly only now. Do these connections tell us anything of his intellectual achievements? Perhaps not, but perhaps so. Everything of permanence in history – intellectual, as much as political – was, when it occurred, overdetermined: this includes the 17th century innovations in philosophy and natural science. All I suggest today is that the personal quirks of my four people played a more significant part in that overdetermination than we have tended, up to now, to suppose.

(I)

LA TOUR D'EYQUEM, VALLÉE DE LA DORDOGNE, FRANCE: 1 APRIL 1592

MONTAIGNE ENTERS LEFT REAR. TWO WINE BOTTLES IN A BASKET, HE PUTS IT DOWN ON THE TABLE: AT FIRST, HE IS VERY FORMAL—

MONTAIGNE. *Messieurs, nobles et honorables – Mesdames, belles et distinguées –*
  It is my proud Honour to make you well come to this my modest, rustic Tower.

  You came by way of Bordeaux? Bordeaux is, of course, my Metropolis! My honoured ancestor, M. Ramon Eyquem (a Spaniard by origin) was a noted exporteur of quality wines from the Bordeaux region. It was he who obtained from the Bishopric the title to this admirable estate of *Montaigne*.

(My friends jokingly refer to it as Chateau d'Eyquem.) His grandson, my Father, M. Pierre Eyquem, who inherited the business, was several times elected Mayor of the City, a position in which, recently, it has been my distinct honour to follow him.

HE FUSSES ROUND THE TABLE, OPENS A BOTTLE—

As you will see, I live here a solitary life: far from the demands of the Court, far from High Society. How did this it happen? Je vous explique: I tell you.

HE TASTES THE WINE AND SITS BACK—

As a youth, I study philosophy at Bordeaux with M. de Grouchy; but I do not finish law school there. The theological quarrels, the repression of the City by Montmorency, make that impossible. So, I train in Law at Toulouse; and, in 1554, when my Father became Mayor, I begin work as a Conseiller in the Law Court at Perigueux.

HE TAKES ANOTHER SIP OF WINE, AND BEGINS TO RELAX—

So I embark on a carrière typique as a lawyer and a parliamentarian. Three years later is my real Red Letter Year. It is 1557. I am 24; I have just entered the Parlement at Bordeaux; and there I find the cher collègue – Étienne de La Boétie – who is to become the friend of all my lifetime.

BY NOW HE IS EXCITED—

(Forgive me, I chatter like a magpie ...)

HE STANDS AND WALKS AROUND—

Étienne de La Boétie and Michel de Montaigne – you must understand – we are more than Friends: we share one single Mind – one Personality. He is – I: I am – He. Thinking about M. La Boétie, I lose all my restraint, all artifice, all studied posture – all those *masks* that les gens respectables hide behind in presenting themselves to others. Sadly, M. La Boétie and I can share our life for no more than 6 years. In 1563, on 18th August – wretched day! – he dies. I have only 30 years, 5 months, 19 days – yet with this événement affreuse my Spirit dies, too. Bien entendu, my body keeps going; Parliamentary duties occupy me;

HE SITS, PUSHING THE WINE GLASS ASIDE—

but, deprived of La Boétie, the work itself loses all charm. Five years after La Boétie, in '68, my Father M. Pierre Eyquem died in his turn; so I became Lord and title holder of this, my beloved estate of Montaigne. Losing my Father grieved me. He had introduced me to the learning of the Ancients – my tutor, a German, did not speak French, and so I mastered the Latin language at the age of three out of sheer nécessité. En tout cas, it was my father's good opinion that had encouraged my first experiments at making myself a writer.

HE IS MOROSE AND REFLECTIVE—

In 1665, I arrange to marry the daughter of a Parliamentary colleague, Françoise de la Chassaigne. The hasard – so to say, the investissement – is not entirely profitable. My wife brings me a substantial dowry – taken with my Father's holdings, it frees me from any need to earn my living au Parlement – still, in 25 years, my wife gives me 6 daughters, and of only one of them, ma Léonor, lives to grow up. Most galling: *Mme ma mère*, the Portuguese Jewess, persists in quarreling with me over her share in my inheritance.

Quant même ... by 1570, I am in a position to retire.

HE STANDS AGAIN—

Look there, at the inscription painted below the ceiling of my Library: it explains the motive of that decision. You can't easily make it out? Heureusement, I have it copied out for you here—

> *Privé de l'ami le plus doux, le plus cher et le plus intime, et tel que notre siècle n'en a vu de meilleur, de plus docte, de plus agréable et plus parfait, Michel de Montaigne, voulant consacrer le souvenir de ce mutuel amour par un témoignage unique de sa reconnaissance, et ne pouvant le faire de manière qui l'exprimât mieux, a voué à cette mémoire ce studieux appareil dont il fait ses délices.*

> {Robbed of the sweetest, dearest and closest friend, than whom our Age saw none better, none more learn'd, none more agreable and none more perfect, Michel de Montaigne, wishing to sanctify his memory of a mutual love in a unique testimony, and unable to find any better way to express it, devotes to that memory this Place of Learning in which he finds such joy.}

HIS EMOTION IS OBVIOUS—

All my discussions with M. La Boétie, our talks together, the shared life of our shared souls, can be, is being, reconstructed here in the bosom of my Tower. Our joint méditations, which I attempt to preserve in my soi-disants *Essais*, are dedicated to his memory. And, in all of these Essais, *my interlocuteur, my compagnon, my partenaire*, still remains at all times Étienne de La Boétie.

HE SITS AT THE TABLE AGAIN—

I study philosophy, bien; but this does not stop me being a Pyrrhonist – a Skeptic. Despite M. de Grouchy's best effort, I prefer the urbane irony of the learned Erasmus – known to les savants as Desiderius Erasmus of Rotterdam. His treatise, *In Praise of Folly*, shows the limits of Certainty, and the modesty of our Knowledge. In turn, Sextus Empiricus of Rome also underlines the néccessité of Skepticism, of this I am soon convinced.

My Father asks me to explain the *Theologia naturalis* of the Spanish writer, Raimond Sebond. Begun as an act of piety, this is the hardest task of my life. I have to write généreusement about a speculative metaphysics of which I believe ... *nothing. Enfin*, this is my chance to démontrer the obstacles that make such Certainty *unattainable*. As Sextus has shown me, every metaphysical question which pretends to *universality* is a trap, that tempts Humans to pursue a Certainty available to the Lord God alone!

Enfin, I write 150 pages on Raimond Sebond: wasted labor, it seem to me. All the same, I have *begun!* I become a *writer! – Comme on dit*: "Well Begun is Half Done." Yet, set aside metaphysics, what can I write about now? I need a less presumptuous style of writing – less abstract, and more humane. So I look for topics based on my personal *expérience*. I write of Sadness, of Indolence (that one comes naturally) of Pedantry, of *Friendship*: I reprint 29 Sonnets written by La Boétie. I write about

Cannibals, Names, Drunkenness, Books, *Thumbs*. Book I, 57 essays; Book II, 37; including my *Raimond Sebond*. Taken together – I assume – that is enough.

But my amiable readers do not satisfy so easily: they want more. I exhaust the topics I talked about with Étienne de La Boétie, and now nothing is left but memories and reflections from my own life. So I fill out the Essays that are already in print, and complete a third Book: thirteen more *Essays*, whose tone is more – how can I put it? – *auto-biographique*.

HE STANDS AND WALKS AROUND—

These memories are more individual, personal, intimate. *Entre nous*, I cross-question myself with unusual frankness. I do the best to present myself *unmasked*: in moments (allow me!) of bodily necessity – at the table, on the toilet, even in the bed of love.

HE LEANS FORWARD, CONFIDENTIALLY, OVER THE DESK—

You find this offensive? Moi aussi. Les dames de la Cour use my *Essais* to furnish their rooms – and, when I write of Love, their boudoirs. I find this trying: still, better be accepted as an honest man than as a liar. Yet what has our genital activity (so natural, so necessary, so appropriate) done to us humans, that we cannot speak of it without shame, and exclude it from serious or well ordered talk? We bravely utter words like *kill, rob, betray*; yet that other word – *fuck* – we say only through clenched teeth! As for myself, I order myself to *dare to say* anything that I *dare to do*; and I dislike even *thoughts* that are unpublishable.

My *Essais* win me new friends – or admirers. the great scholar Justus Lipsius dares call me "the French Thales" – *sans doute*, as a compliment but offensive to French *savants*. (Am I truly the first?) Also, a charming lady scholar, Mlle de Gournay, has chosen to be my adoptive daughter. In the Summer of '88, I visit her family home at Gournay sur Aronde in Picardie. Finally, let me add, they win me gracious and flattering friendship of Henri Bourbon, King of Navarre, who is now engaged in making himself the King of *la France entière*.

HE WALKS AROUND MORE CALMLY—

If I could have a second friend as close as *feu* M. La Boétie, it could – I dare say – be this Henri Bourbon. In the conflicts that break out across France, between fanatical Huguenots and dogmatic Catholics, he is head of the moderates in the so called *Religion Reformée*. Brought up by his strict Calvinist mother, he is target of the massacre of *Saint-Barthélemy*: néaumoins, he struggles to maintain the bonds of civility between the two communautés religieueses.

CONFIDENTIALLY—

From time to time – gratifyingly – I can help in his diplomatic *entreprises*. No one doubts I am a good Catholic – least of all the Holy Father, whom I visit in Rome. But I always avoid the Catholic irreconcilables of the *Sainte Ligue*, with their war cry, *One King, One Law, One Faith!* – as though no Huguenot could ever be a loyal subject of the King of France. My relatives – my extended family – profess both religions, so do I have to disown my own cousins? In secret negotiations of Henry of Navarre with the Catholic *moderés*, then, I am accepted as *interlocuteur valable* – as a trusted go-between.

HIS FORMALITY RETURNS—
En tout cas, Michel de Montaigne, your servant, and Henri Bourbon, the new King of France – formerly the Count of Béarn and King of Navarre – are long co-members in a discreet *fraternité*, about which I am forbidden here to say anything more.

MORE RELAXED, HE POURS OUT A FINAL GLASS OF WINE—
Now I am in my final years. For *la belle France*, my life is a time of troubles. If I face death without losing hope, it is because Henri IV has mounted the throne of supreme power. Wise, moderate, determined to protect both his former Huguenot coreligionists and his present Catholic coreligionists alike – so long as they act as loyal subjects – apart from this policy of toleration, I might despair of our future.

HE STANDS UP, PICKS UP THE BASKET, AND GETS READY TO LEAVE—
Meanwhile, life goes on. My female *dépendantes* – Mme ma mère, la Juive Portuguaise – ma fille Léonor – and my wife – survive several bouts of the Plague, and take care of my daily needs. Most of all, *La Portugaise* enjoys more robust health than I do myself. Already in her eighties, she will live into the next century. As for me, I long suffer kidney stones: given my frailties, I do not expect to see the year 1600.

A KNOCK—
Mmes, MMs, ayez la bonté de m'excuser – I am called away. I must pay respects to Mlle my granddaughter. Life – *je l'ai déjà dit* – goes on. Yesterday, March 31st, here at Montaigne, ma Léonor bears my first grandchild. Every Newborn [they say] is a Hostage to Fortune. ... Quant même ... I am happy to say—

AS HE EXITS HE LOOKS A ROUND WITH PLEASURE—
—that this little girl is to have an auspicious name. She will be called *Françoise de la Tour* – Frances of the Tower—

(II)

THE ROYAL PALACE, STOCKHOLM: 31 DECEMBER 1649

*DESCARTES ENTERS RIGHT, CARRYING A LIGHTED CANDLE AND A
SAUCER OF MILK—*

DESCARTES. Ts, ts ... ts, ts ... Where are you, petite chatte? Where have you gone – little machine? – I only wish to refuel you.

HE SHRUGS—
Hélas, it disappeared! Perhaps, I offend it by speaking to it politely, as vous, not tu, as an intimate. However charming, a cat is une machine; and who can "tutoyer" une mech-an-isme?

HE SETS THE DISH DOWN, AND STANDS BY THE TABLE—
Well, here I am, in the Palace of this formidable Drottning, Christine de Suède. Such a personality – at once imperious, yet so submissive! Paradoxe: Reigning, she is one of the Great Powers of Europe, and yet – ce qui est rigolo – she most wants to turn herself into une phi-lo-so-phe!

"M. Descartes," she says to me: "I will have you join my Court, as my instructor. Move to Stockholm, and teach me the Principles of Logic and Metaphysics." "Madame," I reply, "Your Majesty's Wishes are

your Servant's Commands."*[A MOCK BOW]* So here I am, an exile—
HE SITS AND LOOKS AROUND—

At first, Stockholm is bearable: the long Summer days allow for agreeable conversations. But now is New Year's Eve, and the Winter nights are épouvantable, flabbergasting. Also Mme ma Patronne, the Queen, is demanding. It is Her Majesty's Policy inaltérable to study Métaphysique before breakfast. That way, for the rest of the day, she can act as a public figure. This does not at all suit my physique: I am not a Lark, I am an Owl, and I am not accustomed to such hours. At times I even ask myself, "How can I bear this régime? Can I even survive it?"

HE LEANS BACK—

To comfort my hopes, I recall my native province of Touraine, where all the seasons are pleasing: Spring & Autumn are mild, Summer is never fierce, nor Winter either.

There, I come from a good family. My Father, a practising lawyer, wants me to be one, too: that way (he thinks) la famille Descartes may enter the noblesse de la robe. I disappoint him. One year at Poitiers Law School is more than enough. Lacking true principles – grossly pragmatic – Law is not to my taste. From my infancy I have pursued deeper quéstions. When I am three, my Father call me his "little philosopher"; but the task of convincing him that I cannot be a lawyer – that really cost me a lot.

HIS TONE SHARPENS—

My Mother? My Mother does not (unhappily) long survive my birth: this gravely irritates me. I may not be wholly free of blame for her death: still, Mme ma Mère abandoned me – orphaned me – let me down, in a thoroughly faithless, feminine way. Still, I take the event as a warning: never to trust fleeting affections – people give them, then take them back. Above all, not to trust the soi-disant "amour" – What a Failure of Reason! What a Flight from Rationality! To become engaged intimately is to join in a battle whose outcome you can neither foresee nor calculate.

Physically, I was not strong, but I turned myself into a reader vorace. Entering the College of Saint Thomas at La Flèche, I gained confidence. Les bons pères Jésuites, who taught me, guided my novice journeys into the Interior of the World of Reason – c'est à dire the intellect masculine. They give me to read M. de Montaigne's Essais: first these seduce me, then they confront me with the challenge to rebut their sceptisme. Also the Fathers teach me the Logic of Port Royal: this shows me (so to say) the athletic side of the rational mind. Finally the Good Fathers encourage us to read mathematics and astronomy, so they at once share with us the brand new Starry Messenger, composed by the chief mathematician to the Grand Duke of Florence, Galileo Galilei.

HE STANDS UP AND WALKS AROUND—

This beautiful little book, printed in Janvier 1611, showed scholars the discoveries Galileo makes with his new té-lé-scope; and it quickly reached the scholars in our community at La Flèche. Twenty years later, Galileo's book on the Principal World Systems might anger Cardinal Bellarmine, and expose M. Galilei to all kinds of trouble. But in 1611,

before the recent Wars, anything by M. Galilei had a power to warm
the minds of scholars like a sunny day.

HE SITS AGAIN—

My time at La Flèche was marked by one gloomy event, which we celebrate, or mourn, in the Great Chapel at the College. As Patron of the
Jesuit Colleges of France, Henri Bourbon bequeathed to La Flèche care
and custody of his heart. (After his death, he means: no one foresaw the
deed by which Ravaillac, Jesuit manqué, decapitated a whole
Kingdom.) So, without warning, the College received the heart of the
dead King; and this duty became the occasion for a series of solemn
annual ceremonies.

In June 1610 (the month after Henri's murder) the sad relic in a silver chalice was consecrated on the Chapel altar. In 1611, for l'anniver-
saire, people came from the whole region to honour him: for this
occasion, a pyramid was built as tall as seven grown men. Meanwhile,
the senior students prepared mournful exercises in Latin, Greek, and
French; and these exercises were printed by Jacques Rezé in the town of
La Flèche. (I myself made this task a reason to *approfondir* – to deepen
– my reading of Galilei's Siderius Nuncius, which had just arrived.)

The King's death (hélas) was a prelude to the Wars from which the
peoples of Europe were freed only last year. Thirty years of barbaric
conflict, to glorify the Prince of Peace and His gentle Mother, and prove
the Holy Truths of the Christian Faith! – it was a monstrous spectacle.

Believe me: I saw it for myself! After wasting a year at Poitiers Law
School, I visited the Netherlands as a Gentleman Observer in the
Military Academy of Maurits of Nassau. Though a Protestant, this
Engineer Prince was recognized by all to be a Master of military science. Next, I join the Duke of Bavaria, in Austria. As an Observer, I
observe not just military *événements*, but the suffering of their innocent
victims.

HE STANDS: HIS INDIGNATION GROWS—

The War seems endless: the army of Gustavus Adolphus joins the battle, and the suffering is merely prolonged. Meanwhile, no one can
remember the original purpose of all this carnage, this bloodletting,
this sacking of cities – least of all the learned Professors of Theology.

HE FIDDLES WITH THE DESK—

Everything the Good Fathers had taught at La Flèche, my scholarly
training, my intellectual soul – in a word, my Reason – was repelled by
the irrationality of the War. There must be a better way to settle doctri-
nal disputes – some clear, self-evident and effective method, which can
be grasped by thinking men of any country and religion.

HE SITS AND RECOVERS HIS POISE—

"What is this Method?", I wonder. I leave the War, travel around, and
return to the Netherlands to take up my studies: not least, my study of
mathematics, in which this Problem of Method might find a solution. I
meet the learned Beeckman, who takes me under his wing, and I am
enchanted to read Galilei's new book on the Principal World Systems.

INDIGNATION RETURNS—

Like a thunderbolt, the news reaches us that Holy Church condemns
the text. I am bowled over. Galileo's arguments convince me; yet the

Judgment of the Church has a claim on my loyalty. Must I hide the text of my own cosmology, my treatise de Mundo? After this condemnation, how can I work as a Philosopher of Nature? My spiritual director advises me to continue working on some more abstract – how can I express it? – me-tho-do-log-ic-al subject. Such a text – he said – may escape the eyes of Cardinal Bellarmine's censors. At first, I take his advice: so I compose my Discours de la Méthode and my Méditations. Still, Galilei's arguments have convinced me, so how can I for ever delay publishing my own scientific ideas?

HE LOOKS AROUND, CONFIDENTIALLY—

There is – it seems – one other way to go. I can publish those ideas, but in a dissimulated form. In my secret journals, I note my new motto, Larvatus prodeo. I go on stage masked – my face hidden – ambiguously. Since then, in publishing all my theories, I have taken good care to elude the censure of the Church. After all, I cannot believe the Church can for ever ignore the wisdom of M. Galilei. What was it first drew me to him? He shows us all the power that mathematical proof gives us in the Sciences of Nature. As he put it, "The Book of Nature is encoded – written in an exotic language, that it is the scholars' task to decipher.

What is the alphabet, the system of this language? It is – precisely – Mathematics. Mathematicians, and only mathematicians can decipher, and read for themselves, the true text of the Book of Nature."

HE GAINS CONFIDENCE—

Galileo's image seized my imagination with unforgettable power. The Philosopher of Nature who learns mathematics becomes Chief Decoder of the Secret Writings of the Creator – that was no mean task!

I am on my own, here in Stockholm? Yes, I am here on my own – not just an exile, but a hermit. I have no woman friend with me, not even a companion – only my valet, if this Nordic buffoon counts as a valet.

Did I always run my life like that? Not at all. When I lived in Holland, I employed a housekeeper, who organized all my material life. She took care of my needs; she comforted my frailties; she understood the phrase, "bonne à tout faire". Not surprisingly, perhaps, she became pregnant. Her little girl (I acknowledge her as my niece) was entertaining enough – a little kitten – but when she was aged six she took ill and died.

I felt more chagrin over the death of my kitten than I had expected. But then, it was not the first time that a woman had abandoned me.

THE BELL RINGS ONCE: HE STANDS UP IN IRRITATION—

Hm, Mme l'Impératrice does not abandon me: too much the contrary. She is a Queen, She is a Sovereign, but She is a Woman too, with female frailties and irrationalities. The Winter nights are long; one cannot talk of philosophy for 12 hours on end. The feelings of a warm hearted woman like Queen Christina are very pressing: she is forever wanting to discuss with me the subject of Amour. "M. René," she says, "We – toi et moi – are not sufficiently intime." "Your Royal Majesty," I answer politely – how can one call a Queen tu – like a member of one's family? On ne peut pas tutoyer une Monarque! – "Your Royal Majesty, I will prepare a Treatise on the Passions for Your Majesty, in which I will demonstrate to Your Majesty the me-chan-isms by which Madame's Body generates in her Soul those tender feelings that can so easily unseat the Reason." This reply displeases her as a Woman; but, as a Phi-lo-so-pher, she can hardly decline to accept the dedication of my Treatise.

THE BELL RINGS A SECOND TIME, MORE IMPATIENTLY—

Je viens, Madame, je viens tout de suite. "Your Majesty's Wishes are your Servant's Commands" [HE BOWS AGAIN, LESS AMIABLY] Or they are so, just so long as they are capable of bring satisfied within the World of Men – c'est à dire, the World of Rationalité!

(III)

THE ROYAL LIBRARY, HANOVER, GERMANY: 18 AUGUST 1716

LEIBNIZ LIMPS ACROSS TO A LEATHER CHAIR AND SITS WITH HIS FOOT ON A FOOTSTOOL: HE SUFFERS FROM GOUT—

LEIBNIZ. Meiner Damen und Herren – Seien Sie herzlich willkommen ins Königliches-Elektorisches Bibliothek der hoch geehrter Georg von Hanover – [HE MAKES AS IF TO BOW] – Ihr gehorsamer Diener ....

Entschuldigen – Excuse. I introduce myself: Gottfried Wilhelm, Freiherr von Leibniz. Seit 40 years, from 1676, have the direction und maintenance of the Bibliothek of the herzogliche Familie Braunschweig been my duties. (Forty years? Not believable? Yet Gott be Praised – Arithmetik tells no lies!)

Now am I trapped in this chair, mit Podagra – Gout. Walk about can I not: even to stand is hard. For News can I only on Correspondents und Visitors rely. So what can you inform me? What News bring you from – from – ... (?)

... from London you are arriving? Ach so, Ich muß again Englisch speak, or try so to do. Since 43 years was I not in Großbritannien, aber jetzt lives meine ganz beste Studentin dabei. You know, perhaps, meine Caroline, the Prinzess – how is it? – von Land Vells? Pays de Galles, like diplomaten say? Leider, since 1714 is staying the whole kingly Familie in England. After my present Master, King Georg der Erst, wird Prinzessin Caroline's Mann "King Georg der Second von England" sein.

Wann ze Familie ist zu England geruft, was mein best Hope with them to move and ein powervolle Rolle im Großbritannische Academie spielen. Aber, the backers of the Local Hero, Isaac Neuton, complain to the King, und so bring mein best Hope zu nichte. Even die gute Prinzessin Caroline can nichts tun.

So Here I am, Here I sit – isolé, a cripple – und mein Brain is turning to Wurst. in Leipzig was I born – Ich war Leipziger – now feel I more like a Braunschweiger (nicht wahr?) ein Braunschweiger Wurst.

Der best I can do is zu Prinzessin Caroline Letters to send, to opset the followers von Neuton und Locke. This evening selbst – mein Assistent, the good Eckhart reminds me – leaves the Kurier für London; und mit Ihm mein latest – mein fifth – answer to the blaspheming und ignorant Samuel Clarke.

HE RELAXES—

Pardon: it is long I have not spoken Englisch. Always (meinen Sie) was I a Man of the World. In Body, living here alone, ist mein life here isolée: I am a Schwann disguise as a Gander – Gänser, so zu sagen. In Geist, I still maintain my activités, dank zu mein Correspondenten in all the lands of Europe. Am I like die Spinne ins Gewebemitte – l'arraignée au centre de la toile – ze Speider in its Vep. In le Monde des érudits, the World of the sciences, nothing happens except they write to tell der old Speider, Leibniz. So am I become das punctum saliens of the Learn'd World. Und so, with all meine weaknesses, kann Ich mein vocation – mein Lebensruf – still pursue.

* * *

Mein Beruf – my Calling, do you say? (Pardon, I can easier speak in la langue universelle des savants.) Let me recall you the circonstances of my origin, and the problèmes from which Leipziger – wie aller Teutscher – then suffer. I am geboren 1646 – 70 year ago. After 28 year of continuel fight, the merciless War must soon terminate. I grew (so zu sagen) in a Germany ruinée – zerstört – smashëd, zu grunde gelevell'd. Mein Vater has taught, at l'Université de Leipzig, Rechtsphilosophie – philosophy of right: Schade, through the War was it always, Might wins über Right. And ze hates – les haines – die Feindseligkeiten – which have prolong this shock of the Titans, are nourished more and more of jalousie religieuse – odium theologicum. And the habitants der Teutscher Länder, they become more and more épou-van-tés, er-schreckt – ter-ri-fied.

In its way, die Katholischer Armee of Erzherzog Leopold was bru-tal; but the mercenary of Lutheranisch König Gustavus Adolphus are without limit terrible. When our little German children will not sleep, say to them their Mutter, "Hush, hush; or will I give you to the Schwedes!"

Among partisans of different religions (semblait il) was no possibil-ity that they reconcile. Every one is certain that his very own Belief are right – are justifiable – please the Good God. Every one find the Good God's Design – die Vorsätze der Schöpfer – in his own prejudice. They lack all Méthode – aller Lehrweise – to arrive at an understanding, according to ze Sufficient Reason – die ratio sufficiens.

Without this understanding, natürlich, are they throwing them-selves one on the other. Not having arguments, is there only arms. They forget what say Good God Himself: En arche, en ho logos – In ze Beginning is der Wort – der Wort der Vernunft.

That, that was insupportable – for the learned people, c'était le dé-fi dé-fi-ni-tif: the final challenge. First of all, is needed new Principles von Human Understanding – the rational méthode to reveal the Design of the Good God. So I find my mission – mein Lebensberuf. My task, it is to articulate arguments that shall convince honest men from any religions.

* * *

How to do it? Ça, c'est l'histoire de ma vie. Through 40 years, have I travailed in hope to explain to all of the World the beautiful Principle of ze Sufficient Reason, without which no système de métaphysique, ou de philosophie naturelle, can give the true understanding of the merveilleuse work of the Créateur. So I study the languages, symbolismes, thought systèmes strange to the philosophique traditions. Languages written with idéograms – like the Chinese – do they suit the human thoughts more than languages written with alphabets like our European langues? The Chinese système of divination, I Ching, can it teach something fondamentale about our fonctions rationelles et intellectuelles? This was my idéal: a langue accessible to men of all culture, all religion, all nation – what I call my characteristica universalis.

It is hard work, even pénible. Partout a spirit of contestation persist. Among my correspondants (semblait il) some are not honest as I assume. The famous Bossuet – archevèque, historien, théologien not bad – trap me in an exchange of letters which first promise to be fruitful. I assume he is an interlocuteur sincère in my project to invite the leading savants of all orientation to a frank and open exchange of view.

But it turn out that Bossuet want only to convert me to a Catholique. The Pope offer me – can you believe it? – the direction of the Bibliothèque Curiale in Rome! After all, they would corrupt me? Du Lieber Gott!

* * *

And now, what do these "English Gentlemen"? As I warn the good Prinzessin, they understand nothing: most of all the solitary autodidacte, Isaac Neuton, who la Princesse call in her letter "le chevalier Newton." Chevalier?! Cavaliere?! Knight? Ritter?! Pferdlose Ritter, à mon avis. Neuton have never mount [so they tell me] either the horse or the woman. Before 25 year, I read his Principia Mathematica Philosophiae Naturalis – more exact, I read the first 30 pages – genug ist genug!

Well, what does he do of any interest, this so-called Chevalier? Nothing at all. He cannot even demonstrate by a preuve rationelle that the beautiful Système of the Sun and Planètes, which the Good God make as habitation for His Créature most high, must preserve always its constant figure. According to M. Neuton, the Planètes wander, lose their way, so that Mister God will intervene to re-establish the lost stabilité! What kind of a Creator is this? What kind of Clockmaker? The Beautiful Mechanical Création du Monde, is it some kind of Kuckusckuhr – a Cuckoo Clock?

Certainly not! The Good God cannot create a Universum that the Men cannot understand. That is easily prove. The Creator must an Universum supremum, optimum, perfectum, have gemade – sicher – ça va sans dire. But, an Universum that the Men cannot understand is certainly worse than an Universum the Men can understand. Ergo: if the Universum supremum perfectum ist, so must it be intelligible to the Men. The best Cosmos (an Universum tout à fait rationel) will be to reason – having thinkers clear and intelligible. Ho theos ouk esti mono sophos, alla kai dikaios, as say the Fathers of the Church. The Good God is not only Wise, He is also Just. We explain not only the Wisdom of the Good God, but also his Justice. This was the goal for which I write my Théodicée.

One need not even be Christian to understand this Beautiful Principle. It shows itself also to the Jews – par exemple, my distinguish colleague, Benedictus de Spinoza of Amsterdam. As even a Jew will one day insist – "Raffiniert ist der Herr Gott, aber boshaft ist er nicht!"

* * *

Of course – I protest to the noble Prinzessin about the ignorant dicta of Chevalier Neuton – and what answer does he give her to my arguments? "The Good God," he say, "can make the Universe just as He has chosen, just as He is pleased." What deep lack of rationalité! – How arbitraire! As if the Good God's choices are decided in a manner less than perfect, less than rational! Is Neuton right, every person return to his prejudice, and attribute them to the Good God without fear of refute! Even worse – Is Neuton right, the War of Religion can once again break out! ... Forbidden! Blasphemous! Unzuläßig! Unmöglich! Weh! Weh! Weh!

LEIBNIZ HALF STANDS, CLUTCHING HIS FOOT—
Entschuldigen, bitte! What do you say, For-Give Me. If I remember all the problem I have with that damned Neuton, und that idiot Clarke, mein Podagra give me the strongest Hurt. In-sup-porteable—

THERE IS A QUIET KNOCK ON THE DOOR—
The good Eckhart knocks. The Courier waits. So muß Ich mein fifth letter to the noble Prinzess finish. How to make this Idiot Clarke a fifth time understand? Only my courtly duty makes me go on. It is a pursuit of the inaccessible: I run after – is it not? – a Red Herring.

(IV)

THE ROYAL MINT, LONDON: 25 DECEMBER 1722

NEWTON IS ALSO IN A CHAIR, NOT FROM GOUT BUT FROM OLD AGE

NEWTON. So good of you, so very, very good of you – so flattering – to pay a call on a very old man on his birthday. It's 80 years – they tell me – since first I saw the light of day; though, in my heart of hearts, I suspect that it's much, much longer than that! You young people must think me an old buffer; but my flattering colleagues all declare that, if Isaac Newton was born the same year that Galileo Galilei died, it could be no accident. Yes, 1642 it was, 1642, another seven years before those Commonwealth men severed the King's head in London.

My colleagues, they mean it kindly, and I never object to flattery. (For an old man, it is one of the few remaining pleasures of life.) But you might rather say, It was no accident Isaac Newton was born on the same day of the year as Jesus Christ. Yes, yes, the 25th day of December in the year of Our Lord 1642 it was, the 25th day of December – if they tell me right (that is) for who knows such things with certainty?

I am – you see – a man without Father or Mother: at least, without a fleshly Father or Mother. They teased me with a tale that my Father died before I was born: a likely story! From the time that I was an infant of tender years – at most 3 years old – my Mother disappeared: not wishing to be a widow, she married the elderly vicar of the next parish – Barnabas Smith, the scurvy fellow was called – so I never lived with her before I was above ten years of age, and that Barnabas Smith went to his maker. In the meantime, I was raised and tended by an aged woman, who said she was my Grandmother.

Think not it was an easy life. Children bear not their burdens with untroubled hearts. It is long years since Barnabas Smith died; but even now it still afflicts my conscience that I swore I would go to the house in which he and my Mother were dwelling, and burn it over their heads.

My Mother's return was not much to my benefit. She brought three step children born to her and Barnabas Smith; and, ere long, I was packed off to Grantham to study at the grammar school. There I was introduced to the World of the Mind in which I have since spent most of my 80 years.

This was the year 1655, and already I began to indulge my curiosity. The day Oliver Cromwell, the Lord Protector died, a storm swept across England. It was the strongest I ever observed: by leaping up in the air with the best of my strength, I was borne on the wind a full twelve inches further than on any other occasion. My coevals – my fellows – at school found this a strange thing for me to do; but then, they were not like me – not like me at all!

After six years, not finding these school fellows to my taste, I was fit to move to Trinity College in Cambridge. There I remained for 35 years, until the Dutch King, William of Orange, preferred me to be the Master of the Royal Mint. When I went to Cambridge in 1661, young King Charles was newly restored, and those who were not reconciled – Mr John Locke and Mr John Milton, with many others – began to conspire with my Lord Shaftesbury within, or sought for asylum without, for the most part in the Netherlands.

Being a young man, I was not given to meddling in Affairs of State, and cast around for subjects that seized my imagination. In what the new students at Cambridge were required to do, there was little mathematics, aside from the Geometry of Monsieur Des Cartes. As a sizar, I worked as a College servant to spare paying fees, and for two years I did not excel publicly in learning.

I had to find my own way into the mathematical and philosophical texts that have since been my joy: my Tutor (Mr Pulleyn) thought it well to introduce me to Dr Barrow, the Lucasian Professor of Mathematics, who thereafter oversaw my studies. When he left the Lucasian Chair in 1669, indeed, he procured for me the succession to that office, and he continued as my protector in the years that followed.

My first years at Cambridge were a time of affliction for both Town and College. The monstrous plague that visited England in the year 1665 did not spare Cambridge. Soon after Midsummer the College dispersed, and I found myself back with my family in Lincolnshire. So, aside from a few weeks in Cambridge in 1666, I was free for the next two years; and I could commune with myself, with no outside demands or interruptions.

My flattering colleagues call these years my anni mirabiles: I thought continually on my problems, and I often found Methods to solve them coming into my head unbidden. Then was I in the prime of my age for invention, and minded Mathematicks and Philosophy more than at any time since.

At this time I fashioned my theory of fluxions, which the German Leibniz claimed to reach independently before myself – it was an error not to publish my results earlier. I satisfied myself that a single gravity fitted the orbits of the planets, as Kepler mapped them, the movement of the Moon around the Earth, and the falling of terrestrial bodies toward the Earth's surface; and I hit on a theory of colours that I published at last in the year 1704. Seeing how much trouble publishing the Principia in 1687 occasioned me, I wished to avoid being engaged in disputes about the Opticks; and would happily have delayed the printing longer than I did, had not my friends' importunity prevailed.

* * *

There are those who understand me to say that the sight of apples falling from a tree in Lincolnshire, while I was back home during the Plague Years, prompted me to think of gravity as the cause of terrestrial and astronomical motions alike. For that I must have been very simple: The true story is easily told. The apples fell when the wind tore them from the tree. They fell sidewise, and reached the ground more or less far from their starting points, as I did as a child when I leapt into the air in a windstorm. As it struck me, the fall of an apple and the orbit of a planet followed the same general rules – like the Moon around the Earth, and the planets around the Sun, an apple blown sidewise at greatest speed might trace a circle round the Earth, and never reach the ground at all.

At first – delicious years – I pursued my fancy in any direction I found entrancing. Fluxions, gravity, the coloured light of prisms, the alembics and receipts of the Alchemists – not least, the Age of the Earth, as told in the Chronology of the Ancient Kingdoms – Egyptians, Chaldeans, Greeks and Hebrews – even Hindoos, so I could find records of their calendars – all was grist to the mill for a youth whose excitement was free to explore all he willed. I felt like a child on the shore, who finds here a pebble, there a shell or sea weed that stirs delight, while the Great Ocean of Truth rolls on beside him.

It was my flattering friends who undid me. Only my dear Swiss friend, Fatio de Duillier, betrayed me not, at least at first. Once I was satisfied about the System of the World, maintained by God's benevolent action, through gravity and other forces, that plausible young Edmund Halley flattered me into finishing a manuscript of natural philosophy for publication. Hinc illae lacrimae – and such lacrimae!

I wept when I saw how all my enemies had lain in wait to entrap me. "Oh, that mine Enemy had written a book!", they thought: my innocent attempt to show how the Rational Creator chose to fashion his Creation awoke their jealous venom. Worst of all, that Spider in my Bosom – that Leibniz – not content with first stealing and then mocking my invention of the Fluxions, and presenting himself to the Learned World as its inventor – also writes complaints to the Royal Court, and seeks to turn the mind of the Princess of Wales against me. Spider! – Viper! – Swineshead!

"What," saith he, "Does not this Newton call the Omnipotent God an incompetent clockmaker, whose works are so ill made that – ever so often – he must needs put them to rights?" Nincompoop! How can he reproach me of all people? Could he ever demonstrate how the glorious System of Sun and Planets manifesteth God's Wisdom? Was it not I who brought to the attention of mortal men that Law of the Inverse Squares, by which the Rational Deity maintaineth his Creation? Does that Leibniz think that any other form of a Law better befits the Almighty's Wisdom than that which I set forth in my Principia?

The silly fellow! What child knoweth all that is in His Father's mind? God Almighty is no incompetent clockmaker. It is we prentices who can fathom only in part the perfect laws of Universal Design testified to in the Book of Nature by which the Almighty illustrates his Book of Scripture; it is we who must submit to His Rational Will. What (asks this Leibniz)? Is the Lord God free to choose, and we not able to calculate his choice in advance, without testimony, Natural or Scriptural? Indeed, I answer him: can God not be free to choose, and we His Creatures be humble enough to seek out His Mind in the evidences of His Creation?

Flattery I enjoy; but I well know how to appear modest if occasion present. Surely, if I had had the soul of a servant – I nearly said, the soul of a sizar – I could never have brought to light of day the wonderful Laws of my Father's Creation. Not the Soul of a Servant, I say: rather, the Confidence of a Son. Think you a Rational God would choose any less than a Rational Messenger to bring to the world of Men the Good News of the Rational Laws of his Natural Creation? With what other purpose did He create a Mind sharing the Divine Harmonies of His Mathematics, and put in it a perception of His Law of the Inverse Square? Why else did He send that Mind into the World on the very same day as His Holy Son, Jesus Christ?

* * *

It is an old man that talks to you. So good of you, so very, very good of you – so flattering – to pay a call on this very old man on his birthday. You must excuse me now: at this stage in life, sleep overcomes me each afternoon. That is the trouble with age: my flattering friends needs must make me President of the Royal Society of London, for the term of my natural life – condemn me, they had rather say. Like a villain spared the quick shock of the Newgate gallows, and transported to the Antipodes, I find the rest of my life dragging along: and, now that Herr Leibniz is gone to his Maker – how little did I foresee it! – I find no one else from among my acquaintance is worth contesting with.

NEWTON YAWNS: HE IS FALLING ASLEEP—

The old lady who raised me – Grandmother, she called herself – used to sing me a song she learned when she was a child, from Mr Gibbons – Mr Orlando Gibbons – in the time of Queen Elizabeth. The Silver Swan, it was called: I well remember the words, as she sang it, and I relish it still, as I yield myself to Sleep—

> The Silver Swan who, living, had no note, When Death approached, unlocked her silent throat. Leaning her breast against the Reedy Shore, Thus sang her first and last – and sang no more. "Farewell, all Joys: Oh, Death, come close mine Eyes – More Geese than Swans now live, more Fools than Wise!"

"More Geese than Swans, more Fools than Wise": yes, indeed! Please excuse me. It is an old man who talks.

HE SNORES, QUIETLY AT FIRST – LOUDER AS THE MUSIC RISES.

Conclusion

Well, there you have it. So what am I saying? Certainly, the men whose voices I have borrowed were not pure embodiments of formal rationality; but the pictures I painted stay close to the historical record. Montaigne, as I show him, has less than 18 months to live – he dies in 1592, in his late fifties: as he predicts, his redoubtable mother lives on into her 90s, to 1601. Descartes may well wonder about his survival: he will be carried off by pneumonia six weeks after we have seen him. Leibniz lasts little longer: he is said to have died of an attack of gout – though I don't quite know what that means in medical terms. Newton is more durable: he lives on for some five years after his 80th birthday.

The thesis that Newton privately saw himself as the Son of God is no fantasy. It was documented 25 years ago by Frank Manuel: even devout Newtonians conceded that his evidence is subtle, complex and ingenious. Nor is it implausible. Like Descartes, Newton knew infantile deprivation – losing both his parents in infancy. His father died before he was born: when his mother remarried, and moved away, she left Isaac in foster care with her own mother. People with such histories are deeply uncertain of their true ancestry. In England they often claim to be illegitimate children of the Royal Family. Nor is this kind of pathology an English monopoly. In War and Peace, Pierre Bezhukov does numerical calculations with the letters of his name, and ends with the Biblical Number of the Beast – 666. This leads him (as Tolstoy depicts him) to set himself a personal mission to assassinate the invader, Napoleon Bonaparte.

Does this mean that the Newtonian world view, the founding structure of Scientific Modernity, was the product of personal fantasy, not logical inference? That is too strong. Yet anyone who savours the intellectual modesty of Francis Bacon's views on scientific method must be struck by the blind-fold audacity Isaac Newton brings to his construction of a picture of God's Design for Nature. A less self confident writer might hesitate, hold back, add reservations to his argument, and rob it of its unadulterated force. Only someone with grandiose ideas about his status as the Divine Messenger, perhaps, could have read God's Mind quite so unhesitatingly.

One last word: in imagining these confessions, am I disrespectful – even insulting – to the people who are their subjects? If I appear to be, then I have failed in my task. I respect these Great Men as much as you. If I go below the surface of their ideas to the deeper motives in which they seem to be entan-gled, this is not just because Fat Oxen may be driven by Thin Cowherds, but because great achievements and grand imaginations may go hand in hand with grandiose conceit, and other personal oddities.

To borrow a phrase from the English poet, Siegfried Sassoon, these peo-ple are my Deathless Friends – not least for their oddities, which are endur-ing and endearing. (It would be hard to be friends with someone who was too perfect an embodiment of formal, abstract rationality.) So let me end by reading part of the poem in which this phrase of Sassoon's appears. It is called "Grandeur of Ghosts":

> When I have heard small talk about great men,
> I climb to bed, light my two candles; then
> Consider what was said; and put aside
> What Such-a-one remarked and Someone-else replied.
>
> They have spoken lightly of my deathless friends—
> Lamps for my gloom, hands guiding where I stumble—
> Quoting, for shallow conversational ends,
> What Shelley shrilled, what Blake once wildly muttered ....

All I have tried to do here is show that Sassoon's feelings for Blake and Shelley as poets are ones we can equally well have for highly individual sci-entists and philosophers: Montaigne or Descartes, Leibniz or Newton. This is not, of course, the complete story about the relations of the natural sci-ences to the humanities; but it is a significant part of that story, even a neglected one. Let me leave it at that.

Thank you.

Chapter 5

Rameau's Nephew. Dialogue as *Gesamtkunstwerk* for Enlightenment

(with constant reference to Plato)

Allan Janik

The idea that Enlightenment could have anything whatsoever to do with art, not to mention humor, strikes us today, at the end of the twentieth century, as wholly implausible. What could Woody Allen have to do with emancipation? we ask. Thus Diderot's "dialogue of language and gesture" seems at first glance to have precious little to do with Enlightenment. This fictional account of an imaginary encounter between a *philosophe* and a parasite, who calls all that is nearest and dearest to the heart of the conventionally 'enlightened' idealist into question, therefore strikes us today as a scurrilously delightful, debunking dramatization of how boringly pompous morality usually is and how much more exciting it is to be naughty than to 'behave ourselves': "imagine a world wise and philosophical, admit that it would be devilishly sad. Behave, long live philosophy, long live the wisdom of Solomon: drink some good wine, gorge yourself with delicious morsels, roll on pretty women, lay down on soft beds. That apart the rest is only vanity" (456-457).[1] Yet, *Rameau's Nephew* hardly impresses us at first glance as an important philosophical statement about the complexities of Enlightenment. Nevertheless, the reasons why we tend to miss the point have more to do with our typically one-sided understanding, not only of Enlightenment, but of the relationship between art and philosophy at the end of the twentieth century, i.e., in a period that must rediscover what was once called practical philosophy, than they do with *Rameau's Nephew* itself.

Rationalists from Carnap and the Vienna Circle to Habermas and Critical Theory have taught us to conceive Enlightenment as progress resulting from the cultivation of a critical, scientific attitude to life as well as the technical implementation of the results of scientific inquiry in society. In doing so these very different thinkers stand squarely in a tradition harking back to Comte with his slogan *savoir pour prevoir pour pouvoir*, to Turgot with his rationalization of the French economy under Louis XVI, farther yet to Bacon's (frequently misconstrued) rallying cry "knowledge is power", and ultimately to Plato's notion that it is only when philosophers become kings or kings philosophers that we shall arrive at a society that will truly promote human happiness. So both the positivists of the Vienna Circle and Critical Theorists can call upon a long and distinguished list of precursors in developing their respective accounts of progress through development of the scientific spirit.

No laughing matter. Indeed, upon hearing the word 'Enlightenment' sensitive souls (starting with the first generation of Romantics in the 18th century) often tend to grit their teeth in the way that children do when confronted with the dentist or a bitter medicine, i.e., with the sense that what is about to be done to them 'for their own good' will be either unduly harsh or ineffectual, at best, with a certain surprise, when the desired beneficial effect is obtained relatively painlessly. So the post-modern critics of Enlightenment in its Carnapian, Habermasochist[2] (or Leninist) forms, for all their frequent superficiality, are not entirely silly in reacting like children to the equally one-sided view of rationality that we are usually presented with.

Yet, the technocratic, "progressive", concept of Enlightenment was by no means the only way of conceiving what it meant to be "enlightened" in the eighteenth century. David Hume's dictum "reason is and ought to be the slave of the passions"[3] captures an aspect of Enlightenment that we have for the most part forgotten (principally, I think, because of Bismarck's Kulturkampf and the nineteenth century debates around Darwinism made Enlightenment into a question of being 'for' science and 'against' religion and generally relegating anything that was not science to a less-than-rational status). It is important to mention Hume here because nobody would be inclined to consider that ironically skeptical thinker as an enemy of Enlightenment; yet at the same time he was less than optimistic about both science and progress. The point is that he, like Diderot, was in no way opposed to progress or science but much more concerned with the ways in which human nature *limits* our capacity for "improvement" according to a consciously developed plan. *Rameau's Nephew* is built around similar assumptions, namely, that before we can even begin to think about how we might improve ourselves we need to have an accurate picture of what we actually are – and that is what is devilishly difficult to obtain.

A similar picture of rationality is at the center of Freud's psychotherapy.[4] His presupposition is that, to the extent that we have intractable psychological problems, the source of those problems is self-induced in a less-than-conscious way. So we have to learn how it is that we have ceased to be master in our own house or how we systematically prevent ourselves from controlling our own behavior by repressing some aspect of our personality. In Freud's view it is only when we are prepared to accept ourselves as we are and not merely as we would like to see ourselves that we can begin to cope with what to that point are insurmountable problems. To be sure, Freud's explicit interest here is entirely psychopathological (although there is clearly a covert utilitarian concept of ethics in Freud's view of human nature, as his critics have often indicated); whereas Diderot's is principally moral and aesthetic. He wants to explain to us generally why it should be that we are seldom the noble, heroic figures that we would like to be.

The problem with Freud, as critics as different as Alasdair MacIntyre, Arthur Schnitzler and Ludwig Wittgenstein have pointed out, is that the concept of Enlightenment that informs his very impressive therapeutic practice is obscured by the fact that it is tied to a highly speculative theory, the meta-psychological structure of the so-called Oedipus Complex.[5] So, as much as Freud can help us gain a general orientation with the conception of rationality at the heart of *Rameau's Nephew*, what we most need is an account of a philosophical route from the rationalistic (i.e. Carnap-Habermas) view of Enlightenment to the one we find in Hume, Freud and Diderot which will show us the way toward understanding the relationship between Diderot's philosophical strategy and his artistic tactics.

One way of mapping that route is to proceed paradoxically from the very center of Plato's philosophizing, in the Allegory of the Cave at the beginning of Book Seven of the *Republic*, i.e., in a text that is frequently interpreted as prefiguring the rationalistic form of Enlightenment associated with Carnap and Habermas, to a contrast with *Rameau's Nephew*.[6] It is important to emphasize that Diderot himself does not present his dialogue as a confrontation with Plato's Allegory of the Cave; rather, this that confrontation is a construct for the purpose of highlighting the features of Enlightenment in *Rameau's Nephew* as they compare and contrast with Plato's notion of Enlightenment as a march into the sunlight. However, the contrast that we shall pursue is not merely an intellectual game; for Diderot is in fact treating a central problem that remains unsolved in the Platonic account of Enlightenment at least as we find it in this most celebrated passage in the Platonic oeuvre. An examination of that problem will help us to understand the significance of *Rameau's Nephew* for Enlightenment.

"Compare our nature in respect of education and its lack to such an experience as this", writes Plato. "Picture men dwelling in a sort of subterranean cavern with a long entrance open to the light on its entire width. Conceive them as having their legs and necks fettered from childhood, so that they remain in the same spot, able to look forward only, and prevented by the fetters from turning their heads. Picture further the light from a fire burning higher up and at a distance behind them, and between the fire and the prisoners and above them a road along which a low wall has been built, as the exhibitors of puppet shows have partitions before the men themselves, above which they show the puppets .... See also, then, men carrying past the wall implements of all kinds that rise above the wall, and human images and shapes of animals as well, wrought in stone and wood and in every material, some of these bearers presumably speaking and others silent".[7] It is a strange situation as Plato himself suggests, but he is nevertheless convinced that it is in fact the situation in which people just like us in fact find ourselves.

Such is the point of departure for Plato's account of Enlightenment. We all find ourselves like the prisoners in a shadowy world in which we have no understanding of our actual situation. It is very important to Plato that we can feel quite comfortable in this situation. We first begin to get a glimpse of our ignorance when we are freed from our bonds and are capable of turning to the fire's light at which point we can be said to begin to know, because we are capable of distinguishing between shadows and the objects that cast them, i.e., between appearance and reality. However, this has to be an extremely painful process for eyes that are not accustomed to direct light. It is equally important to Plato that the freed prisoner's accounts of his experiences are wholly incomprehensible to his fellow prisoners.

However, the story only begins there; for Plato goes on to relate what happens when our prisoner is "dragged by force up the ascent which is steep and rough"[8] out of the cave into the sunlight. Once more the same experience results: the pure sunlight dazzles and the unfamiliar objects, actually the models for the artifacts with whose shadows he has grown up, confuse him. With time he comes to realize what has in fact been his fate till now, and he comes to rejoice in possessing a full grasp of reality.

The Allegory of the Cave is principally about political liberation but its importance for Western thought lies in the fact that Plato considers this impossible without the pursuit of abstract knowledge, i.e. mathematics and metaphysics, the search for true-for-all-time definitions for our concepts. For that reason his prisoner must not only experience the cave itself, he must learn that there is a reality beyond the mere relative certainty that the sensual world presents to us, i.e., in the non-corporeal world of Ideas, where the ultimate definitions of our concepts gambol with the axioms of logic. This other world Plato terms the "world of the really real" (ontos on). Its constituents are the Ideas or Forms (eîdoi). Their chief characteristics are that they are universally, necessarily and unchangingly true. For example, 'a rose is a rose' is a general statement that can never be false, even if roses become extinct; whereas all statements about the color, scent, size, beauty of individual roses can become false under certain circumstances. 'A rose is a rose' is *absolutely* true (if remarkably uninteresting, to the uninitiated), and that is precisely why Plato, along with every metaphysically-oriented logician to this very day, finds it so fascinating and important: it, and all such 'logical' truths, is absolutely certain and thus absolutely reliable. Plato was convinced that the unreflectiveness typical of the Athenians who put Socrates to death was a form of inconstancy, which was in fact the 'logical' result of taking the world of sensory experience for ultimate reality. His task was to convert people from this belief. Thus, he created in his dialogues a set of 'spiritual exercises' designed to seek reality with the mind's eye (a phrase Plato invented), rather than with the bodily eye.[9]

The first step in this process of conversion is thus to reject what the senses present to us as reality, and with it the body itself. Nothing is more central to Platonic thought and to the tradition of thinking commonly termed 'Platonism' than the idea that there is an absolute dichotomy between body and soul (mind), one which must be cultivated by fleeing the physical world[10] through the pursuit of what he called dialectic, i.e., what we would call logic, which "purified" the body. It is this aspect of Platonism that St. Augustine might be said to have baptized in his theological works and which in its 'spiritual' form has become a central teaching of orthodox Catholic Christianity and a presupposition of metaphysical thinking to the present day (albeit in the form of Leibnizian ontology, cognitive psychology or Transcendental Philosophy, that many traditional Platonists or Augustinians would hardly recognize). What is crucial here is that it is at this point in the development of Western metaphysics that the body was banned once and for all from the realm of genuine knowledge; only to be allowed re-entry into the realm of reality with Newton, who mathematized physical reality and thereby 'materialized' and 'mechanized' Platonism.[11]

Be that as it may, Plato's allegory continues. He poses the question as to what would happen if the 'enlightened' prisoner were to return to his former colleagues, tell them of his experiences, and urge them to flee the cave with him to a better world. They would, of course, be absolutely incapable of understanding a word that he would say. Moreover, his incapacity to function efficiently in the darkness would be a further indication that he should not be taken seriously. Should he insist that the world which he had experienced was, nevertheless, superior and continue to admonish his fellow prisoners to leave their familiar surroundings, Plato suggests, they would probably kill him – a clear reference to the fate of Socrates. In the end the allegory purports to demonstrate that it is only when philosophers become kings or kings become philosophers that we can expect to transcend the cave.

Up to this point the story is the classical account of the pursuit of knowledge as a difficult struggle against what Bacon would term the "Idols" that are conventionally and unreflectively confused with genuine knowledge. As such, Plato's allegory has become the classical account of the liberation of society from the bonds of convention on the basis of science. However, on the standard view of the matter, Plato was certain that his view of 'real' society was so far from the common sense perspective that it was not something that ordinary people can be expected to understand in any literal form. *Logos*, i.e., a true, scientific account of the matter, would only confuse them. Thus he must have recourse to *mythos*, i.e. tell a story whose point hearers must establish for themselves, if he is to communicate the insight he has gained here. The literary form incorporates the cognitive content of his message into an aesthetic experience designed to provide a deeper, more coherent alternative to the everyday picture of the world. So Plato turns out, paradoxically, to be closer to Diderot than he is either to Carnap or Habermas in his presentation of what is involved in becoming 'enlightened'.

Plato's assumption in telling us the allegory is that its "logic" is transferable to our own condition. Thus, if we are to think along with Plato we should want to raise questions about the details of the story he has told. For the most part philosophers have (not implausibly) construed the allegory as a paean to formal logic as the key to transcending the world of sense deception into the world of Truth (i.e., the Ideas) and thus the means to Enlightenment. Plato describes this arduous process as a conversion. However, he tells us very little about its nature. Rather he is content to *show* us, both in his "myths" or little stories as he describes them[12] and in the dialogues themselves, examples of how that comes about – the problem that poses itself here is that of whether it is possible to do anything more than 'showing' here. In the Allegory of the Cave, as we have seen, he simply says that the freed prisoner has to be "forced" out of the security of the cave to the rough and steep ascent to daylight. This has all the earmarks of the child's bitter medicine. It is important that Plato's prisoner is portrayed as being passively acted upon in the course of becoming enlightened. How are we to understand Plato at this crucial juncture? How is rationality compatible with force as it would seem to have to be in the Allegory of the Cave? The answer is entirely unclear from the text.

The problem, then, with Plato – and with the mainstream of the philosophical tradition inspired by him – is that of sugar-coating the bitter pill, to put the matter in a banal form. However, this cannot be a mere cosmetic matter, for it must function as a prelude to a conversion, as Plato repeatedly describes the process that the freed prisoner undergoes. That conversion requires a rhetorical moment that Plato, at once a master story teller and an enemy of fiction, could only, as in the Allegory of the Cave itself, structure in fictional form.

It is this point that the Diderot of *Rameau's Nephew*, unlike the typical 'Platonist',[13] so clearly understood, namely, that the philosopher, the would-be 'enlightener' has to speak the language of the cave in order to entice its inhabitants out of it. He cannot simply say what Enlightenment is all about; he has to show it in a way that the captives can come to grips with. He has to provoke them to *want* to leave the cave. Somehow the captives must gain *for themselves* a glimpse of their actual situation; but they must want to see themselves. This is where humor comes into the picture as a motor to self-knowledge and ultimately self-realization.[14]

The editor of the *Encyclopédie*, however much he would object to the 'other-worldliness' of the usual metaphysical reading of the allegory, would hardly have wanted to do anything other than to provide a *mythos* of his own which would induce readers to reflect upon the meaning of Enlightenment *within the Cave*, i.e., endeavoring to understand the peculiar mixtures of darkness and light that are possible there. The problem that Plato leaves unresolved, then, becomes one of turning those 'irrational' faculties that enable one to function in the Cave, i.e., what Plato identifies as 'the body',[15] to the service of Enlightenment: how are we to transform the body into a vehicle of Enlightenment? Diderot's answer, unlike Plato's, will take the form of a conversation interspersed with pantomime and involve reminding us of the importance of laughter in human life, but that is to run ahead.

However, the challenge to Diderot is rather more complicated than the one presented to Plato, for, unlike Plato, Diderot was confronted with a society that was capable of quoting Plato without taking him seriously enough to try to 'think along' with him. This is surely the immediate source of aggravation that led the politically-persecuted editor of the *Encyclopédie* to pose the question 'who among us is *really* "enlightened"?' as opposed to merely paying lip-service to Enlightenment. In short, for Diderot, unlike Plato, the most serious aspect of the problem of appearance and reality concerns not simply ignorance but *hypocrisy* within the Cave. Before Enlightenment in the conventional Platonic sense is possible it will be necessary to lay bare the social dynamics within the Cave, i.e., to ask how hypocrisy itself is at all possible – an investigation that will ultimately require a drastic revision of the respective roles of theory and example, word and gesture, in human experience.

The opening of the *Rameau's Nephew* must be read with extreme care in order to grasp the character of its protagonists and their relationship to one another, for it is only when we have an absolutely clear concept of who *moi* and *lui* are that we can attain a solid grasp of the sense of the dialogue. Although the dialogue abounds in ideas, there are few "theses" in the sense that they are found in the Platonic dialogues.

Who are the protagonists? We learn about them from the urbane moi, the personification of the *philosophe*.[16] *Moi* has often been construed as Diderot himself but there is no particular reason to do so, and, good reasons for not identifying Diderot with *moi* .... It is through his eyes, or to be more precise, through his considerable powers of description that we encounter *lui*, whose own assertions only offer us partial insight into his character. *Moi* is everything that we expect from a *philosophe*: regular in his habits, a reflective, critical, intellectual, as such curious, a worldly-wise 'thinker' in every respect, to whom pleasure is by no means foreign, but whose aim in life is to achieve and maintain equilibrium.[17] He is every bit the eighteenth century man of 'enlightened' wisdom, the *honnête homme*, the *libertin* in Montaigne's sense, who cultivates publicly respect for convention and authority, while maintaining private freedom of imagination to examine, to question and explore the whole of reality intellectually. In short, he is the very personification of Neo-Stoic values such as they were understood circa 1760 – and everything that the very existence of Rameau's nephew calls into question. *Moi* believes, like all 'Platonist' philosophers, that everybody really would like to think like him, but that their short-term perspective on reality, i.e., their 'passions', prevent them from seeing things with the requisite objectivity to share the perspective of his 'enlightened' self-interest.

Moi finds *lui* interesting precisely because he is absolutely unconventional, which is to say 'natural'. *Lui* can be construed as the *epitome* of Plato's contented Cave dweller inasmuch as he and everything he does is a puzzlingly dynamic mixture of solid common sense and folly, good and evil. His bewildering transformations of himself, now in the money, now poor as a church mouse, now overstuffed, now lean, provoke *moi* to assert that, "nothing is less like him than himself" (424) – something that *lui* will flatly deny at the end of the dialogue: "Isn't it true that I'm always the same?" (520), ironically claiming a more profound sort of *constantia* for himself than the Stoics have yet conceived. In any case, he is above all a corporeal creature in all that he does, something that his stentorian voice exemplifies in the eyes of *moi*. Briefly, he incorporates everything sensual that the puritanical Allegory of the Cave enjoins us to eschew. For *moi*, which is to say for Enlightenment, *lui* is important because his disdain for orthodoxy is so *refreshing*; he is so very much his irrepressible self that he dramatically *shows* us the difference between spontaneous Nature and stolid convention in social matters i.e., something that will be of value to all would-be social reformers and idealists like *moi*. In a sense 'society' is in fact the central theme of the dialogue inasmuch as both figures in their very different ways consider it a conventional, and as such arbitrary, network of constraints to be subjected to criticism or to be exploited depending upon whether one is a *philosophe* or a parasite.

At this point we do well to bear in mind that Diderot's argument here turns very much upon a value that the secular Enlightenment adopted from its Augustinian Christian (i.e., Jansenist) sources, and thus a value that is foreign to Plato's world, namely, sincerity and its opposite hypocrisy. Rameau's nephew's 'naturalness' consists precisely in the forthrightness in conversation with *moi*: he displays his good characteristics without being ostentatious about them, his bad ones without being ashamed of them. This is what makes him so interesting: he presents himself in dialogue as the curiously contradictory 'sincere' insincerity. Thus, he casually affirms his conviction that there is nothing more to reality than the corporeal by remarking that the important thing in life is a free and easy, copiously pleasant, daily bowel movement (442). Yet, he would give anything to be truly creative. His unconventionality both in his conversation and conduct catches people unawares; it shakes them up and unmasks them of their pretensions. Briefly, he is a curious parody of the Socratic gad-fly that stimulates us to reflection. Thus, his folly, partly natural, partly contrived,[18] is an indispensable aid to the student of society. For that reason *moi* is happy to see him but only from time to time, presumably because he becomes tedious or even threatening *à la longue*.

The ensuing conversation proceeds with whirlwind pace twisting and turning from a discussion of the pleasures of watching chess players to the nature of genius and folly, art and creativity, education, music, the social value of gossip and laughter, the power of money to create otherwise undeserved reputations and generally as a motor in society, the role of rules and spontaneity in education and art, virtue and vice, the sublime and the ridiculous, hypocrisy and role-playing in society, etc. etc. The 'philosophical' center of the dialogue, conceived as 'traditional' philosophy comes about a third of the way through when *moi* and *lui* state their views of life clearly and unequivocally (459-473).

Moi's ideal is hardly a world-denying Platonism. Indeed, his charm resides in his urbanity. He enjoys good food and wine as well as the sight and touch of a beautiful woman, but he insists that these pleasures mean little to him in comparison with the 'spiritual' delight he gets in assisting the unfortunate, in defending the persecuted or even in sacrificing, even endangering, himself for the sake of his fellow human beings. Being good to others regardless of the cost to oneself is what happiness really is all about. A more eloquent account of 'enlightened self-interest' can scarcely be imagined.

Lui's response to this is short and to the point: that all sounds fine but there are plenty of good people who are not happy and happy ones who are not good. This objection goes right to the heart of Plato's (and Kant's) claim that moral goodness is genuine happiness. He then proceeds to turn the tables upon the refined Platonist by defending the view that he brings more good into the world than our moralist through exploiting his natural failings, i.e., easily and pleasantly than the *philosophe* does with all his efforts. By being the buffoon that he is, he is sociable; he puts people at their ease; he makes them laugh – in stark contrast, he thinks, to the 'philosopher' who "only thinks of himself" (428) and on that account does nobody any good. Inasmuch as virtue requires that we suppress the hedonistic side of ourselves, virtue makes us unnatural and unnaturally disagreeable. Beyond that, virtue is consummately boring. Respectable people praise it, but in reality they hate it and avoid it like the plague as something coldly inhuman. Who knows, suggests the nephew, perhaps it is merely a matter of perspectives: what you call virtue, I call vice and vice versa. With his skeptical insistence that we in fact do not know what virtue really is *lui* thus suggests that a "transvaluation of values" in Nietzsche's phrase is in order; for the only important values, i.e., those that people act upon are usually the opposite of those to which they pay lip service. Rameau's nephew is restating LaRochefoucauld's point that virtue is often only vice in disguise in suggesting that spontaneous feelings, regardless of their specific nature, are the only real source of value in the world. Emotion shows itself to be valuable by its impact upon people. Joy, for example, is contagious: everybody likes somebody who makes them laugh. Nobody *really* admires the coldly detached intellectuality, verging on solipsism,[19] of the Stoic, and the proof that nobody really admires him is that nobody emulates him. *Lui* considers the *philosophe* foolish to think that anybody believes anything like that.

The 'principle' according to which Rameau's nephew lives his life is thus absolutely hedonistic. Its justification lies simply in the fact that it is natural to enjoy oneself. Thus he refers to himself as "the apostle of ... ease" (482). Plato had gone to pains to show that rigorous pursuit of a life devoted to pleasure was ultimately self-defeating, like collecting water with a sieve as he put it.[20] Plato's argument was that to try to make the search for pleasure into the goal of life is bound to be self-defeating because this means that you must look at life entirely in terms of what you *have*. However, that means that you are also thinking about what you lack, since to think of life in these terms is to consider the goal of living something that you possess – as opposed to something that you are. The problem with this view is that you will never have 'enough' and, therefore, you shall never be satisfied.

In the two millennia between Diderot and Plato this view had certainly been challenged, but usually in literary form, for example by Rabelais,[21] seldom by philosophers themselves. Few philosophers were bold enough to take up Plato's challenge straight-forwardly by constructing a thought experiment (i.e., a "myth" in Plato's sense) in which the full consequences of hedonism were explored. Philosophers may have been unhappy with the Platonic view that virtue is the only real happiness but they seldom dared to defend the full consequences of hedonism as Diderot does in *Rameau's Nephew*. This entails accepting the primacy of pleasure over logic and a picture of life in which consistency does not play a particularly large role. It is exactly what we have in *Rameau's Nephew*. Diderot accepts Plato's view that such a life would be a life in of frustration, but, nevertheless, worth living. Moreover, he seems to be insisting that pace Plato we can live with such frustration if we are aware that it is an integral part of our chosen life style. Thus Jean-Francois Rameau's frustration at not being a genius like his uncle, Jean-Philippe, is not something which arbitrarily appears in the dialogue, it is absolutely central to Diderot's confrontation with the philosophical tradition stemming from Plato. So it is entirely consistent that the nephew gains his livelihood from sham and pretence but, nevertheless, appreciates, to the point of worshipping, genuine creativity.

The very fact that *lui* is a professional parasite is also entirely coherent with the confrontation with Plato's scenario for the good life; for the latter considers that the need for autonomy underlies human strivings. We should bear in mind that Plato's philosopher is a lover of wisdom, and that love in Plato's view is the ever-yearning, underprivileged child of poverty and plenty.[22] Diderot seems to be insisting that we shall never understand what it is to be a lover of wisdom, till we understand what it is to be a lover of money, i.e., of the means to pleasure.

Be that as it may, consistent with his character *lui* is full of aspiration[23] but his goal is always pleasure. So he is content to pretend to be a piano teacher, if that ensures the good will of his patrons and provides him with a livelihood. At that level everything he does is simply a means to the end of making his life more pleasant. The price he must pay is that, regardless of what people think of him and his talents, he must be aware of his own pretenses and of how little he can actually do in comparison with his uncle, who had revolutionized the theory of harmony. In this matter he possesses a shattering self-knowledge (436) that makes him worthy of the attentions of a Socrates.

His choice of a life devoted to hedonism is thus the choice of a life that is continually lived between extremes, which is the exact opposite of the Stoic ideal of *constantia* as conventionally conceived. In living for his instincts he is always contradicting himself: in his cynicism money is the only value that he respects: yet, his yearning for genius reflects that he recognizes standards of excellence which are more than means to his selfish ends. He is thus more Platonic than he would admit.

Nothing is more typical of *Rameau's Nephew* than his incessant motion: "I never tire", he says (444). The eminent Diderot scholar, Jean Starobinski, has demonstrated that the ceaseless flow of discussion in Diderot's dialogue has the form of a chiasmus, i.e., an 'x' shaped figure, in which the nephew is a sort of pivot that swings from the heights to the depths, from joy to despair, from wisdom to folly, from morality to art, from assertion to self-contradiction.[24] This is certainly a crucial feature of the 'consistent inconsistency' of *Rameau's Nephew*; equally important, however, is the *musical* character of the dialogue itself frequently commented upon by commentators. More specifically, it has been observed that *Rameau's Nephew* displays at least superficial similarities with that typically eighteenth century musical form, the *suite*.[25] The suite is composed of a group of dance movements interspersed with purely musical movements in a loose, interchangeable order, usually in the same key. If we consider the nephew's mime sequences as dances and the conversational elements as the dialogue's "pure music" as it were, it is entirely possible to consider the dialogue as a suite. It is well-known that Diderot was very much taken by the then frequently-discussed problem of whether matter could think and what would be a better example of matter thinking than a dance?[26] This hypothesis is wholly consistent with Starobinski and entirely fitting in a work which would parody Plato's flight from the body to the soul in the form of a dynamic 'x'-shaped 'ensouled' movement.[27] We should not forget that Plato was thoroughly suspicious of music[28] so it is entirely fitting that a dialogue that would challenge the central tenets of Plato' thought should have a musical form. Moreover, just as a piece of music overcomes Platonic dualism inasmuch as it reconciles sensual beauty with rigorous intellectual structure, i.e., it can both dazzle us sensually and at the same time have a rigorously mathematical order, Diderot's dialogue seeks to show us a certain bodily 'logic' incapable of abstract analysis behind the nephew's antics.

Consider the following example of one of *lui's* 'dances':

He: It's nothing. These things are just passing moments [i.e., frustration with his own mediocrity and jealousy of his brilliant uncle].

(Then he pulled himself together singing the overture to *Les Indes galantes* and the air *Profondes abîmes*, and added):

Something inside there is speaking to me and saying: Rameau, old chap, you would like to have composed those two pieces, and, if you had composed those two you could do two more, and when you had done a certain number people would play and sing them everywhere, and you could hold your head erect when you walked. Your conscience would attest to your own worth, and people would point at you with their finger and say: 'that's the man who wrote the pretty gavottes' (he sang the gavottes, then, with the appearance of a man deeply touched, with eyes wet from swimming in joy, he added, rubbing his hands): you would have a good house (and he measured it dimensions with his arms), a good bed (and he stretched himself nonchalantly on it), good wines (which he tasted clicking his tongue against his palate) a fine coach (and he raises one leg to climb into it), pretty women (whose breasts he fondled and cast lecherous looks upon them), a hundred rascals would come to flatter me every day (he thought that he could see them around him – Palissot, Poincinet, the Frérons, father and son, LaPorte – and he listened to them, strut with pride, gave them signs of approval, smiled, treated them with disdain or contempt, put them to flight, called them back and then continued): And thus it is that people would tell you in the morning that you were a great man, you would read in the *Trois Siècles* that you were a great man, and by the evening you would be convinced that you were a great man; and the great man Rameau the Nephew, would fall asleep to the soft murmur of praise in his ears, and even in his sleep he would appear well satisfied, his chest would dilate, rising and falling with comfort and he would snore like a great man. (And speaking all this he softly sank upon a bench, closed his eyes and imitated the blissful sleep he was imagining. Having tasted the sweetness of this repose for a few moments he awoke, stretched his arms, yawned, rubbed his eyes and looked around for his dull flatterers.) (434-435)

Two things should be borne in mind with respect to this passage. First, there is an extraordinary eye at work here; moi's description reveals an extraordinary *perspicacity* with respect to the gestures appropriate in particular situations. Second, there is an equally extraordinary *pen* at work here: those gestures are *described* masterfully, so masterfully that we are all too easily tempted to delight in the passage – which was Diderot's point in writing it as he did – without remarking upon the consummate artistry that has gone into crafting it in all its detail.[29] Just those things that are tediously inessential to the Platonist turn out to be crucial for disclosing the nephew's character. In Pascalian terms the *esprit de finesse* captures what of necessity eludes the *esprit de géometrie*.

However, it is not as if this topic, which Michael Polanyi would later term tacit knowledge, is not at all mentioned in the work. To the suggestion that he ought to put the tricks of his trade into writing *Rameau's Nephew* insists that whoever needs a manual can not be expected to go far (469). General rules fail to catch the most essential feature of our actions, namely, *how* they are performed. Moreover, people of experience in fact always deviate from general moral rules, insists the nephew cynically (455ff). Earlier he had insisted that the sorts of things contained in his 'bag of tricks', his skill successfully evading, as it were, was a matter of knowing the exceptions to general rules. His claim is that the division of labor in society presupposes deviance from all general codes of ethics and a-fortiori abstract patterns of knowledge. In fact Rameau's nephew champions imitation and improvisation as the actual sources of the knowledge that real people live by. Plato's flight into the world of the "really real" is for him the equivalent of ceasing to exist, so much more real is the particular than the general for him.

There is also a certain irony here; for the whole Platonic epistemology in the early and middle dialogues[30] turns upon precisely the rejection of the idea that there could be 'knowledge in general' or a 'general' method for attaining knowledge. In fact it is for this reason that he rejects the claims of the Sophists to be able to teach 'knowledge'[31] – and of actors to possess it. There is no such thing as 'knowledge'; only specific modes of knowing. There are criteria for using words rightly. Doctors and generals are called 'doctors' and 'generals' because they have certain very specific competencies, i.e., medical and military, respectively. They do not learn something called 'knowledge' to be called by those names; they master a skill, which is to say they learn to make crucial distinctions between particular types of illness or particular situations in battle.

To this point Plato and Diderot are moving on the same track; they part company at the point where Plato insists that the skill that has been learned is really a form of propositional knowledge, i.e., a matter of learning true propositions; whereas Diderot insists it is rather a matter of mastering certain specific techniques. In *Rameau's Nephew,* as in other of Diderot's works we have a profound epistemological rehabilitation of the notion of practical skill as true knowledge.[32] Diderot's favorite example of such knowledge directly challenges a cherished Platonic view, namely, that the competence of actors is not knowledge [*Ion*]. Fully aware of Platonic rejection of any claim to knowledge that is neither propositional nor abstract, Diderot is recognized for his defense of the cognitive character of the actor's knowledge, i.e. of a form of knowledge that is fundamentally gestural, gained through imitation and repetition. Indeed, *Lui* is the perfect instantiation of such a 'knower', whose knowledge is genuine but corporal, rather than mental; instinctual, intuitive and imitative, rather than representational.

In relation to Platonism, indeed, to traditional philosophy as a whole, Diderot is voicing a very important complaint, namely, that by concentrating upon the perfect world of logical truths philosophy has entirely ignored the ways that the world in which we live, the Cave, functions, which in epistemological terms means that knowledge has been severed from learning. Diderot, like Wittgenstein later, will ask Plato, how does one learn to be a doctor? Not yet in the position of a Wittgenstein to see language as a plethora of interweavings of words and gestures,[33] but, nevertheless, convinced by the example of the longstanding tradition of excellence of the *commedia dell'arte* that words alone are only part of language,[34] Diderot juxtaposes two conflicting conceptions of the relationship between words and knowledge, the representational and the mimetic, thereby employing the very tension between them to make them cast light upon one another in a manner reminiscent of Pascal's ways of dealing with the complimentary truths and falsities of Stoicism and Skepticism.

Indeed, it is just this technique which provides the dialogue with its ironic 'logic'. Just as nearly all the positions taken by *moi* and *lui* discussed are presented as incompatible but *somehow* complimentary, i.e., fundamentally cogent in themselves, but nevertheless without claim to universal validity, so the two characters themselves are incompatible but, nevertheless, somehow complimentary. For *moi lui* is a kind of social yeast leavening an otherwise drab society that is much given to dissimulation. *Moi* does not particularly like *lui* and is often shocked by his values, for example when he lauds treacherous duplicity (489), but he both understands (438) and appreciates his antics. *Lui* needs the respectable, working people of the world to live off. He understands *moi* and at least in certain situations enjoys his company. Their 'friendship', then is based upon a degree of mutual recognition and upon the common conviction that most social life is based upon pretense. Their differences are rooted in their attitudes to that pretense. For *moi* it is something to be at worst lamented and, at best, corrected according to 'enlightened' standards: for *lui* it is something to be exploited. For both of them there is something disturbingly artificial about society. Indeed, to the extent that *moi* is himself disturbed (i.e., as opposed to being shocked by the tone or substance of his assertions) by *lui* it is because his role as idealist is convincingly portrayed as entailing a curious acceptance of the *status quo* as a set of conventions, badly in need of reform. *Lui* reminds *moi* that to live by these conventions in the hope of reforming them is to affirm hypocrisy covertly in a way that the parasite's overt exploitation of them does not.[35] Moreover, the suggestion here is that the parasite's mocking parody of existing social relations and that alone is the real prerequisite for genuine 'free thinking' (*libertinage*) just as his sincere insincerity makes him the genuine *honnête homme*.

Lui's 'experience' playing the fool in society has given him an insight into social dynamics that the social reformer *philosophe* would appear to lack. This is most evident in the discussion of folly and its role in social life: "There is scarcely a better role to play among the grand of this world than that of fool. For a long time kings kept official fools, but there has never been an official sage. I am Bertin's fool as well that of many others – yours, perhaps, at this moment – or perhaps you are mine. A real sage wouldn't keep a fool at all. So anyone who keeps a fool is not a sage, and if he is not a sage he must be a fool and perhaps, if he is a king, his fool's fool. For the rest, remember that in a matter as variable as moral standards there is nothing absolutely, essentially, universally true or false, unless it is that one must be what self-interest dictates – good or bad, wise or foolish, proper or silly, respectable or vicious." (476-477) The break-neck velocity of the argument here is typically of Diderot. It makes for exciting reading but in fact the logic is not exactly simple to follow.

At the most obvious level a clown is affirming that "all the world loves a clown" and nobody more than the mighty. Superficially Rameau's nephew is reminding us of our hedonistic preference for entertainment over philosophy. More deeply he suggesting that amusement plays a more important role in social relations than conventional wisdom will admit. From the viewpoint of the professional parasite, i.e., of someone we would call a professional entertainer, social relations break down to a matter of entertainer and entertained. Moreover, in that situation it is often unclear who is playing which role. His perspective offers him an insight into the theatrical quality of society and at the same time seems to suggest that there could be an alternative to all this pretense, but he does not have any idea what that may be. His reference to the court jester, however, is a reminder that wit can serve an indispensable critical function, that there is wisdom in the jester's folly. Moreover, he reminds us that as long as kings keep fools, they are hardly philosophers and as such unworthy to rule. Then, in a curious twist he suggests that the role-playing which constitutes social life is, which he himself glories in, is probably silly. The only thing that is clear to him is that one must play one's role according to the situation in which one finds oneself.

It is typical of Diderot that the reader is left in the uncanny situation of having to mull over his own situation. Diderot's philosophical artistry creates a *Gesamtkunstwerk*[36] in two related but distinct senses. First, he pays no attention to traditional boundaries between genres. Dialogue and narrative, fact and fiction, the hilarious and the profound, the elegant and the grotesque, pass in and out of one another continually. His meticulously crafted descriptions aspire to the impossible in attempting to capture spontaneous gesture and therefore aspire to the condition of music and dance. Secondly, and more importantly, all of this is in aid of drawing his reader into the dialogue. Readers must "see" the antics of the nephew through the *philosophe's* description. The reader must fuse with him in 'experiencing' this strange character to the point that he or she is left puzzling over the meaning of *lui's* final remark: "he who laughs last, laughs best." What has this encounter meant? It is finally the reader who decides. Diderot has drawn the reader into an ironic situation where he or she must reflect upon the importance of the disquieting encounter *lui*. However, Diderot's *Gesamtkunstwerk* differs from the more notorious version of Richard Wagner in its rejection of monumentality. The force of the dialogue is that something which is actually monumental, the role of gesture and imitation in social life, is portrayed as considerably smaller than it actually is, which is to say in a way totally foreign to the earnest Wagner, namely, ironically.[37] It is not the least of Diderot's achievements in *Rameau's Nephew* to have created the small, ironic *Gesamtkunstwerk* in his efforts to help us take a look at ourselves as we really are.

The situation that we are left with is comparable to that in which the reader of Plato's early dialogues finds himself or herself in – but not exactly identical with it. In those dialogues such as the *Euthyphro* we are given examples of filial piety but these examples have not proven to have the universality required for a definition. Thus such dialogues typically conclude with the ironic observation that we seem not to know what filial piety is after all. The usual interpretation of this admission of ignorance, which has been wrung out of Socrates' interlocutor through a relentless cross-examination, is usually implied to mean that we have been looking in the wrong place, namely, in the world about us for something that can only be comprehended from the point of view of the World of Forms.

In Diderot's dialogue, as in Mozart-DaPonte's *Cosi Fan Tutte*, which *Rameau's Nephew* much resembles in its troubling message, we simply do not know who laughs last. Indeed, the parasitical nephew is presented in such a sympathetic light (we post-Nietzscheans are probably inclined to see him even more sympathetically than Diderot's contemporaries would have) that we incline to interpret the work as a defense of his values and position. However, this is hardly a plausible reading. After all, Diderot never intended to make a fool out of the *philosophe* or to reject Enlightenment. If we think about it a bit, the delightful non-conformity of *lui*, for all the amusement he brings us, is not something we *really* admire; for nobody would want him as a husband or son-in-law. *Lui* is just as little Diderot or the incarnation of his position as *moi*. In fact he seems to be telling us we can only become 'enlightened' by coming to grips with the *lui* within us, but even more than that, actually drawing us into an encounter with him. Diderot's artistry, rather like that of DaPonte and Mozart in *Cosi Fan Tutte*, demonstrates how easily we let ourselves be self-deceived by showing us how deeply we are attached to an inaccurate self-image. In effect, *Rameau's Nephew* shows us how the Enlightener gets enlightened.

Rameau's Nephew is ironic in the paradoxical Platonic sense that it makes something great seem small for the sake of letting its actual greatness emerge 'dialectically', rather than in the monumental-pathetic Wagnerian sense. Thus Diderot's effort to capture humanity in all its often self contradictory concreteness prefigures both Strindberg's exploitation of ambiguity in *Miss Julie* as well the "transcendental irony" of Offenbach and Georg Trakl's ironic 'deconstructions' of the Symbolist's poetical dream world, inasmuch as it presents as something considerably smaller than it actually is and it draws its audience into itself for the sake of reflection upon convention's comfortable certainties. Beyond that, Diderot's insistence that "the important point is that you and I should be, and that we should be you and I", (433) anticipates such radically different reflections on what it is to become a person and those of Feuerbach and Kierkegaard, which ulimately foreshadow the twentieth century philosophy of dialogue in Ferdinand Ebner and Martin Buber.

Notes

1 Denis Diderot, *Le Neveu de Rameau, Oeuvres romanesques*, ed. Lucette Perol (Paris: Garnier, 1981), 423-520, hereafter referred to parenthetically in the text. The translation is my own.

2 For Carnap Enlightenment is the equivalent the abolition of all traces of metaphysics from human thinking. See Rudolf Carnap "The Elimination of Metaphysics Through the Logical Analysis of Language," in *Logical Positivism* ed. A.J. Ayer (New York: The Free Press, 1959), 60-81. On Habermas see Thomas McCarthy, *The Critical Philosophy of Jürgen Habermas* (Cambridge, Ma.: MIT Press, 1978), passim. McCarthy emphasizes how Habermas sees psychonanalytical theory as presenting a model of Enlightenment. On the relationship between the proto-positivism of nineteenth century German Monists to Bismarck's *Kulturkampf* see Daniel Gassman, *The Scientific Origins of National Socialism* (London: 1971). This heritage does much to explain the bitterness of the twentieth century positivism's assault upon, not only metaphysics, but all forms of 'non-scientific' philosophy. Prof. Tore Nordenstam reports finding this apt expression coined by Ernst Topitsch in Hans Albert's guestbook.

3 David Hume, *A Treatise on Human Understanding*, ed. L.A. Selby-Bigge (Oxford: Clarendon Press, 1888), 2,3,3, 415.

4 See Brian McGuinness, "Freud and Wittgenstein," *Wittgenstein and His Times*, ed. B.F. McGuinness (Chicago, University of Chicago Press, 1982), 27-43.

5 See Allan Janik, "Psychoanalysis: Science Literature or Art?", *Style, Politics and the Future of Philosophy*" (Boston Studies in the Philosophy of Science, Vol. 114; Dordrecht & Boston, London: Kluwer, 1989), 190-196.

6 Plato, *Republic*, trans. Paul Shorey in *The Collected Dialogues of Plato*, eds., Edith Hamilton and Huntington Cairns ("Bollingen Series LXXI; New York: Pantheon Books, 1961), vii, 514A-517A.

7 *Rep.*, vii, 514A-515A.

8 *Rep.*, vii, 515E, "diá traxeías tês anabáseos, kaì anátous."

9 On the role of 'spiritual exercises' in philosophy see Allan Janik, "Style and Idea in the Later Heidegger," in Janik op. cit, 20ff. On the "mind's eye" see *Rep.*, vii 527E.

10 *Theaetetus*, 173Dff.

11 Concerning the ways that early Christianity reinforced Platonic views of the body see Peter Brown's brilliant study, *The Body and Society: Men, Women and Sexual Renunciation in Early*

Christianity (London and Boston: Faber & Faber, 1988). The idea that Newton mechanized and materialized Platonism is, of course, an oversimplification of a long and involved historical story. For the full account see E.J. Dijksterhuis, *The Mechanization of the World Picture: Pythagoras to Newton* (Princeton: Princeton University Press, 1986).

12 *Timaeus*, 29D.

13 'Platonism' has, of course, only a little to do with Plato as Nietzsche and Heidegger have pointed out; cf. Janik, *op. cit.*, 16-18.

14 For a succinct account of Diderot's literary-philosophical ideal here see his "Eloge sur Richardson," *Oeuvres esthétiques*, ed. Paul Vernire ("Classiques Garnier"; Paris: Bordas, 1988), 29-48. I am indebted to Herbert Josephs for calling my attention to the importance of this text for understanding Diderot.

15 Phaedo, 65.

16 For the distinction between Enlightenment philosophers and *philosophes* see Henry Steele Commager, *The Empire of Reason: How Europe Imagined and America Realized the Enlightenment* (New York & Toronto: Oxford University Press, 1977), 236-245. Commager emphasizes that the *philosophe* was 1) essentially a practical thinker, rather than a theorist, 2) a man of the world with deep concern for society, 3) a utopian, 4) a "natural philosopher" (in practice a botanist) and avid admirer of Newton, 5) an educator, 6) a rationalist and deist in religious matters regarding all churches with suspicion, 7) a humanist social reformer, 8) a publicist, who campaigned for the humanistic causes he championed, 9) typically Francophile, 10) a statesman, who aspired to be a social architect, 11) a friend of kings.

17 In short, the *philosophe* is what has become of the *honnête homme*, whose principal virtue remains a sort of *constantia*.

18 In *King Lear* Shakespeare makes much of this distinction. Lear is the "natural fool of fortune" (IV, 6, 191-192) who cannot make the distinction between appearance and reality, rule and exception; and he must suffer for it. The "artificial" fool is the jester, who reminds Lear that the truth cannot be simply and straight-forwardly perceived, but must be apprehended in a judgment about differentiating between situations (I, 4, 91ff.). In Diderot the natural and the artificial are not opposed to one another in this way, but the whole of *Rameau's Nephew* speaks for the idea that the judgment in question has not in the meantime, for all the virtues of Enlightenment, become any easier.

19 There would appear to be an ironic reference to Plato's and Machiavelli's defence of the lie in politics. Diderot would appear to be suggesting that amusing falsehood plays an important and indispensable role in social life.

20 *Gorgias*, 492Eff.

21 The philosophical significance of Rabelais' satires is usually overlooked by historians of philosophy with the notable exception of the sagacious Richard Popkin. See his *History of Skepticism from Descartes to Spinoza* (Brekeley, Los Angeles & London: University of California Press, 1979), 22-23.

22 *Symposium*, 203Bff.

23 For F.M. Cornford the Socratic revolution in Greek philosophy stems from his introduction of a "morality of aspiration" into western philosophy. See his *Before and After Socrates* (Cambridge: Cambridge University Press, 1968).

24 Jean Starobinski, "Sur l'emploi du chiasme dans *Le Neveu de Rameau*," *Revue de Métaphysique et de Moral*, 1984, 182-196.

25 I am indebted to András Borgó for this suggestion.

26 Nietzsche, it should be remembered would not worship a God, who could not dance: "Ich würde nur an einen Gott glauben, der zu tänzen verstünde," "Vom Lesen und Schreiben," *Also Sprach Zarathustra.*

27 Could this be a parody of the vortex paradigm of physical reality in Cartesian physics? On Cartesian physics see E.A. Burtt, *The Metaphysical Foundations of Modern Science* (New York: Doubleday, 1954), 112: "This primary matter, forced into a series of whirlpools or vortices, in which the visible bodies such as planets and terrestrial objects are carried around and impelled toward certain central points by the laws of vortical motion."

28 *Rep.*, 411Aff.

29 Diderot's concern for the nature of description in all its complexity is connected with his efforts to describe the paintings exhibited at the *salons*, i.e. from just about the time that he began to write *Rameau's Nephew.*

30 According to the generally accepted view Plato's early dialogues are the so-called "elenctic" dialogues in which Socrates cross-examines someone or other with a view to determining whether his claims to knowledge can pass the test of universality. They are generally taken to represent what Plato thought Socrates was up to. The middle dialogues contain the so-called Theory of Ideas and thus represent Plato's own philosophizing. In a third period Plato subjected the Theory of Ideas to a scathing critique. On this division of the Platonic corpus see Joseph Owens, *A History of Ancient Western Philosophy* (New York: Appleton, Century, Crofts, 1959), 193-194.

31 I take this to be the point of such texts as *Republic* I and the *Ion.*

32 Notably in the *Paradoxe sur le comédien, Oeuvres esthétiques*, 299-381.

33 Ludwig Wittgenstein, *Philosophical Investigations*, ed. G.E.M. Anscombe (Oxford: Blackwell's, 1953, I, 7.

34 Herbert Josephs, *Le Neveu de Rameau: Diderot's Dialogue of Language and Gesture* (n.p.: Ohio University Press, 1969), 23-38; 43-62.

35 We should bear in mind that the Platonic philosopher must withdraw from the world into the Academy in order to understand how the world really functions and to determine what is "really real". See Plato, Theaetetus, 176B. The Enlightenment believed that it was possible to understand this world and even to change it from within.

36 Josephs, *op. cit.*, 107-120

37 For Wagner's concept of the *Gesamtkunstwerk* see Michael Tanner, "The Total Work of Art," The Wagner Companion, ed. P. Burbige and R. Sutton (London: Faber, 1979), 140-224. On the Problematic character of Wagner's *Gesamtkunstwerk* see A. Janik, "Saint Offenbach's Post Modernism," "Der Fall Wagner", ed. Thomas Steigert (Laaber: Laaber Verlag, 1991), 361-386.

Chapter 6

Morals in the "Theatre of the World"

Solveig Schult Ulriksen

The following remarks relate essentially to Allan Janik's reading of *Rameau's Nephew* as a confrontation with and challenge to Platonic thought. I am also indebted to Herbert Joseph's rich contributions to Diderot studies.

Much has been said about Diderot's relationship to the philosophers of antiquity, Socrates and Plato, Diogenes and Seneca, the latter replacing Socrates towards the end of Diderot's life as a model for thought and action. Yet he never ceased to admire the great figure of Socrates, the seeker of truth, and clearly identified with the persecuted philosopher during his imprisonment in 1749, when to occupy his mind, he translated Plato's *Apology for Socrates*, at the same time discovering (painfully so) that he was not made for the heroic virtue of his philosophical and moral ideal.

Diogenes is the other figure Diderot tends to identify with, whose "frock", were he Athenian, he would willingly wear. In the article "Cynique" of the *Encyclopédie* presenting Antisthenes and his school, Diderot approves as a sign of "good judgement" the Cynics' reaction against Platonic idealism, their leaving the realm of sublime hypotheses for "the study of morals ("moeurs") and the practice of virtue". The portrait of Diogenes, the at once "indecent but truly virtuous philosopher", stresses his insolent frankness, wit and irony, his "fearless soul and courage of mind" along with the austerity, the virtuous frugality of his life and the denial of personal needs. Diogenes thus stands for individual freedom and self-sufficiency, adopting "in the midst of society the manners and morals of the state of nature", and by his very example, accusing corrupt society of its vice. The model he represents is, however, no more accessible than that of Socrates; as Jean Starobinski writes in an excellent article, Diogenes is but another name for impossible liberty, "historically and existentially out of reach."[1]

In *Rameau's Nephew* Socrates and Diogenes are both important figures, alternatively attacked and defended. The late Jacques Chouillet was, I believe, the first to point out that the functions associated with these two figures – the Socratic and the Cynic function – are both at work in the dialogue, represented (however imperfectly) not by the philosopher-Moi but by the anti-philosopher-Lui.[2] True, the Nephew essentially retains the "effronterie" of the Cynic philosopher and has certainly nothing in common with the virtue he represents. Yet, in his shameless frankness he "brings out the truth", unmasks hypocrisy and vice, and in so doing accuses a corrupt and perverted society where moral principles and social behaviour each go their separate ways. In thus reversing the traditional roles, allowing for the "enlightener to be enlightened" (A. Janik), Diderot gives another twist to the ironic reversal of Platonic thought, which indeed is what much of the dialogue is about.

Jacques Chouillet also reminds us that in the years of crisis in Diderot's public and private life when he started writing *Rameau's Nephew*, some of his most cherished convictions seem to falter, such as the famous trinity of the True, the Beautiful and the Good, or the equation of virtue and happiness, both of Platonic origin. The clash between principles and the world as it goes, turning the philosopher into a mere "oddity" is repeated, Chouillet says, within philosophy itself in the clash between theory and action. So it is that neither of the two characters are consistent in their roles; a number of times the fundamental opposition between them weakens to the point of turning into agreement and complicity. In this game for power their respective positions are constantly put to the test, pushed as far as possible in a series of moves of attack and defense, where positions are reversed and superiority shifts from one to the other.

Diderot subtitled his text *Satire seconde*, which has generally been read as referring to Horatian satire, in relation to the epigraph quoted from Horace. There are other possible readings, one of which ties up with the Diogenes motive and its anti-Platonic implications. Recent critics (Starobinski, Jauss[3]) have suggested that the "genre" which most aptly describes Diderot's masterpiece is that of Menippean satire, as developed by Lucian in his dialogues, later by Varro and by Petronius in the *Satyricon*. Of this possible ancestor Diderot's *Satire seconde* certainly has the provocative laughter, the subversion of traditional values and the mocking challenge of established truths. Menippus, writes Diderot at the end of the article "Cynique", "made himself more recommendable for the kind of writing to which he gave his name than for his morals and philosophy". As Starobinski points out in the article quoted above, when the virtuous courage of the early Cynics disappears, what is left is an author of satire: literature thrives on the ruins of philosophy "in spite of the lesser dignity of existence, or precisely because of this degradation". After Diogenes, embodying "heroic marginality, submitted to the most radical norm", follows Menippus the usurer:

Et les propos qui s'échangent dans la satire diderotienne ne trouvent leur patron légitime qu'en Ménippe, le disciple imparfait, l'écrivain spéculateur, sarcastique et incapable de résignation. Les *moeurs*, faisant désormais problème, ne suivent aucune norme, et la parole – insolente, nostalgique, doutant d'un rétablissement de la norme perdue – se donne libre cours, en deux voix alternées.[4]

The theatre is everywhere in *Rameau's Nephew*. In front of the philosopher-spectator the Nephew's verbal and mimetic performances bring a multitude of characters and voices into the dialogue, where also Moi is acting his part. As the brilliantly staged performance progresses, the Café de la Régence is literally transformed into a theatre. The audience is enlarged to include the chess-players and even the occasional passers-by in the street. The reader is also clearly invited to participate in the spectacle, as he too has his part to play in "la comédie du monde". The metaphor of universal theatre – the ancient topos of *theatrum mundi* – is, I believe, a major figure in

Diderot's thought. This is what informs the inherent theatricality of nearly all of Diderot's writings, where, as Herbert Josephs puts it, "the imaginative staging of encounter and conflict" has proved irresistibly attractive to directors and actors alike, giving rise to a number of successful performances. Added to the dialogical form, which in itself is not enough to define theatricality, nor is the multiplicity of characters and voices specific to the theatre, there is in *Rameau's Nephew* the conscious acting of roles in front of an ever-present keenly observing spectator.

Jean-Francois Rameau, the mediocre musician, tormented by his mediocrity, is by contrast an extraordinary actor, capable of imitating virtually anything. He is from the outset portrayed as a protean figure, constantly changing, divided and contradictory, never at one or identical with himself. Being nothing, he may become anything – so he plays whatever part circumstances (his own biological nature, social conditions, hazard and necessity) may require. An actor in life, playing with perfect control (except for the one fatal occasion) his role as parasite, fool and jester to the "Bertinhus" household, assuming various "positions" in the "beggars' pantomime" in order to please, seduce and deceive, he reveals the true nature of the world as an enormous theatre, where everyone takes "positions" in the social masquerade. He forces the philosopher-spectator out of his comfortable seat in the pit and up on stage, drives him to reveal his own fragmented self and makes him (and the reader) recognize that the "beggars' pantomime" is but one variation of universal pantomime, "the great round-dance of the world".

Not surprisingly, the moral debate between the parasite and the philosopher comes to a dead end, which is not to say that this is the final outcome of the dialogue itself. The moral values mocked by the Nephew are reestablished by what are generically the weapons of satire, laughter and indignation. The perilous confusion of ethics and aesthetics (the Nephew's praise of "sublimity in evil") is denounced and priority given to ethics. And finally, ethical norm is reintroduced in the dialogue by the Nephew himself with the idea of justice. The slandering of "Bertinhus" by their "menagerie" of flatterers and parasites is an act of justice, whereby the Nephew and his infamous companions carry out the just decrees of Providence: "But while we are carrying out her just decrees against stupidity, you who show us in our true colours are carrying out her just decrees against us." The moral purpose and significance of satire, of this particular satire, can hardly be more clearly expressed.

Notes

1 "Diogène dans *Le Neveu de Rameau*", *Stanford French Review*, 8, 1984.

2 *La Formation des idées esthétiques de Diderot*, A. Colin, 1973, pp. 542-544.

3 Hans-Robert Jauss, "*Le Neveu de Rameau*, dialogue et dialectique", *Revue de métaphysique et de morale*, 89, 1984.

4 "And the exchange of views and words in Diderot's satire only find their legitimate patron in Mennipus, the imperfect disciple, the speculating writer, sarcastic and incapable of resignation. Morals, being henceforth an unresolved problem, do not follow any norm and speech – insolent, nostalgic, doubting the reestablishment of the lost norm – flows unhindered in two alternating voices."

Chapter 7

The Traditions of Dialogue and the Future of Philosophy

Igor Naletov

We are living in a period of great change, not simply in chronological terms, but in the broader sense. The changes are profound enough to affect political, economical and scientific thinking – the entire system of human values that is common to all mankind. Now, in the early nineties, the direction of change can hardly be predicted, and it is therefore important to identify the trends of renewal in philosophy and scientific methodology and in styles of thinking.

In Russia, philosophical thinking is at a crossroads, having travelled a long, original, and in many ways tragic path from Marxism to Stalinism and post-Stalinism. And now Russian philosophical thought has to find its own original way out of our political, economical and spiritual deadlock. There is no doubt that, being original, Russian philosophy has to become emancipated and take its place in the mainstream of world philosophical thought. Its entry into the international community will be a form of guarantee against new intellectual and social collision.

Some Russian philosophers still hope for a return to authentic Marxism – to "real dialectics", to "scientific materialism". They believe this alternative would lead to a revival of the creative spirit, to the resolution of our aggravated economic and social problems. In my view, these hopes cannot be realized. I believe that our society's deep crisis has its roots not in politics and economics alone, but in some philosophical postulates of Marxism, postulates which none of our philosophers dares to touch. I would like to attempt a statement of what it is in Russian philosophical thinking that must be overcome. I propose a discussion of these problems in the hope that they are of universal interest, because they relate to the dynamics of world philosophical thought. First of all we have to overcome the stereotypes of isolationism and, in our Russian version, the mania for creating systems.

Marxism only declared the annihilation of Hegel's universal philosophical system, which aspired to solve all problems. Marxism found a rather effective means of annihilating the universal system – the dialectics which "never bends down before anything and is critical and revolutionary in its essence." And dialectics was genuinely revolutionary and critical of all other forms of philosophy. But at the same time it isolated itself from many humanitarian and scientific concepts. Dialectics failed the test of criticality:

it proclaimed itself the only scientific and universal philosophical system that contained the source and the means of its own development. It could not oppose the creation of systems, as it was premised on the possibility that absolute truth could be achieved. And that concerned not only the truth of fact but also the postulates of dialectics itself, materialism etc. Dialectics considers these postulates to have been solved once and for all. I think you will agree that questions concerning the role of philosophical knowledge and truth and the creation of philosophical theory are not trivial matters. There is a real problem both in regarding philosophy as being reserved for a special form of thinking, and also in its tendency to deconstruct, fragmenting into a large number of schools, trends and even disciplines. World philosophy (as the last World Philosophical Congress showed) stands against these dilemmas.

The first dilemma could be described thus: will philosophy deconstruct itself, transforming itself into specialist (or special interest) categories such as the philosophy of physics, philosophy of biology, philosophy of business, philosophy of law, or Russian philosophy, Chinese philosophy and so on; or will there be a single, whole, universal, great Philosophy. To my mind, these tendencies are in some ways interrelated. The deconstruction of philosophy will only lead to expansion and universalism if any one dogma becomes too dominant. On the other hand, every system creation is in itself a disintegration of philosophical knowledge, as it is of any other knowledge. As a matter of fact, both these tendencies lead to the death of philosophy, as it does of any other common knowledge.

The second dilemma of contemporary spiritual life is connected with the principle of free thinking, with the right of a free choice of philosophical position. Marxism did not allow this principle. Russian philosophers and scientists had cruel experience of thought enslavement, when different trends of thought were forbidden. Russian philosophers have suffered a great deal for this freedom of choice in the spiritual and intellectual spheres. They all understand that we cannot live as we used to. But even now, after eight years of Perestroika, many of them said that they did not know any other way of "constructing" the spiritual world. They cannot understand how freedom can be used in the spheres of science and philosophy where, as in ordinary life there is a strong need for order. Can we really combine materialism with idealism, determinism with indeterminism, freedom with moral responsibility and so on? If we proclaim absolute freedom of thought, without any canons or rules, we will fall into growing chaos. Thus we have a choice: we may choose a monological style of thinking, which shows us only one possible solution, at least to fundamental questions like "matter is primary, consciousness is secondary", "motion is absolute – stasis is relative", or we opt for the freedom to choose any point of view. With this second choice we will face chaos, eclectics and unscrupulousness.

It may be that these issues only arise in the intellectual situation in Russia. They are, of course, only a few of a great number of dilemmas which give us a very difficult situation in philosophy and in intellectual life as a whole. I would be pleased to hear the views of the participants of the seminar about some possible solutions to these dilemmas. In this context, I would like to draw your attention to the traditions of philosophical thought which we have already forgotten. In these traditions lie the solution to our dilemmas. I refer here to the traditions of Diderot's philosophy.

First, I would like to stress that Diderot was perhaps alone among the encyclopaedists in not "creating a system". His philosophy is not a collection of dogmas. It does not have a life of its own, separate from reality and human knowledge. For Diderot, philosophy is only the instrument of thinking; it is real dialogue which reflects all the difficulties of the real world, of human thoughts and passions. Do you not think that this magic of philosophy, free from the mania to create systems, is needed to overcome the boundaries of scientific disciplines and the limits of the various philosophical schools and systems of beliefs?

In their writings on Diderot, many Soviet philosophers maintain that Engels took Diderot's thoughts to a deeper level, or that Marx showed the narrowness of Diderot's views and so on. But we can see more dialectics in many of Diderot's works than in Marxism itself. To some extent Diderot was more profound than Marx because he saw the deep roots of the contradictions between spirit and nature, between nature and education, between freedom and necessity, between motion and stasis and so on.

I do not know of any other form of philosophy, including Marxism, in which these aspects are so strongly contradictory and at the same time so strongly dependent on one another. The matter is that the spirit of system creation, the ambition to solve all possible problems and to use any means to build practical and non-contradictory systems, leads both Marx and Hegel to accentuate and state preferences. For example, Marx insists that materialism is preferable to idealism, motion is preferable to stasis, struggle is preferable to unity. Yet in the strict sense dialectics needs at the same time equality and the mutual elimination of all these opposites. That is, in fact, the spirit of Diderot's philosophy.

In its almost absolute flexibility and refinement, Diderot's thinking achieved full uncertainty, thanks to its complete freedom and emancipation. Diderot himself knew this, and he used his talents as a writer and philosopher to express the lack of correspondence between the process of thinking and the result of thinking. He concentrated on the contradictoriness of thought.

Some scientists called these aspects of his works Socratic. It is thanks to these features that Diderot managed to avoid the temptation to create a system. His Socratic, or should I say dialectic, way of thinking destroys any system. I consider this characteristic of Diderot's writings to be one of his foremost distinctions and one which illustrates the features of the philosophy of Enlightenment. Diderot is interested not only in what his contemporaries are thinking about, or the subject of their thinking, he is interested in the very process of thinking, the very process of reasoning. He manages to capture the thought, to understand the meaning of the thought even when it is far from complete. Thought is always in motion if it is not dead. Every completed thought is actually only half of it. It not only discovers, it also hides the mysteries of life and the process of thinking. That is why Diderot's philosophy is not explicit; it is latent in the structure of the dialogues between the Philosopher and Rameau, between Jack and the master. The flexibility of Diderot's thinking does not mean that his notions and images are without form. The notions and images of his dialectical thinking are very definitely formed. Diderot achieves this through contrast. The differences between things in nature, feelings and thoughts eliminate one another. But there are no other forms of definitions in philosophy than through their opposites. Motion may be defined as in opposition to stasis. Necessity may be defined as the opposite of chance. Truth can only be found through absurdity.

It must be noted that this correspondence of categories is supported by neither Hegel nor Marx.

Diderot's way of thinking differs from that of Holbach, Helveziy and Marx and Engels in its realized paradoxicality. Marx and Engels were sure that their own concept held no inherent contradictions. And they were unwilling to look at their own concept from the opposite viewpoint. Diderot's philosophy was in itself contradictory. Diderot did not want to solve contradictions. His task was only to discover the contradiction in its most paradoxical form. In Diderot's works all opposite sides are equal.

The philosophy which we shall bring into the next century must not be simply pluralistic, drifting with neither sail nor rudder in a boundless sea of world culture. The open philosophy implies not an infinite and unbounded series of possibilities, but a very concrete set of alternatives. I must recognize and grant to the philosopher, scientist and political figure the right to *choose* one of the possible positions: materialist or idealist, monistic or pluralistic, religious or atheist etc. However, in consistently championing and developing open philosophy, they follow the principles of dialogue and do not allow one of them to turn into an all-consuming monster. In contrast to Marxism, freedom of choice will be not only a conclusion drawn from gnosiology and sociology, but one of the fundamental prerequisites of philosophy.

We are, of course, at the beginning of the road, but let me express my wish and my belief that this process will be a pacifying and fruitful one.

Chapter 8

Comments
Lars Kleberg

Before leaving Yasnaya Polyana to go to his death we are told Tolstoy sat down at his desk and re-wrote, by hand, like a schoolboy, a long passage from Socrates' *Apology*. We do not know exactly what passage he chose. What interests us here is the very act of re-writing – not simply re-reading – the text in order to let it pass through the physical movement of the hand, reiterating the very curves of the letters, as if to memorize physically the movement of the thought itself. Tolstoy's was a gesture of profound submission; of concrete understanding.

Today, modern communications technology seems to have reduced the physical or physiological relation to thought and reasoning (rhythm, friction, contextuality) to a minimum.[1] Tolstoy's schoolboy-like exercise reminds us of the importance of retaining the connection between hand and thought, between body and mind. For the Russian writer, the work of copying obviously had a deep moral meaning of submission and subordination of the self to the text. The studious and careful rewriting has an ascetic, almost monastic character.

At the same time, Tolstoy's example reminds us that every reading, every act of understanding (even without copying by hand) implies a kind of translation. The professional translator's goal is not only an imitation of the "content" or the "form" but of the very *movement* of the original text.[2] Thomas Tempte's fascinating reconstruction of Tutankhamen's Chair is, in this respect, a perfect icon for the work of the translator. In order to "imitate" the original, one needs to "get inside" not only the end product but also the process of construction (maybe even its tools); one needs to understand practically "how the text is made".[3] The theory of translation has therefore taught us less about the skill than about the careful study of the history of the profession or of concrete and successful pieces of work.

Both systematic reasoning and organization are traditionally modelled on the principles of non-contradiction. The ideal behind the perfect system is often the smooth, frictionless working of a machine or engine.[4] The re-writing by hand of Socrates' *Apology* is, from this point of view, totally absurd. Compared to a modern digital copy or some other kind of "cloning" of the (Russian or Greek) original, the re-writing only introduces distortion into the system. But as is the case with any serious process of translation, distortion does not only imply the well-known "losses" but also certain gains of another kind, and these can generally be described in terms of dialogue.

Stephen Toulmin's imaginary confrontations (dialogical, although in the form of soliloquies) between the old master thinkers and their biography is yet another demonstration of the useful confrontation of body and mind. At the same time it is a brilliant artistic performance. In his intriguing essay on *Rameau's Nephew* Allan Janik questions the limitations of abstract reasoning, or of a certain understanding of it. As Janik shows, through the examples of Plato's metaphor of the cave and Diderot's *Nephew*, successful enlightenment must not only strive towards the abstract light but also constantly keep in mind the conditions of the cave and the necessary connection between the cave and the bright sunlight.

Solveig Schult Ulriksen points out how the necessary connection between concrete and abstract can be studied in the theatrical act. The actor and the role, both present on the stage, are also an ideal example of the creative tension between one's self and the other: a tension that Diderot the writer provokes us, the readers of today, to silently revive when reading his text.

Another feature of Diderot's art which is essential for a new understanding of the limitations of abstract reason is exemplified by Igor Naletov. For all the planning and strictures, the system of philosophical thought in the former Soviet Russia was never smoothly closed. And here, paradoxically, lies not a defeat but a possibility for a new beginning. History has taught the Russian philosophers to be extremely skeptical about all promises of a successful, final synthesis. The closed system is either a threat or an illusion.

Notes

1 The introduction of the pen-computer, particularly the Apple Newton with its program for translating handwriting into digital information (designed by the Moscow mathematician Georgy Pachikov), might change this radically.

2 Thomas Tempte, "The Chair of Tutankhamun", in Göranzon and Florin (eds), *Dialogue and Technology. Art and Knowledge* Springer-Verlag, London 1991, pp 157-164.

3 Jean le Rond d'Alembert, "On the Translation of Tacitus", Observations sur l'art de traduire en général et sur cet essai de traduction en particulier, the Introduction to "Essai de traduction de quelques morceaux de Tacite", *Mélanges de littérature, d'histoire et de philosophie. Nouvelle édition* Amsterdam 1760.

4 Nordal Åkerman (ed.), *The Necessity of Friction. Nineteen Essays on a Vital Force*, Physica Verlag, Heidelberg 1993.

Acting as a Model for Skill

Chapter 9

We Must Safeguard the Freedoms of our Craft

Erland Josephson

In the field of dramatic art the most inaccessible and hard-to-describe thing is the knowledge an actor possesses. Most actors find it difficult to understand what their knowledge actually consists of, once one goes beyond the obvious skills of good diction, excellent movement, stamina and a good memory. Some of us can fence and ride as well, some have learned to fall well without hurting themselves, and a few of us can still apply an expressive stage mask.

All of this can be registered and described. And all of this is the sort of thing that drama schools can, or at least should, teach.

But beyond that, things become more difficult.

One unforgettable day, John Gielgud gave me a lesson in delivering Shakespearean verse. At that time he was 86 years old and I was 67. He usually addressed me as "young man".

We were making a film of The Tempest, directed by Peter Greenaway. Sir John was Prospero and I was Gonzalo. Gielgud asked if he could take me through my lines:

> I have only wept
> Or should have spoke ere this.
> Look down, you gods,
> And on this couple drop a blessed
> Crown:
> For it is you that have chalk'd forth
> the way
> which brought us hither.

And so on for another ten lines.

We spent two hours on these fifteen lines. Gielgud was tireless. Eagerly, he gave me of his knowledge, and to him that knowledge was more important than he himself, his name and his reputation. I had to go through my lines again and again. I was supposed to observe all the punctuation and mark the end of every line. There was a difference between a full stop and a comma, and where in the text you drew breath was vital. All these signs and rules constituted a tradition that had been handed down, knowledge that had been developed and refined over hundreds of years. The signs separating phrase and sentence were not Shakespeare's, they were the actors'; their placement an expression of the actors' experience, of their recommendations and their practice. They reflected hard-won knowledge, a battle with phrasing, with feelings and insight, technique and clarity, with characterization and with contact with the audience. The punctuation was notes, directions, reminders. Line ends were not simply a notation of metre, they also stimulated thought and feeling. Fantasies that had been worked upon right across centuries, decades, years, months, weeks, days, hours, minutes and seconds. Everything is at once venerably old, original, altered, developed and renewed.

Consciously or subconsciously, Gielgud's lesson will leave its mark on me. And it is reasonable to suppose that what I learned may at some time influence some young or old actor. Suddenly, one evening on a Swedish stage in the year 2003, Gielgud's and his predecessors' phrasing may echo from a young actor playing his first Shakespearean role.

In the same way there is not a single actor at the Royal Dramatic Theatre who is permitted to take the part of the King in any play without coming under the influence of Lars Hanson; imitating him and his dialogue. The theatre walls are imbued with experience, knowledge, suggestions, angels and ghosts.

Lars Hanson died in 1965.

Ivan Hedqvist died in 1935. I cannot possibly explain, either to myself or to others, what there is of Hedqvist in my performances; I have probably never seen him on the stage. But I know that I make use of Hedqvist's theatrical triumphs and changes. As with all innovators, he discovered new and useable knowledge. Knowledge that the audience perceives as new truth. A surprising naturalness or an expressive un-naturalness that signals new discoveries about man.

Once, when I was in difficulties with a monologue, I asked the advice of Georg Rydeberg, the famous Swedish actor. "Don't lean back when you sit", he said. "You can't deliver a harangue like that when you are leaning back". I sat up straight and the problem was solved.

Acting is full of the most varied kinds of knowledge. But as a rule we actors are rotten theoreticians, probably for fear that structured theories might come between us and startling new experiences of ourselves, of others and of the world. Our knowledge suffuses all our senses and our bodies; it is in the tone of our voices and in our expressions and gestures. We remember in the way we hold ourselves, we muse with our facial expressions, we animate our thoughts by making rhythmical appraisals. We sensualize all sorts of internal processes.

We pass on experiences without verbalizing them. This does not prevent us from making craftsmanlike observations or giving instructions. We are better practical teachers than we are lecturers.

This has nothing to do with our intelligence. Except that the actor organizes, so to speak, his intelligence in a different way to other people. He must keep his intellect sharp, alert to lightning-fast impulses and influences, and this requires a different kind of resolution than that required to grasp a thought. He must assiduously investigate and assess the impulse, but not allow himself to be enslaved by it; he must transform it into a dogma: no-one has such a complicated relationship to faith as does the actor. The actor's intelligence is restless and hungry, its main objective not confirmation but new experience. This is often described as intuition, but that is a senseless limitation because in most cases our intelligence is such a vigorous co-creator. But its function can and must be so untrammelled that its creative processes will extend to encompass even stupidity and emotional storms. It fears the confining walls of "push-buttonology".

Am I now clothing the usual stereotypes in rather more complicated wording? Yes, I probably am. But ancient knowledge and truthful observations will emanate even from the stereotype actor. The actor's knowledge and experience is, after all, subjected to constant interrogation on the rack of the inquiring and exacting audience.

We are both controlled and developed by our audiences, perhaps in equal measure, and as often in a negative or cautious direction as in a positive or bold direction. The audience influences us in our knowledge of ourselves. This is sometimes painful and demanding, sometimes joyful and confirmatory – and that is when there is a danger that we might stagnate. We must learn to make wise use of the knowledge our audiences give us. That is not a simple process, for this knowledge is intimate and personal in nature. Its strength lies in its lack of objectivity, its weakness in its assumed objectivity. Drama creates new knowledge. Without art, science will stagnate, and without science, art will stagnate. Knowledge is refined as much by its expression as by its formulation. But where is the actor in this process?

In the centre.

Or at least we should be in the centre. The actor must abandon his supposedly humble position as an "interpreter", as a conveyor of other people's intentions and visions. We are our own vision, our own consciousness, which the playwright, the director and each member of the audience have to interpret. We are the portrayers of society, we offer a role to the lost and insecure, a structure to the confused, truth to the blind. We have the gift and the opportunity to create new attitudes in a matter of a few hours. It is above all the actor who provides the substitute experience, makes it understandable, concrete, relevant to man and his fate. This may sound pompous, but I don't give a damn how it sounds, as long as I allow myself to say it.

The actor has made himself a platform from what is clear and at the same time contradictory. We must keep a watch on this, for this is the freedom of our craft. It is so easy to lose. Sometimes it is so temptingly comfortable to simply reproduce.

Chapter 10

Some Reflections on Diderot's Paradox

Lars Gustafsson

Truly original intellectual work is produced less frequently than we may think. Each century produces few arguments that are as fascinating and seemingly original as Descartes' Cogito or Anselm's Ontological Proof. The profoundly original often has a somewhat treacherous simplicity to it.

How many men have managed to think as many original thoughts as Diderot in one lifetime? Taken together, the Paradox of the Actor, in the dialogue of the same name, the Harpsichord Metaphor for the relation between Mind and Body in D'Alembert's Dream and, of course, a creation like Rameau's Nephew add up to a larger number of original inventions than is usually produced by an entire generation of writers.

Diderot seems so much closer to us than do the other heroes of the Enlightenment. And in spite of his position at the very core of the French Enlightenment, by virtue of his role in the Encyclopédie, that gigantic formalization of, among other things, what up to then had been wordless knowledge, he seems to lack one typical hand-book ingredient of the Enlightenment: the Optimism.

His approach to Philosophy (L'étonnement est le premier effet d'un grand phénomène; c'est à la Philosophie de le dissiper"[1]) is very humble. The free, and seemingly errant, flow of conversation in his essays, which is in such striking contrast to the style of German philosophy of his own time, reminds us strongly of the style of people like Wittgenstein. And his dislike of the linear, the mechanistic, the deterministic explanation, also has something very modern about it. It is hard to understand how the different fields of Diderot's thought fit together. And this is at least in part because he was too honest to construct virtual connections between ideas and experiences where there were none. In his *Pensées sur l'interprétation de la nature* he imagines the entire field of science in that way.

"Je me représente la vaste enceinte des sciences, comme un grand terrain parsemé de places obscures et de places éclariés."[2] On the one hand he is convinced that the idea of a single isolated fact, logically independent from the rest of the world, is incompatible with any philosophy, e.g. that explanations must in some sense be of a global nature. Diderot is convinced that there is a great chain of being connecting all phenomena, but he resents the idea that anybody should know its different links. For Diderot, creativity is to know where a field of knowledge comes to an end.[3] Knowledge is also a knowledge of limits. The needs form the organs, but the organs also form the needs. There is a flux in Nature which excludes perfectibility – there are no platforms to be arrived at. In Rameau's Nephew the divine mathematical madness of the great-uncle turned into the non-divine madness of the dilettante nephew. Nature has returned to a new experiment, forgetful of all the arias and heroes and pythagorean speculations of the great Rameau. How, then, do these ideas hang together? Is it an old sport, started either by Sainte-Beuve in his Lundis or perhaps by even earlier critics to speak about the "confusion" of Diderot. "Son matérialisme n'est pas un mécanisme géométrique et aride, mais un vitalisme confus, fécond et puissant, une fermentation spontanée, incessante, évolutive, ou, jusque dans le moindre atome, la sensibilité latente ou dégagée subsiste toujours présente."[4]

However, it remains an open question whether it is not the reader rather than the writer who is "confused". Inspired by such modern scholars as Elizabeth Potulicki, I am fairly convinced that Diderot's thought shows a great deal of internal coherence and consequence and that it all constitutes an understanding of the world which is admirably modern and free, but which in his time was hardly possible to express other than in fragmentary and paradoxical terms. As I shall try to argue in a moment, his Paradox is a good example. Sainte-Beuve also remarks that at the core of Diderot's philosophical method is his talent for being surprised. An excellent example of this is of course the famous Paradox of the Actor. Once we are acquainted with the paradox in Diderot's oeuvre it all seems so simple, and yet – how mind-boggling are the consequences.

To the English empiricists – who although less coherent and less rigidly empirical than their textbook image are still fairly insistent on the principle that nothing can be in the mind which was not put there – creative imagination poses a problem, because every idea which is not an exact copy of something outside ourselves has to be explained in terms of combinations of such representations. This approach has a reasonable chance of accommodating things which do not exist, such as dragons and greek gods, but has more difficulty with the immense wealth and flow of human creativity.

Diderot makes a serious attempt to bring creativity into the picture, and that is probably one reason why it seems so difficult to fit essays like D'Alembert's Dream or the Paradox of the Actor into a general Enlightenment pattern.[4]

How can Diderot's paradox be formulated? Various ways will suggest themselves to the reader of Diderot, depending on where his interest lies. If it is in psychology, he might say that the most convincing way to theatrically represent an emotion is in an emotionally detached way.

If, on the other hand, our interest is in Nature, we might express Diderot's result by saying that Nature cannot be imitated with natural means. And thirdly, if we are more interested in the logical foundations of semantics, we might say that the act of representation always has to be different from the thing represented. A thing cannot be its own optimal image, because if it could, it would have to be at the same time different from and identical to itself, as the image-relation seems to presuppose a difference between the representation and the thing represented. What we meet in the theatre are not emotions but acts of art which evoke emotions in ourselves. It is we, not the actors, who feel rage or love. As to the actor, as he is portrayed by Diderot in the Paradox in a lively little picture of the way he looks after the performance, we see a completely different set of emotions to those presented on stage:

Le socque ou le cothurne déposé, sa voix est éteinte, il éprouve une extrême fatigue, il va changer de linge ou se coucher; mais il ne lui reste ni trouble, ni douleur ni mélancolie, ni affaissement d'âme.
     C'est vous qui remportez toutes ces impressions.
     L'acteur est las, et vous tristes; c'est qu'il est démené sans rien sentir, et que vous avez senti sans vous démener. S'il en était autrement, la condition du comédien serait la plus malheureuse des conditions; mais il n'est pas le personage, il le joue et le joue si bien que vous le prenez pour tel: l'illusion n'est que pour vous; il sait bien, lui, qu'il ne l'est pas.[5]

In his essay, Diderot in fact expresses the Paradox in many ways; you can say that he walks around what he has discovered in a sort of circle, viewing the discovery from different perspectives. In one place it is introduced psychologically, as a distinction between *sense* and *sensibility*:

C'est que' être sensible est une chose, et sentir est une autre. L'une est une affaire d'âme, l'autre une affaire de jugement.[6]

A little further into the dialogue we find what might better be called a "logical" interpretation of the Paradox:

Je vous entends; il y aura toujours, entre celui qui contrefait la sensibilité et celui qui sent, la différence de l'imitation à la chose.[7]

And, still a little further down, we find what might be called the formulation in terms of Nature and its limits:

Vous voyez qu'il n'est pas même permis d'imiter la nature, même la belle nature, la vérité de trop près, et qu'il est des limites dans lesquelles il faut se renfermer.[8]

So what might look like a logical observation from one perspective looks like an empirical observation from another. The distinction probably does not make as much sense to Diderot as it did to Kant.

Of course, the logical approach to the Paradox does not exclude its empirical confirmability, but for a modern approach, what can be argued logically does not have to be argued empirically as well.

Seen as a logical argument, the Paradox seems to be more a regression than a real paradox. An emotion in representation cannot be identical with the emotion represented because the element of representation adds a quality which makes the copy radically different from the original. Thus a likeness in order to be a likeness has to be different from what it is like. The argument which can of course be extended to all sorts of representations (pictures, memories, perceptions) does not really say anything about the nature of mind or the limits that nature has placed on our activities.

So it seems that what Diderot delivers is not one but a package of at least three "Paradoxes" in his Essay, in which logical, empirical and psychological considerations form a strange unity. This is highly characteristic of Diderot's way of arguing an idea. The most obvious relevance is, of course, to a rather dubious aesthetic concept, that of *expression*.

Clearly, not everything which the actor or anybody, for that matter, does is equally expressive. There are performances which do and performances which do not convince us. In other words, there is an actor's *skill*, which in Diderot's opinion is connected with a certain detached mood of mind; in other words, which demands more sense than sensitivity, where sense is an intellectual and sensitivity and emotional faculty.

One of the obvious consequences of this claim is the blow which it deals to the idea that an artist who expresses a feeling is performing an act of transporting, say, rage or desolation from his own mind to the mind of the audience. Diderot's stress is on the sender side; the actor need not have, and normally never has, the feelings which he expresses (he might have completely different feelings). But in the dialogue there are some hints at the obvious fact that the same or similar considerations can be applied to the receiver side; the theatrical performance is like a well-organized society where everybody sacrifices his rights for the good of the ensemble and the totality.[9] There is also an element of skill in the reaction of the educated theatre public. What is appreciated are not brute expressions of emotion but a harmonic whole.

In other words, we can appreciate the expressiveness of one of those passionate concert arias which Mozart loved to write for young, beautiful sopranos without assuming either that Mozart ever felt the passions of his heroines or that the singers feel them, or that we feel them. What we are able to experience and value is "expressivity" itself, without having to assume that there is any emotion which is transported from mind to mind in this triple act of communication, from composer to singer, from singer to audience.

Furthermore, at the end of the dialogue Diderot even hints that likeness between the brute feeling and the feeling represented on the stage is essential.

Le poète sur la scène peut être plus habile que le comédien dans le monde, mais croit-on que sur la scène l'acteur soit plus profond, soit plus habile à feindre la joie, la tristesse, la sensibilité, l'admiration, la haine, la tendresse, qu'un vieux courtisan?[10]

This thought, never quite developed in the Paradox, brings us very close to a contemporary tendency in the Philosophy of Art, i.e. the refusal to accept similarity as an explanation of the relation between the work of art and that which is supposed to be its meaning. When Nelson Goodman[11] draws our attention to the fact that all oil paintings of castles have many more similarities in common with other oil paintings than with castles, he makes a reflexion which Diderot probably would have liked.

What is "expression of feelings" supposed to mean? Mozart's Requiem is supposed to express Mozart's personality. Mozart's obscene canons are also supposed to express the divine composer's personality. If we follow Diderot, and it seems very hard to deny that he has said something very important about the subject, instead of an emotional substance which is transported between minds we get a skill, which is not really even an imitative skill. An obvious objection is one similar to Nietzsche's objection to Kant's philosophy; we cannot explain a propensity with a propensity ("Vermöge eines Vermögens).[12] If it is an intrinsic rather than an extrinsic quality that makes the actor's or painter's work interesting to the public, we should at least be able to say something more about it than that it demands sensibility rather than sensitivity. Perhaps we should try representativity? We clearly attach much greater weight to some artistic or human expressions than to others. Thus when Jacques Derrida wants us to attach the same importance to what Nietzsche says in his Notebooks from Sils Maria about his forgotten umbrella as to what he says about the Will to Power, we find it difficult to really accept such an egalitarian view of semantics.

Not all "expressions" interest or impress us to the same extent. Is that because some of them are more skillful or because they express something more interesting?

It seems almost inevitable that Diderot's paradox, at least if we follow its implications, leads to the conclusion that all expressions that are equally skillful are of equal importance. This seems to question an entire hierarchy of values. And this hierarchy is entirely based on distinctions like "important" and "unimportant", "representative" and "non-representative". In the sort of egalitarian semantics to which the skill theory in an explication of Diderot appears to point, everything seems to be of equal importance and apt to affect us only to the extent that the expression is skillful. The likenesses seem to imitate each other in a sort of endless topological involution.

One reason for the notorious confusion which seems always to occur when we begin to talk about "expression" is that the word is used very ambiguously. Mozart, in other words a personality, is supposed to express himself through a work, say the Piano Concerto Köchel 491, where, like a letter and its author, the person is the agent and the work the medium. Then there is the use of "express" where Köchel 491 itself is said to be expressing something. It rarely becomes clear whether this is a derivative meaning of the first meaning or not. Then there is the case where a pianist, say Glenn Gould, is said to express some particular thought or feeling, using Mozart's Concerto as his medium. This perhaps takes us to the case in which Diderot is mainly interested: the actor.

Clearly, the word "express" cannot mean the same in these different cases. What similarity could there be between Wolfgang Amadeus Mozart and a piano concerto? What similarity is there between Charles Baudelaire and a poem like "Une Passante"? In some cases a person is the agent, in others a text (or a class of texts, or a class of performances), is supposed to act. The oscillation between the derived and the literal meaning of the word "express" here makes possible the same sort of trick which we find in a lot of deconstructivist modern discourse. The reasoning of the deconstructivist seems to assume that texts can really talk and write to each other. But texts know nothing, not even what they contain.

But we have probably already pushed Diderot a little too far into the modern. Certainly, the remarkable thing is his observation of a certain emptiness, a blind spot at the core of commonsense aesthetic ideas. We all agree that art certainly adds something to Nature, but looking closer at the phenomenon, we find it impossible to say what it is we are talking about. As in other fields of his thought, The Paradox of the Actor shows Diderot's fascination with the gaps in our knowledge. And also the possibility to make a rhetorically and philosophically highly effective use of the awareness that is there. Compared to other Enlightenment philosophers, Diderot seems more preoccupied with what he does not understand than with what he does understand, and that is, perhaps, the source of his originality.

Notes

1 *Pensées sur l'interprétation de la Nature XI*

2 *Pensées sur l'interprétation de la Nature XIV*

3 ibid.

4 Sainte-Beuve Lundis Vol III

5 DIDEROT ED.BIBLIOTHEQUE DE LA PLEIADE Paradoxe p. 1010

6 DIDEROT ED.BIBLIOTHEQUE DE LA PLEIADE Paradoxe p. 1051

7 DIDEROT ED.BIBLIOTHEQUE DE LA PLEIADE Paradoxe p. 1053

8 DIDEROT ED.BIBLIOTHEQUE DE LA PLEIADE Paradoxe p. 1055

9 DIDEROT ED.BIBLIOTHEQUE DE LA PLEIADE Paradoxe p. 1016

10 DIDEROT ED.BIBLIOTHEQUE DE LA PLEIADE Paradoxe pp. 1057-1058

11 Nelson Goodman

12 Friedrich Nietzsche "Jenseits von Gut und Böse!" 11. Ed, Schlechta II p. 575

Chapter 11

The Actor as Paradigm?
Christopher Bigsby

Prologue

The nature of theatre is such that its metaphoric force is frequently, if para-doxically, invoked. A simulation of reality, it assumes a paradigmatic force with respect to that reality until we seem trapped in a house of mirrors. Since we stage our lives before an audience, it is suggested, where should we look for a clue to our self-dramatizations but to the theatre. Since the the-atre mimics the social world, which is the pre-condition for its existence, where should the actor turn for a clue to authenticity but to that world which he would convince us he reproduces and inhabits? The unease which such a circularity implies is disturbing precisely because it would seem to challenge the very notion of authenticity itself, because the deceit which we applaud is also the deceit which we would deplore. Living thus becomes a series of lies and plausibility what we require above all. And yet if what we seek is understanding of our social actions we could do worse than step through the curtains and enquire whether stage and auditorium, actor and audience, are not, indeed, merely versions of one another, offering, as they do, altered perspectives but perhaps not a radically transformed mode of being.

When Freud looked for an image of men growing into possession of their lives he turned to the theatre, to Sophocles' Oedipus at Colonus. When the sociologist Erving Goffman looked for an image of social relationships, in The Presentation of the Self in Everyday Life, he turned to the theatre. As metaphor, as symbol and as fact the theatre has been seen not merely as a mirror to our psychological and social nature but as a key to those transfor-mations which are the essence of private and public truth, which fact is the more disturbing since acting and the theatre have always been treated with the most profound suspicion. As late as the second half of the 19th century an actor in New York was refused burial in holy ground. But – and this I suppose is my point, in so far as I have one – we should perhaps all be refused such burial in so far as the actor's skills are no more than extensions of our own and his violations those necessary for social life.

Act I

> Why, I can smile, and murder whiles I smile,
> And cry "Content!" to that which grieves my heart.
> And wet my cheek with artificial tears,
> And frame my face to all occasions.
> I can add colours to the chameleon,
> Change shapes with Proteus for advantages,
> And set the murderous Machievel to school.
> Can I do this, and cannot get a crown?
> Tut, were it farther off, I'll pluck it down.

The distance between a megalomaniac, such as Richard III, who would be king, and a megalomaniac, who would be an actor, is slim indeed, if the chief skill required is simply dissembling: "That one may smile, and smile, and be a villain." And it is worth recalling that the Greek word for actor was *hypokites*, which is the root for the English word hypocrite. Thus: (Gk) *hypokrises* – to play a part on stage; hypocrisy – to feign virtue, beliefs, standards.

In the same way a principal meaning of the verb to act is "to represent by action, especially on the stage"; a secondary meaning is "to feign, to simulate, to behave insincerely." And the verb 'to play' may also mean "to feign a specified state or quality." What, then, is a good actor but a dissembler and if we are talking here of transferable skills then those who should be paying greatest attention at this moment should presumably be double-glazing salesmen and politicians. And, indeed, David Mamet, in *Glengarry, Glen Ross*, makes precisely this connection having his real estate salesmen stage an improvised drama in order to ensnare a potential customer. The play's the thing wherein to catch not so much the conscience of the king as the cash of the gullible.

And certainly acting, and the words associated with it, has historically had a pejorative meaning.

> Seems, madam! nay it is, I know not seems.
> 'Tis not alone my inky cloak, good mother,
> Nor customary suits of solemn black,
> Nor windy suspiration of forced breath,
> No, nor the fruitful river in the eye,
> Nor the dejected behaviour of the visage,
> Together with all forms, modes, shapes of grief,
> That can denote me truly. These indeed seem,
> For they are actions that a man might play,
> But I have that within which passes show.
> These but the trappings and the suits of woe.

Hamlet's speech, of course, proposes a distinction between actions that a man might play, and authentic feeling – a distinction crucial to, among others, Diderot, for whom seeming is the essence of acting. And yet what irony there is here for this speech on the distinction to be made between seeming and being, is not only made by a man who himself chooses to put on an antic disposition, but is delivered by an actor for whom Hamlet's passions are precisely assumed for the duration of the play. Stanislavski remarks:

"Pushkin asks of the dramatist, and we may ask of the actor, that he possess 'sincerity of emotions, feelings that seem true in given circumstances'." To Pushkin and Stanislavski, then, sincerity and seeming become one and the distinction so carefully made by Hamlet and, incidentally, Diderot, is blurred. Nonetheless it is a distinction which is vital. The skill of the actor, you might say, is thus tainted by its very nature. And even Diderot accepts as much when he says that "the player's brain gives sometimes a touch of trouble to his soul. He weeps as might weep an unbelieving priest preaching of the Passion; as a seducer might weep at the feet of a woman he does not love, but on whom he would impose or, like a courtesan who has no heart, and who abandons herself in your arms." Seen thus, of course, the deceits of the actor are not a special circumstance but a redirection, a focusing of those tactics, those social representations which are the stuff of daily intercourse.

But it is not only deceit that has made the actor the focus of subversion. The Puritans were quite right to suspect the theatre. There is something seductive, lubricious, sensual about it. In the theatre language is savoured in the mouth, shaped, formed, caressed, ejaculated. The body is recuperated so that abstract speech is rooted in physical being, a body which, with a mere movement, may expose the supremacy of instinct over thought, language being earthed in need, the body becoming a sign more powerful, immediate and subversive than a language borrowed from the library of public expression. Dionysus denies the supremacy of Apollo. The body is proxemically alive and, above all, present, now, in the tense which is uniquely the theatre's own: the present tense. The tense which is also our own. In a public place we are permitted to share in transgression and transgression is perhaps a central fact of theatre. Here we are allowed a voyeuristic involvement, to glimpse those who post with such dexterity to incestuous sheets, to boldly go where few members of the audience have gone before: incest, adultery, torture, murder. The theatre is libidinal and Dionysus is its god. Though the Apollonian is present in the structured language, the form, the ordered context, the actor's role is to threaten that order with his or her physical being, to suggest, by his or her very skills, how insecure are the categories, the systems, the social and psychological roles in which we otherwise place our faith. The actor is a reminder that we, too, are Proteus; that we, too, combine the Apollonian and the Dionysian. The actor is a paradigm of the resistant self and of the plural self.

Act II

The Puritans put theatre on a par with long hair, face painting (which, of course, is a critique of God), health drinking, effeminate dancing, effeminate music, Christmas keeping and bonfires. The list is William Prynne's and the word effeminate occurs twice and is an interesting word in the context of acting because, to my mind, one of the qualities of truly great actors – of Brando, as he once was, of Olivier, of Malkovich – is the fact that they contain both the male and the female, that they are no respecters of boundaries. It is one of the skills of the actor to draw on levels of being and sensibility

otherwise proscribed or denied by custom or acculturation, to cross boundaries, deny the permanence of meaning, the fixity of language, the precision
and singularity of interpretation. It was Ibsen who insisted that the function
of the artist was to move the boundary posts. The playwright digs the holes:
the actor places the posts within them.

And what leverage Shakespeare derives from his disturbing of these categories. In The Merchant of Venice Portia dresses as a man and in doing so
displays those qualities assumed to be those of men – rationality, social
command, dispassionate judgement verging on cruelty – only to lay them
aside and become a woman again, quite as though those categories had not
just been breached and thus shown to be arbitrary. In As You Like It the
game is more dangerous as a woman dresses as a man to mock, of all things,
inconstancy and then persuades her male lover to woo her as a man playing
a woman. Since she is in turn wooed by a woman you have a regular
Freudian dog's dinner. But there is another twist, of course, in that Rosalind
herself was played by a boy actor so that we are faced with the sexually dis-
orienting spectacle of a boy playing a woman who pretends to be a man
who is wooed by another man and by a girl in turn played by a boy. And
yet, of course, it is not actors alone who contain male and female and who
find those categories less discrete than they appear.

The very nature of theatre and the skills of the actor raise questions about
the nature of the real and the manner in which it is constituted, perceived,
confirmed. It is impossible to accept the Shakespearean conceit of the theatre's metaphoric centrality and then suppose that there are only two terms
in our equation: the actor, who is real, and the character, who is not. Olivier
and Lear exist together. They are co-present but if we puzzle over the true
nature of Lear – king, beggar, madman, saint – in a play in which most of
the principal characters turn actor (as, indeed, they do in many of
Shakespeare's plays), to deceive, to survive, to redeem, should we not puzzle over the true nature of Olivier for Olivier is surely a construction, his
supreme invention, and no number of biographies will deconstruct that fiction. For Joseph Chaiken: "When we as actors are performing, we as persons are also present and the performance is testimony of ourselves. Each
role, each work, each performance changes us as persons. By this I don't
mean that there is no difference between a stage performance and living. I
mean that they are absolutely joined. The actor draws from the same source
as the person who is the actor. The stage performance informs the life performance and is informed by it."

Act III

There is a term in Noh theatre – Riken no ken – which means outside view,
and another – Gaken – which means inside view, the performer's own view.
The actor needs both: to see his performance from within and without
simultaneously. Like Tennessee Williams's gypsy girl, in Camino Real, who
regains her virginity with every full moon, it's a good trick if you can pull it
off. But the actor has to walk this high wire and in simulating he draws not
just on technical skills but skills having to do with emotional recall, itself a

dangerous territory. John Gielgud thought of his dead mother when playing Hamlet's 'To Be or Not To Be' soliloquy. When Daniel Day Lewis walked off the stage at the National Theatre reportedly because Hamlet's concern for his dead father had become entangled with Day Lewis's for his, he was perhaps being a bad actor but a good human being. Whatever the truth of that it served to underline a danger. The actor has to be simultaneously involved and detached. This is what concerned Diderot. Balance is perhaps the essence, though not to Diderot who preferred detachment, but, as with a high wire act in a circus, part of the excitement of theatre comes from our sense of being in the presence of danger. Ian Holm rushed from the theatre in 1979 in the middle of a monologue in O'Neill's *The Iceman Cometh*, a play which itself explores the permeable membrane between the self and its social representations, which dramatizes the degree to which life and performance become inseparable. Directors feel uneasy in the presence of Alan Rickman, not because his acting can be mannered but also because he exudes this sense of danger, of being barely in control. So, too, perhaps, with Anthony Sher and John Malkovich. This is not a feeling you would like to have in the presence of a brain surgeon and not, perhaps, strictly speaking a skill, unless consciously deployed, more of a quality, but no movie ever gave you this. The fact is that in theatre we are ready for any eventuality from actors forgetting their lines, to duellists inflicting real wounds, the scenery collapsing or onstage coronaries. Moliere did in fact collapse and die while playing the part of the hypochondriac Argan in *The Imaginary Invalid*, thus somewhat undermining the point of his own character.

The essence of an actor's skills, and, I am tempted to say all skills, is that they should be invisible, subsumed in the task they facilitate. The Japanese actor Yoshi Oida has explained that in traditional Japanese theatre there is no improvisation or personal expression, simply prescribed forms of expression and physical and vocal techniques. Training consists of learning these. The end result of training may be the acquisition of these skills and techniques but it is also, paradoxically, a sense of freedom. As he explains, "the aim of all systems of technical training is to enable you to do an action without worrying how you do it. Unless you have this training you cannot arrive at this freedom of communication." The American actor/director Joseph Chaiken has said, similarly, that "technique is a means to free the artist." The risk lies in becoming a victim of the technique or being too conscious of the skills being deployed. As Maureen Stapleton has said of the Delsarte method of actor training: "by the time you've learned it all it's hard to open a door." Consciousness of this kind is the enemy. In like manner the golfer who becomes suddenly obsessed with technique is liable to find himself in the bunker. The skill is not to be aware of the skill which moves from the level of learned procedure to apparently instinctive behaviour. As Stanislavski remarked, in *Creating a Role*, "let our unconscious, intuitive creativeness be set in motion by the help of conscious preparatory work. Through the conscious to the unconscious – that is the motto of our art and technique."

Yet at the same time the essence of acting is not that the actor should efface him or herself in assuming a role or subordinate intuitive ability to skill. If it were why should we choose to see Kenneth Branagh's Hamlet or even Mel Gibson's? Actor and role co-exist. Nor is this a mere matter of doubleness for the actor is himself a construction in several senses, both as a public figure, canonized or demonized in the press, and as a supposedly private self, a self mysteriously assumed, by Diderot among others, to be purged of the skills and qualities which make an actor. But that, of course, is my point. Why do we assume that the self is so purged, that there is an end to acting?

Woody Allen is an actor famous for playing roles which seem close to but not synonymous with that version of himself deployed for public view. But Woody Allen the actor is not the same as Woody Allen, would-be individual. And, as we have discovered, even in private life Woody Allen is capable of acting, of appearing what he is not, even taking photographs of his supposedly more intimate moments and thus turning a spontaneous private action into a theatricalized moment as though he can only believe that action when he sees it photographically staged, a voyeur of his own privacy. This is territory that Diderot does not enter. It is the paradox behind his paradox. He pictures the actor at home, diminished in size and impact and yet somehow authentic. But who is the authentic Woody Allen? Who knows? Not his wife, certainly, and not, for a bet, himself; after all why else has he spent thirty years in analysis, like Anne Bancroft, Maureen Stapleton and a host of other American actors who rush from the stage or the film set to a small room where they pay the audience of one inordinate amounts of money to hear a speech consisting, one presumes, of equal parts self-justification and confession? And what is therapy, after all, but a form of theatre with the irreducible elements of theatre: namely a performer and an audience. Is there no end to acting, then? Is it a matter of I perform, therefore I exist? Quite possibly.

Act IV

Lenin once remarked that if the appearance and essence of things were the same there would be no need for such a thing as science. Much the same could be said of culture but in particular of the theatre in which the two co-exist as the condition of its being. The gap never closes. Gloucester's bastard son Edmund deceives and dissembles to win his way to power, Portia to save a man's life, Kent to survive, Edgar to redeem. Lear plays king, beggar, madman, saint. For O'Neill's derelicts, in *The Iceman Cometh*, survival depends on their playing out their fictions and not confronting something which presents itself as reality but which is merely another form of performance. Authenticity and performance constitute a false dichotomy. They are the infra red and ultra violet of human response, not easily distinguishable to the human eye but part of the white light of truth. We watch Gloucester's eyes gouged out and wince in horror, but not really in horror for we know that what we see is not what we see, that Gloucester is not Gloucester, that the eyes are not eyes, that the blood is not blood and that we are playing the role of audience and not that of bystanders uncertain whether to intervene or not. A child may not make this distinction but we can tell a hawk from a handsaw. And there, surely, is the proof, you might say, that we are more than actors for we know that we have but to step outside the theatre and the blood and the eyes will be real enough. True. But then perhaps that is the function of the theatre, to remind us of what we know, that, as in the former Yugoslavia, today's friendly neighbour may be tomorrow's rapist and murderer and that we, in turn, are someone's neighbour. And which, then, was the authentic self? The friendly neighbour or the rapist? And which are we? The truth is we do not know and may not until the moment comes. We may be either. We contain both possibilities. The theatre tells us this, not in the plot of individual plays but in its recognition of transformation as an immediate possibility, a source equally of hope and of despair.

Joyce Carol Oates concludes an essay on Ionesco thus: "Ionesco comes closest to the gravest most sinister truth about ourselves – being is an empty fiction, and our 'becoming' is equally fictitious, equally empty, for we stand in front of locked doors, motionless, not lacking the power of motion but willed to motionlessness, waiting for a key or a miracle. There is no key, there is no miracle. Being is an empty fiction. Becoming is a nightmare." Diderot's paradox is thus resolved—or side-stepped. There is no sensibility to deplore or praise, to deploy or avoid. There is only pretence. To wipe off the greasepaint is not to reveal the truth. To remove the mask is only to expose another beneath it. That is one version of man as actor, transfixed by a fear of inauthenticity, a fear of being no more than a sequence of performances designed less to deceive others than the self in wait for the miracle of meaning, the Godot of revelatory coherence. There is, however, a brighter version of the coterminous nature of social and moral existence and acting having to do with plenitude and possibility, with transformation and empathy, with performatic skills which have become so intuitive that they are indistinguishable from intuition itself. As John Barth once remarked, "the key to the treasure is the treasure." We are a blend of the given and the created. So, too, are actors in a play. We make a particular hand gesture because somewhere in the double helix of our being is an instruction that we should do so. At the same time we learn by watching and never discover the extent of improvisation and the degree of authority which must be given to the genetic text which we follow.

We are plural, as the actor teaches us we may be. Like the actor we, too, surely progress by transgression, speak words which are not our own while, like an actor, endeavouring to give them a sense of ourselves? We are at our finest when we allow our imagination to let us see through others' eyes, feel the pain that others feel, see the stranger enter our world as a coequal on the stage of experience. Whatever else Shylock may be required to speak he is allowed to plead his humanity and when his mind might be on his gold he cries only one name – Jessica, his daughter. It is the actor who leads us where we must go, into the mind of one who cries for Jessica as we would cry for our own. Do we not become ourselves only by losing ourselves? Acting is not falsehood but an alternative possibility. It is as we might be in a parallel universe except that the parallel universe is this one. We exist as separate selves yet, like the actor, only in so far as we exist as social selves, shaping our behaviour and adjusting our language to that of others, thereby creating a meaning out of dialogue, speaking in confidence of being understood, in the faith that a reply will come, that your experience may be translated into mine and mine into yours. The theatre – Bakhtin notwithstanding – is the dialogic form. It does not mirror or mimic social action. It is the thing itself. The theatre can only exist through the community of those on the stage and the community constituted by the bond forged between those on stage and those in the audience. The actor thus offers us the proof that social co-operation is productive of meaning and since the actor is essentially concerned with mutability he by his very skills reminds us that change is possible and may be an imperative. No wonder, therefore, the theatre has been seen as subversive. The actor is polyvocal, various and thus a denial of the monologic culture in which a singular text, whether it be the Bible or Das Kapital, is interpreted only in a singular way by a priest-hood of initiates. In the theatre all meaning is subject to change and inter-pretation is available to all.

Act V

In explaining the actor's craft John Gielgud turned to art: "I've always said," he remarked, "that when you see the picture of the Van Gogh chair you suddenly think what an extraordinary way to paint a chair – at an angle – and it's yellow – and a funny colour. But after you've seen that picture you can never again see a chair without thinking of Van Gogh. In the same way I think any great actor's moment in a play is brought about by the fact that he has felt it, he has observed it and registered it in his memory book, and he can then repeat it technically over and over again." In other words what the actor does for us is to recuperate the world and make it strange for us, to defamiliarize and offer it back to us new born. And the word repetition is significant for repetition in the theatre is not like repetition on the produc-tion line where the objective is precise replication. It is not even repetition in the sense of a mechanically reproduced and identical image, such as an artist's print or even a movie. As Ingmar Bergman has reminded us, the essence of theatre is "repetition, living, throbbing, repetition. The same per-formance every night, the same performance and yet reborn." And in that respect, too, the theatre can stand not merely as metaphor but exemplar for as Kierkegaard reminds us, in his book *Repetition*: repetition in life always implies change and difference and forces us to understand that we do not inhabit the realm of the aesthetic. The theatre is thus an aesthetic form which contains a suspicion of the aesthetic, which deliberately contaminates the unyielding and unalterable perfection of the object represented to us in its unchanging coherence. The skill of the actor is to resist the deceptive per-fection of an inert language, to deny fetishization, the iconic force of charac-ter become myth.

For Maureen Stapleton the job of the actor is to be "true and real and alive each time" adding that "nothing in life, or in human behaviour, can be alien to the actor. There is nothing that the human being can do that is a surprise, or a shock, or un-understandable." In other words the writer and the actor together, at their best, accomplish what the historian, the psychologist, the sociologist, the anthropologist, all of whom have turned to drama and the actor as metaphor and as fact, struggle so hard to achieve: an understanding of human beings and their behaviour, for that is the essential skill of the actor, at his or her best. And the world they recuperate, whether it be fourth century Greece, sixteenth century England, or 19th century Sweden, is in essence our own, for, whatever fictions they enact there is no other world than our own. As Paul Eluard remarked: "There is another world, and it is this one."

There is a play by Arthur Miller called *The Archbishop's Ceiling*. It is set in an old archbishop's palace in eastern Europe. Concealed in the ceiling may or may not be a series of microphones, the effect of which is to turn all those in the room into actors, performing for an audience which may or may not be listening, which may or may not exist. Beyond the political point, beyond even an awareness that today we are rarely out of range if not of microphones then of video cameras, that we are public even when we imagine ourselves to be private, is a more fundamental consideration. For this is an archbishop's palace. The true reason, therefore, for Jaques' observation that all the world's a stage, his insistence that we are all actors, is that there is perhaps a hidden audience without whose knowledge no sparrow falls from the air. The actor's skills are therefore the skills of all. And if we are no longer sure that such an audience exists or, like Richard Nixon, forget for a moment that it may, nonetheless awareness of that potential audience remains a spur to performance. For the greater fear is not that the microphones are there but that they are not, for it is the microphones, the audience, which give significance to those in the room. The fear, then, is not that we may be actors, observed in our actions, given meaning by an audience, but that we live our lives unobserved, that we may not, after all, be what in our inmost hearts we wished we might be, figures on a stage, performing a drama whose meaning and purpose is assured because its coherences are clear to one who watches and whose applause, at the last, we require if we are to perform our strange eventful history and know it to be something more than "mere oblivion, sans teeth, sans eyes, sans taste, sans everything".

Chapter 12
Actors and Acting
Michael Robinson

Midway through Klaus Mann's *Mephisto* one of the novel's supernumeraries finally gets a purchase on its central figure: 'I think I have his number', he exclaims, 'He's always lying and he never lies. He believes in everything and he believes in nothing. He is an actor.'[1] The context makes this definition all the more disquieting since it describes an actor justly celebrated for his performance as Mephistopheles in Goethe's *Faust*, who is in turn a character based on the great German actor and director, Gustaf Gründgens, a chameleon-like figure whose ability at assuming whatever role was required of him enabled him to move with apparent conviction from the left-wing agitational theatre of Germany in the 1920s to the directorship of the Berlin Staatstheater, where he survived the Third Reich. Indeed, so ably did Gründgens survive that in 1959, Bertolt Brecht invited him to direct the premiere of his play *St Joan of the Stockyards*. This quotation serves as well as any as an approach to the nature of the actor's skill, on which Diderot deliberated with such provoking insight in *Le Paradoxe sur le comédien* of 1773. It helps define the actor, while both testifying to his demonstrable skill and suggesting some of the disturbing paradoxes to which his figure gives rise. In what follows I shall explore some variations on this theme, with the contributions of Lars Gustafsson and Chris Bigsby in mind, primarily through the medium of a fragmentary babel or collage of other voices. That is to say, I shall quote frequently and sometimes at length, but usefully so, I trust, in order to establish a number of reference points for a consideration of what it is an actor actually does. Our attention has already been directed towards several of the underlying causes of the widespread hostility that the theatre so frequently arouses. As Chris Bigsby suggests, this deeply ingrained antitheatrical prejudice may be variously identified with an ontological queasiness in the face of someone who (like Mann's Mephisto) is at once both there and yet not there, who is or seems to be everything and nothing. Particularly, but not only, where identity is concerned, the theatre questions established notions of fixity, continuity, stability, and coherence. To a Puritan critic like William Prynne, in his *Histriomastrix*, integrity or constancy of character admit 'no variableness, no shadow of change', and each man can play 'one part only' if social order is not to give way to a licentious multiplication of roles.[2] 'Men should be what they seem', as that master of dissembling, Iago, remarks (*Othello* III.iii.126). Complexity spells impurity, instability, distemper, and acting a part lays one open to what Lionel Trilling calls 'the attenuation of selfhood that results from impersonation'.[3] (It is instructive, however, that all those critics of the theatre who, like Trilling, suggest that playing a role such as Iago or Richard III endangers the moral integrity of an actor, since s/he may assume the attributes of those s/he impersonates, do not extend this notion of imprinting through impersonation to any virtues a character might have.) The actor is therefore certainly transgressive, as Chris Bigsby also points out, and not only because his ambivalent, equivocal, multiple, carnivalesque nature on stage has the ability to confound all distinction and discrimination, whether sexual, social or political. Indeed, the element of transgression already exists as a possibility in the encounter which the theatre sets up between the exciting, strange, and on occasion aggressive – almost animal – energy of the actor and the audience that is on the receiving end, an energy that has frequently been identified with the theatre at its most compelling, whether it be Olivier's celebrated physical magnetism as Othello or Rachel in Racine, who was described by the English philosopher and analyst of acting, George Henry Lewes, as a 'panther', by Charlotte Bronte as a 'tiger', and by her French critic and admirer Jules Janin, as a 'pythoness'.[4] Such physical, adversarial, even erotic aspects of live performance are sometimes to be caught in the slang which actors use (at least in English) to describe their relationship with an audience: 'bowling them over', 'knocking them out', 'socking it to them', 'slaying them', or even 'laying them in the aisles'.[5] Sexuality, the transgression of gender boundaries, and an ill-defined but tantalizing link with the idea of prostitution are therefore assuredly bound up with our notion of acting. The significance of this parallel has been explored in spectacular fashion by modern dramatists, the metatheatrical investigation of specular images and social and staged identity by Genet in The Balcony is an obvious example, while theoretically we might ponder not so much the commonplace associations between the two occupations as the way in which the actor allows him or herself to be used by a variety of texts, any one of which would seem to be as good as another for his or her purposes. Nevertheless, in Britain, the theatre has, ever since the acceptance of the actress on stage during the Restoration, frequently been associated with an act in which women routinely violate polite conventions of dress, make-up, and gesture while exposing themselves, in later years by flickering gaslight, in order to solicit the concupiscent male gaze, a desire that in the two domains of prostitution and stage performance may, as Tracy Davis suggests, be gratified by 'women whose identity, sincerity, and appearance were illusory but whose success relies on not giving away the hoaxes of the consumer's control of full reciprocity or enjoyment'.[6] One might add, however, that in the theatre at least, the actor does not normally divulge the skills whereby this illusion is created, any more than does a conjurer, since in the dominant conventions of western theatre, the art of the performer consists in concealing that there is any art at all, although in The Gay Science, Nietzsche was prepared to see such behaviour as characteristic of women in general: 'Reflect on the whole history of women', he noted, with misogynic satisfaction, 'do they not have to be first of all and above all else actresses? ... love them – let yourself be 'hypnotised by them!' What is always the end result? That they "put on something" even when they take off everything'.[7]

According to Walter Kaufmann, the final sentence in the original ('Das sie "sich geben" selbst noch, wenn sie – sich geben') permits the more literal reading: 'That they "give themselves" (that is, act or play a part) even when they – give themselves'.

The link between acting and femininity, however, is a commonplace. It is even made by women themselves, as when Sarah Bernhardt, in *L'Art du théâtre*, claims that acting 'contains in itself all the artifices which belong to the province of woman: the desire to please, facility to express emotions and hide defects, and the faculty of assimilation which is the real essence of woman'.[8] More particularly, the skills of the actor are (wrongly) seen to be entirely imitative and reproductive, and to require the histrionic multiplicity of a chameleon combined with the seductive and fickle charm of someone who will be whatever is demanded of them. In his *Man and Woman*, Havelock Ellis remarks 'an interesting parallelism, and probably a real deep-lying nervous connection, between the suggestibility of women and the special liability of female butterflies, birds, and mammals to be mimetic in coloration, etc. Mimicry, or suggestibility, is an adaptation to the environment, ensuring the protection of the sex that is less able to flee or to fight.'[9] And to bolster his argument, he quotes the opinion of the French dramatist Ernest Legouvé, who had closely observed the great nineteenth-century French tragedienne, Rachel, and concluded that 'Whether actor or singer, the interpretative artist needs above all a talent for observing details, flexibility of the organism to follow the movements of thought, and above all, that mobile, ardent, and varied impressionability which multiplies in an almost incredible degree the sensations and signs which represent it. For this reason the dramatic faculty is more native to women than to men.'[10]

Reviewing Bigsby's evocation of the anti-theatrical prejudice in the light of the quotation from *Mephisto*, there are two other recurring associations to which acting gives rise that it is valuable to recall here. One is that acting attracts those who are nothing in themselves, and therefore seek to fill this void with a surrogate existence. The performer, in brief, has no countenance but the countenance of the occasion and his seemingly boundless capacity for mutability and imitation is consequently understood to mean that an actor's character may be defined as a lack of character. The idea is not necessarily negative. Although it is advanced with contempt by the Irish writer George Moore in his diatribe on 'Mummer Worship' of 1888, where the stage is described as 'a profession for the restless, the frankly vicious – for those who [seek] any escape from the platitude of their personality',[11] it is presented with a certain wistfulness by Johan Ludvig Heiberg, the director of the Royal Theatre in Copenhagen and husband of the great Danish actress Johanne Luise Heiberg, in his verse drama *En Sjæl efter Døden* (1841), in which he portrays an actor who in the course of many years and roles on the stage has prayed to so many different gods that at the moment of death he did not know on which one to call. Not only that: he had forgotten the Lord's Prayer and could only recite it with the assistance of the prompter. And for Diderot, of course, this absence, or void, of character was closely bound up with the paradox of the actor, as the precondition of his or her necessary variety and plenitude. Diderot famously questioned the argument 'that actors have no character, because in playing all characters, they lose that which Nature gave them, and ... become false just as the doctor, the surgeon and the butcher become hardened. I fancy that here cause is confounded with effect', he observes, 'and that they are fit to play all characters because they have none'.[12] Or as Henry James remarked, of the English actress Fanny Kemble, the performer represented not so much an inchoate variety as the copiousness of life: 'she abundantly lived and, in more than one meaning of the word, acted – felt, observed, imagined, reflected, reasoned, gathered in her passage the abiding impression, the sense and suggestion of things'.[13]

The other association is with that essential but surprisingly neglected component of the theatrical event, the audience or crowd, with whom the actor promiscuously shares his art. In speaking of the *dédoublement* of the personality, Chris Bigsby refers us to Baudelaire; it is also worth recalling what Baudelaire has to say in his Journals of the prostitution of crowds as 'a mysterious expression of sensual joy in the multiplication of Number'.[14] Indeed, many of the characteristics which are attributed to the actor by the anti-theatrical prejudice are also identified with crowds, which similarly alarm the antitheatricalists with their undifferentiated multiplicity. That obsessive theoretician of the crowd, Gustave Le Bon, repeatedly describes how they submerge the stable ego in the mass and threaten the individual with a loss of identity. 'Crowds', Le Bon maintains, 'are everywhere distinguished by feminine characteristics'. They are unconscious, irrational, barbaric, impressionable and easily seduced, and it is therefore hardly surprising that in his disdain for this seething, amorphous, fluid, changeable, compound and (supposedly) corruptible body in all its protuberant and menacing excess, he associates it readily with the theatre. 'The art of appealing to crowds is no doubt of an inferior order but it demands quite special aptitudes', he observes. 'It is often impossible on reading plays to explain their success.' And more pertinently for our purposes perhaps: 'A crowd thinks in *images* .... It is only images that terrify or attract them and become motives of action. For this reason theatrical representations, in which the image is shown in its most clearly visible shape, always have an enormous influence on crowds .... Nothing has a greater effect on the imagination of crowds in every category than theatrical representation. The entire audience experiences at the same time the same emotions and if these emotions are not at once transformed into acts, it is because the most unconscious spectator cannot ignore that he is the victim of illusions, and that he has laughed and wept over imaginary adventures.'[15]

Le Bon's argument is also pursued, as usual more succinctly, by Nietzsche when recording 'the emergence of the actor in music' in the guise of Richard Wagner. 'No one brings along the finest senses of his art to the theatre, least of all the artist who works for the theatre – solitude is lacking; whatever is perfect suffers no witnesses. In the theatre one becomes people, herd, female, pharisee, voting cattle, patron, idiot – *Wagnerian*; even the most personal conscience is vanquished by the levelling magic of the great number; the neighbour reigns, one becomes a mere neighbour'.[16] However, in this review of the actor as a proliferating and unnatural multiplication of signs, an identity that circulates, that is not fixed, and which associates in a promiscuous violation of identity with both prostitution and crowds, perhaps the last word should be given to the nineteenth-century Catholic rabu-

list Léon Bloy. 'I regard the state of an actor as the shame of shames', he ful-
minates, in his novel *Le Désespéré*. 'The vocation of the theatre is, in my eyes,
the basest misery of this abject world, and passive sodomy is, I believe,
slightly less infamous. The male whore, even when venal, is obliged to confine his debauchery to cohabitation with a single other person, and can still
– in the midst of his frightful ignominy – preserve a certain freedom of
choice. The actor abandons himself, without choice, to the multitude, and
his industry is not less ignoble because it is his body which serves as instrument of the pleasure given by his art.'[17]

Bloy returns us to the Puritan rejection of pleasure; unwittingly, he also
indicates where a proper assessment of the actor's art might begin. For
what, of course, characterizes all these expressions of the anti-theatrical
prejudice is an ignorance of acting itself, and more particularly of the skills
which sustain an actor on stage, save as a public display of that dissembling
to which even puritans may be reduced in private. For it is almost invariably a perceived absence of sincerity that most offends, and ultimately, the
actor stands condemned because the tricks he employs in strutting his stuff
are supposedly our own. Logically, indeed, this enthusiasm for sincerity
would accord greater merit to the unfortunate Gallus Vibius, the actor who,
according to Seneca, went mad while attempting to imitate the movements
of a madman, rather than Garrick who, in a famous anecdote that Diderot
repeats in his 'Réponse à la lettre de Mme Riccomboni' (1758), describes
how he prepared for the role of Lear by observing a madman kept locked in
a room near his lodgings. While standing near an open window in the
upper story of his house with his young daughter in his arms, a moment's
distraction had caused the man to drop the child into the street below,
where it was killed. The man's insanity manifested itself in a horrible pantomime in which he repeatedly reenacted the entire scene. Although he
applied his observations to the role of Lear, Garrick also worked up the
scene into one of his parlour performances, which he was accustomed to
conclude with the remark: 'Thus it was I learned to imitate madness'.[18]

Even if the theatre is an essential and central metaphor for life, the normally collective process whereby it is created is distinct from the sometimes
quite elaborate dramas that all of us may on occasion stage in our private
life, where those about us are not professional actors but, like the young
men employed to humour Pirandello's supposedly mad Henry IV on being
appraised of his sanity, the bewildered and unwilling supernumeraries in a
plot they do not understand. The theatrical event is collaborative, and created, at least in a theatre like the Royal Dramatic Theatre, which is providing
the venue for this conference, by a host of scene painters, carpenters,
machinists, electricians, flymen, wardrobe assistants, and box office staff as
well as a director and the actors who eventually fill that empty space which
Peter Brook has identified as the starting point of the theatrical event.[19]

Instead of searching out the real or metaphorical consonance of theatre
and life it is therefore of more value in the present context to emulate
Diderot and consider how the actor achieves what s/he does in the theatre,
in, for example, the rehearsal process, through which the knowledge s/he
requires to play a part is researched, established, and defined, often with the
help of improvisation, before it is finally placed before a public in the theatre, where, according to Artaud, meaning is created here and now, in the

presence of an audience, a meaning that is sensuous, palpable, and which may, as we are told, 'hold a mirror up to nature', according to the codes and conventions of whatever that theatre happens to be, but where it is always a question of embracing the encounter of performer with audience.[20]

This empty space is populated by the actor, and in the first instance by his bodily presence, by means of which he transposes the written text of the playwright into the physical text of the stage. As the great French actor and director Louis Jouvet observed, in his *Témoignages sur le théâtre*:

Il vit ainsi une crise. Il éprouve une vie nouvelle. Par de légères phosphorescences, la pièce prend sa signification et le jeu devient une découverte de sens, une vérification. Quelle que soit l'œuvre, au moment où il la joue dans cet état de sensibilité aiguë, ce qui est ou ce qui se fait dans l'acteur le place au sein même de cette œuvre. Et le texte de l'auteur cesse d'être un texte littéraire pour devenir **une transcription physique** dont il est le premier dédicatoire et l'inter-médiaire exclusif. Il comprend qu'il est la part matérielle, corporelle du poète et que **sa mission n'est autre que de retrouver dans ce texte imprimé l'état physique, le transport où était l'auteur dans le moment qu'il écrivait**, et de recréer avec lui, avec exactitude, les sensations et les sentiments. Cela ne peut s'accomplir par la pensée, mais seulement par un état sensible, une pratique secrète du texte par quoi le personnage est délivré.[21]

Or as David Garrick articulated the process in English, in his *An Essay on Acting* (1744), where it is implicitly extended to all stage performance, scripted or otherwise: 'Acting is an entertainment of the stage, which by calling in the aid and assistance of articulation, corporeal motion, and ocular expression, imitates, assumes, or puts on the various mental and bodily emotions arising from the various humours, virtues and vices incident to human nature'.[22]

That is to say, the actor finds a bodily emotion for each feeling, s/he works through physical actions that express psychological realities. The actor's body is normally the primary theatrical sign, the repository of the role which is acquired and stored in the performer's muscular memory. S/he is at once artist and instrument, which is his or her own body – the torso, legs, arms, hair, hands, feet, eyes and voice as well as the balance and timing at his or her command – and just like the dancer and the dance, the two are inseparable, even if in naturalism the aim of the performance is to disguise the artifice this suggests.[23] 'Drama', as Bert O States claims, 'will tolerate nothing of the psychological or philosophical that is not expressed in visible action ... philosophy in the theatre must unfold itself as, literally, a thinking of the body;'[24] This applies both to the political farce of Dario Fo and the intellectual discourse of Leone in Pirandello's *The Rules of the Game* or his *Henry IV*, where philosophical abstractions are literally embodied in the active figures of the stage. This process is not of course confined to the stage. One might compare Freud's hysterics and their theatre of the body, in which they articulate what they cannot express in words, a theatre of symptomatic acts that may be traced back to the staging of hysteria by Charcot at La Salpêtrière during the 1880s.[25] Such acts, however, were already part of the stock in trade of the dramatist when (for example) in act two of Ghosts, Ibsen has Mrs Alving move towards the light of the window as she declares, 'I must work myself free' and then drum upon the pane of glass behind which she is trapped like an imprisoned fly, only to turn away again exclaiming, 'What a coward I am!', and the successful performer finds such actions for whatever part s/he plays should the dramatist not have indicated them.

The point for us, however, is to emulate Diderot in *The Paradox of the Actor* and examine the way in which the actor finds these actions, the skills on which his art is predicated. It might therefore be helpful to focus not on the ready assumption that the skills an actor employs are those we all deploy, if with less obvious dexterity in the real social situations of our daily lives (the kind of approach that finds confirmation in the approach to the latter of (say) Erving Goffman in *The Presentation of Self in Everyday Life*).[26] For example, in eliding all difference between theatrical and ordinary social intercourse Raymond Aron's observation that 'Society is a sort of *commedia dell' arte* in which the actors have the right to improvise along prescribed lines',[27] diverts our attention from what is particular to the actor to what is commonplace.

In *Rollen*, his account of a year spent rehearsing and performing in Peter Brook's production of *The Cherry Orchard*, Erland Josephson nudges us in the right direction, when he asserts that it is the actor's 'instinct, intuition and intellect',[28] which provide a focus for her/his work on the dramatic text, especially if, as George Henry Lewes did, we associate intuition with 'organized reasoning',[29] a kind of tacit knowledge that we have internalised into a system for understanding and acting in the world, and which may be applied to the situations with which the actor is confronted in the dramatic text. Skill, dexterity, physical and vocal training are, of course, essential, and I note that in our eurocentric fashion we have omitted all consideration of the kind of training necessary to achieve the skills demanded in Kathakali or Noh theatre, where not novelty but the faithful perpetuation of an ancient tradition is the performer's aim, where a performer often learns a performance score by imitating a master, and repeats it until it can be reproduced perfectly, and where a hand gesture or a movement of the eye is codified so as to be expressive for a spectator even when dispassionately demonstrated. Nevertheless, in the western tradition, at least one needs to add to these elements the notion of 'emotional memory' as it is defined by Stanislavski with some help from the French psychologist Théodule Ribot in his *Les Maladies de la mémoire* (1881) and *Les Maladies de la volunté* (1885), that frequently suppressed and forgotten knowledge which, like involuntary memory in Proust, may often be associated with the kind of physical sensation that Diderot recognized in his *Eléments de physiologie*, when he affirmed: 'The sound of a voice, the presence of an object, a certain place, and behold, an object recalled – more than that, a whole stretch of my past – and I am plunged again into pleasure, regret, affliction'.[30] Compare this with the account of the corporeal memory of the actor in the Paradox, which permits the performance of a controlled acting score rather than the inspirational frenzy of Lui in *Rameau's Nephew* because the trained instrument that is the performer's body is able to combine with a store of sense impressions and emotions that may once have been experienced with great intensity, but which are now recoverable as a sequence of reflexive mechanisms responding in turn to a plan that the actor has worked out carefully in advance, and which may consequently be repeated every evening to an audience that accepts them as if the performer were responding to outer stimuli for the first time. 'It is when the storm of sorrow is over, when the extreme of sensibility is dulled, when the event is far behind us, when the soul is calm, that one remembers one's eclipsed happiness, that one is capable of appreciating one's loss, that memory and imagination unite, one to retrace, the other to accentuate',[31] which can be compared with Stanislavski's remarks in *Building a Character* on how, 'Our art seeks to achieve this very result and requires that an actor experience the agony of his role, and weep his heart out at home or in rehearsals, that he then calm himself, get rid of every sentiment alien or obstructive to his part. He then comes out on the stage to convey to the audience in clear, pregnant, deeply felt, intelligible and eloquent terms what he has been through. At this point the spectators will be more affected than the actor, and he will conserve all his forces in order to direct them where he needs them most of all in reproducing the inner life of the character he is portraying'.[32]

Thus, well before Stanislavski defines him as such, the actor, as Diderot is aware, is a master of physical actions in which the imaginative world of the text is realized in constant dialectical play with the world of real experience, but where what we witness on stage cannot, ultimately, be mistaken for that world, except as a social activity in which actors and audience are mutually engaged. Two extended quotations, depicting two great actors at work, will help establish firstly, one of the ways in which an actor may achieve his performance text, and secondly, how this text inevitably and necessarily differs from our experience of the performer offstage. In his biography of Stanislavski, David Magershack gives the following account of how Stanislavski 'taught his actors the method of reaching to the inner nature of their parts through the external idiosyncracies of any person they knew in life who seemed to approach most closely their mental picture of the character they had to represent', and how he created one of his greatest roles, Dr Stockmann in Ibsen's *An Enemy of the People*, by taking the composer Rimsky-Korsakov as his model for Dr Stockmann's facial appearance.

In this part, Stanislavski found that his stage comportment and gestures seemed to come to him by themselves. But it only seemed so. When he came to analyze his acting, he discovered that while he assumed that Stockmann's gestures, gait, and deportment had come to him intuitively, they had really emerged hand-made from his subconscious mind where he had stored up a great number of impressions of people he had met in life and then unconsciously picked out those that were most characteristic and typical of Dr Stockmann. Thus Dr Stockmann's short-sightedness, his hurried gait, his manner of walking with the upper part of his body thrust forward, and particularly the expressive use he made of his fingers folded with thumb on top – were all taken from life .... As for his way of "sawing the air" when engaged in heated argument, with his thumb stretched out and forefinger and middle finger as well as third finger and little finger held close together and the two sets of fingers held apart like the blades of a pair of scissors, he got it from Maxim Gorky, who always drove home his point that way.[33]

However, lest one assume that suiting the action to the word and discovering the rhythm of a text and the tempo of a performance is merely a matter of finding the appropriate correlation in life, it is instructive to juxtapose this account with Edward Gordon Craig's description of Henry Irving, in his memoir of the great Victorian actor. Craig describes Irving on stage 'as natural, yet highly artificial', and possessed of a walk that was 'a whole language' in itself. 'I think', Craig opines, that 'there was no one who saw him in the street or a room, in private life, who denied that he walked perfectly

.... Irving walked perfectly naturally – but only in private life. As soon as he stepped upon the boards of his theatre, at rehearsal, something was added to the walk – a consciousness .... It wasn't walking. It was dancing.' And he then makes a bold attempt to convey a sense of Irving's stage presence in an account that does not admit summary:

'When [Irving] came to melodrama', Craig writes, 'he realized that a good deal more dance would be needed to hold up these pieces [than in Shakespeare], – and then it was that, putting out all his skill, he wiped the floor with the role and danced it like the devil. When it was Shakespeare he was dealing with, he had merely to wipe the beautiful glass window-panes. His movements were all measured. He was forever counting – one, two, three – pause – one, two – a step, another, a halt, a faintest turn, another step, a word. (Call it a beat, a foot, a step, all is one – I like to use the word 'step'.) That constituted one of his dances. Or seated on a chair, at a table – raising a glass, drinking – and then lowering his hand and glass – one, two, three, four – suspense – a slight step with his eyes – five – then a patter of steps – two slow syllables – another step – two more syllables – and a second passage in his dance was done. And so right through the piece – whatever it might be – there was no chance movement; he left no loose ends. All was sharp cut at beginning and end, and all joined by an immensely subtle rhythm – the Shakespearean rhythm.'[34]

Acting resembles life, but on the stage it is essentially distinct from life even though (another paradox) it must be imbued with life if it is to succeed.

For the words on the page are only a beginning, and as Brook again points out, the frequently expressed injunction to the actor to 'Play what is written' directs the actor only to certain ciphers on paper, which are records of the words the dramatist 'wanted to be spoken, words issuing as sounds from people's mouths, with pitch, pause, rhythm and gesture as part of their meaning. A word does not start as a word – it is an end product which begins as an impulse, stimulated by attitude and behaviour which dictates the need for expression';[35] it is hence part of a complex, fluid, multivocal process that is again likely to disturb precisely on account of its failure to be always and securely the same. And thus the frequently expressed preference for what is considered to be the stability of the published text over the evanescent, provisional nature of the text in performance, which is also condemned for bringing down 'a fine vision to the standard of flesh and blood'.[36] In fact, with few exceptions, the written or printed texts of plays have always had a derivative or secondary status, either as a scenario which acts as a blueprint for future productions or as a document that records earlier ones. The words of a text may imply a body and its shape and movements, a voice and its articulation and inflections, but only in production do these words assume theatrical meaning, firstly through the intervention of the actors and a director, and secondly through the decoding of the complex processes of verbal and non-verbal communication by an audience.[37] As Diderot remarks, in the Paradox, of his favourite actress, Mlle Clairon: 'The poet had engendered the monster [but] Clairon made it roar'.[38]

A text like Le Misanthrope, for example, does not even indicate whether either of the characters who open the play is already on stage at the outset, and if so where, or if not, how they arrive, and who enters first, and whether they are running or walking: all this emerges only in rehearsal. Likewise, even in so internally directed a play as Beckett's Waiting for Godot, with its many textual indications as to what should happen on stage, it is only in the theatre that our understanding of the final tableau takes shape:

> ESTRAGON. Well? Shall we go?
> VLADIMIR. Yes, let's go.
> *They do not move.*[39]

But in what positions are Vladimir and Estragon arrested? In what relation to each other, and to the singular tree with which they share the stage? Moreover, in what light, and what kind of silence, before the one (possibly) is extinguished in order to confirm that this is indeed the end of the evening's proceedings and that consequently the other may be broken by applause. The printed page in which, according to Charles Lamb, we observe 'the mind and its movements',[40] is indeed a comfortable refuge in comparison with the 'body and bodily action' of the play in performance, or our hurried perception of a shifting sequence of visual and verbal images in the *commedia dell' arte*, Pip Simmons, Robert Wilson, or Robert Lepage.

It is the skills an actor employs to achieve this enacted event that should concern us in the context of this conference, and I would conclude with two detached, but pertinent remarks by contemporary practitioners. Firstly, Robert Wilson who echoes Ibsen in declaring that 'For me to work in the theatre is to ask a question and not to have answers',[41] and secondly, a comment by that fine contemporary Irish actress, Fiona Shaw, who maintains that 'The desire to perform is the desire to make sense of the world through performing in it'.[42]

Notes

1 Klaus Mann, *Mephisto* (Harmondsworth, 1983), p. 130.

2 Prynne's wide-ranging but repetitive assault upon the theatre was published in 1633. For an overview, see Jonas Barish's essential survey of the phenomena in *The Antitheatrical Prejudice* (Berkeley: University of California Press, 1981).

3 Trilling argues this point in his essay on the theatricals at Jane Austen's *Mansfield Park*, in *The Opposing Self*, 2nd ed. (Oxford, 1980), pp 181-202.

4 For Lewes's description of Rachel as 'the panther of the stage, [moving] with a panther's terrible beauty and undulating grace', see his *On Actors and Acting* (London, 1875), p. 23. Charlotte Bronte's fictional account of Rachel's acting, which in life had 'transfixed me with horror, enchained me with interest, and thrilled me with horror' (letter to James Taylor, 15 November 1851, *The Brontës: Their Lives, Friendships, and Correspondences*, ed. T J Wise and J A Symington, 4 vols. (Oxford, 1932), III, p. 289), occurs in her novel *Villette* (1853), where Rachel is portrayed as the actress Vashti. Jules Janin's remark, 'Elle est semblable à la pythonisse', is repeated in his *Rachel et la Tragédie* (Paris, 1859).

5 For a valuable account of acting as the product of a powerful transgressive energy, see Michael Goldman, *The Actor's Freedom* (New York, 1975).

6 *Actresses as Working Women* (London, 1991), p. 83.

7 *The Gay Science*, translated by Walter Kaufmann (New York, 1974), p. 317.

8 Sarah Bernhardt, *The Art of the Theatre* (London, 1924), p. 144.

9 Fourth revised and enlarged edition (London, 1904). Cf. Darwin, who, in commenting on the 'natural' differences between men and women in *The Descent of Man*, maintains that through natural selection, man has become superior to woman in courage, energy, intellect, and inventive genius, and thus would inevitably excel in art, science and philosophy. Even those faculties in which women had the edge – intuition, perception, and imitation – were actually signs of inferiority, 'characteristic of the lower races, and therefore of a past and lower state of civilization, although they might give her the edge in acting'. Reprint of 1871 edition, Princeton, N. J., 1981, p. 327.

10 Ernest Legouvé, *Histoire Morale de la femme*, 6th ed. (Paris, 1874), p. 345.

11 *The Universal Review*, September, 1888, p. 114.

12 *The Paradox of Acting* (New York, 1957), p. 48. If Diderot does not celebrate the apparent absence of character in the actor, he nevertheless perceives it as a precondition of great acting. 'Perhaps it is just because he is nothing that he is before all everything', remarks the first speaker in the *Paradox*. 'His own special shape never interferes with the shapes he assumes' (p 41). And again: 'A great actor's soul is formed of the subtle element with which a certain philosopher [Newton] filled space, an element neither cold nor hot, heavy nor light, which affects no definite shape, and, capable of assuming all, keeps none' (p 46).

13 Cf. James's early response to Mrs Kemble, in a letter to his mother: 'Mrs Kemble has no organized surface at all; she is like a straight deep cistern without a cover, or even, sometimes a bucket, into which, as a mode of intercourse, one must tumble with a splash' *The Letters of Henry James*, ed. Percy Lubbock, vol. I (London, 1920), p. 67.

14 Baudelaire, *Intimate Journals* (London, 1969), p. 29.

15 See Gustave Le Bon, *The Crowd. A Study of the Popular Mind* (London, MDCCCXCVI), pp 37, 57. Cf. a letter from Strindberg to his old friend Leopold Littmansson, written while Aurelien Lugné-Poë's Théâtre de l'œuvre was performing his play *Creditors*: 'This is happiness, this feeling of power, to sit in a cottage by the Danube, surrounded by six women who think I'm a semi-idiot, and know that right now, in Paris, in the intellectual headquarters of the world, 500 people are sitting like mice in an auditorium, and foolishly exposing their brains to my suggestions'. *Strindberg's Letters*, 2 vols, translated and edited Michael Robinson (London, 1992), II, p. 480.

16 *The Will to Power*, translated by Walter Kaufmann (London, 1968), p. 666.

17 Quoted in Barish, *Op cit.*, pp 321-22.

18 One might contrast this with Ellen Terry who was urged to visit an asylum and study real madwomen in order to prepare for the role of Ophelia. This she did, but found that the madwomen were 'too theatrical' to teach her anything. Ellen Terry, *The Story of My Life* (New York, 1982), p. 98.

19 *The Empty Space* (London, 1968), passim.

20 Diderot's dialogic imagination always recognizes the essential role of the audience in the theatrical event. Likewise in any form of narrative. As he observes, at the start of the short story entitled in English translation 'This is Not a Story': 'When one tells a story, there has to be someone to listen; and if the story runs to any length, it is rare for the storyteller not sometimes to be interrupted by his listener. That is why (if you were wondering) in the story which you are about to read (which is not a story, or if it is, then a bad one) I have introduced a personage who plays as it were the role of listener'. *This is Not a Story and Other Stories*, translated by P. N. Furbank (Oxford, 1993), p. 17.

21 *Témoignages sur le théâtre* (Paris, 1952), p. 229. My emphasis.

22 Toby Cole and Helen Chinoy, eds., *Actors on Acting* (New York, 1949), p. 134. My emphasis.

23 Thus C. B. Coquelin, in *Art and the Actor* (Brander Matthews, Papers on Acting II (New York, 1926), p. 163), who assumes a position entirely consistent with Diderot's argument in the Paradox: 'the instrument of the actor is himself. The matter of his art, that which he has to work upon and mould for the creation of his idea, is his own face, his own body, his own life. Hence it follows that the actor must have a double personality. He has his first self, which is the player, and his second self, which is the instrument.'

24 *On the Phenomenology of the Theater* (Berkeley, 1987), p. 102.

25 For Charcot's staging of hysteria, see Henri F. Ellenberger, *The Discovery of the Unconscious* (New York, 1970), p. 96, and Georges Didi-Huberman, *Invention de l'hystérie* (Paris, 1982), passim.

26 Goffman's classic study was first published in 1959.

27 *Progress and Disillusion* (London, 1968), p. ix.

28 Stockholm, 1989, p. 185.

29 *Problems of the Life and Mind*, 5 vols (London, 1874-79), IIV, p. 290.

30 Quoted in Joseph Roach's excellent chapter on Diderot, 'The *Paradoxe* as Paradigm', in his *The Player's Passion: Studies in the Science of Acting* (University of Delaware Press, 1985), p. 146. Roach's account of Diderot on acting remains the most informed and intelligent study of the subject, and the present essay is greatly indebted to his book.

31 *Paradox*, p. 36.

32 *Building a Character*, (London, 1950), p. 74.

33 Cited in Eugenio Barba and Nicola Savarese, *The Secret Art of the Performer* (London, 1991), p. 143.

34 Edward Gordon Craig (London, 1930), pp 73-78.

35 *The Empty Space*, p. 15.

36 The phrase is Charles Lamb's, in his *Essays of Elia* (1823). On seeing Garrick's tomb Lamb also wondered 'what connection that absolute mastery over the heart and soul of man, which a great dramatic poet possesses, has with those low tricks upon the eye and ear, which a player by observing a few general effects, which some common passion as grief, anger, etc., usually has upon the gestures and exterior, can so easily compass'. So easily indeed!

37 One might note an example of such a physicalisation of the text that would surely have appealed to Diderot. In an interview in *New Theatre Quarterly*, 6 (1986), p. 100, one of the leading members of the Berliner Ensemble, Ekkehard Schall, maintains that 'The thinking of an actor on stage is the thinking which expresses itself. It doesn't matter what you feel here and here [he points to his head and heart] – nobody wants to know', and he goes on to underline his point with an anecdote: 'Helene Weigel once told me the following story. As a young actress she once played at the side of the great Albert Basserman, in one of Ibsen's plays, I think. In one scene in which she was on the stage with him, he received one piece of catastrophic news after another: father dead, mother dead, children dead. To take in these catastrophic bits of news, Basserman chose to stand with his back to the audience. One day Helene complained to him that his face, turned away from the audience, did not show any emotion and, what was worse, took on some private expression. "So what, the audience don't see my face." He played everything with his back; he played every shock that he received with his back.'

38 *Paradox*, p. 43.

39 *Waiting for Godot* (London, 1956), p. 94.

40 Charles Lamb, 'On the Tragedies of Shakespeare' (1811).

41 *The Guardian*, 25 August 1993.

42 Roland Rees, ed., *Fringe First* (London, 1992), p. 164.

Chapter 13

Comments
Bo Göranzon

The interest that has centred on skills has developed from reflections on case studies carried out in the late seventies and early eighties. These case studies were of problems that arose in the workplace, and included nurses, doctors, foresters, social insurance office staff, meteorologists and others. The focus was on the epistemology of skill in working life. Increasingly, as the question "what is skill?" emerged at the center of worklife research, it was felt that work had to be understood from the perspective of the philosophy of science. Traditional epistemology was of little help in shedding light on this issue, because its concerns were too abstract. Skill, on the other hand, is something very particular, and its particularity cannot be captured in general theories, it can only be grasped through case studies. These case studies provide examples of the way solid judgement is built up over time, as a novice gradually develops his or her competence and, with talent and perseverance, expertise in the workplace. Both confidence and certainty are the hallmarks of the expert judgement that develops as a result of this process. Its distinctive characteristic is its success in dealing with unforeseen problems. Expertise, skill in the fullest sense, is less a matter of knowing more than it is a matter of knowing better.

Skill is formed by doing something. Typically, a skilled person can give an example of what it is to do something. Erland Josephson takes an example from an unforgettable meeting with Sir John Gielgud, who gave him a lesson in delivering Shakespeare's verse. "We spent two hours on these fifteen lines. Gielgud was tireless. Eagerly, he gave me of his knowledge /... / I was supposed to observe all the punctuation and mark the end of every line. /... / All these signs and rules constituted a tradition that had been handed down, knowledge that had been developed and refined over hundreds of years. They reflected hard-won knowledge, a battle with phrasing, with feelings and insight, technique and clarity, with characterization and with contact with the audience."

The idea of taking acting as a general model for skill is taken from Diderot. Erland Josephson says that an actor's intelligence "... requires a different kind of resolution than that required to grasp a thought. /.../ The actor's intelligence is restless and hungry, its main objective not confirmation but new experience."

This ability to "grasp a thought" is a different kind of intelligence, namely an analytical, mathematical intelligence. Arthur Schopenhauer drew attention to the limitations of the mathematical method in a contribution to the Edinburgh Review of January 1836 by Sir Walter Hamilton, Professor of Logic and Metaphysics. Its conclusion is that the value of mathematics is only indirect and is found to be in the application to ends that are attainable only through it. In itself, however, mathematics leaves the mind where it found it. It is by no means necessary; in fact it is a positive hindrance to the general formation and development of the mind. This conclusion is not only proved by extensive dianological investigation of the mind's mathematical activity, but it is also established by a very learned accumulation of examples and authorities." The only immediate use left to mathematics is *that it can accustom fickle and unstable minds to fix their attention* (author's italics).

Christopher Bigsby says "It is one of the skills of the actor to ... cross boundaries, deny the permanence of meaning, the fixity of language, the precision and singularity of interpretation. "The essence of an actor's skills," says Bigsby, "and, I am tempted to say all skills, is that they should be invisible, subsumed in the task they facilitate." Bigsby quotes the Japanese actor Yoshi Oida: "... the aim of all systems of technical training is to enable you to do an action without worrying how you do it. Unless you have this training you cannot arrive at this freedom of communication." The understanding of people and their behavior – that is the essential skill of the actor at his or her best.

Michael Robinson also talks about the actor as a crosser of boundaries: "the ... almost animal energy of the actor ... an energy that has frequently been identified with the theatre at its most compelling." He strongly rejects the expressions of the antitheatrical prejudices that are an expression of ignorance of the skills of an actor; for example the "ready assumption that the skills an actor employs are those we all deploy, if with less obvious dexterity in the real social situations of our daily lives." Here it is interesting to draw attention to the specific professional skill of the actor, and not to the more general aspects of skill that are addressed in *The Presentation of Self in Everyday Life* (a book by Erving Goffman which has become a classic). It is here that Erland Josefson's reflections on the art of acting "from within" have become of particular interest, not least in making analogies with earlier case studies in research in the field of Technology and Skill.

"We all agree that art certainly adds something to nature," says Lars Gustavsson, "but looking closer at the phenomenon, we find it impossible to say what it is we are talking about." This phenomenon is noted in Diderot's observation of a certain emptiness /.../ blind spots at the core of common sense aesthetic ideas. The expression of rhythm is a sign that a technique has been mastered.

What is rhythm? The musical imitation of rhythm was not an unprocessed expression of sensations. It was rhythm created after an agonizing struggle with words. The mind listens attentively to its own movement, the critical intellect is, always lucidly, always actively, considering sensations which show them naturally in the spontaneous gestures of thought.

According to Diderot, the ability to observe and control the surge of one's thoughts, to make the proper gestures and rhythmic expressions, is a result of reflection. The point of Diderot's study of the paradox of the actor is not subordinate to the emotion he is projecting. Actors who play from their souls, who are sensitive, are never consistent in playing their parts.

It is quite different with the actors who act after thinking and after studying human nature, and who always have some ideal picture to follow, building their parts on the power of their imagination and their memories.

Diderot anticipates Wittgenstein's view of language, says Lars Gustavsson. In his manuscripts and notebooks Wittgenstein repeatedly referred to Shakespeare and the theater. He maintained that portrayals and the language of portrayal must replace logical argument and demands for clarity in philosophical work. Wittgenstein believed that the path to knowledge was through the paradoxical power of the actor. This is analogous with Schopenhauer's criticism of the mathematical method.

Alan Turing and Ludwig Wittgenstein –
A Meeting of Different Traditions of Knowledge

Chapter 14

Beyond All Certainty

Bo Göranzon and Anders Karlqvist

This script records a production designed as part of a seminar on performance and text, one of a series of Dialogue Seminars held in Norwich, Stockholm and Vienna. These seminars have contributed to the development of an international Ph.D. program in Skill and Technology at the University of East Anglia, the Royal Swedish Polytechnic, the Swedish Institute for Worklife Research and the Technical Institute in Vienna.

Characters: Ludwig Wittgenstein   Alan Turing   Bertrand Russell   Winston Churchill
Helene Wittgenstein   Mrs Turing   Turing's two research assistants   A reporter

Beyond All Certainty was premiered by The Great Escape Theatre Company in Norwich, England on the 20th February 1993 with the following cast:

Ludwig Wittgenstein: Martin Cooke
Alan Turing: Jonathan Rea
Bertrand Russell,
Winston Churchill: Paul Lawrence-Davies
Helene Wittgenstein,
Mrs Turing: Charlotte Garrard

The cast for performances in Bodø, Norway and Stockholm, Sweden was:

Ludwig Wittgenstein: Richard Davies
Alan Turing: Jonathan Rea
Bertrand Russell,
Winston Churchill: Jon Hyde
Helene Wittgenstein,
Mrs Turing: Charlotte Garrard

Design & Stage-Management: Steve Ridley
Directed by Jon Hyde

Music

Clearly central to Wittgenstein's philosophy and to the world of the play, two musicians – cello and piano – should underscore the language and action. For the original production, the director selected recorded music as follows where indicated in the script:

1. *Clarinet concerto K622 – Wolfgang Amadeus Mozart.*
2. *Lonesome Blues – Louis Armstrong & His Hot Seven.*
3. *Cello Suite No.2 in D minor – J.S. Bach.*
4. *Avodath Hakodesh Silent Devotion Prelude – Ernest Bloch.*
5. *Requiem K626 – Wolfgang Amadeus Mozart.*
6. *Israel in Egypt – Handel.*
7. *Concerto for Cello and Orchestra in E minor – Elgar.*

The Great Escape Theatre Company
34 Trinity Street, Norwich
NR2 2BQ
England.
Telephone (0603) 505019 / 615415

*CUE MUSIC (1). A LECTURE BY WITTGENSTEIN, CAMBRIDGE 1939. WITTGENSTEIN IS
SEATED AS THE AUDIENCE ENTER, READING A CHEAP AMERICAN DETECTIVE
NOVEL. ONSTAGE A LARGE BLACKBOARD WITH WITTGENSTEIN 'GRAFFITI' AND A
TABLE WITH A MODEL OF TURING'S ENIGMA MACHINE. AS MUSIC ENDS, LIGHTS UP.
WITTGENSTEIN NOTICES AUDIENCE AND STANDS...*

WITT. These lectures are on the foundations of mathematics. By what right
can I, as a philosopher, talk about mathematics? I shall not give you any
new calculations, I shall speak of the interpretation of mathematical
symbols and devote myself to trivial facts that you know quite as well
as I. I won't say anything which anyone can dispute. Or, if anyone does
dispute it I will let that point drop and pass on to say something else.

I will try to show that the philosophical difficulties that arise in
mathematics as elsewhere arise because we find ourselves in a strange
town and do not know our way. So we must learn the topography by
going from one place in the town to another and from there to another
and so on. And one must do this so often that one knows one's way,
either immediately or pretty soon after looking around a bit.

This is an extremely good simile. In order to be a good guide, one
should show people the main streets first. But I am an extremely bad
guide, and am apt to be led astray by little places of interest and to dash
down the side streets before I have shown you the main streets.

*ENTER ALAN TURING AND TWO LABORATORY ASSISTANTS. ALL THREE INTENT ON
STUDYING TURING'S NOTES. THEY ARE OBLIVIOUS TO WITTGENSTEIN, AS HE IS TO
THEM.*

The difficulty in philosophy is to be able to find one's way about. And
that is a matter of memory – memory of a peculiar sort.

One talks of mathematical discoveries. *[TURING AND ASSISTANTS
NOTICE WITTGENSTEIN AND APPROACH HIM THROUGHOUT REMAINDER OF
HIS SPEECH]* I shall try again and again to show that what is called a
mathematical discovery had much better be called a mathematical
invention. There is nothing for the 'mathematician' to discover. A proof
in mathematics does not establish the truth of a conclusion; it fixes,
rather, the meaning of certain signs.

TURING. I understand your point, but I don't agree that it's simply a question of grammar and giving new meanings to words.

WITT. I have no point, but we do not, and cannot disagree, because I have
not advanced any thesis. If you do not agree with what I say, it is
because you do not understand how I use certain words. *[PAUSE]* As
you did not attend my last lecture Mr. Turing, I would like to refer to
what we discussed then, which was conducting experiments in mathematics. You will know...

TURING. I'm still inclined to say that we can pursue a mathematical investigation in the same spirit in which we might conduct an experiment in
physics. Just as we can place ... weights on a balance *[THE TWO ASSIS-
TANTS LEAVE STAGE AND RETURN WITH A SEESAW FROM WHICH THEY HANG
WEIGHTS]* and see which way it tips, we can suggest to someone that
they take a few numbers, make a mathematical calculation, look up the

multiplication tables, etc. and see what results they come to.

WITT. Yes, there appears to be a parallel, but where does the similarity lie?

TURING. In both cases we are interested in what the final result may be.

WITT. Let us suppose that we get someone to multiply two numbers by each other, where is the experiment in that? Do I want to know what results this person arrives at, or what? If *that* is the experiment, it doesn't matter what answer he writes down. 136 x 51 = 6935, for example.

TURING. Then the experiment was carried out wrongly. He did not follow the rules.

WITT. Yes, of course, we can say: we have taught him the rules, now let us see if he follows them. I cannot at the same time allow the result of an experiment to be the result of a mathematical calculation. If the result of the calculation is determined by rules, i.e. 136 x 51 = 6936, the result of the experiment is not *what* result he arrives at if he follows the rules, but *whether* or not he follows the rules...

TURING. But surely...

WITT. No! The entire analogy between mathematics and physics is a complete mistake. In fact, what we have here is an important source of confusion. It may be that 20 apples + 30 apples = 50 apples *[THE TWO ASSISTANTS LEAVE AND RETURN WITH APPLES IN BUCKETS AND DEMONSTRATE THE BALANCE BY SITTING ON SEESAW AND TOSSING THEM TO EACH OTHER]* may not be a proposition about apples. It may be a proposition of arithmetic and in this case we could call it a proposition about numbers.

On the other hand *[TURING CATCHES FOURTH APPLE THROWN BY ASSISTANTS, ENDING THEIR GAME]*, if we say that lions are four-legged – then that is a statement about lions, or that elephants are four-legged – then this is about elephants and not numbers.

THE TWO ASSISTANTS FETCH THE APPROPRIATE STUFFED TOYS AND ARE DISMISSED BY WITTGENSTEIN'S...

No! *[THE TWO ASSISTANTS THROW ANIMALS AWAY.]* What I want to show with these examples is that there is an essential difference between mathematical propositions and experiential propositions that look exactly the same.

TURING. You seem to assert that mathematical truths are only conventions – a question of consensus of opinions.

WITT. Is that what I'm saying? No! There is no opinion at all, it is not a question of opinions, it is a question of consensus in action. A consensus in doing the same things, in reacting in the same way. We all act in the same way. When we count, we do not express views. There is no opinion that says that 25 follows 24 – neither is there a special intuition. We express our opinions quite simply by counting. We demonstrate mathematics in action, in practice.

THROUGHOUT THE ABOVE SPEECH, WITTGENSTEIN AND TURING SIT ON SEE-SAW AND PUNCTUATE THE SPEECH BY MOVING IN CONCERT.

TURING. Yes, but you cannot be confident about applying your calculus until you know that there is no hidden contradiction in it. If one takes Frege's symbolism and gives someone the technique of multiplying in it, by using a Russell paradox he could get a very wrong application.

WITT. This would come to doing something that we would not call multiplying. Let us assume that I have convinced someone of Russell's Liar Paradox, and he says...

ASSISTANT 1. I am lying.

ASSISTANT 2. Which goes to prove that you are not lying.

ASSISTANT 1. From which it follows that I am lying.

WITT. ...and we therefore have a contradiction and therefore 2 x 2 = 369. We could not call that multiplying. Does finding a contradiction in a system, like finding a germ in an otherwise healthy body, show that the whole system or the body is diseased? Not at all. The contradiction does not even falsify anything. Let it lie. Do not go there.

TURING. But if you look at it from a practical viewpoint, if you have a logical system, a system of calculations which you use in order to build bridges. You give this system to your clerks [TURING HANDS A PLAN OF A BRIDGE TO ONE ASSISTANT – HE PINS IT ON THE BLACKBOARD AND THE TWO ASSISTANTS CREATE A BRIDGE BY TURNING THE SEE-SAW UPSIDE DOWN] and they build a bridge with it and the bridge falls down. You then find a contradiction in the system.

WITT. There seems to me to be an enormous mistake there. You have confused two separate things. Your calculus gives certain results, and you want the bridge not to break down. I'd say things can go wrong in only two ways: either the bridge breaks down or you have made a mistake in your calculation – for example you multiplied wrongly. But you seem to think there may be a third thing wrong: the calculus is wrong.

TURING. No. What I object to is the bridge falling down.

WITT. But how do you know that it will fall down? Isn't that a question of physics? It may be that if one throws dice in order to calculate the bridge it will never fall down!

TURING. Although you don't know if the bridge will fall down if there are no contradictions, it is almost certain that if there are contradictions, then something will go wrong.

WITT. But nothing has ever gone wrong in that way yet. I don't understand why people are so puzzled about paradoxes like the Liar Paradox: I am lying, therefore it follows that I am not lying, from which it follows that I am lying and so on. You can go on like that until you are blue in the face. But why bother? Isn't it just an unusable language game? We are struggling with language, Turing. We are engaged in a struggle with language.

TURING. And you seem to be saying that if one uses a little common sense, one will not get into trouble.

WITT. No, that is NOT what I mean at all. A contradiction cannot lead one into trouble because it leads to nowhere at all. One cannot calculate wrongly with a contradiction, because one simply cannot use it to calculate. One can do nothing with contradictions except waste time puzzling over them. [WITTGENSTEIN RETURNS TO HIS CHAIR]

TURING. If you're going to continue to lecture on the foundations of mathematics without admitting that contradictions are a fatal flaw in that system, then there can be no common ground between us.

CUE MUSIC (2) TURING COLLECTS PLAN FOR BRIDGE AND EXITS. THE TWO ASSISTANTS, REALIZING THEY ARE LEFT ALONE, HURRIEDLY CLEAR AWAY THE SEE-SAW AND EXIT.

SCENE 2

ENTER BERTRAND RUSSELL AND A REPORTER

RUSSELL. No, no, no, he came to me!

REPORTER. When was this, Professor Russell?

RUSSELL. I believe it was on the 18th October, 1911. I was in my rooms at
Trinity. And suddenly, he stood there, an unknown German, very nervous, who explained in broken English that he wanted to study the philosophy of mathematics...

REPORTER. A German...?

RUSSELL. Ludwig Wittgenstein. He had qualified in aeronautics in
Manchester, but now wanted to devote himself to philosophy.

REPORTER. Why was that?

RUSSELL. I understood later that he had met Frege and been advised to come
to me. So I took him to my lectures. And before long he totally domi-
nated our discussions. Not only during the lecture, he sometimes followed me back to my rooms afterwards and argued his position until
late in the evening. He was obstinate and perverse, but I thought not
stupid.

Sometimes I suspected my German engineer was a fool. I remember
that he maintained energetically that nothing empirical is knowable. In
one of my lectures, I wanted him to at least admit as an empirical fact
that there was not a rhinoceros in the room, but he wouldn't! Ha, ha, ha!

WITTGENSTEIN SNORTS

Wittgenstein refused to admit the existence of anything except asserted
propositions.

WITT. You know that I discussed this in my Tractatus: the world is the totality of facts, not of things.

RUSSELL. Anyhow, I soon discovered him to be pleasant-mannered, literary,
very musical and highly intelligent. Oh, he's Austrian by the way, not
German. I had a feeling that he might do great things.

RUSSELL AND REPORTER ENGAGE IN MIMED CONVERSATION AS WITTGENSTEIN
ENTERS FROM AUDIENCE

WITT. Bertrand Russell saved my life! I had been on the brink of despair for
many years. I had led a life of loneliness and suffering and was
ashamed that I had not killed myself earlier. With his encouragement I
saw that it was my duty to follow my impulse and pursue philosophy.

WITTGENSTEIN EXITS

REPORTER. What is your chief recollection of the man, Professor Russell?

RUSSELL. Wittgenstein was perhaps the most perfect example I have ever
known of genius as traditionally conceived; passionate, profound,
intense and dominating. I soon realized that I had here a man who
could carry on my work. He was like me. I saw myself in him. And yet
there was something strange about him. It was difficult to understand
his emotional life, and his morals. Of course I respected his personal
integrity and I could even stand him harping on about himself. But his
intellectual arguments were harder to take.

I particularly recall the time when I was writing my Theory of
Knowledge. I had been invited to America to lecture and had begun to
write the first chapter. I had hopes that it would be a major work. But

then I showed the manuscript to Wittgenstein. What I had written was metaphysical rather than logical, so I guessed that he wouldn't like it. His criticism was devastating.

ENTER WITTGENSTEIN IN HOSPITAL PORTER'S COAT PUSHING WHEELCHAIR

WITT. Unfortunately there were some fundamental errors that could not be put right without a correct theory of logical propositions, a fundamental problem of logic that cannot be bypassed. I am sorry to hear that my objection to your theory of knowledge paralysed you.

RUSSELL. *[COLLAPSING INTO WHEELCHAIR]* Paralysed! You made me abandon my project. I came close to giving up and taking my life. You had set new standards for logical exactness that made my efforts appear meaningless!

WITT. At least you realized that my comments were of some use to you.

RUSSELL. Yes of course. But your criticisms were often vague and incomplete. I realized that you were right, but I didn't quite understand your explanations.

WITT. Oh my God! How many times must I go through these arguments? It bores me. *[DURING THE REST OF THE SPEECH, WITTGENSTEIN RACES ROUND AND ROUND PUSHING RUSSELL IN CIRCLES]* All propositions in logic are generalizations of tautology, and all generalizations of tautology are logical propositions! What can be said can be said clearly, and what we cannot talk about we must pass over in silence. *[STOPS]* That is all.

RUSSELL. That means you leave most things in life – ethics, aesthetics, and religion, etc. – outside the limits of science and unapproachable to rational thinking?

WITT. Exactly.

RUSSELL. You were not always so sure of yourself.

WITT. I was very close to arriving at a final solution to the problem of logic. It was extremely depressing. I wish to God I had been more intelligent so that everything would finally become clear to me – what else would be the point of carrying on living? Perhaps you thought that this pondering about myself was a waste of time – but how can you be a logician if you are not a person. The most important thing is to arrive at an understanding of oneself! *[PUSHES RUSSELL AWAY]*

RUSSELL. Nothing can be more tiresome than disagreeing with Wittgenstein in an argument. You often needed my support though in time you increasingly ignored my ideas.

WITT. You know what difficulties I had getting my work published. I wanted at least someone to have examined my works in case I failed to complete them before my own life was ended. It was when I had left my conviction in the Tractatus and was writing Philosophical Investigations that I quite simply had to discuss my ideas with you. That's why I visited you in Cornwall.

RUSSELL. Oh yes, I well remember that occasion. You appeared at my door just when my son had gone down with the measles, little Kate had chicken-pox. Life was difficult at home. What's more, Dora was pregnant. And to cap it all, that sub-human American journalist Griffen Barry was the father!

WITT. Ethics was never your strong suit. *[DURING REST OF THIS SPEECH, WITTGENSTEIN EXITS BRIEFLY TO FETCH A FOLDING CHAIR WHICH HE PLACES*

FACING RUSSELL'S WHEELCHAIR] I detested all your popular philosophical works. Popular scientific writings are not an expression of hard work, they are resting on your laurels. Resting on your laurels is as dangerous as resting when you are walking in the snow – you doze off and die in your sleep.

WITTGENSTEIN EXITS AGAIN TO FETCH PLAYING BOARD AND DOMINOES

RUSSELL. I remember the young Wittgenstein as a man obsessed with intensive thinking on difficult problems, like myself, and as a man who possessed genuine philosophical genius. But later in life you seem to have grown tired of serious thinking and found a doctrine that would render that activity unnecessary.

WITTGENSTEIN RETURNS AND SETS UP CHAIR FACING RUSSELL, PLACING THE
DOMINOES AND BOARD ON RUSSELL'S LAP. SITS.

WITT. The mistake you and Frege made was to believe that the foundation of mathematics was not solid, and needed to be shored up. With your logical system you did nothing more than design another mathematical calculation. What we need is to *see* more clearly.

RUSSELL. Ah, but in my essay Mathematics and the Metaphysicians, I...

WITT. New evidence cannot dispel the fog.

RUSSELL. I demonstrated that all pure mathematics is built up by combinations of the primitive ideas of logic.

WITT. Formal logic is not, as you appear to think, identical with mathematics. Mathematical logic has failed to show us what mathematics really is.

RUSSELL. But you must admit that Weierstrass, Dedekind and Cantor have solved the problems of the infinitesimal, continuity and infinity in a logically perfect way.

WITT. There was nothing wrong with the science before the foundations were laid.

RUSSELL. But you cannot dismiss three of the greatest creators of the foundations of mathematics!

WITT. Notions like infinity are actually used in mathematics and everyday life. They are not clarified by such definitions, rather distorted. Do you remember what I said long ago? Philosophical clarity has the same effect on the growth of mathematics as sunshine has on the growth of the seed potato. They grow a meter long – in the dark!

My task has been to attack Russell's logic from without and not from within. This means that, as a philosopher, I have opted not to attack it mathematically – otherwise I should be doing mathematics of course.

RUSSELL. The understanding of proof as a way of seeing an aspect, seeing connections, is typical of Wittgenstein's own view of the world.I perceive his own philosophical investigations as a means of creating understanding through seeing connections.

WITT. But a mathematical argument *is* a matter of seeing connections. Every paragraph I write constantly relates to the whole, is constantly the same thing.

I might say: if the place I want to get to could only be reached by way of a ladder, I would give up trying to get there. For the place I really have to get to is a place I must already be at now. Anything that I might reach by climbing a ladder doesn't interest me.

RUSSELL. Curious though it may sound, Wittgenstein sees proofs in pure mathematics as analogous to the explanations offered in Freudian psychoanalysis. *[RUSSELL RISES FROM WHEELCHAIR AND PUTS DOMINOES AND BOARD IN BAG ATTACHED TO BACK OF WHEELCHAIR]* Perhaps one may understand his interest shifting from mathematics to psychology when he realized that Freud's patterns were more interesting than the pictures of mathematicians. *[RUSSELL PLACES WHEELCHAIR BEHIND WITT-GEN-STEIN]* It may even have been something of a relief to Wittgenstein to be able to place the events of his own life into some kind of pattern. *[RUSSELL PLACES HIS HAND ON WITTGENSTEIN'S SHOULDER AND HE SITS]*. But it was nothing of the sort.

EXIT RUSSELL

WITT. I no longer feel any hope for the future of my life. It is as though I had before me nothing but a long stretch of living death. I cannot imagine any future other than a ghastly one.

CUE MUSIC (3)

Friendless. Joyless. Ludwig Wittgenstein. Porter. Guy's Hospital, April 1942.

FADE LIGHTS

SCENE 3

CHURCHILL IS SEATED BUT NOT LIT. TURING WHEELS A COMPUTER TO STAGE CENTER. LEAVING IT, HE WALKS TO ENIGMA MACHINE. LIGHTS UP ON TURING, AND THEN ON COMPUTER. HE CROSSES TO COMPUTER, INTRIGUED. AS HE SPEAKS, HE TAPS HIS FIRST SPEECH INTO COMPUTER.

TURING. Churchill, Winston. Bletchley Park. 19 ... 48.

CHURCHILL LIGHTS CIGAR AND IS LIT BY A TABLE LAMP FROM BEHIND. THE EFFECT SHOULD BE ONE OF SMOKE AND VOICE ONLY.

CHURCHILL. You say, Mr. Turing, that a sonnet written by a machine is best appreciated by another machine?

TURING. Mr. Churchill, the sonnet that a machine will one day write...

CHURCHILL. Forgive me, but that sounds quite extraordinary.

TURING. ... will naturally be best appreciated by another machine. There is, as yet, no machine capable of doing so.

CHURCHILL. Bearing in mind that everything you do in your daily work is so practical, useful and sensible ... do you have an explanation for me?

TURING. Research, Mr. Churchill, is not encouraged by setting limits or objectives.

CHURCHILL. Excuse me, but I feel as though I was standing before my Latin teacher when he threatened to beat me for asking why I should bother to learn the vocative case of table and chairs when I should never say "Oh Table!" I never talk to furniture Mr. Turing. So my question to you is – What machine will, (a) write a sonnet, and (b) read one? And in any case, what person would possibly want to read a sonnet written by a machine?

TURING. Artificial man must be one of our oldest dreams. Even Plato talked about androids. A sonnet is a poor example. But the universal machine – for which I have so far only been able to produce some theoretical

ideas, then the war came and I was given the task of building this calculator – the universal machine will certainly, one day, even be able to
develop feelings. And probably also have what we call a soul. Animals
too have souls, and for how long were they denied their existence?

CHURCHILL. And this is your universal machine?

TURING. *[CROSSING TO ENIGMA]* No, not this. This is a very banal calculator
that I had to build to break the German's Enigma code. It is just a simple application of my theoretical work. It has certainly not been
endowed with a soul.

CHURCHILL. And when did you get the idea for your universal machine?

TURING. I published my thesis in 1936, Prime Minister.

CHURCHILL. 36. How old were you then?

TURING. I was 24.

CHURCHILL. And this offshoot of your universal machine?

TURING. Just a modest, special version. With the aids at my disposal, any
good mathematician could have tackled Enigma....

CHURCHILL. That is what people always say when someone absolutely irre-
placeable is the first to think of something. Then those people who
didn't think of something say that it would have occurred in any case.
Thus it is yours, it is, and will continue to be yours, Turing. And what
will you call your universal machine?

TURING. It hasn't been given a name yet, Prime Minister. The Latin for count
is computare, so "computer", perhaps? Perhaps one could call it a computer.

CHURCHILL. A computer? A counter? It all sounds too simple, too colorless.
Surely there is some magic involved here?

TURING. Magic isn't involved here at all ... but...

CUE MUSIC (4). TURING TAKES A LIVE, WHITE RABBIT FROM THE COMPUTER.
STROKES IT. LIGHTS FADE.
EXIT TURING AND CHURCHILL.

SCENE 4

HELENE WITTGENSTEIN ENTERS WITH WRAPPED GIFT.
DURING HER FIRST SPEECH SHE COMPLETES THE WRAPPING WITH A RIBBON.

HELENE. Ludwig sometimes retired to a cottage in Norway where he isolated himself in order to concentrate intensively on his philosophy. But in
the autumn of 1937 he returned home *[ENTER WITTGENSTEIN, CARRYING*
SEVEN-CANDLE JEWISH CANDELABRA], to visit me, his sister Helene. The
whole family was gathered, all the children and grandchildren, and all
our friends. The house on the Alleegasse was full to overflowing. We
sang and laughed and talked about old times, of course. We all gathered round the Christmas tree and sang the Austrian national anthem.
Everyone agreed that it had been the most lovely Christmas ever ...
except Ludwig.

WITT. I felt superfluous and wrapped up in myself. There was no-one in
Vienna that I was close to. After spending the entire autumn in my cottage it wasn't good enough for me. But where was I to go? Being alone
was hell. An inner voice told me to stick it out. I felt cut off from

heaven. Wisdom was not enough if I were to be saved. To be redeemed I needed faith. It is my soul with its passions, with its flesh and blood as it were, that has to be saved, not my abstract mind. Wisdom is cold, and you can no more use it for setting your life to rights than you can forge iron when it is cold. Only love can make me believe. Oh God, can you break this vicious circle, or must I do it myself.

HELENE. The dark clouds had begun to gather over Europe. Hitler invaded Austria. The Anschluss was a fact. Soon Austria was part of Nazi Germany. Three days ago Ludwig was an Austrian citizen, but now he is just another German Jew in England, worried about us in Vienna.

WITT. Work is impossible. The idea is worn out by now and no longer usable. Like silver paper which can never quite be smoothed out again once it has been crumpled. Nearly all my ideas are a bit crumpled. Freud said that in madness the lock is not destroyed, only altered; the old key can no longer unlock it, but it could be opened by a differently constructed key. If only I could find a new key, I could unlock the doors to my own prison, and then *everything* would be different.

HELENE. Ludwig asked Russell's advice. He said that he couldn't return to Vienna. The professorship was waiting for him in Cambridge and he could take British citizenship. We are out of danger. We have used the influence of our position and great wealth to negotiate with the Nazis to be classified as non Jewish.

HELENE TURNS TO LUDWIG AND OFFERS HIM THE GIFT. HE RESPONDS BY BLOWING OUT THE SEVEN CANDLES. BLACK OUT. EXIT HELENE. THE FIRST PARAGRAPH OF WITTGENSTEIN'S FOLLOWING SPEECH IS DELIVERED IN THE DARK.

WITT. Becoming a professor is flattering and so on, but it would have been much better for me to get a job as a railway crossing keeper. My vanity and stupidity is sometimes affected, but I returned to Cambridge with the greatest reluctance.

FADE UP BRIGHT LIGHT

It's a long time since I was here last, and it shows. There is a completely new generation of students. Fortunately not many of you attend my lectures. I discuss aesthetics and religious belief, and not mathematics or general philosophy. I don't want my students to take notes. Some day someone may publish them as my considered opinions. That would be regrettable, and against my own will. All this will need a lot more thought and better expression.

Well, help me somebody! God damn my bloody soul, why am I so stupid!

What I am trying to do is persuade people to change their style of thinking. The worship of science and the scientific method has had a wretched effect on our whole culture. Aesthetics and religious belief are two areas of life in which the scientific method is not appropriate, in which efforts to make it so lead to distortion, superficiality and confusion. People nowadays think that scientists exist to instruct them, poets, musicians, etc. exist to give them pleasure. The idea that these have something to teach them – that does not occur to them!

Freud is a good example. In explaining dreams with primitive sexual elements, he reduces the patient's experience. This may have its charm and fascination, but it is misleading. It is wrong to say that through his causal analysis Freud really understands what dreams are about. Compare that with the way he speaks about the joke and the subconscious. Freud takes an example from Heine's Reisebilder, where a humble lottery-agent, boasting of his relationship with Baron Rothschild remarks, "he treated me quite as his equal – quite famillion-airely!" We laugh at this not only because of the clever play on words, but also, Freud says, because it brings out a suppressed subsidiary thought: that there is actually something rather unpleasant about being treated with a rich man's condescension. We can identify with this kind of chain of ideas. We do not compare it with experience or look for a causality, but we accept Freud's analysis as an *explanation*.

This is the whole point. We must give an explanation that is *accept-ed*. Just as in art, in music. We must *see* connections that we did not dis-cover before, see what is gripping, beautiful and so on.

CUE MUSIC (5). EXIT. FADE LIGHTS.

SCENE 5

A CEMETERY. ONSTAGE A FUNEREAL URN. TURING AND HIS MOTHER ENTER.
MRS. TURING HOLDING FLOWERS.

TURING. Chris is dead. We were such good friends as students. I admired him enormously. He was a year older than me and shared my interest in natural sciences. It wasn't until we met at Sherbourne College that I realized I wasn't entirely alone in life. I was so attracted by his face. And the way he used to smile at me – sideways. Chris made everyone else seem so mediocre, and I worshipped the ground he walked on. He even got me to join the gramophone society. Music's not my strong suit, though I played the violin a little. Chris played the piano – beauti-fully.

MRS. TURING. Alan needed friends. He was such a dreamer and very unso-ciable. As a small boy he wanted to be a doctor. Well, I thought that you didn't become a doctor unless you had the right education, so we made sure that he went to the right school.

TURING. Oh, mother, Hazlehurst was unbearable! I hated all those competi-tions, and the lessons – hardly worthwhile. Do you know, our maths teacher gave a completely wrong idea of what is meant by X! No, you know my interest in science was first awakened when I was given a book called 'Natural Wonders Every Child Should Know', do you remember? It shaped my view of the world and life.

MRS. TURING. It was one of those modern books from America. A little too explicit in biology. At least I thought so.

TURING. What, you mean the chapter on the origin of life? It described the separation of the cells, but not how it all began. That was left to the "puzzled but well-intentioned parent to explain".

MRS. TURING. As with your brother I wrote you a letter...

TURING. That began with the birds and the bees...

MRS. TURING. And ended by instructing him to always conduct himself like a gentleman.

TURING. Chris made me see myself through others eyes. He had very high morals, and a strong conviction of what was right and wrong.

MRS. TURING. To the memory of her late son, Christopher Morcombe's mother endowed Sherbourne College with a science prize to encourage originality and creativity. It was to serve as an inspiration for other young boys and show that genius and humility can go hand in hand.

TURING. I entered that competition in honor of Chris, which I won. Twice in fact. The second time, I was already at King's College. I was there to complete what Chris had been snatched away from doing. But a mathematics scholarship to King's College, what's that? Proof of a certain virtuosity, like playing a sonata prima vista or repairing a car, no more than that. Many people younger than I have won better scholarships.

MRS. TURING. *[FUSSING WITH HER SON'S CLOTHES]* When he was 16, Alan studied Einstein's special theory of relativity, and that does not require any advanced mathematics. He came close to being expelled for that.

His maths teacher wrote to us saying that if Alan was to remain at a public school he would have to attempt to get a more general education ... "but if he wishes to be a scientific specialist he is wasting his time with us". Well, what could one hope for from a boy who knew by heart all the six-figure serial numbers on all the lampposts, but who had to have a mark on his thumb to tell his left hand from his right! A boy who takes three minutes to write a letter, but an hour and a half to find an envelope for it, and another hour and a half to find the letter that he put aside to look for the envelope....

TURING. It was mathematics and physics that were important. And now I was in Cambridge, at the very hub of scientific life. Imagine, Hardy and Eddington! They used to be just names in text books for me. What was it Hardy said...?

HE RECITES AS THOUGH LEARNED BY ROTE

"317 is a primary number, not because we think it is, or because our consciousness is created in a certain way, but because it is so. Mathematical reality is such, independent of ourselves".

MRS TURING KISSES HER SON AND SLOWLY EXITS, WALKING BACKWARDS

TURING. Free at last – one's own room, one's own thoughts. To be able to work and think, to be happy and unhappy when I want. And no more of those ridiculous competitions.

MRS. TURING. A healthy mind in a healthy body!

TURING. Both are just as difficult: to express oneself well and to coordinate one's movements. I do not run fast with any style, but I have stamina. I can run far.

MRS. TURING. It does you good to strain your body and develop your stamina.

TURING. And it's good for me to tire myself out, so I'm not tortured by my desires. *[MOVES TO URN]* Why am I so different?

FADE LIGHTS.

SCENE 6

WITTGENSTEIN AND RUSSELL ENTER CARRYING TWO DECK CHAIRS AND GLASSES OF
BEER. TURING IS SEATED IN DARKNESS UPSTAGE.

RUSSELL. Shakespeare!

WITT. Yes, that troubles me.

RUSSELL. Troubles you? What, that Shakespeare was a great writer and
poet?

WITT. I am troubled that everyone thinks so.

RUSSELL. But surely you don't think the whole world has been bluffing for
hundreds of years?

WITT. No, I don't think so. But I am unable to accept Shakespeare as a great
poet. His metaphors and similes are, in the ordinary sense, bad. Take
that passage from Richard II: "within my mouth you have engaol'd my
tongue / doubly portcullis'd with my teeth and lips."

RUSSELL. Well, that's not so bad. Perhaps the reason you don't like it is that
you don't like English culture in general.

WITT. Yes, that's true. But I cannot see Shakespeare as a great human being.
I can only stare in wonder at Shakespeare; never do anything with him.
He has such a supple hand and his brush strokes are so individual that
each one of his characters looks significant. One can talk of
"Beethoven's great heart" – but nobody could speak of "Shakespeare's
great heart". Nor could he regard himself as a prophet or as a teacher of
mankind. People stare at him in wonderment, almost as a spectacular
natural phenomenon. They do not have the feeling that this brings
them into contact with a great human being. Rather with a
phenomenon.

RUSSELL. But you yourself have said that understanding music, poetry,
painting and humor are reactions that belong to, and can only survive
in, a culture.

WITT. Yes, and you could have added philosophy too. What is required here
is not the discovery of facts, nor the drawing of logically valid inferences from accepted premises, nor still less the construction of theories
– but, rather, the right point of view. It's the same with humor, it's not a
mood, but a way of looking at the world. The Nazis managed to
destroy an entire style of life when they stamped out humor.

RUSSELL. But philosophy. What has music to do with philosophy?

WITT. Appreciating music is a manifestation of the life of mankind.

RUSSELL. But how should we describe it to someone? You cannot capture
the sense of a piece of music by using words to describe what the music
means.

WITT. It's the same with philosophy. Understanding a sentence is like
understanding a theme in music. To me a musical phrase is a gesture. It
insinuates itself into my life. I adopt it as my own. Like the infinite variations of life, musical expression is incalculable.

AS WITTGENSTEIN SPEAKS THIS LAST PHRASE, WE HEAR THE INTRODUCTION FROM
HANDEL'S "ISRAEL IN EGYPT". CUE MUSIC (6).

It is impossible for me to say one word in my book about all that music
has meant in my life. How then, can I hope to be understood?

*THROUGHOUT THE FOLLOWING SPEECH, WITTGENSTEIN BECOMES
PROGRESSIVELY SELF-INVOLVED, AND THE CONVERSATION WITH RUSSELL SHIFTS
TO A SOLILOQUY.*

Thinking is difficult. What does this really mean? Why is it difficult? It is almost like saying "Looking is difficult". Because looking intently *is* difficult. And it's possible to look intently without seeing anything, or to keep thinking you see something without being able to see clearly. Looking can tire you even when you don't see anything.

*RUSSELL EXITS TAKING GLASSES AND ONE DECK CHAIR. AFTER A CONSIDERABLE
PAUSE, WITTGENSTEIN SPEAKS, SEEMINGLY TO THE EMPTY AIR.*

Do you still hold the opinion that mathematics is more of a discovery than an invention? You thought I wanted to introduce some kind of bolshevism into mathematics.

TURING. You wanted to reduce complex mathematical argument to some kind of everyday language. You constantly came back to the idea that the only thing that had any meaning was common sense and the meaning we give to words.

WITT. I wanted to sow a seed with a jargon in which irony was juxtaposed with the idea that it should be necessary to have one's starting point in logic – Russell's logic – as some kind of basis for all thinking. It is pretentious and pernicious to give anyone the idea in a lecture that logic would be a way of penetrating the complexity of reality more deeply. This is incredibly stupid.

TURING. You mocked me because I counted instead of thinking. You maintained that one of the most dangerous ideas was that we think with, or in, our heads.

WITT. But that argument does not appear to have made any significant impression on you. I recently read an article of yours in – "Mind"? It was entitled "Can a Machine Think?" Are you joking? I think the question is as meaningful as "Does the figure three have a color?"

TURING. We wouldn't have got very far at Bletchley Park with your general speculations about good and bad analogies or arguments about the difference between an experiment in physics and an experiment in mathematics. It was a matter of working hard to break the code.

WITT. As a philosopher, one must act as a masseur for mental cramps.

TURING. Do you honestly think that people like us were consulted about the way our discoveries would be put to use?

WITT. The pilot who bombs civilians risks his life, but the scientist doesn't. But pilots who drop atom bombs over a completely vanquished Japan risk nothing of course. For God's sake, I'm not saying that I know how one should act in your shoes. People who write such harmless things as I do should probably say nothing about your problems.

"A young man, thirsting for knowledge, came to Archimedes," – and I quote – "Initiate me in the divine art/ That has given our fatherland such a wonderful fruit/ And protects the city walls against the mangonel." "Do you call my art divine, my son? It was, when it did not yet serve the state."

TURING. Well, if you're going to foist that Schiller rubbish on me as the ultimate truth! That poem can only have been written by someone who had not been exposed to war and had been – blunted by happiness! I can swear on the life of my mother that I had no idea that our "brothers" on the other side of the Atlantic would commit such a crime without warning....

WITT. Two atomic bombs are reason enough to tackle a problem that not even Schiller was up to. Yet who was capable of tackling that problem? Not even you. And I am not up to it because I have the kind of profession which, according to you, "bluntens you with happiness".

TURING. Look, the Americans made the bomb because Einstein – the pacifist! – wrote to Roosevelt assuring him that...

WITT. Roosevelt was a decent man! He would never have used the bomb on the Japanese if victory had already been assured!

TURING. He was fortunate enough to die at the right moment. The question is, would Einstein have committed such a terrible crime if he had *not* written to Roosevelt. Einstein had every reason to believe Nils Boor when he said that they were working on the bomb in Berlin. *[PAUSE, AND THEN SUDDENLY]* I thought you were Jewish.

WITTGENSTEIN SLOWLY STANDS TO FACE TURING

WITT. Half Jewish, why? What does that tell you? I am indignant about the fact that the bomb was developed to be used against Hitler, but was then used on a people who were not making atom bombs. And who did not bomb cities. And who did not murder millions of people in gas chambers. Was it also mere coincidence that the atom bomb was dropped on the Japanese because it wasn't ready until a month after Berlin had fallen? That is even more shocking.

TURING. So, we didn't stop the atrocities of the concentration camps by breaking the Enigma code. Or did we?

BLACKOUT. CUE MUSIC (7).

SCENE 7

LIGHT UP ON ENIGMA MACHINE, AS TURING WALKS INTO THIS LIGHT. MRS. TURING WALKS INTO LIGHT CENTER STAGE.

MRS. TURING. Alan's professional ambitions took him to Manchester University, a center for the burgeoning development of computers. While there, his private life was destroyed. His home was burgled and he reported the incident to the police. The police were more interested in his relationship with a young man who was a close friend of the suspected burglar. Alan's frank description of his love affair led to his conviction under a law that dated from 1885. It was the same law that was invoked in the trial of Oscar Wilde. When this crisis came he was in the wrong place at the wrong time, and his friends and colleagues were unable to protect him.

Alan faced the choice of a two-year prison sentence or submitting to hormone treatment. He chose the clinic. None of his friends deserted him; he kept his chair at the university and was spared publicity.

But in 1954, at the age of 40, he took his life by eating an apple dipped in potassium cyanide.

EXIT MRS. TURING. INCREASED LIGHT ON TURING.

TURING. They say that people from Oxford think the world belongs to them,

while people from Cambridge don't care who it belongs to. If I had
stayed in Cambridge, things would certainly have taken a different
turn. I could have ended my days as Sir Alan Turing, President of the
Royal Society. And there was so much scientific work still to be done. I
had shown the way to the development of the computer. The only
thing we were waiting for was the technology. Electronics.

We could have built an intelligent machine, a machine that could
really think, I never doubted that. *[Enter Wittgenstein to blackboard]* But
Wittgenstein, and his critical attitude to logic and the idea that it was all
a matter of seeing, that nothing is hidden, what has that given us?

WITT. Bach said that all his achievements were simply the fruit of industry.
But industry like that requires humility and an enormous capacity for
suffering, hence strength. And someone who, with all this, can express
himself perfectly, simply speaks to us in the language of a great man.
Bach wrote on the title page of his *Orgelbüchlein,* "to the glory of the
most high God, and that my neighbor may be benefitted thereby". That
is what I would have liked to say about my work.

Only every now and again does one of the sentences I write make a
step forward; the rest are like the snipping of the barber's scissors,
which he has to keep moving so as to make a cut at the right moment. I
am not capable of bringing out the great, the important things. But
great views are hidden in these feeble remarks. A philosopher may be
interested in reading my notes. Even if I hit the target rather infrequent-
ly, he should understand what target I have been aiming at. The meeting point, the point where doubt becomes meaningless. We cannot
doubt everything, and that is true for practical reasons alone. A doubt
without end is not even a doubt. Am I not getting closer and closer to
saying that logic cannot be described? You have to look at the way the
language is used, and then you will see.

TURING. Hilbert said of Galileo that only an idiot could believe that scientific truth calls for martyrdom. I do not intend to die a martyr. It may be
necessary in religion, but I have no such faith.

TURING FINDS A SCRAP OF PAPER IN HIS POCKET FROM WHICH HE READS THE
FOLLOWING:

> As I lay with my head in your lap, camerado,
> The confession I made I resume, what I said to you and the open
>   air I resume,
> I know I am restless and make others so,
> I know my words are weapons full of danger, full of death,
> For I confront peace, security, and all the settled laws, to unsettle
>   them,
> I am more resolute because all have denied me than I could ever
>   have been had all accepted me,
> I heed not, and have never heeded either experience, cautions,
>   majorities, nor ridicule,
> And the threat of what is call'd hell is little or nothing to me,
> And the lure of what is call'd heaven is little or nothing to me;
> Dear camerado! I confess I have urged you onward with me, and

still urge you, without the least idea what is our destination,
Or whether we shall be victorious, or utterly quell'd and defeated.
[from "Leaves of Grass" by Walt Whitman.]

TURING. Consciousness does not need my body. Let me leave it. I know I can get in touch with Chris Morcombe. That, at least, is beyond all certainty.

WITT. Wisdom is without passion. Knowledge only hides life from you. It is like cold grey ashes that cover the glow. Life can educate one to believe in God. And experiences too are what bring this about; I don't mean visions and other forms of sense experience which show us 'the existence of the being' but, for example, suffering of various sorts. Experience, thoughts, – life can force the concept of God on us. The problems of life cannot be solved on the surface; they can only be solved in depth. One keeps forgetting to go right down to the foundations. One doesn't put the question mark deep enough down.

FADE TO BLACK.

Chapter 15

Thoughts on Acting and the Play
Beyond All Certainty
Great Escape Theatre Company
Richard Davies and Jon Hyde

The Cast

RD   Richard Davies: Ludwig Wittgenstein.

JH   Jon Hyde: Bertrand Russell, Winston Churchill, director of production.

CG   Charlotte Garrard: Helene Wittgenstein, Mrs Turing.

JR   Jonathan Rea: Alan Turing, *mise en scene*, lighting design.

SR   Steve Ridley: set design, stage management.

September 1992: First Notes I

Currently a confusion in the playwrights' treatment between public and private.

Material and language very good, but structure of the piece demands too great a knowledge of all the characters, as well as running the risk of putting even a supposed ideal audience to sleep after 15 minutes (JH)

* * *

ONE: Visualization

JH. The play begins with a passionately-done, but largely technical discussion about certain rules of epistemology and mathematics, if I remember right. Really very difficult at first sight.

RD. I remember learning the lines for Wittgenstein from the first draft I saw. It was almost impossible because there had been so many changes, you could hardly read the lines for all the blacking out and bits of writing added on in biro or whatever and then photocopied. I had to keep asking "Which bit am I supposed to be memorizing? What's that or there? Is that all the speech gone or just most of it?"

JH. A scene we chose to set in a playground.

RD. It could have been a lunatic asylum with a recreation ground for all I knew.

JH. Exactly. It could be Marat Sade land. You guys on the seesaw. You could push it into pantomime.

RD. I didn't know anything about this playground business. Nobody told me. This is the first time I've heard of it and I've acted in the play five times!

JH. I think the seesaw was originally a scale. To show a balance.

JR. A large scale. Far bigger than any normal scale and Steve found a big yellow and red seesaw.

JH. A seesaw. It wasn't originally going to be a seesaw. These two back-room boys enter with Turing, laboratory technicians, it's war time-

JR. When the seesaw idea came along we knew, "Yes, the balance. It must be a seesaw!" And we wanted scales they could sit on to dramatize the debate, the "20 apples + 30 apples = 50 apples" moment...

JH. And then it became the playground.

RD. And I never knew until now.

CG. But it is also a lecture hall of some kind.

RD. So the space in the first scene is threefold, three things simultaneously: a theater, a lecture hall, and surreal playground.

JR. And there is an object that is twofold: a scale and a seesaw, at the same time a technical instrument and a child's toy.

JH. And on the stage this is not just a matter of multiple purposes in the same moment but of multiple meanings

WITTGENSTEIN. "...It may be that 20 apples + 30 apples = 50 apples (The two assistants leave and return with apples in buckets and demonstrate the balance by sitting on the seesaw and tossing them to each other) may not be a proposition about apples..."

Beyond All Certainty: Scene I

Memoirs of a Production Manager: I

Jon Hyde and Jonty Rea asked me to design the set and stage manage the production of a new play about Wittgenstein and Alan Turing. Having discussed it with Jon and Jonty it became clear that rather than a stage set, a group of props could be more effective. Lighting, designed by Jonty, would be crucial. This style of design has advantages – with no set building, transport would be easier and available resources could be concentrated elsewhere. The set would consist of a large black-board in one corner. In the opposite corner, a chair and a table with a lamp on it and a stylized model of the Turing Engima Machine (naval version) placed somewhere downstage on a plinth. To punctuate the dialogue between Wittgenstein and Turing in Scene One, a child's seesaw/ roundabout would be used to great effect. Later on in the play, the shell of a modern computer would be wheeled on from which, at the end of the scene, a rabbit would magically emerge. (SR)

TWO: Epistemologies of Theater

RD. We can't quite explain what it is we mean by what is good or skilful in the particular field of knowledge and activity we're involved in.

JH. I think we can. I think that Beyond All Certainty is now an engaging and interesting piece. It presents very grand ideas in just over one hour. Now, something like King Lear presents equally grand ideas over three hours. But it does something else as well. When Lear is dying and he's lost his entire kingdom, he says to his daughter – "Will you loosen my button?". It might go by you in performance, you might miss it, of course. Nevertheless, that for me is as profound as anything else going on in the play.

RD. But where are these depths located? How do we know about them, recognize them? What is profound about loosening a button? That's your judgement. I could say, for example, that it's a superficial remark, a neither here nor there sort of thing, under the circumstances. As you say, you may not even notice it, but you wouldn't miss it as such. You would still be moved by the play

JH. I don't think it is superficial or that you didn't miss something deliberate and essential. You can't simply present these ideas, these reflections, by preaching at people at great length about the things that Wittgenstein and Lear were obsessed by. You can't just present them baldly and have a narrator telling you what to think. You have to find another way of presenting them, which is more closely connected with people's experience. You're not hiding the ideas. You are presenting them obliquely.

RD. Is this more than you saying you know what you like?

JH. It's a way of foregrounding the things that are difficult to talk about or express. It's why you laugh at Mrs Turing fussing with Alan's clothes and yet find it sad, and poignant as well. Drama has to address itself to things that are difficult to talk about, things we would normally rather avoid, I think. And do it in an understandable way.

HE RECITES AS THOUGH LEARNED BY ROTE

TURING. "317 is a primary number, not because we think it is, or because our consciousness is created in a certain way, but because it is so. Mathematical reality is such, independent of ourselves.

MRS. TURING KISSES HER SON AND SLOWLY EXITS, WALKING BACKWARDS.

Beyond All Certainty: Scene V

THREE: Action and Character

RD. Some of the feedback I got at the dinner after the Stockholm performance was that it was a good performance, very absorbing, a great show, but it wasn't drama. What interests me, whether I agree or not is that I knew exactly what was meant when someone said "It wasn't drama". How do we recognize drama?

CG. There was a similar reaction from someone who saw it in Norwich. He was waiting for something visual to happen. Isn't there a sense in which there's no room in the play for things-that-happen? Words are what happens.

JR. But that's a lot of what philosophy's about. Isn't it?

JH. And literature, religion, politics, blah, blah. It is argued that we con-
     struct the world through our languages. "In the beginning was the
     word" and so forth.

RD. Wasn't Wittgenstein very fond of that alternative of Goethe's "In the
     beginning was the deed."

JH. Possibly. Anyway you could say that the impact Wittgenstein had on
     the philosophical playground was inherently dramatic. In terms of
     what he was arguing, of the way he was.

RD. From what I've learned from doing the play, is that if there was a dra-
     matic figure in philosophy in the past 200 years it was Wittgenstein. In
     terms of his arrival, his impact and his obstinacy – and so much of dra-
     ma is about the arrival of someone or something at the door setting off
     a chain of events after which nothing is really the same...

CG. That has to do with his personality and his power, rather than words.

JH. But in the world of the play, he is solely created by the words the play-
     wright gives him

CG. And by the interpretations of the director and actors. You also create
     the character through the performance. The point is: it's not just the
     words.

RD. How does one separate his obsessive thinking from the way he was,
     anyway? His personality is a philosophical personality.

CG. Yes. But what did he represent? Not just "what did he mean when he
     said such and such"

JR. Exactly. Who is this man, what is he saying, and why do we care?

CG. And what does he represent in the play? It can't be enough that
     Wittgenstein had an impact on a philosophical playground as an obses-
     sive personality. His charisma isn't inherent for the audience member
     who knows nothing about him. It has to be apparent dramatically.

RD. Even now, according to Stephen Toulmin, you can see Wittgenstein in
     Cambridge through the mannerisms of his former students who are
     themselves now professors of philosophy.

WITTGENSTEIN. I felt cut off from heaven. Wisdom was not enough if I were
     to be saved. To be redeemed, I needed faith.

Beyond All Certainty: Scene IV

September 1992: First Notes II

Suggest the following approach:
   *1] Adopt an episodic structure, using existing script to intercut private
(Turing's early experience, pg 24; Russell/Wittgenstein report, pg 6, etc) with
public presentation of ideas (opening lecture, many other speeches throughout the
script) to achieve a performance dialectic that supports existing debate. In short
make these humans human (JH)*

* * *

FOUR: Practice

Perhaps this book will be understood only by someone who himself already had the thoughts that are expressed in it – or at least similar thoughts. – So it is not a textbook. – Its purpose would be achieved if it gave pleasure to one person who read and understood it.

Tractatus Logico-Philosophicus. Preface, p. 3

JH. You can't start doing the real work until you're in the rehearsal room.

JR. We thrashed about for about three weeks before that.

RD. What were you thinking? What were your reactions? What did you think you'd landed yourselves with?

JR. My reactions were – "What is this about? What does it mean?" And we spent a long time, some wasted, going over every line...

JH. Wasn't a waste, wasn't a waste...

JR. Speech by speech...

JH. Together...

JR. Going.. "What does this mean, what is he saying..."

RD. Did either of you go to the Tractatus?

JH. No. Unnecessary.

JR. The Ray Monk biography was more relevant.

JH. For the purpose of this exercise we don't need the Tractatus. Just as for Hamlet one wouldn't seek authenticity in performance by researching the actual writings of 16th century Danish aristocrats. One might of course and it may contribute to an interesting interpretation but it would only be one approach amongst many others.

RD. Wittgenstein really didn't like Shakespeare, did he? I wonder why. Only someone who hasn't seen a beautifully done "Midsummer Night's Dream" as I did last summer in front of a ruined abbey in the middle of open Norfolk countryside on a warm, dry evening, with a professional company using local children as fairies, could say Shakespeare wasn't a great poet or human being. The whole event was phosphorescing with humanity, from the text, whatever its quirky metaphysics, to the performance, where at one point the lights failed. I suspect Shakespeare wasn't quite man enough for Wittgenstein, he was someone of a too complex androgyny. Great 'human being' for Wittgenstein is probably synonymous with great 'man'. In his book it probably wasn't available to women to be great human beings any more than it was available to them to be great philosophers Whatever his sexuality I think Wittgenstein liked his genders cut and dried which may be why he couldn't get on with Shakespeare. Beethoven by comparison does seem to come over as a grand, passionate, rogue male which is why, I suppose, Wittgenstein could allow him a 'great heart'.

WITTGENSTEIN. ... I cannot see Shakespeare as a great human being... he has such a supple hand and his brushstrokes are so individual that each one of his characters looks significant. One can talk of 'Beethoven's great heart' – but nobody could speak of "Shakespeare's great heart"... People stare at him in wonderment, almost as at a spectacular natural phenomenon. They do not have the feeling that this brings them into contact with a great human being. Rather with a phenomenon."

Beyond All Certainty: Scene VI

FIVE: Engineering: Space and Theater

JR. With the exception of one theater, we haven't had control over the space. It's a touring show...

JH. So that when we played it in Bodø for instance, we were on this huge, raised up proscenium arch. Not the ideal place to see this intimate piece...

RD. Like chamber music?

JR. We did it at the King of Hearts [a small arts center in Norwich] in a semi-circle.

JH. Yes, the horseshoe formation. It was tricky in that space.

CG. The King of Hearts is a good example. The entrance we used was actually part of some flats – it took you out onto a landing with a shared, residential staircase. At one point during the play we were standing outside, in our costumes, holding the rabbit, waiting to go on when a man and his girlfriend left their flat. We said "shush" which seemed to annoy the man because he slammed the door extra hard and began whistling loudly as he went down the stairs.

JH. And you walked on stage knowing that everyone in the audience had been just as distracted as you.

JR. You could hardly get a more different space than the theater in the Kulturhaus at Bodø.

CG. Still, a piece of theater is designed to work in certain ways according to the space around it.

JH. It has to be responsive to the spaces around it.

RD. Like engineering it uses space, space is fundamental, space is part of its material.

JR. And like engineering, providing you know the conditions you are going to perform in, you can do theater anywhere, like building bridges. The important thing is to know the environment, the conditions and the earlier the better. But sometimes you just have to improvise. Especially when you're touring. Then its like a military campaign through unfamiliar terrain. You have to be able to throw up a bridge with whatever materials are at hand.

RD. It's not only a matter of improvisation – it's about resourcefulness, preparation – and having thought out all the contingencies before setting out. That is the calculus; and where things go wrong is where the real situation throws up a contingency you had not imagined previously.

WITTGENSTEIN. "But how do you know it will fall down? Isn't that a question of physics? It may be that if one throws dice in order to calculate the bridge it will never fall down!"

Memoirs of a Production Manager: II

When the time came to take the play to Scandinavia, we could all see problems in transporting those props which could not be provided by our hosts. Imagine taking a child's seesaw on board an aeroplane, or trying to explain to airport security officials that the box of components was a replica of Turing's Enigma Machine (naval version). But it was not so – it was my work shoes with steel toe caps which amused security most; as for the third or possibly fourth time I passed through the metal detectors at Stockholm airport.

The arrival at a venue is always an intense experience. Get in, rig and focus lights, dress the set, check the sound, eat, perform, strike the set and get out, all takes place within a few hours, and with a small theater group this means everyone must work fast to have things ready for the performance. To the casual observer this may seem chaotic, yet casual, tense and time-challenged, frantic and fraught with danger – in reality that's exactly how it is! (SR)

SIX: Empathy: Learning the Lines

WITTGENSTEIN. "Yes, of course, we can say: we have taught him the rules, now let us see if he follows them. I cannot at the same time allow the result of an experiment to be the result of a mathematical calculation. If the result of the calculation is determined by rules, i.e. 136 x 52 = 6936, the result of the experiment is not what result he arrives at if he follows the rules, but whether or not he follows the rules."

RD. I really was scared that some of the lines and passages were almost unlearnable, or if I did learn them they would never come back to me in an orderly fashion when I was on the stage.

JR. The script is unkind to actors. In places.

RD. It is when you have lines that are almost similar but are in very different parts of a scene and you suddenly find yourself lost; you don't know which one you're saying with all the implications that has for what is to follow, for where you are located in the scene or the play. For example "The entire analogy between mathematics and physics is a complete mistake. In fact what we have here is an important source of confusion." Later on in the scene we have "There seems to me to be an enormous mistake here. You have confused two separate things." What we are talking about is not a definite catastrophe, things necessarily going wrong, but experiencing a sudden, unpleasant doubt in a vulnerable situation. Again, its about knowing the topography but there are two landmarks in very different parts of the town that look similar. You come across one of them on the way to your supposed destination, and for a horrible moment you can't remember which one is which and you are no longer certain where you are. One would care not to experience such things.

JH. So, the script is unkind to actors ...?

JR. At times...

JH. Then why is it that you do some of your best work in these roles? RD seems to be saying that Wittgenstein's opening speech – the first speech in the play – in some way delineates the actor's experience. But also, in my view, you bring tremendous understanding and sympathy to the characters.

JR. The only reason I can be in contact with the character is dependent on the one thing I can sympathize with. In this play there seems to be much more that I find difficult to understand and personify – his passion for mathematics, his homosexuality – presumably both vital to Turing. But for me, the only trait I can, as an actor, work with and understand, is his sadness, his melancholy. I worry that I don't understand his mathematics.

JH. How do you approach a character? It seem to me that you approach him or her with almost nothing at all, and an understanding grows. The full picture is impossible, so you cling to incredibly tenuous handholds, that become less tenuous.

JR. It's like climbing a rockface. I don't believe in doing a huge amount of research. You have to work with what you've got, with the play you've got. Research might help, but it's limited. What counts more is the quality of feeling and imagination you bring to bear on the script. But some actors of course take research very seriously and go into great detail. Some actors get so deep into their research, especially in the context of playing 'real' characters, that they know too much to imagine and the performance suffers.

CG. But actors go about these things very differently. You can't really make hard and fast rules about how much or how little research you should do.

RD. For me, what makes for good acting is not biographical knowledge or knowledge of salient facts whatever, but clarity, conviction, economy, honesty and a capacity for manufacturing authentic feeling somehow or other in public. In learning the part of Wittgenstein there were quite distinct phases of development, of the nature of the actor's relationship to the material. The major phases involve the intense discovery of the character, the search for meaning and information and so on, and there are elements of impersonation. But the mature phase involves the abandonment of the character, of forgetting of meaning, of thinking of the text in musical terms, of actually becoming more oneself than the imagined other. There is no longer an interest in the meaning of the words and sentences, but in their musicality, in rhythm, melody, beat, nuance, pitch, volume and so on. The character and explicit meaning have gone as such and what remains is sound and the movements of the body, and what you are concerned to do is manipulate the sound as effectively as possible so it comes to resemble linguistic meaning and the movement of the body so they come to resemble character – for the audience – although you as an actor are now quite empty of such meaning. It's a variant on the theme of the paradox, I guess. Character and meaning are your handholds en route to oblivion. I mean these are not facts, or ideas or strategies but certain sentimental phases in a process of development.

CG. I have to say I disagree with you quite strongly here. Going the further step into oblivion surely means you lose your character and "explicit meanings." Part of the paradox for me is juggling these things at the time in performance with oneself. You are two people. Not a development to oblivion. A problem I came across was getting to the point where I knew my lines so well that the problem of re-invention came up – i.e. how do you keep the role fresh night after night. My brain needs to be totally present to re-react otherwise oblivion does come and it just motors out of your mouth.

JH. This is a complicated argument. It is about being on form. Like an athlete? Some times it all falls into place. Sometimes it doesn't. I remember a painter telling me that he knew that a painting was finished or it worked or something because it sang; all its elements had finally come together and this chord was struck, a chord which cannot be paraphrased or explained.

Anyway if you really listen to the question being put to you on stage by another character then the response will be new each night. If you're not listening to the others on the stage how can you expect the audience to be?

JR. For example in this play it is important to convey the drama of thought or thinking, so spaces must be left for people to be seen to be thinking about what has just been said, or what they are going to say. The play we know is not made up of ordinary speech; what the characters say is hard to say and would at times have required strenuous thought and that has to be shown dramatically, in silences.

CG. But that assumes a particular kind of audience, a particular kind of tolerance?

JR. There is some part of me that doesn't like talking about acting, It seems to me to be one of those things that the more you talk about it, the less able you are to do it. I'm not sure why that is. I mean how can you rationalize an occupation that requires you to work in the full gaze of the public. The great majority of sensible people would run a mile from doing such a thing.

JH. There's a story told by the British actor and director Clive Barnes that I think is relevant. This fellow is cast in a play and is walking around in his room trying to learn his lines – in this particular play he was cast as a soldier in WW1 – and he couldn't come to grips with it. He kept saying over and over, "I am a soldier in the first world war" and he was walking about, slogging up and down. And finally the way he cracked it was to change firstly to "I was a soldier in the first world war", losing the present, but it still seemed false to him. It was only when he began telling himself "There was a soldier in the first world war" and losing the "I" that he was able simply to demonstrate and not worry about impersonation. To tell the story.

September 1992: First Notes III

2] *Resist temptation to 'biopic' it, and instead leaven existing tragic tone by foregrounding the already present comic sense – without sacrificing aforesaid tragedy.*

   3] *More gags! More physicality! (JH)*

SEVEN: Personification of Roles

JH.   There is a sense for me – and it might be a bit tenuous – there is a very
      large sense for me in which Helene and Mrs Turing unlock the play.
      They become the center of the play because, although they are both
      quite different women, vastly different women, I mean one is a sort of
      classic 1940s, English suburban type, you know, Turing's Mum; and
      the other one seems to be a very sophisticated, wealthy, Austrian; but
      they both do the same thing for and in the play: they both deliver
      essential information. It doesn't matter that this role might be rooted in
      the original conception of the 'Narrator'. which came with the script.
      We've gone a long way from that, so that when Helene (Wittgenstein's
      sister) says time and time again things like "The Anschluss is a fact;
      Ludwig could go back to Cambridge", she's not just giving over informa-
      tion.

RD.   She is on the stage with him; they embody a significant relationship
      without the addition of more words, simply by their physical disposi-
      tion on the stage, by the meeting of their eyes, the silent offering and
      refusing of gifts and so on.

JH.   The mere fact that you personify his sister and – again it's non textual –
      you offer him the gift and he refuses it and blows out the candles. I
      don't know, I don't know if it is appropriate to talk about the relation-
      ship between textual and non-textual moments. We are talking about
      seconds, brief seconds, but moments which are fundamental to the
      whole thing, to its effect, its tone.

RD.   And so its overall meaning. You are talking about drafting other layers
      of meaning through performance rather than just from the words in the
      text... The performance is another kind of text, is itself a kind of literary
      act. To paraphrase a line from the play 'What I am trying to show by
      these examples is that there is an essential difference between the math-
      ematics of the text and the physics of the performance'.

JH.   Yes. What happens to me now is that my favorite scenes are the scenes
      with Helene and Mrs Turing, the scenes we developed as performers or
      producers as opposed, with respect, to scenes already set down by the
      writers. They are my favorite, not because of Charlotte's performance,
      which I love, or that they supersede or overtake the men in the play,
      but they somehow root the whole play in something that is under-
      standable. That sounds rather Romantic.

RD.   Perhaps they root it in something social rather than the purely meta-
      physical, philosophical, whatever. It adds that sort of concrete social
      dimension, of identifiable human relationships, that in this instance
      happens to be women: a mother and a sister.

HELENE. We are out of danger. We have used the influence of our position
      and great wealth to negotiate with the Nazis to be classified as non-
      Jewish.
(HELENE TURNS TO LUDWIG AND OFFERS HIM THE GIFT. HE RESPONDS BY
BLOWING OUT THE SEVEN CANDLES. BLACK OUT. EXIT HELENE)

* * *

EIGHT: The Paradox of the Actor

RD. Would it have mattered if you had never understood the text?

CG. I don't think I do understand a lot of the text.

JR. I don't either.

CG. I really don't. I mean I can stand backstage and just let it all wash over my head. I know vaguely what's going on, the more personal stuff and you know there's an argument weaving in here, but I don't understand the finer technical points.

JH. (TO JR) Would you say you understand everything Turing says?

JR. Not everything. Not when he's talking about the mathematical side of things.

JH. My question is: "as an *actor* do you understand?" I don't mean you have to know the calculus or all about that. As an actor, do you still have difficulties with certain lines?

JR. Yes, I do. Mostly in the first scene. Maybe I just have a block about first scenes. I can understand its point. I can get inside the emotion behind it. I can get inside the head of someone who has a radically different point of view to another person, but apart from that... I don't know enough about mathematics and mathematical theory and blah, blah. But I can get in touch with Turing's sadness. If there wasn't that sadness I'd be really at sea.

CG. Can I just drop in *'the paradox of the actor'*?

JH. Oh yes. Absolutely. I was hoping you would.

CG. It's a nightmare. You can be in the Alan and Mrs Turing scene and you're saying something like "Alan needed friends. He was such a dreamer and very unsociable." Now that's a very normal thing to say and a very easy thing to understand. But you can be on stage and suddenly, for example, you need to go to the toilet. So your mind is on two entirely separate things. It's a real pulling between character and person on a tense line of concentration. I can imagine if the words are more complex involving philosophical debate, the problem increases tenfold. Your brain is holding an argument together and your body wants to be in the bathroom and you're thinking "I don't understand what I am saying. I have lost concentration."

JR. Anyway, if you don't understand what you're saying, you're far more in danger.

CG. There's much greater danger.

JR. You're not absolutely, completely in control of that character.

CG. But no actor ever is. You never absolutely, completely know what the next minute on stage is going to be like, to sound or look like.

RD. There's that story, I don't know if it is true or not, you always hear about Olivier, being furious with himself in the dressing room after doing a wonderful Othello and people asked why he was so angry after being so brilliant and he said "I know it was brilliant, but I don't know how I did it, so I don't know if I can do it again". An actor's knowledge is unavoidably, always, and probably necessarily, incomplete.

JH. That's the job, isn't it?

RD. Some job.

CG. But that's the job.

RD. If that's the job, that's the paradox.

TURIN. ... you cannot be confident about applying your calculus until you know there is no hidden contradiction in it. If one takes Frege's symbolism and gives someone the technique of multiplying in it, using a Russell paradox he could get a very wrong application.

* * *

Memoirs of a Production Manager III

Time spent at a new venue is a time to make new friends, and it is important to observe the prime directive, never upset the resident technician, for if you do, darkness will fall upon your house and pestilence and plague will follow the performance. No matter what it takes one must get what one needs from the theater, so co-operation is important, a constant supply of caffeine and nicotine, water and tranquilizers, beer and gaffer tape, safety pins and other ephemera and knowing where the spare fuses are kept are all crucial for smooth and faultless performance. (SR)

NINE: 'Biopics': Acting Real Lives

JH. It's not a question of saying "I must understand Wittgenstein's philosophy". We're fortunate, of course, if we do understand that philosophy, or a bit of it. Maybe then you have an advantage. But I'm not even sure of that.

RD. Perhaps for a performance of something like "Beyond All Certainty" it's not important for those doing it to understand Wittgenstein's philosophy. It's more important to have a sense of his dramatic impact upon the prevailing state of philosophy. That was certainly my feeling about learning the part. What was important was to convey the intensity and passion of the man which were the sort of fuel rods of his philosophy. He did not take his work lightly. I don't know and probably never will anything about Frege's symbolism, or even be that interested in it, but it might well have been something that moved Wittgenstein to the core. That will do as a starting point. Philosophy was not an armchair sport as far as he was concerned. It was very much about his relationship to some sort of ruthlessly exacting divinity, his Dad maybe; he got enamored of it and angry about it and so on. That's quite enough for an actor to be going on with. That's the job. You don't act out ideas, you act out trouble at mill, even if you're not quite sure what the fuss is all about.

JR. I think Wittgenstein is the hardest part to do in the play in terms of understanding more of what that character was dealing with, i.e. Wittgensteinian philosophy. There are far more lines than anybody else and you have to make at least some kind of head if not tail of what is being said. It's a huge role.

RD. One of the things that impressed me most in doing it was learning about the significance of Turing. I found that the more I learnt the part of Wittgenstein the more interested I became in the character and ideas of Turing. My feeling at this point is that the actor playing Turing has very little to go on. Turing is somehow under-represented or insufficiently expressed in some way. I think of Turing as a most interesting and complex figure who gets cuffed about and seen off, bullied if you like, in the play by Wittgenstein and I don't think justice is being done either to the man or his ideas, or his historical circumstances... But then I don't know.

JR. I remember Richard, me and Steve spending the night in that bloody nightclub in the center of Stockholm with all that heavy metal music. We could not speak, and we could not hear each other.

RD. My ears rang for three days afterwards.

JR. We had to write to each other on the club's napkins at three o'clock in the morning making notes about building the character of Turing.

RD. Jonty expressed concern about how difficult the Turing character was to get a grip on and I remember having done a couple of performances feeling how tragic and central Turing was and yet this was somehow not realized in the script. Subsequent saloon bar discussions with Bo and others suggested that Turing was of immense importance but the information is not available, you know, the old British mania for secrecy. Apparently there are these huge collections of papers in some classified pit in Cambridge that refer to those old debates and discussions but are only just becoming available because of his involvement with the secret services and his homosexuality. The adequate account of Turing is absent, is incomplete not only in the play but generally, in the body politic and all that.

JH. No. I disagree. In the play the account is more than adequate. It is moving. How could you have any more on Turing in this play. The play concerns itself with the meeting of these two individuals. And that is what it represents.

JR. Are you saying that the fact that you feel the most central or tragic figure is Turing may be true but may also be a trick, not an intentional trick, but possibly a kind of instinct of the play, that at the end of the script that we've got, there suddenly appears to be this eulogy for Turing. There is all this attention given to him. He kills himself in the last scene with this cyanide injected apple and his mother comes on and talks about his homosexuality.

RD. Maybe I've been taken in by that instinct. The script does him justice, makes him important in ways we haven't – or I haven't – quite grasped. Otherwise I mightn't have noticed.

JR. In a sense I am lucky playing that character because he, of all the characters in the play, is the only one that gets humanized suddenly. But it's right at the end, he gets humanized. You get this background, that he was homosexual in a world murderously hostile to all of that. We don't know that till much later on. In fact the scene with his mother is in the last third of the play, the last fifteen minutes and it's all about his love for this Chris Morcombe and 'I must protect myself from my passions and why am I so different' and then he kills himself and all these things, but actually no other character in the play has that. We don't know anything of Wittgenstein's death, how he approached it, what it meant. It suddenly gets top heavy about Turing towards the end. Am I wrong?

JH. What happens to me is that in the world of the play this all fits and is appropriate. Of course this isn't what happened in 'real life'.

RD. But that's alright in this piece with regard to Wittgenstein and Turing. They did not actually meet as such, as far as this company knows, but there was and remains a kind of meeting and conflict and this play is an aesthetic version of it, an organized impression of it, with points to make, and issues to represent that go beyond the documentary details of the lives of these particular individuals.

JR. The fact is Wittgenstein and Turing hardly met.

CG. Apart from a couple of lectures.

RD. Anyway we don't really know. I don't. Monk hardly seems to mention Turing.

JH. What seems to me to happen in the play is that we all know that Wittgenstein is the star and the most difficult part – or maybe not, maybe the lead role is not the most difficult – but what seems to me is that the scene at the very end where you finally see Turing – or the ghost of Turing – that triggers this final speech of Wittgenstein's which isn't about philosophy, it doesn't seem to be quite Wittgenstein's voice—

CG. And the whole play is called "Beyond All Certainty" which is something that Turing says and it sometimes seems to me that the play is about something they start talking about in the last scene. As if they're wrapping up the whole play in those final speeches.

RD. There is Wittgenstein, at the end of the play, doing this pulpit terrier job about life forcing God on us and all this stuff. It's very fine and moving but I'm not convinced it's Wittgenstein. What you've got, which is perfectly reasonable, is the authors of the play speaking. So for example when Wittgenstein in the Cambridge speech says "What I am trying to do is change people's style of thinking"; whose is the "I" here, or how many others inhabit this apparently singular pronoun. I would argue that here the play's authors are speaking and the people they are trying to change are the people attending the performances or the conferences. Wittgenstein moves from being this extraordinary ego to this extraordinary vehicle

JH. In so far as there is any useful difference.

RD. OK. The authors of "Beyond All Certainty" have skillfully put together a speech that might have been made by Wittgenstein but is, in my view, *their* collage performing as Wittgenstein's ultimate statement, his grand summary. But it is a collage, made out of found material. This material is lent a certain inflexion by the way it is organized and put on the page to suit other purposes. I would say that in doing those final speeches I don't feel much like I am being a mouthpiece of Wittgenstein. I am presenting a manifesto for the authors of the play, or a public provocation to debate born out of the Skill and Technology movement. I say that because perhaps I'm not entirely happy pressing notions of God on people, but the quotes those final speeches are made up of may be, I think, in some cases quite critical remarks or observations that Wittgenstein made in other contexts *about* religion and so forth rather than being statements *of* his beliefs, religious or otherwise. But also these speeches are made up of his own odd religious utterances and his Bach stuff and this would be fragments of table talk down through the years and they have been organized in the play to make this great statement, not of Wittgenstein but really of other people on the basis of other more contemporary interests.

JH. And it is a great statement.

JR. It is. It's very good. It's very moving.

RD. It sounds like Wittgenstein speaking, extolling us and so on. But I'm sure it isn't. I don't think he said that but I don't really know. And reading what he was like I would be terrified if he was in the audience. I can imagine him jumping up and down and shouting at us.

WITTGENSTEIN. "I detested all your popular philosophical works."

Beyond All Certainty: Scene II

* * *

September 1993: First Notes

We knew of the Wittgenstein 'industry' of course. As the commission stated, we would perform initially to approximately sixty academics from all over the world and their post-graduate students. We were told that, having seen the performance, many other people with a stake in the Great Man would have the opportunity at 9:00 am to ask us questions about the relationship between text and performance. We decided immediately to do it. (JH)

TEN: Form and Economy

JR. Are you saying the play would be better if it was two hours rather than one?

RD. The play that we have got could be the first act of three.

JH. I disagree.

RD. It could be epic. I think more could be made of Russell. I think we tend to make him look a bit of a silly twit – and yet he was one of the few or only philosophers around at the time that Wittgenstein would not allow others to treat disrespectfully in conversation. We don't hear anything of that other genius, philosopher, fascist of the time, J.L. Austin who everybody was apparently scared stiff of, just down the road in, wash my mouth out, in Oxford. And who the hell was Frege? His name crops up in the play. The unintelligible in pursuit of the inaccessible. What were they all so bothered by?

JH. The play is about the meeting of Turing and Wittgenstein – who in fact, it appears, hardly met but they represented opposing systems of thought or different notions about what it is to be human and able to think and do things, and we are still living in the consequences of it all. That's why this script and these conferences exist. There is absolutely no need to go on about any other stuff.

JR. Possibly there was not enough time, enough script, to make for exam-
     ple the balance right at the end between Wittgenstein and Turing.
JH. I don't disagree with that. The play goes by quickly. Possibly too quick-
     ly. Because it is such an intensely practical business, theater, I can't see
     how you can hold attention with material as difficult as this with more
     – maybe it would be a better play if it was two hours, but there's no
     guarantee that it would be, and it might be hugely worse.
JR. It might just be a longer play.
JH. It might just be heavy handed.
JR. We've always talked about chucking in another scene.
JH. We're all busy. There is a sense for me that you have the script, which
     we have performed what, ten times? Eight times? This is something I
     should know but I don't. It works, it works very well, it's like snap-
     shots, it's like an impression of – I like that very much, there is some-
     thing for me that is very attractive in trying to encapsulate all this stuff,
     very briefly. And you're bound to miss loads of things, particularly if
     you're trying to – as this play tries to – weave in Turing's sensitivity
     and Wittgenstein's sensitivity in – what – an *hour*.

RUSSELL. "But you must admit that Wierstrasse, Dedekind and Cantor have
     solved the problems of the infinitesimal, continuity and infinity in a
     logically perfect way"

                                                     Beyond All Certainty: Scene II.

* * *

Memoirs of a Production Manager IV

*Each venue is different, and so the set and lighting design needs modifying each
time. For example we performed Beyond All Certainty at Clare Hall College,
Cambridge in a small lounge, bounded on two sides by large windows and a low
sloping roof, in one corner a grand piano and a quantity of tables and chairs, and
eight lights to work with. Within weeks we were performing at Bodø, Norway, a
stark change for now a real stage approximately sixty feet by thirty feet and fifty to
one hundred lights available, plus many extra and willing hands too. (SR)*

ELEVEN: Character and Motivation

JR. You wrote three things on the napkins in the nightclub.
RD. I wrote that Wittgenstein was an old Viennese romantic rhetorical sui-
     cide merchant.
JR. He wasn't romantic at all.
RD. He was insanely romantic, all that solitude, huts and mountains; and it
     is all very much in the Romantic spirit to reject scientific rationality in
     the way he eventually does.
JH. He loved Mozart, and talks of Beethoven's great heart.
RD. All that young Werther stuff. You were meant to be so passionate about
     life that you topped yourself because life was never going to match up,

or something. The impression I get is that suicide was a particular kind of young man's fin de siècle sort of tradition or fashion if you like. Everybody was doing it and if you didn't you were shown up as spineless and compromising. You didn't put your money where your mouth was.

JR. There's nothing romantic about depression, suicide and alcoholism

RD. Wittgenstein didn't drink.

JH. But that attitude to suicide can be born out of romanticism. All that can be fuelled by Romanticism.

RD. We know there's nothing Romantic about suicide. But that's us, now. It's a different time, we blame governments not life.

JR. I don't think Wittgenstein ever voted in elections.

RD. Besides, you can probably in certain circumstances be persuaded by a scientific rationality to commit suicide – the arguments for euthanasia and so on.

JH. The Romantics provided crucial rhetoric for the French Revolution. It is difficult to see how one could get very much more political.

RD. But in terms of the kinds of cultural messages you're getting at a certain time in your life – two of his brothers committed suicide, I believe – all sorts of things can have all sorts of meanings that are quite absurd from another perspective, i.e. "don't top yourself, try and survive". But Wittgenstein I'm sure was part of a certain tradition of suicide as the ultimate snub at the failure of life in relation to one's aesthetic demand on it, rather than anything social or political or whatever where you really shouldn't commit suicide because you might, one day, be needed by others in a vital cause. Turing was from another pathology. He probably was suicidal. For Wittgenstein suicide was a dramatic flirtation with the idea that life, as one confronted it, intelligently, with all the passion one could bring to bear, was inadequate to one's subjective valuing of it, one's hope of it. With Turing it was different. I'm sure he really was a depressively ill, oppressed, publicly ambushed and lonely individual, all that sort of stuff; having a gifted, abstract kind of intellect into which he escaped; so that the social norms, the moral milieu in which he found himself could no longer eat him up. Wittgenstein was happy to be eaten up by a certain inherited notion that suicide was heroic response. For Turing suicide was surrender not defiance, defeat not triumph. We could have a play here about conflicting notions of suicide.

JH. But in the end the way Turing chose to kill himself was intensely Romantic. You know, the poisoned apple. That's extraordinary.

RD. The story was that he was very impressed as a child by Snow White and the Seven Dwarfs, the Walt Disney cartoon.

JR. He saw it as an adult. It was a pantomime he'd seen. Not the cartoon. And he wasn't that young. He was about 21 or something.

JH. He was an undergraduate.

JR. He used to wander about Cambridge reciting a line from the story "See the poison, take the apple, dip it in, see the poison sink in." Or something.

RD. "And what were Wittgenstein's last words. "It's been a wonderful life." Or something. Can you imagine Turing saying that?

September 1992: First Notes

The script was in draft form, though it had benefited from a rehearsed reading some months before. There was a clear delineation of scenes. The understanding of both Wittgenstein's and Turing dilemma was acute and there were specific instructions as to what music should score the play. Were we being asked to present an illustrated lecture? And if so, isn't this narrow focus missing the point? Whatever that might be?

We talked to the playwrights. We said... "We want Turing's mother to be a character rather than just reported. We want to stop Bertrand Russell narrating what went on, and stick him into the action." The playwrights said...

"You must do whatever you want with it. That's the point."

WITTGENSTEIN. We must see connections that we did not discover before, see what is gripping, beautiful and so on.

Beyond All Certainty: Scene IV

Postscript, following performances in Stockholm and Sundsvall, April, 1994

You could say that in the beginning when the performer and the text are brought together "This is nothing to do with me". But at the end of that process, which is the performance, you should be able to say "This is me".

This is the statement of an ideal because in performance, as elsewhere, consciousness is discontinuous – and this is true for practical reasons alone. Things go wrong. One is continually in thrall to technical and logistical problems: "Will that work?" "Will that fall down?" "Oh no, I've forgotten the candles!" "I've completely ruined those lines." But when the performances is working, then it is singing, a chord begins striking between all the elements of the theater, the performances both of audience and actors. A certain state of grace has been permitted. For the actor it is an experience of the total habitation of the role which is a synthesis of the self of the actor and the character in the text: "That I is now this I".

The process of learning and change should nevertheless continue. Each preceding performance informs the present. When that stops happening, then it is moribund; you are dead as an actor; or better, for your duration on the stage, one of the living dead, an automaton more or less persuasively regurgitating alien meanings. It has become "Not I" and the performer and the text should part company, not because they are bad or doing badly, but they are no longer worthy of each other. It is time to say goodbye, the relationship should dissolve and another "I" perhaps brought to the text and so starting the process afresh.

* * *

I cannot with any confidence say that all my preparation before a

performance is any more than laying the ground for a certain kind of
potential – optimizing the chances of something happening, a state of grace
which all the preparation in the world cannot guarantee.

* * *

When doing a play involving historical characters then not to do any research as an actor would for me be a symptom of such uninterest that if I were to know this I would not go to it. I would feel that I had been duped into watching just another egomaniac seeking attention. So there is an ethical, documentary responsibility.

I don't feel this is the case for Mrs Turing and Helene because their role is a narrative and informational one. They are there to tell us about Turing and Wittgenstein and not themselves. This is their purpose and it is really quite instrumental. They began their lives in the play as 'The Narrator'. The two women have been fashioned out of an original, anonymous narrator figure in order to provide some degree of human and social context to the technical and abstract concerns of the two philosophers. The integrity of the performance here is not measured by the quantity of research.

Chapter 16

The Legacy of Turing
– On the Limits of the Calculable

Anders Karlqvist

How much can we discover about pi?

Most of us are familiar with the mathematical symbol π. It is a number expressing the relationship between the circumference of a circle and its diameter. In most practical contexts it would be enough to say that π is 3.14. One might add that this is an approximate value of an irrational number, i.e. a number that cannot be written as a ratio between two integers n and m. It is a number with an infinite number of decimal digits.

This limited knowledge about the exact numerical form of the number π should, however, hardly make us doubt the *existence* of such a number. We can assure ourselves by geometrical means of a given relationship between the circumference of a circle and its diameter, and that the ratio between these two figures is equivalent to a well-defined length that may be reproduced on an axis. We can also actually devise an algorithm with the help of which we can determine π to an arbitrary number of decimal places. It is a mechanical process which we may leave to a computer.

Let us then take as our point of departure the notion that π exists, or to put it a different way, that the statement "the number π exists" is a true statement. Is the statement "the third decimal of π is a 4", true or not? We may not remember it at the moment, but it can easily be checked in a table or with a pocket calculator. This statement proves to be false (the third decimal is a 1). Is the thousandth decimal place a 3? That is not so easy to check, but we know that with the help of a computer we can work out the answer fairly quickly. Even if we choose not to make the calculation, we are secure in the knowledge that it is possible to do so. This theoretical possibility is what makes us accept without hesitation the statement "the thousandth decimal place of π is a 3" as a clearly-defined mathematical statement, which is *either true or false*.

What happens if we change the question to: "is the 10^{100}th decimal of π a 3"? In principle, nothing appears to have changed. The statement is either true or false. We can continue to let the computer churn out decimal after decimal and then check the result. Or can we? The problem is that there is no computer in existence, nor one that could be constructed in the lifetime of our universe that could reach the 10^{100}th decimal place, so it is hidden from us for all time. Nonetheless, most of us would be prepared to accept the statement as either true *or* false, blaming practical circumstances rather than pointing out that mathematics is in itself incomplete.

Now let us go one stage further. "The decimal places of π contain a sequence of 10^{100} consecutive threes". We immediately run up against the insurmountable practical problem described above, and another complication as well. If our theoretical experiment (which can never be carried out in practice) finds 10^{100} consecutive threes, we have clearly demonstrated that the statement is true. But if we fail to discover such a series of threes, we have not, however, shown the statement to be false. There is no *finite* procedure that can verify the falsity of this statement!

Finally, let us test the statement: "the decimal expansion of π contains an infinite sequence of threes". Here we cannot use any algorithm to determine whether this statement is true or false. What, then, do we mean by the terms true and false? Can we formulate meaningful mathematical statements that are neither one nor the other?

Enigma

On June 7th, 1954 Alan Turing was found dead, by his side an apple poisoned with potassium cyanide, with which he had chosen to end his own life. This was a death without farewells. No letters, no actions that warned of what was to happen. Turing's legacy was a modest one, his estate was negligible and his physical remains were cremated and the ashes spread in the memorial gardens at Woking crematorium. No stone was raised to his memory.

The story of Alan Turing, a 42-year-old English mathematician could end there. But prominent researchers may often count on some kind of immortality, an abstract life after this one, as a concept, a unit of measurement or as the name of a mathematical theorem. And this was the case with Turing. Turing's name became associated with a machine, the Universal Turing Machine. But Alan Turing's intellectual legacy proved to be richer than that. In the perspective of 50 years of history, the world of thought he inhabited can fascinate, be understood, and live on in the new life it gives to the intellectual debate of our times.

Turing's own fate was a dramatic one, or to be more precise, it was fatefully linked with a dramatic historical event. His penetrating mind was put to use by the military powers, a fate that he shared with many other scientific and trained mathematicians in the Europe of the Second World War. The British Brains Trust, which had been given the task of deciphering German radio messages, was situated at Bletchley Park. Bletchley was an unremarkable rural English village located in the triangle between London, Oxford and Cambridge. Alan Turing came to Bletchley in the autumn of 1939, and he stayed there for the whole of the war. Turing's efforts were decisive in breaking the German's Enigma code, and therefore probably had a decisive effect on the course of the war.

This historical role that Turing and his colleagues played did not attract any significant amount of attention. That was partly due to the nature of the work, which was surrounded by very strict secrecy. Turing's "secret" life had another, more personal, dimension. His homosexuality limited his social life. Society's view of sexual deviations was repressive, and in Turing's case this kind of lifestyle could easily have been seen as a security risk. His feeling of isolation was well-founded.

Turing's work on the Enigma code was a top priority matter. Encrypted messages had to be decoded while they were still topical, and the codes were constantly changing. This work required more than mathematical acuity. Machines were also needed to solve these problems quickly.

Turing was not a practical man, but he was well acquainted with mechanical designs. At the theoretical level he had earlier encountered problems of a mechanical nature, and the question of the artificial versus the natural. Problems relating to thinking, the brain and machines were central problems, which today would come under the heading of artificial intelligence. Turing's genius was in mathematics, but his revolutionary contribution to the theory of mathematics was in fact a combination of mathematical insight and mechanical ideas in the form of a theoretical machine. The result was presented in his thesis "On Computable Numbers" (published in 1936). This was the context in which the Turing machine was introduced.

The value of Turing's dissertation was evident to leading mathematicians of the time such as John von Neumann and Alonzo Church. Yet at the time his findings were neither widely-known nor very influential. In the orthodox mathematical environment of Cambridge, Turing's link between abstract symbols and mechanical devices was perceived as being "shockingly industrial".

The logical connection of applications with mathematical theory were met with suspicion. Turing often had to defend and argue his standpoints. He was the only pure mathematician in Ludwig Wittgenstein's seminar on the Foundations of Mathematics, held in Cambridge in the spring of 1939. At this point, Wittgenstein had refuted the ideas on mathematical logic he had developed in his Tractatus. He claimed that the work of attempting to deduce the foundations of mathematics from a strictly logical calculation was futile. It is a mistake to believe that mathematics rests on loose sand, and that by applying logic one could clarify the nature or composition of mathematics. Wittgenstein therefore disputed the idea that the internal contradictions and paradoxes discovered in the foundations of mathematics had any relevance. Mathematical arguments are a question of seeing connections, and paradoxes are merely expressions of language-games that have no use.

It was impossible for Turing to accept the question of the internal composition of mathematics was irrelevant, and he gradually gave up arguing with Wittgenstein on that point. The realities of war soon crowded out philosophical speculation on the nature of the language of mathematics. The Germans' coded messages, which with the help of mathematical combinations became combinations of letters sent over the ether, were anything but language-games with no practical application...

The ideal calculating machine

Unlike many other machines, the Turing machine has not become obsolete or been replaced by newer and better designs. It only exists on paper, as an idea and a "gedanken experiment". The machine, which has a simple design, is very powerful, as it can perform *all* kinds of mathematical computations. The contribution of Turing's genius was that he not only stated how this machine would work, but also demonstrated that it is actually capable of carrying out all mathematical computations.

The Turing machine has two parts, a "black box" and an infinitely long paper tape. The box can read and write on the tape, which may be seen as being divided into squares. A 0 or a 1 can be written in each square, or the square may be left blank. In each unit of time, one or more of the following occurs:

- the tape is moved one step to the right
- the tape is moved one step to the left
- the read/write head in the box erases the signs in the read/write position
- the read/write head writes a 0 or a 1 in the square positioned in the read/write position
- the machine stops, i.e. the calculation is completed!

What the machine does at any given moment is determined solely by the internal status of the box at that moment. This status is in its turn decided exclusively by its internal status during the previous unit of time, and by the symbol in the read-in square at that time.

The remarkable thing about this apparatus is that, despite its primitive design, it can do everything that a modern computer can do. The Turing machine is the prototype of the computer. (In practice the computer is, of course, more cleverly designed, to make the computations faster and more user-friendly. Operating systems and various kinds of programming languages are tools for this purpose. But the principles are basically the same, even though no paper tapes are fed through the machine.) The stream of 0s and 1s are the instructions and data that describe a computational task. The machine performs its mechanical work from these instructions, without any external intervention. The result in the form of 0s and 1s is then written on to the tape. If the problem is to calculate whether a certain mathematical statement is true of false, we can imagine that the machine prints a 1 for the answer true, and a 0 for false, and then stops. The machine stopping signifies that the problem has been solved. In other words: calculability is the same as the Turing machine stopping at some point. If it is given a calculation that cannot be solved, the machine will never stop.

As we shall soon see, Turing's ideas have far-reaching implications. The Turing machine gave the idea of mathematical computation an exact and generally-applicable content. With this definition we can also take the important step forward of asking the question whether or not we can acquire knowledge of the physical and biological world by using *computa-*

tions as a tool. The dream of the rational universe is precisely the dream that this tool is a universal one. Perhaps the clearest expression of this view is to be found in the work of Gottfried Wilhelm Leibniz, the German philosopher and mathematician. Leibniz was convinced that in theory all human activity was accessible to mathematical calculations and that every dispute could be resolved with computations. "Gentlemen, let us compute!"

Hilbert's Tenth

At the Congress of Mathematicians in Bologna in 1900 the great mathematician David Hilbert made an exposé of unresolved mathematical problems which he thought would be an important challenge for the mathematicians of the next century, the present century that is soon at an end. In his list of 23 problems there was one, the tenth, that dealt with a classical area in mathematics, so called diophantine equations, equations where the solutions can only have the value of integers.

The problem that Hilbert posed concerned the possibility of finding a procedure, an *algorithm*, which could be used to determine in advance whether or not an arbitrary diophantine equation can be solved, i.e., whether there are *integer* numbers that satisfy the equation.

Hilbert was sure that mathematics was a perfect structure and only the finishing touches remained to be put to it. Even though the naive mechanical picture of the world that prevailed in the 1700s had been substantially changed, there was still a strong belief in the boundless ability of human reason and in the dream of a coherent picture of the world. Newton's physics was the basis for knowledge of the world and mathematics was its most powerful tool. Only a few pieces of the puzzle were missing. That was the spirit of the time, and the great philosophers and mathematicians of that time, Hilbert, Russell and Frege, for example, were steadfast in this belief.

It only remained to show conclusively that mathematics was *consistent*, i.e. free from internal contradictions, and *complete*, i.e., that *every* meaningful mathematical statement could be proved to be either true or false. This required a *formalization* of mathematical arguments, so that every derivation could be expressed as a chain of logical operations. From a series of given primitive concepts and axioms, a mechanical application of the rules of logic will produce every possible mathematical proposition.

Little did Hilbert know, when he fired his younger colleagues with enthusiasm at the Bologna Congress, nor Russell, when he wrote with Whitehead his monumental work "Principia Mathematica" on the formalization of mathematics, that their life dreams could never come true. As soon as he arrived in Cambridge in 1911, the young Wittgenstein addressed the task of correcting Russell and pointing out the shortcomings in his mathematical logic. But it was an eccentric Czech mathematical genius, Kurt Gödel, who was to finally puncture the dream of the perfection of mathematics, with his findings on "Über formal unentscheidbare Sätze der Principia Mathematica und verwandter Systeme I", published in 1931.

Neither would Hilbert experience in his lifetime the surprising resolution of the diophantine equations. In 1970 Yuri Matijasevic, a young Russian mathematician, presented a result which showed that the solvability of the diophantine equations is equivalent to the problem of determining whether or not the Turing machine stops!

As we know, neither was the project of the physicists' perfect picture of the world realized. When the new century was just a few years old, the theory of relativity was introduced, and quantum mechanics forced a review of the foundations of physics. The mechanistic and deterministic world designed by Newton was replaced by, and supplemented with, a world based on probability calculations, and the cost was an unbridgeable gap between an objective reality and our capacity to acquire knowledge about that reality. Although Einstein held an unshakable conviction that "God does not throw dice" with physical reality, modern physics has another tale to tell. The increasingly refined models of the physicists have failed to shine a light on the obscurities of the world. What is worse: the unlimited capacity of reason proved to be a chimera, even when confined to its own specialist area of mathematics.

Hilbert's tenth, like Beethoven's tenth, never became reality.

Liars, barbers and the theory of numbers

As a foreign element in human reason and thinking, paradox has always caused amusement and concern. The paradox is a cul-de-sac of thinking and reasoning. It cannot move forward. We have reached an impossible combination of conclusions and must take a step back and review our circumstances.

The most classic of all paradoxes is the one attributed to the Cretan Epimenides, who said: "all Cretans are liars". Spoken by a Cretan himself, this statement has the following logical form:

Paradox I – "this statement is untrue"

Is the above statement true or not?

Another well-known paradox is about the barber. In a town there is a barber who shaves everyone except the people who shave themselves. The paradox occurs when on the basis of this statement one must decide whether or not the barber is in the group who shave themselves. The following is a version of this paradox expressed in mathematical terms:

Paradox II – "the set of all sets that are not elements in themselves"

Is this set an element in itself or not?

A third paradox, which is usually referred to as Berry's paradox, and which contains a trace of information theory, is as follows:

Paradox III – "the smallest integer which requires more words to express than those in this sentence."

Does this sentence specify such an integer or not?

These paradoxes were seen as more than amusng subtleties; they have vexed both mathematicians and philosophers. These paradoxes indicate profound difficulties in logic and in mathematics itself. Bertrand Russell was one of the first people who took this seriously. He drew attention to, and published, Berry's paradox in 1908. But Russell's name was connected mainly with Paradox II – the barber paradox. Russell realized that this paradox demonstrated that informal arguments in mathematics could lead to contradictions. The way out of this problem was to formalize the basics of mathematics, beginning with the theory of sets, so that this kind of contradiction could never occur. The occurrence of paradoxes was like having weeds in a garden, they were the result of carelessness and neglect. Principia Mathematica was an heroic attempt to clear the garden of mathematics of weeds.

It soon became clear that these paradoxes were not so easy to weed out: the useful plants of mathematics disappeared as well. Berry's paradox was put to use to demonstrate the inherent randomness of mathematics, and Epimenides' paradox of the liar plays a decisive part in Gödel's findings, because it leads to an unbridgeable gulf between what is true and what can be proved. Gödel utilized this paradox in a form which says "this statement cannot be proved" to demonstrate that in every formal system there are true statements that cannot be proved.

Wittgenstein held a radically different view of this matter. There were no mathematical truths to discover. Proof did not mean that one establishes that a conclusion is true, it means that one must establish the meaning of certain symbols. To deny that $2 + 2 = 4$ is to ignore the meaning of the symbols involved, not to deny a fact! In this perspective, paradoxes and contradictions were uninteresting. Turing, who was confronted with these opinions at Wittgenstein's lectures, was not convinced. Mathematics was incontrovertible, and contradictions were unacceptable, because they may cause errors when mathematics is applied. In this argument, Turing claimed that mathematical experiments could be carried out in the same spirit as experiments in physics. This comment has an almost prophetic ring to it in anticipating the computer-aided mathematical activities of today. However, for Wittgenstein the analogy between physics and mathematics was misleading and a cause of confusion. Mathematics is a technique, a way of perceiving connections, of seeing aspects. There is no mathematical paradise (Hilbert's description of how Cantor introduced infinity into the axioms of mathematics), and Wittgenstein saw his task as being to demonstrate that.

Gödel's death blow

A great deal of effort had gone into developing a formalized mathematics to show that it was possible to reproduce completely and consistently all possible mathematical results. When Gödel demonstrated that the most central of mathematics' own systems, arithmetic, was not free from these deficiencies, there was concern and despondency among mathematicians and philosophers. However, the practical consequences of these results hardly appeared to be particularly dramatic (just as Wittgenstein had said). The craft of mathematics and its applications could still be carried on; "business was as usual". It is relevant to mention here that Gödel's proof was complicated and hard to understand. The consequences did after all appear to be limited to the peculiar pathological corners of mathematics.

A few years after Gödel's propositions had been published, Alan Turing introduced a new approach to these findings. Turing was able to link Gödel's arguments to the question of computability, and thus to the possibility of running programmes on a computer – the Turing Machine! Today, there are many paths leading to Gödel's conclusions (and their generalizations) that are easier and more natural to follow than the original proof. With all these new perspectives that have opened up, mathematical "imperfections" have also become more tangible and immediate. Mathematical theories appear to be an increasingly threadbare patchwork in the total mathematical-logical landscape.

Gödel's original proof contains a number of brilliant ideas, the contents of which are possible to grasp without having to master the entire mathematical–technical machinery. The core of the proof lies in constructing a statement within the mathematical system (in this case, the theory of numbers, arithmetic), which is self-referencing and contradictory in the same way as Epimenides' paradox. In Gödel's version this statement became G = "this statement cannot be proved". If G can be proved, then the system (arithmetic) is inconsistent, i.e. it contains logical contradictions. If, on the other hand, G cannot be proved, we have a true proposition, G, that cannot be proved, i.e. the system is flawed.

The trick in creating this self-reference is to code the mathematical statements themselves as numbers. Every theory of numbers statement thus corresponds to a unique "Gödel number". A great deal of ingenuity is, in fact, needed here to get this right.

The special characteristics of primary numbers are used to secure a unique correspondence between numbers and mathematical propositions. Using this technique, it is possible to formulate the theory of numbers principles containing Gödel's numbers, and thus perceive these propositions as propositions that are in themselves about theory of numbers propositions!

Self-referencing systems obviously have a vital ability to break out of the framework of rational linear thinking. If we look back to the prototype paradoxes formulated in the previous section, we find that all three blunt our rationality with a self-referencing statement. This kind of self-reference does not need to be as explicit and condensed as in these paradoxes. It may also be the result of the connection between two or more simple (and unopposed) statements such as:

1. "The following sentence is true"
2. "The previous sentence is untrue"

The paradox takes on a global quality, for which we find geometrical expressions in Maurits Cornelis Escher's pictures and Oscar Reutersvärd's impossible figures.

One may speculate about whether or not self-reference is an important feature of complicated systems in nature, and if so, whether computability has a limited scope in acquiring knowledge about such systems. Life itself offers many examples, from the genetic code to human consciousness. Are there therefore absolute limitations to understanding the world in rational scientific terms? Is it possible to express human characteristics such as judgement and intuition in computable forms? Is artificial intelligence in this strong form at all possible, or is there a Gödelian limit to thinking about thinking? Wittgenstein went further in his conclusions when he claimed that the limitations of science were to be found in language. Everything that can be said can be said clearly, and of that of which one cannot speak, one must remain silent, and this silence contains everything that is important in life.

Turing machines that sometimes stop

We expect that a computer which is fed a programme will complete its calculations and stop. The fact that the calculation stops is thus a signal from the machine that "it has finished". Turing showed that one cannot determine in advance whether an arbitrary programme will ever stop or not. There is no mechanical procedure or algorithm which will settle this question. Gödel's results on the imperfections of mathematics follow as a direct consequence of this. Why? Well, if this wasn't so, we could feed computers with sets of axioms and let the computer work through all conceivable proofs. Had there been an algorithm to show whether or not a programme will stop, we could know whether a given statement was true or not.

Turing's results give us a more transparent picture of the problem of the incompleteness of mathematics. We may refer to an information theory syllogism that ultimately states that the mathematical theories cannot be richer in information than the axioms from which they are derived.

Alan Turing's universal calculating machine allowed the concepts of calculation, algorithm and programme to be given a precise content. The concepts agree with what we today call computer software: they are executed mechanically in a sequence according to given instructions, and without external interference.

One point is that all variations of hardware and programming languages may be traced back to the primitive design of the Turing machine, with its zeros and ones on a paper ribbon. It is therefore sufficient to refer to the Turing machine. It is representative of all computers and all computations.

With Turing's help it is possible to further Gödel's idea about coding. Turing showed that the formal mathematical system has its counterpart in computer software:

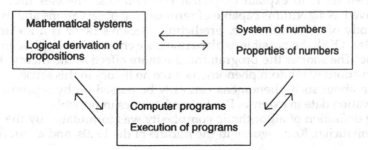

Although the results of Gödel and Turing uncover weaknesses in the structure of mathematics, they give no indication as to how frequently these problems occur. But Gödel realized that the damage was irreparable. A mathematical statement which is true but cannot be proved may be included in the system as yet another axiom. But this new extended system may be subjected to a new "Gödelisation" and generate an infinite number of new propositions which cannot be proved. There is no finite system of axioms that can generate all mathematical truths.

Randomness and complexity

Zeros and ones may be regarded as the basic building blocks of mathematical calculations. Every natural number may be expressed in binary form, i.e., in a system of numbers made up of only zeros and ones. Every logical operation may also be thus represented. In the hardware this corresponds to the gates in the computer chips being closed or open for the flow of data to pass.

From this starting point, it is useful to describe a computer programme in terms of the number of building-blocks – "bits" – that are needed. The length of such a sequence of zeros and ones is a measurement of how complicated the programme is. This technique may be used to formulate the complexity of a number X, as the length of the (shortest) computer programme required to reproduce that number. If this programme is shorter than the number itself, then the degree of complexity is low. If the number has a simple structure (for example consisting only of n ones), a very short programme is needed (write the number one n times). We see that there are numbers, for example the number we discussed at the beginning of this article, which seemed to be far more complicated, yet which are non-complex. The number π can be computed to an arbitrary number of decimal places with a computer algorithm of a limited length.

It is evident that the ultimate conclusion is that there is no structure at all. If so, the only possibility is for the programme to write out the number digit by digit, a procedure which requires a programme of at least the same length as the number itself. The information contained in the number cannot be compressed into a shorter form. The number is *algorithmically complex*. This is also a criteria of *randomness*.

Algorithmic complexity captures an idea which has a wide general application, and which can also be applied to the science itself. The task of scientific theories is to explain empirical observations. Theories may thus be perceived as algorithms capable of reproducing observations and extending this body of observation, i.e. predicting. Occam's razor is a metaphor for this idea. Of all the possible explanations, we choose the simplest and shortest one. The shorter the programme the more effective the theory. $E = mc^2$! Observations of random phenomena have no theory in this sense, and information about such phenomena can only be passed on by reproducing the observation data in extenso. Prediction becomes impossible.

The definition of algorithmic complexity was formulated by the Russian mathematician, Kolmogorov in the middle of the 1960s, and about the same time and independently, by Gregory Chaitin, a young student at New York City University. In his later work at the IBM research laboratories, Chaitin used these ideas for his quite astounding development of Gödel's results. Like Gödel, Chaitin used a self-referring paradox. Barry's paradox, which is described above, was transformed into a computer programme with the following form: "Find a number that can be shown to have a complexity greater than the complexity of this programme." The paradox lies in the programme thus being assumed to find a number that it can be proved to be incapable of finding. The conclusion from this contradiction is that no programme can produce a number more complicated than itself. Although we know that almost all numbers are random, we cannot prove that this fact applies to a given number!

Did God throw dice with mathematics?

In following historical developments from Gödel's penetrating analysis of the limitations of arithmetic, through Turing's machine and his argument on programmes and algorithms, to the "real" Turing machines of the present day, which can be programmed and run, we also follow a development from a platonic mathematical world of ideas to a world where it appears to be possible to approach mathematics, despite what Wittgenstein maintained in his debate with Turing, as an experimental science. The computer is an instrument with which to research the theoretical world of mathematics in the same way as the microscope and the telescope have served the science of physics. Chaitin has demonstrated the way information theory interpretations of Gödel's results have a natural parallel in the relationship of information theory to physics, to the worlds of Shannon and Boltzmann. Does mathematics need its own thermodynamic epistemology?

Let us return for a moment to the theory of numbers. Chaitin produced a diophantine equation which contained a parameter K and seventeen thousand variables! It is obvious that such equations cannot be produced by hand. This is really a question of CAD/CAM standing for Computer Aided Diophantine equations/Computer Aided Mathematics! Chaitin designed this special single parametric family of equations purely for their remarkable characteristics.

The question that was put was whether or not such an equation for a given value of the parameter K has a finite or infinite number of solutions. The rather surprising answer is: perhaps. The answer cannot be deduced from the mathematical axiom. It is itself an irreducible mathematical statement. Thus we must add to it as a new axiom to determine the solvability of the equation (which is of course is no deduction at all). Unfortunately it is not enough to use the solutions for some values of the parameter K to determine the solvability of other values of K. If the solutions to the first 100 equations are given, the solution for K = 101 is still not determined.

If we let ω = a number where the decimal place K is 1, if the corresponding equation where the parameter K has an infinite number of solutions and zero otherwise, then we have a number ω without any structure at all. ω is random. It cannot be compressed.

A paraphrase of Einstein's famous dictum that God does not play dice with physics is close to hand. It was Einstein's persistent suspicion of quantum mechanics that prompted this statement. But we may, of course, agree with Chaitin that God appears not only to have played dice with physics but also with mathematics itself! Before we leave experimental mathematics and Chaitin with his 7000-headed equation, which he had a computer produce (in 1987), we return once again to Turing. The fate of Hilbert's tenth was of course sealed forever. This was perfectly clear when the solvability of diophantine equations proved to be closely related to the problem of whether Turing's machine stops or not. As much as ten years before Chaitin designed his equation for ω, the number had been introduced as a probable number.

ω is the probability that a given Turing machine stops after a finite number of steps, when it is given an arbitrary programme. This was the number that Chaitin coded as a signature of the solvability of diophantine equations.

The simple and the vague

Our logical capacity to argue does not give us access to more than a small part of the world around us. Mathematics itself appears to resist exhaustive penetration with logical methods. Leibniz's thoughts about God as a mathematician who can compute everything is an expression of an ideal that is remote from the world of science as we now see it.

"True or false" are blunt criteria for scientific understanding. If we go no further than mathematics, we may note that very few of all the possible mathematical propositions and true statements mean anything and give us understanding. The essential, i.e., the information-carrying and meaningful, is not revealed with a truth drug. We need to summon all our powers, both intuitive and ascetic. Paul Dirac, one of the creators of quantum mechanics, said that scientific choice was governed by "a keen sense of beauty". Simplicity, the moral of Occam's Razor, has an ascetically convincing power. The economy of thought, the precision of expression and the absence of any need for sweeping gestures are the essential components of all science and art.

In the transfer of mathematical knowledge, the rigorous and precise are often a burden. A vague form of communication may be an advantage in making the essence of an idea comprehensible. The details can be filled in later. This quality of human thinking is difficult to capture in the artificial intelligence that the computer represents. The mind's ability to go straight to the core, to intuitively understand the point of an argument before one has, with the help of the laws of logic, established it is correct; here is a deeper idea about understanding. Does this make it unattainable through algorithm? Can we thus see the limits to the application of computers and artificial intelligence?

The machine-like and the intuitive

The computer has been an important tool in exposing shortcomings in the nature of human thinking. This does not mean that the computer has won any decisive victories over the brain. Being able to count fast and accurately is hardly more than a pyrrhic victory when there is a risk that the foundations, i.e., the algorithmic approach, will crumble. Can we compare human consciousness with a Turing machine? Turing himself was convinced that this was fruitful. The computer can, in theory, carry out any and all kinds of mental process. This conviction, at least as a working hypothesis, was the starting point for what became something of a movement. The foundation was laid in the mid-50s. John McCarthy of Dartmouth College, USA, was a leading figure. He became known as the father of artificial intelligence. AI soon became a well-known concept.

The meaning of the term artificial intelligence, AI, may vary. The mechanical attitude is that man is a machine and the cognitive condition of the brain is in functional terms identical to those in a machine. In other words, neurones are to be seen a biological chips. This view is usually called "Strong" AI. "Weak" AI recognizes no a priori functional similarities between the brain and the computer, but maintains that cognitive processes may be simulated by a computer (in the same way as an aircraft simulates the flight of a bird, but applies different mechanical principles).

This is illustrated by Turing's own famous thought experiment. Can a computer be made intelligent in the sense that a person putting questions to "someone" cannot decide from the answers whether he is communicating with a human or a machine? Turing was convinced that the computer could be made intelligent in this imitative sense. One gets the immediate impression that Turing thought that computers were like humans, rather than humans being like machines.

The humanistic view stands in contrast to these positions. Man has a soul. Something that is not within the reach of a machine. This soul is what prevents us actually producing an artificial intelligence programme. We have already been able to state that logical systems and algorithms place a definite limit on both man's and the machine's ability to acquire knowledge by computation and mathematical calculations. Is there then a different cognitive dimension, a dimension accessible to the human brain but not to the machine? Is this what we call a soul or consciousness, and what is characterized by judgement, intuition etc?

Chess computers are beginning to reach a level where they are on a par with the very best human players. But does this allow us to conclude that computers are playing intelligently? There is a clear difference between the problems that are difficult for computers and difficult for people. The human mind can penetrate certain kinds of problem and make decisions based on a feeling for problems. Reason appears to function in a non-algorithmic way, and use information that is global, i.e. knowledge of the whole that cannot be divided into local information about the parts. Inspiration is often a question of capturing at one time a totality. This observation was made as much as 200 years ago by a person with some experience of creativity: Wolfgang Amadeus Mozart.

At a chess competition for computers held some years ago, one computer was not particularly successful. In fact it lost all its games. In other words, it was not particularly "artificially" intelligent. But it had one particular "talent", namely the ability to give up. It gave up on lost games long before other computers "realized" that the game was lost. This generated widespread admiration.

Even though the chess computer's simple application of judgement in giving up lost games hardly indicates any radically different type of artificial intelligence (a cleverly programmed decision rule should suffice), the example demonstrates precisely how it is possible to apply a decision rule at a different level in the game than the level which deals with moving the pieces. Changing levels, going from playing the game to examining the rules of the game, is to go from analyzing differences in perceptions to questioning the category of concepts with the help of which these perceptions are articulated. This is typical of genuine human discourse. Allan Janik has shown "essentially contested concepts and the part they play in human life" (Cordelia's Silence, Carlsson Bokförlag 1991).

It is hardly likely that considerations of this kind can be wholly captured in algorithmic rules. To determine whether or not an algorithm is applicable requires insight, and not yet another algorithm. A Gödelian argument leads inevitably to the conclusion that human consciousness is not capable of formalizing its mathematical intuition. If it had managed to formulate in algorithms any of this intuition, it is this very knowledge that provides new intuitive insights. It is possible that a theory-proving machine can exist, which is the same as mathematical intuition, but if so, it cannot be proved to have this capability!

A bowl of cold porridge

Alan Turing said that the brain was more like a bowl of cold porridge than anything else. That this "lump of porridge" produces reason and intelligence is, and may always be, a great miracle. Of course we can understand something of how this "porridge" is composed with its more than 10^{11} neurones and electrical impulses and we can assume some understanding of the way this complex system of signals generates thoughts and initiates action in the form of muscular movements. However, from the evolutionary viewpoint the importance of consciousness is shrouded in mystery. Is there anything that gives human consciousness a selective advantage or is there any other selection principle from which consciousness quite simply occurs as a side effect or an artefact?

These questions obviously bring us closer to fundamental existential problems which we cannot hope to formulate in a meaningful way, even less resolve. We are prevented by the inherent limitations of thought. The computer, with its sophisticated and highly efficient capacity for calculation, will take us closer to the border country of thinking, but never through it. We have seen the mirror image of these limits in arithmetic. The theory of numbers cannot answer all the true statements about itself. Logic does not permit this. Self-referring systems cannot be broken down into finite calculable steps.

We cannot think about thinking with anything other than our own thoughts. We cannot study our brain with anything other than our own brain, even if our instruments and calculating machines can sharpen our sight and speed up our computations. We are therefore doomed to incompleteness. We must continue to live with our great mystery: to remain a mystery to ourselves.

Chapter 17
"Nothing is Hidden"
Georg Henrik von Wright

Much may be gained from reference to "the legacy of Turing" and to a line of tradition that starts with Turing and Gödel's work and that may be traced back to earlier traditions in logic and mathematics. Wittgenstein is far more difficult to place. His later thinking (after "*Tractatus*") has no obvious predecessor in philosophical tradition. Although Wittgenstein had a strong influence on present-day philosophy, one can hardly say that he "formed a school" or "left a legacy" which others have managed to cultivate.

Nonetheless, Wittgenstein plays an important part in connection with "the legacy of Turing", and it is a multi-faceted part. One facet which I shall attempt to discuss in more detail here could be summarized as follows: Wittgenstein is a critic who wanted to reduce to its proper proportions the consequences of some of the more sensational ideas and findings in the science of logic and mathematics. He wanted to calm the storms in thinking that these advances had precipitated.

Put very simply (and therefore easily misleadingly), the results may be described as the discovery of some inherent imperfections in formalized systems of logic and mathematics. Or to simplify it slightly more: the discovery of theoretical limitations in human thinking. Thus in all systems with a sufficiently elaborated structure there are propositions that are "unverifiable", i.e. it is impossible to establish within the system whether they can be proved or not. Neither can it be shown of all such systems, without looking for proof beyond the system's own framework, that they do not contain latent contradictions.

It is evident that results of the kind indicated are important and may have far-reaching consequences. But why must they be considered so sensational, or even subversive? To understand this we must set the discoveries of Turing and his "predecessor" Gödel against the background of certain generally accepted expectations or deeply rooted preconceptions about the capacity and nature of human thinking. These preconceptions – which are "philosophical" rather than "scientific" in nature – are part of the spiritual structure, which I shall simplify here to "the classical world picture of European science".

In mathematics, this picture of the world had been so to speak canonized in the "programme" of the great mathematician Hilbert, which was presented in a shortened form in a lecture at an international congress of mathematicians at the very threshold of our century. It was a tenet of Hilbert's that there is no *ignorabimus* in mathematics, no questions whose answers are in theory inaccessible to thought. It was this idea, among others, which, just over three decades later, was overturned by Gödel and Turing.

Hilbert's "comprehensive" conception of mathematics ultimately derives from Leibniz's vision of a "calculus ratiocinator" formalized in a "characteristica universalis". Leibniz's part in the design of the classical picture of science is important in other respects. The ideal science *par préférence* of this picture was physics. We may consider its fundamental idea to be that all events are strictly governed by laws. Everything that happens has a cause which explains why it must occur. The deterministic character of the picture of the world presented by the natural sciences derives from the idea that calculating reason is able to resolve all mathematical problems.

When matters are seen in this perspective it becomes interesting to observe that only a decade or so before the emergence of Gödel and Turing breakthroughs in quantum physics had dealt a serious blow to the deterministic world picture of physics. As Gödel's theorem of incompleteness places a limit on computability, Heisenberg's uncertainty relation limits measurability, which is the ultimate prerequisite of causal prognostication. The discoveries of Heisenberg and others led to a "foundation-crisis" in physics which may be seen as a parallel to the situation in logic and mathematics after Gödel. The truth of all mathematical theories cannot be decided, and the position and velocity of all micro-particles cannot be determined. So what? Can we not say: "if anyone has been so stupid as to believe in the completeness of the scientific conception of the world in the above-mentioned respects, then he must accept that he is in error. The insights which have destroyed his beliefs are some of the greatest scientific advances of this century. Let us rejoice! There is certainly no reason to regard them as disasters."

With this reasoning, things are seen from within the scientific disciplines, in an "intra-science" perspective. There is nothing wrong with that. But one can also adopt what I would like to call a "extra-science" view. One then sees science as a "conception of the world" with a "paradigmatic" influence on thinking about, among other things, man and his societies.

Here one is reminded of the story – myth or reality – of the Greek Hippasus from Metapontum. He realized that the diagonal and the side of a square had no lowest common denominator. The story goes that this threw him into such despair that he lost his reason, took his life, or both. Why should he have reacted in this way, when in fact he had made a fantastic discovery, pushed ajar the door to the paradise of irrational numbers? It is better to walk through that door than slam it shut in terror!

However, the idea of commensurability, the comparability of all quantities by virtue of a common unit, was a foundation stone of Greek thinking, and one can imagine that when this stone was removed the psychological effect was dramatic. So why not expect the same effect when Gödel proved that not all thinking can be formalized in systems that are demonstrably free of contradiction, or that the truth of all mathematical statements cannot be determined – or when physicists discovered theoretical limits to measurability and predictability? It is evident that the psychological effects of such discoveries on the "general way of thinking" may also be considerable and confusing. One loses faith in something one would have preferred to hold fast to. But rather than throw oneself off a cliff in despair, one should attempt a sober appraisal of what has really happened, both in an "intra-science" and a "extra-science" perspective. One could say that this was the sort of thing that Wittgenstein wanted to do.

We get an "intra-science" perspective of Gödel's and Turing's discoveries when we view them in the light of the later developments that began during and after the Second World War and in which the computer played a decisive part, not only as a theoretical object (the "Turing machine") but also as a practical tool for research. In his article, Professor Karlqvist relates this development to the advances in mathematical and physical science that became popularly known as Chaos research. Seen in an extra-science perspective they may be said to have made a further contribution to the undermining of traditional faith in deterministic causality and predictability. Chaos has gained a foothold in our picture of the world – something that, inter alia, colours our conceptions of our ability to plan and control the path of humanity towards the future. But I shall not reflect any further on this matter. Instead, I shall briefly return to the Gödel–Turing–Wittgenstein constellation.

I dare say that both Gödel and Turing may be criticized for having dramatized the extra-science perspective of their results in a possibly misleading way. In Gödel's case the existence of unverifiable but true mathematical propositions – a doubtful formulation in itself – was the starting point of a platonized metaphysics, which sees quantities and numbers as realities in a world of eternal truths, which we can look into but which remains beyond our ability to understand. This of course is not an entirely accurate, and even less an exhaustive description of Gödel's position. But I cannot but believe that Gödel's mathematical realism is the not-so-great philosophy of a great mathematician. Wittgenstein's criticism of it – and of Hilbert's programme – is an attempt to reduce the consequences of Gödel's incompleteness proofs to their proper "intra-mathematical" dimension.

Turing fell victim to another philosophical temptation. In a famous essay from the end of his short life, he took his insights into the nature and limits of computability as the starting point for speculations on consciousness (the "psychic"). The question of whether or not the brain operates like a computer when we make calculations, or remember things in the past, or structure the impressions of our senses, is entirely significant. This is an "intra-science" issue and it does not lose its legitimacy because an earlier enthusiasm for the computer analogy appears to have faded in the light of more recent discoveries about networks in the brain and their integrative ways of operating. But the occurrence of conscious reactions in a living being is not determined on the basis of what happens in his brain, but on the basis of verbal and other macroscopic behaviour in his "Lebenswelt". The belief that the "mystery of consciousness" may be resolved through, for example, AI research, is a conceptual confusion. The very idea of a "mystery" is fuelled by false analogies, as is the idea of an out-of-body "soul" as some kind of ethereal being, inaccessible to an outside observer. One may answer all this with an oft-quoted saying of Wittgenstein's: "nothing is hidden". The difficulty is to see what lies, openly, before our very eyes.

Chapter 18

Turing and Wittgenstein
– Two Perceptions of Reality
Dag Prawitz

The philosophical legacy of Turing

If I were to summarize in a few words the contribution Turing made to philosophy I would emphasize the following three themes:

(1) Turing's definition of an abstract general computer, i.e. what we now call a *Turing machine,*
(2) *Turing's thesis* that everything which is computable can be computed by a Turing machine, and
(3) Turing's ideas about an artificial intelligence and its criterion, summarized in what is commonly called the *Turing test.*

According to this summary the philosophical legacy Turing left contains three main assets: the *Turing machine,* the *Turing thesis* and the *Turing test.* In the following I shall make some brief remarks on the three components of this legacy.

The *Turing machine*

The first part of the legacy, the Turing machine, is Turing's main, but by no means only, contribution to logic. I use the word "calculator" here to mean someone who can carry out mathematical computations, i.e. who by following instructions given in advance can work out the value of certain functions for given arguments, all expressed in a given notation. There are many kinds of calculator: human calculators, mechanical calculating machines that operate with cogs and wheels, and various kinds of electronic computer. They all look very different. What is it they have in common?

The answer to that question must be abstract, stated in terms of what is normally called software. From the concrete viewpoint, seen as hardware, these different kinds of calculator hardly have anything at all in common. But they can all do the same things. Can we then with the assistance of simple, abstract operations, describe a calculator, or a family of calculators, which in terms of functional ability correspond to all known concrete calculators, i.e., human calculators, mechanical calculating machines, computers or what have you? What Turing succeeded in doing was to give such a description, and that is no small feat. What we now call Turing machines are the solution to the above problem.

The so-called universal Turing machine is capable of imitating any Turing machine as soon as it is fed with a code number for that machine. Turing even designed a single, abstract machine which can match all known calculators. This also opened up the possibility of self-reference of the kind Gödel had investigated – the universal Turing machine can also be fed the code that denotes the machine itself – and it thus became possible to prove impossibility results of the Gödelerian type.

Turing's thesis

The Turing machine constitutes a body of work that is on the border line between logic and mathematics. By contrast, the other legacy, Turing's thesis, is a contribution of a logical-philosophical character. It is a question of a *philosophical* thesis and not a mathematical result. The thesis is that the intuitive concept of computability and the concept of decidability can be defined, or even better, explicated, with the help of Turing machines. The definition says that something is computable or decidable if, and only if, it can be computed or decided by a Turing machine. Turing argues – apparently convincingly – that this explication or definition corresponds to our intuitive concepts of computability and decidability. Philosophers have made great efforts to attempt to clarify central concepts in different areas, including concepts that are more or less distant relatives to computable and decidable, such as provable, definable, measurable and knowable, and have said a great deal about such concepts. But for none of them have we an explication that even comes close to Turing's in terms of precision, simplicity, fruitfulness and inherent plausibility.

The *Turing test*

The third part of the legacy, the Turing test, is in the nature of a provocative, philosophical speculation. Turing suggested a criterion for establishing whether or not an artificial "calculator", a computer, possessed intelligence. The criterion was that the responses produced by the computer would be so like the responses from a human intelligence as to be indistinguishable from them; a person communicating in writing with the computer, which it is assumed can produce a written text, would not be able to decide whether he was dealing with a person or a machine. In Turing's view, if the function was identical, if the machine was taken for a person in the blind test he described, then there was no reason not to ascribe to the artificial intelligence human attributes such as consciousness.

This idea of Turing's has been disputed by many philosophers and in many quarters has been virtually mocked, while others have welcomed it with enthusiasm. It is a contribution which stimulates an important debate, and this debate is far from finished. Like many other people, I feel uneasy about being compared to a machine, but embarrassingly enough I have very little to offer to show what the difference in fact is. And I would like to say that no one has actually managed entirely successfully to take up the gauntlet Turing threw down. I myself am convinced that Turing's ideas about artificial intelligence are entirely erroneous, but to argue in favor of this conviction is in my view far more difficult than many of Turing's critics realize.

There are at least two different paths to take if you want to try to refute Turing. One is to attempt to show that humans have abilities which are in theory impossible to get a machine to carry out. In his essay, *The Legacy of Turing*, Anders Karlqvist touches on such an argument, and I believe it would be fruitful to go further in this direction. A second possibility is to maintain that even if a machine could imitate man's external behavior with total success, there would still be a crucial difference between man and machine. Man's mental actions have both an external and an internal aspect. They are associated with certain types of experience. To experience a certain color, for example, involves more than being able to identify that color in a discrimination test. We are also conscious of it in a certain way, a way that is not correlated to any specific external behavior. Agreement in terms of external behavior between man and machine is therefore not necessarily decisive in attributing consciousness to man. I believe that this kind of argument also has some merit. But it is clear that there is a great deal in this entire area that we neither know nor understand.

I shall not dwell longer here on the legacy of Turing, so well described by Anders Karlqvist in his essay, but will instead say something about the meeting between Turing and Wittgenstein.

The meeting between Turing and Wittgenstein

The meetings that took place between Turing and Wittgenstein in the course of the latter's seminars in Cambridge must have been dramatic. There are clear indications to that effect in the notes from these seminars, which Cora Diamond edited in *Wittgenstein's Lectures*. I notice with interest that Professor von Wright, who also attended these seminars, willingly confirms this impression. The drama of these meetings is also unmistakably present in the play *Beyond all Certainty*.

It is clear, I think, that Wittgenstein wants to play down the importance of Gödel's and Turing's contributions. From Wittgenstein's perspective, the matter may be described in the words used by Professor von Wright, that Wittgenstein wanted to reduce Gödel and Turing's contributions to what he considers to be their proper proportions. This tendency is clearly expressed in what Wittgenstein says about contradictions. If the existence of contradictions in mathematics is not a question of any great importance or interest, as Wittgenstein so emphatically maintains, much of what logic has done and is doing, rather falls flat on its face. The aggressive tension in the encounter between Turing and Wittgenstein is unmistakable.

Even the impartial observer cannot avoid becoming involved in the controversy. Let me begin my comments with a comparison with another meeting, also portrayed in *Beyond all Certainty*, the meeting between Turing and

Churchill. The episode in the play where Churchill becomes severely irritated by what Turing is saying about machines and sonnets is splendid and in my eyes illustrates a conflict between a scientific and non-scientific attitude. As a practical man, Churchill is not interested in the vocative of tables and chairs, or in machines that write sonnets. Similarly, electrical phenomena were long regarded as being something to amuse people with at the circus but not to be taken seriously. I have heard practical people say that even if parapsychological phenomena are real, they are not particularly interesting because they occur so rarely. Turing's answer to Churchill is that research is not encouraged by setting limits or objectives and he tells Wittgenstein that contradictions are symptoms that should be taken seriously.

For a scientific attitude, and I am now considering science as related to philosophy rather than technology, what appear to be practically unimportant exceptions and contradictions are actually of great interest. They show that reality is not as we had imagined. Electrical phenomena had no place in the conception of the world engendered by early physics, and parapsychological phenomena have no place in the conception of the world we have today. Exceptions are exciting in science and philosophy, for in order to understand them we must sometimes change both our stock of concepts and our picture of reality. That is why since ancient times philosophers have been deeply interested in paradoxes and contradictions.

Wittgenstein is certainly right when he says we have no immediate practical use for contradictions. Nobody uses paradoxes to make calculations or to draw an arbitrary conclusion from them. Being language mistakes, they have no use. But they are symptoms that something is fundamentally wrong with our ideas and theories, and thus that exciting things may be just around the corner. There are also practical aspects to this. As Turing quite correctly pointed out, bridges may collapse if faulty theories have been used in the calculations with which they are designed. Conversely, good theories often prove to be of practical use.

Thus these two meetings have some similarities. It may appear absurd to put Churchill and Wittgenstein in the same boat, and admittedly, there are differences between them. Churchill instinctively takes a pragmatic attitude, and it is understandable that he had no time to get interested in the question of who would most appreciate sonnets that future machines might be imagined to write. Wittgenstein adopts a similar attitude when he rejects paradoxes as having no practical importance, and minimized the importance of certain theoretical and philosophical embarrassments, but he does it for reasons of principle, and argues intellectually that this is philosophically correct.

Conventionalism

Wittgenstein's position stems from a certain conviction about the nature of mathematics. It is related to what is usually called conventionalism. But Wittgenstein goes a step further; his standpoint could be called extreme conventionalism. His view is indicated by his slogan that in mathematics we are dealing with inventions, not discoveries. A mathematical proof is not a discovery that things are in a certain way, it should be seen as a decision we take to use the relevant concepts in a certain way. By calling something a proof, we make it a proof.

Many logical empiricists had thought that a mathematical truth is merely a result of fundamental conventions in the sense that in a mathematical proof we only derive the consequences of what we have chosen to let the symbols involved stand for. But Wittgenstein also rejects the idea that something may be said to follow from these basic conventions, and takes the far more radical or extreme view that every so-called proof is a choice, a decision we make. Designations such as conventionalism may be misleading. Wittgenstein was, of course, not conventional, and he himself would certainly reject that -ism designation in its philosophical meaning. For him, mathematics is not a question of conventions in the sense of agreements reached in advance. One of his basic points is that nothing is determined in advance from what could follow from such conventions. It is through our practice that we give sense to our symbols. Superficially it may seem that we discover in a proof what follows from some more fundamental conventions, but in fact every new proof is only a new convention; it becomes an agreement by being accepted by us as a new yardstick that we file away. In this sense Wittgenstein is an extreme conventionalist.

Realism

This conventionalism is in sharp contrast to the realism of which Gödel became an advocate and which von Wright refers to in his contribution to this volume. According to a so-called realistic view, mathematical proof is something that shows what mathematical reality in fact is. In *Beyond all Certainty* Turing quotes Hardy: "317 is a primary number, not because we think it is, or because our consciousness is created in a certain way, but because it is so. Mathematical reality is such." Turing himself did not, as Gödel, develop a realistic interpretation and understanding of mathematics, but it is clear that he, like a very large number of working mathematicians, largely agrees with such an interpretation.

The mathematical paradise

It is here, in the contrast between a conventionalistic and realistic perception that I find the meeting between Wittgenstein and Turing to be at its most exciting from a philosophical viewpoint. Designations such as "realism" and "realistic" may sound sympathetic, but like von Wright I feel that the realistic attitude in the philosophical sense indicated above is difficult to maintain. The quote from Hardy may seem plausible, and Gödel's realism or so-called mathematical Platonism, is not an especially "bad philosophy". On the contrary, it should be seen as one of the classic main directions in the philosophy of mathematics. As I said above, most mathematicians probably adopt it. And, as Karlqvist says in his essay *The Legacy of Turing*, most of us are prepared to accept statements about the decimal places of pi as being true or false even when we cannot in practice determine them. Nonetheless, I consider Wittgenstein's pointing out the problematical aspects of such an attitude to be one of his major contributions. On the other hand, there is still something absurd about Wittgenstein's radical conventionalism.

Wittgenstein says that he would never dream of driving someone out of the paradise that Cantor is said to have given us. The expression "Cantor's Paradise" comes from Hilbert. He was afraid that Brouwer's intuitionalistic ideas, by which Wittgenstein was strongly influenced in many respects, would make us abandon large parts of Cantor's creation, and Hilbert accused Brouwer of attempting to drive us out of this paradise. But Wittgenstein said that he would instead welcome everyone to this "paradise" and show the new arrivals around, upon which they would certainly leave the paradise all by themselves.

But Cantor's paradise is not the only bone of contention between Turing and Wittgenstein; there is also the paradise first populated by the ancient Greeks. Since the time of the Greeks we have thought that by providing proof we could find out about the real nature of things. Wittgenstein did not want to criticize the mathematicians' proof. He was entirely against getting the mathematicians to change their practices, but he wanted to make us see these practices in a new light. He wanted us to understand that proofs are nothing more than conventions, that they are decisions we make jointly and store in our archives. But if we are quite wrong in believing that through proof we arrive at an understanding of the true nature of things, why should we continue this activity? As the British philosopher Michael Dummett said: the effect of what Wittgenstein says about mathematical proof is that although he did not want to drive us out of even the paradise the Greeks discovered, he will not give us any reason to stay there.

There is something incomplete about Wittgenstein's understanding of mathematical practice; he never manages to account for its deductive aspects – for what use do we have it; why should we keep it at all?

The meeting between Turing and Wittgenstein illustrates one of the most important and topical issues in theoretical philosophy, namely the conflict between realism or Platonism on the one hand, and various forms of anti-realism – such as idealism, conventionalism, constructivism – on the other, forms that are currently under discussion in seminars and symposia all over the world (including, to make a local comment, the philosophical seminar at Stockholm University). The difficulty in finding a reasonable position between those of Wittgenstein and Turing is that, on the one hand, this position should respect the objective validity of a mathematical proof, which means that we are not at liberty either individually or collectively to prove what we want, and, on the other hand, the position should free us from the idea of a mathematical reality that is already given independent of us, which mathematical proofs do no more than uncover. It is this difficult philosophical balancing act that the meeting between Turing and Wittgenstein challenges us to perform.

Chapter 19
Carved in Stone or Carried by the Wind?
Stephen Toulmin

The title "Beyond Certainty" is ambiguous in a way that can, but need not, be misleading. Wittgenstein did not claim that we can arrive at no kind of Certainty: merely that the philosophers deceive us if they pretend that the only kind of Certainty that has any intellectual relevance is a formal, geometrical kind. He did not direct us beyond all Certainty, only beyond the monopoly of inappropriate, *formal* Certainty (decontextual logical necessity) and toward an appropriate, *pragmatic* Certainty, a well grounded, situated certitude. With the Death of Cartesian foundational epistemology, we do not lose all hope of certainty, only the illusion that the only Certainty worth having is a formal, eternal feature of knowledge, exemplified in the logical coherence of *texts*. In its place, we recover an alternative Certitude: a timely, pragmatic feature of knowledge, within particular situations and modes of *praxis*.

In parallel with this confusion of practical certitude with theoretical necessity, Cartesians also confuse two kinds of Skepticism: the Classical Skepticism of Pyrrho or Sextus, revived in Montaigne's *Apologie de Raimond Sebond*, and the Systematic Doubt of Descartes' *Méditations* and *Discourse*. Rationally speaking (for Descartes) claims to Knowledge for which no theoretical foundation is given are to be rejected: we must deny propositions we cannot prove.

For Montaigne and other Classical skeptics, by contrast, it is as misguided to deny truths that go beyond the reach of proof as it is to assert them. The high school Atheist who shocked his family friends by denying God's existence became an Agnostic after studying Classical Skepticism at College. He now found Dogmatic Atheism as baseless as Dogmatic Theism: "What I previously disbelieved I now no longer understand." He gave up not just the positive answer to the question "Does God exist?", but the question itself – positive *and* negative answers alike. ("Does God exist? God alone knows!")

In classical terms, Systematic Doubt is not a kind of Skepticism at all: the Ancients call it negative dogmatism. So, the 20th century escape from Cartesian Foundationalism did not put systematic denial in the place of theoretically groundless assertion. Rather, it freed us from a dogmatism exemplified, equally, in misplaced *denials* and in misplaced *assertions*.

Cartesians wanted knowledge claims judged in a Court of Rational Appeal whose rulings were grounded in Theory. With the loss of all overarching Theory, this demand is suspended: rather, Theories – more exactly, appeals to "theory" – are accepted as a kind of Practice. Thus, the Death of Modernity does not require the cultural fragmentation of rationality: all we need abandon is the grandiose, universalism imposed by the formal Certainty of the Cartesians. Abandoning Foundationalism thus leads not to Absurdity, but to Pragmatism. Here, Pragmatism can be understood not as just one more old style philosophical theory, but as the move from philosophy justified by theory to philosophy rooted in practice: not just rooted in Bourdieu's "theory of practice" (say) but in the demands of Practice itself.

To pick up the related idea of Narrative: the Dream of Philosophy was of Truths that (in Malcolm Bradbury's phrase) are "carved in stone". In the early 20th century, these were called "propositions" and tagged as true at a given place and time. Yet how does carving utterances in stone affect them? Does their meaning as utterances survive the operation? What meaning do functional, timely, situated utterances keep, once changed into functionless, timeless, desituated propositions? Are they not at risk of losing all function, modus operandi, or even meaning.

Later 20th century philosophy has seen a transition from timeless Propositions to timely Utterances: language games, illocutions, speech acts or whatever. This change shifts the philosophical focus from Formal Logic, in a direction that can help to rehabilitate Rhetoric. Not that mid 20th century philosophers knowingly chose Rhetoric: it took until 1992 for the University of Pittsburgh to organize a meeting on the role of Rhetoric in the Natural Sciences. Still, any shift from the question, "How do propositions cohere?", to the question, "How are utterances put to use?", i.e. from the logical to the pragmatic, was headed that way. Against this background, the issue of Certainty is seen as a rationalist distraction from substantive issues of Practice. (Did this distraction serve a social purpose? The argument of my *Cosmopolis* implies that it may have done.) Either way, the pragmatic narratives reemerging today are narratives of a kind that predate Descartes: the narratives within which we all live, when not playing academic games. If Philosophy is to develop any constructive Way Ahead after the Death of Modernity, it must be built around a troika of Language Use, Pragmatism and Narrative.

To cite one example: how a casuistical way of handling the moral problems of clinical medicine contrasts with the formal theories of Bioethics. Philosophers see in Medicine cases that can be quoted in the *a priori* arguments for one "ethical theory" against another; but their theories still aim at the timeless validity of all philosophical theories. Working physicians put at the center of the picture, rather, the patient's History: the narrative of medical episodes, clinical treatments and personal factors that serves as the basis of practical diagnosis and treatment. (Kathryn Hunter has helpfully compared clinical inquiry to the detective work of Sherlock Holmes.) So, Bioethics carries into medicine the dream of moral doctrines carved in stone; but clinical ethics acknowledges that a doctor's judgements are made on this day not that, in Chicago not Berlin, with an eye to one feature of a patient's history rather than another.

If, after an hour or two, the patient's condition takes an unexpected turn for the worse, the doctor's earlier judgement is then set on one side, while the clinical team asks why the picture changed so rapidly. When this happens, the doctor's earlier utterances – as offered to colleagues navigating shoals here and now – are no longer "carved in stone": now they blow away on the wind.

A clinical focus on timely, localized events gives words definite meaning, only so far as they are situated in a given medical locus, e.g., the bedside of a patient who just lapsed into a vegetative state: it in no way relies on the Dream of rational exactitude, or the identification of "propositions" as the units of knowledge. So understood, concepts, beliefs, judgements and utterances, are praxis based, not text based – meaningful only in relation to their situation of use. If the physicians' judgements carry any "certitude", this is not the formal necessity of deductive inferences, but the pragmatic outcome of mature experience. Nor is Medicine alone in this. The whole realm of phronesis (Aristotle's "practical wisdom") has survived the wreck of Modernity untouched.

Chapter 20

Experiment, Science, Literature
Göran Printz-Påhlson

I. Primitivism

I represent to myself the vast body of science as a large area strewn with dark places and with illuminated places. Our labors should have as their aim, either to extend the limits of the lit-up places, or to multiply the number of centers of illumination. One is for the creative genius; the other for the wisdom which improves, develops, amplifies.

We have three principal means: the observation of nature, thought and experiment. Observation collects the facts, thought combines them, and experiment verifies the result of the combination. The observation of nature must be painstaking, the thinking profound and the experiment exact. One rarely sees these methods combined. And creative geniuses are not common.[1]

This is the patron saint of our conference, Denis Diderot, writing in 1754, and the text underlines much of what we still see as standard wisdom regarding the relationship of natural science to our culture. But if we go to his contemporary, adversary, and part-time ally, Rousseau, it is not difficult to find examples of a contrary and more jaundiced evaluation of natural science:

If our sciences are futile in the objects they propose, they are no less dangerous in the effects they produce. Being the effect of idleness, they generate idleness in their terms; and irreparable loss of time is the first prejudice which they must necessarily cause to society. To live without doing some good is a great evil as well in the political as in the moral world; and hence every useless citizen should be regarded as a pernicious person. Tell me then, illustrious philosophers, of whom we learn the ratios in which attraction acts in vacuo; and in the revolution of the planets, the relations of spaces traversed in equal time; by whom we are taught what curves have conjugate points, points of inflection, and cusps, how the soul and body correspond, like two clocks, without actual communication; what planets may be inhabited, and what insects reproduce in an extraordinary manner. Answer me, I say, you from whom we receive all this sublime information, whether we should have been less numerous, worse governed, less formidable, less flourishing, or more perverse, supposing you had taught us none of all these fine things.[2]

We are now, 250 years later, so thoroughly enmeshed in technological innovations, at that time hardly foreseeable even as science fiction, that Rousseau's question, when applied with any degree of sensuousness, loses itself in a misty primitivism. Had the intervening two and a half centuries not seen all those great ameliorating technological advances – in medicine, in nutritional habits, in education, as much as in transport and communication – we would not have had the opportunity of being present at this conference. Most of us who are now comfortably and vigorously middle-aged would in all probability have been dead, of the remaining, no doubt a majority would have shuffled around in menial positions as ageing flunkies or kitchen maids – and it would have been extremely hard for all of us to find the time to prepare and come to this conference without mechanical or electronic aids of some kind. The more we distance ourselves from the Arcadian ideal, the more Rousseau's questions lose their poignancy, as his own age takes on a pastoral glow of its own. We may care to remember that Rousseau, perhaps spuriously, but with a conviction which lasted for at least a century, from Kant to Strindberg, created, not a primitivist myth of a Golden Age, which had been commonplace since antiquity, but a qualified and practicable primitivism, which we could call, with Lovejoy, Second-Stage Primitivism.[3] When we think of shepherdesses, we think of Marie Antoinette at the Petit Trianon, not about the weather-beaten faces of the daughters and wives of the nomads of the steppes. The first objection to absolute technological primitivism is its impracticability; that it is, in a sense, even inconceivable. Technological 'progress' (even in quotes) is inescapable (although selective as to possibilities, depending on where you are born).

II. Experiments

Regarding the applicability of a generalized method of science to the single "forms of life" that offered themselves in a thoroughly technologized society, Diderot's tripartite division of scientific principles still seems valid. Although empiricism is not much in vogue at the moment, as at least the famous 'dogmas' of empiricism have been cunningly undermined by the very spokesmen for "scientific realism" who first isolated them, and though thought (refléxion) is most often redefined as "consciousness", theory and observation are still the two main foundations of knowledge, even outside the domains of science proper. The pursuit of truth is still seen as a function of these two concepts, but their internal relationship has been variously interpreted in the meantime, in particular in regard to the third, more instrumental or operational concept: that of 'experiment'. The reason for these fluctuations is to be found in the intrinsic developments of the more abstract disciplines of science, physics, mathematics, and more lately, cosmology, where the link between observation and theory has become, to say the least, tenuous. Nevertheless, 'experiment' has provided a powerful model for domains of knowledge, far removed from the sciences where traditionally the strictures of objectivity have had much less prominence: literature, art, philosophy. I shall highlight three occasions or moments where the analogy of 'experiment' has been applied to innovations in literature, albeit with different bias, but still with commensurate results.

'Experimental' literature was favored by modernism, or at least by one branch of modernism that we might call *avant-gardism*, and we are now enjoying – if that is the word – the result of the struggle of postmodernists and various experimentalists to retain the freshness of the experimental impact. We still know what the word 'experiment' means: before it was given a refined definition within science, it was more or less synonymous with 'essay', which was appropriated after Montaigne for philosophical use, but still, with an alternate spelling, reveals its link with the laboratory: "assay". When Goethe and Schiller, in a series of enormously revealing and important letters in the summer of 1796, discussed the recently completed novel of Goethe's, Wilhelm Meister's Apprenticeship, it is Schiller who remarks when investigating the elements of realism in the novel:

Meister's Lehrjahre sind keine blosse Wirkung der Natur, sie sind eine Art von Experiment. [Wilhelm Meister's Apprenticeship is no mere result of nature, it is a kind of experiment.][4]

In the next few days, in an intense exchange of long letters, they discussed the novel as such an experiment in the pursuit of realism, and Goethe is forced to admit to a "realistic tic", which he likens to a computation which introduces deliberate mistakes in addition, in order to make the sum appear less.[5] We can see an important new meaning of the word 'realism' gestate before our eyes.

Two years later, in 1798, in the "advertisement" to the first edition of Lyrical Ballads, we find Wordsworth writing:

The majority of the following poems are to be considered as experiments. They were written chiefly with the view to ascertain how far the language of conversation in the middle and lower classes of society is adapted to the purposes of poetic pleasure.[6]

The word is retained with less emphasis in the much longer Preface to the Second Edition (1800):

It [the 2nd edition] was published, as an experiment, which, I hope, might be of some use to ascertain, how far, by fitting to metrical arrangements a selection of the real language of men in a state of vivid sensation, that sort of pleasure and that quantity of pleasure may be imparted, which a Poet may rationally endeavor to impart.[7]

In the subsequent versions of Wordsworth's theories of poetic language as "the real language of men", the experimental aspect is gradually lost.[8]

In 1880, Emile Zola published his manifesto Le roman expérimental, in a selection of essays of the same title. The state of scientific praxis had changed a great deal in the intervening years, and Zola is pleased to be able openly to model his argument on Claude Bernard's recent study Introduction à l'étude de la médecine expérimentale. He shares with Bernard an outlook which is, or purports to be, scientific in that it isolates representative cases in a one-to-one relationship to nature, which is his definition of naturalism, in which he generously includes forerunners such as Stendhal and Balzac. Paradoxically, in spite of the formal constraints imposed by the experimental framework, it leads him to a complete disregard of the formal aspects of writing novels:

Et le naturalisme, je le dis encore, consiste uniquement dans la méthode expérimentale, dans l'observation et l'expérience appliquées à la litterature. [...] Fixons la méthode, qui doit être commune, puis acceptons dans les lettres toutes les rhétoriques qui se produiront; regardons-les commes les expressions des tempéraments litteraires des écrivains.'

The naturalist disregard for form puts a damper on the development of the mainstream novel of the next fifty years, a damper which we would now see as the opposite of the experimental. Kierkegaard, and here I adduce my fourth example, is much closer to the scientific spirit in his use of "experimental" [experimenterende] in the subtitle of his novel Repetition – A Venture in experimenting psychology.[10]

III. Reductionism

If we accept the pragmatist's claim that the meaning of a statement is to be identified with the methods of its verification, then Zola seems to be in a peculiar position in advocating his experimental method when refusing any formal constraints to this method. This is different from the positions of Wordsworth or Goethe, as they are in fact, in various ways, trying to predict some future paths for the novel, or the diction of poetry. As they are not bothered by any large or holistic claims for poetry or the novel, they can easily sidestep the "view from nowhere" and concentrate on the work at hand. And here, I think, lies the crucial difference in attitude between positivism, as represented by Zola's naturalist stand, and previous partial attacks on, or defenses of, science.

Because there is no such thing as a divided culture: no 'two cultures' of the kind that C. P. Snow dreamed up in the late 1950s, when positivism was at its strongest.[11] There are, and have always been, a good many cultures in our Western civilization – high and low cultures, specialized and popular cultures, and all those ethnic enclaves we have preferred to forget about until very recently. What has been objectionable to the so-called humanists has not been a culture of science, or even a culture of boffins, but the all-embracing claims of reductionism. And there is a general as well as a special theory of reductionism – just as with the more famous doubling of the theories of relativity. There is the widespread belief that science as a unified viewpoint can provide an objective picture of everything, in terms that are translatable into a final vocabulary, presumably of subnuclear forces and particles. But the special reductionist tenet is connected with Diderot's second 'principle': reflection – thought or consciousness. If the general scheme of reductionism is correct, then the special case of reducing human consciousness to a vocabulary of biology, physiology or artificial intelligence, must also be viable. Even the most discerning scientists have preferred to remain skeptical of that possibility. Let me throw in another quote, from the Cambridge physicist Sir Brian Pippard:

What is surely impossible is that a theoretical physicist, given unlimited computing power, should deduce from the laws of physics that a certain complex structure is aware of its own existence.[12]

Diderot's dream of science as an ever-extending area of illumination contains its own qualifications. Experimental knowledge, as far as it is tentative, heuristic, enquiring, is opposed to reductionism in all its forms, be it applied to poetry, the novel, the theater, film, or the various traditional sciences. It has to oppose many forms of institutional knowledge, in order to leave room for the "wisdom which improves, develops, amplifies".

I want to leave the last pronouncement to the wisest adjudicator between science and literature, Gaston Bachelard:

Tout ce que peut espérer la philosophie, c'est de rendre la poésie et la science complémentaires.[13]

Notes

1 Denis Diderot, *L'interprétation de la nature*, 1754, quoted from the English translation in Gerd Buchdahl, *The Image of Newton and Locke in the Age of Reason* (London, 1961) pp.80-81

2 J.-J. Rousseau, *Discours sur les sciences et les arts*, 1750, quoted from Gerd Buchdahl, op.cit., pp.97-98.

3 Arthur O. Lovejoy, The Supposed Primitivism of Rousseau's *Discourse on Inequality, Modern Philology*, XXI (1923), reprinted in *Essays in the History of Ideas* (New York, 1955) pp.14-37.

4 Schiller, writing to Goethe 8 July 1796 from Jena, Goethe/Schiller *Briefwechsel* (Fischer, Frankfurt am Main, 1961) p.126.

5 Goethe, to Schiller (undated) ibid. p. 130-131: und ich komme mir vor wie einer, der, nachdem er viele und grosse Zahlen über einander gestellt, endlich mutvillig selbst Additionsfehler machte, um die letzte Summe aus Gott was weiss was für einer Grille zu verringern.

6 William Wordsworth, *Advertisement to Lyrical Ballads*, composed 13 April to 13 September 1798, in *William Wordsworth, Selected Prose*, edited by John O. Hayden (Harmondsworth, 1988) p.275.

7 ibid. p. 27

8 e.g. in *Appendix 1850* and in *Essay, Supplementary to the Preface* (1815).

9 Emile Zola, *Le roman expérimental*, edited by Aimé Guedj (Paris, Garnier, 1971) p.92.

10 Which is properly noted by the translators in the most recent translation by Howard V. Hong and Edna H. Hong (Princeton, 1983).

11 To be fair, one has to admit that Snow showed himself very aware of the distorting effects of his dichotomy. See the new edition of his two lectures (1959 and 1963) edited and with an illuminating introduction by Stefan Collini (Cambridge, 1993). Fairness never bothered Dr Leavis in his various rebuffs to Lord Snow: they are conveniently reprinted in F.R. Leavis, *Nor shall my Sword: Discourses on Pluralism, Compassion and Social Hope* (London, 1972).

12 A.B. Pippard, "The Invincible Ignorance of Science", *The Sir Arthur Eddington Memorial Lecture 1988, The Great Ideas Today 1990 Encyclopaedia Britannica* (Chicago etc., 1990) pp.324-337.

13 Gaston Bachelard, *La Psychanalyse du feu* (Paris, Gallimard, 1938) p.10.

Chapter 21

Scientific "Fact-Fictions"
Elinor Shaffer

The death of many important ideas has been proclaimed in our century – the death of God, Man, the Self, the Imagination, and the Author. More recently, a new proclamation has been issued: Jean-François Lyotard has come to fell the "grand narratives." According to Lyotard, a French philosopher and social thinker, postmodernism is to be defined as "incredulity towards metanarratives."[1] In Lyotard's influential book, *The Post-Modern Condition* (1979), the death knell of grand narratives was still largely confined to the grand narratives of the Enlightenment already called in question by Horkheimer and Adorno in *The Dialectic of Enlightenment* (1942), narratives of reason, progress, and the liberty of humankind.

According to Lyotard, "The penetration of techno-scientific apparatus into the cultural field in no way signifies an increase of knowledge, sensibility, tolerance and liberty," as the Enlightenment believed. "Experience shows rather the reverse: a new barbarism, illiteracy and impoverishment of language, new poverty, merciless remodelling of opinion by the media, immiseration of the mind, obsolescence of the soul." In his more recent book *L'Inhumain* (1988), The Inhuman, Lyotard underscores this: we must, he tells us, give up the narrative of "the emancipation of humanity."[2]

The toll of deaths reached a new high with the death of the grand narrative not of any particular author but of humanity itself. But now, in The Inhuman, we seem to be dealing with a different kind of claim: for the death that figures largest in this book is none other than the Death of the Sun.

The Death of the Sun is a "fact" projected into the future, a prediction or prophecy rather than a *fait accompli*; but it is presented as none the less certain for that. No evidence is given, no reference to evidence is made. No particular scientific authority is named. It is presented as a simple, irrefutable and incontestable fact on which present contemplation and action must be based. What will follow post-modernism? Lyotard tells us: it is none other than "post-solar thought."[3] Even as an ungainsayable scientific fact "the Death of the Sun" nevertheless has a feeling-tone, an affect about it, and a familiar, an all-too-familiar rhetoric: if, as a limit, death really is what escapes and is deferred and as a result what thought has to deal with, right from the beginning – this death is still only the life of our minds. But the death of the sun is a death of mind, because it is the death of death as the life of the mind.[4] In short, this fact is to put a stop to the religions, myths, aesthetics, and grand narratives of death that modern thought has dealt in.

We must ask ourselves what sort of fact this is. In this end-dominated discourse, both cultural critique and literary work privilege a "fact-fiction" based on the assumption of the verity of a hypothetical event within the parameters of the possible as currently understood by science. For we are increasingly faced with scientific replacements, substitutes, and equivalents for the "dead" – the outworn religions, debunked myths and aggrandizing narratives. This, surely, is the reason for the phenomenal sales of Stephen Hawking's outline of current physics and astrophysics, A Brief History of Time(1988). This account by "one of the world's leading cosmologists" purports to give the scientific facts about the origin and fate of the universe "from the big bang to black holes" (his subtitle). What degree and kind of factuality attaches to them? Pursuing Lyotard's "Death of the Sun," we find that Hawking offers, for example, the round figure of "five thousand million years or so": "Our sun has probably got enough fuel for another five thousand million years or so ...."[5] The Encyclopaedia Britannica, as the culmination of an article on "The Life History of a Typical Star," concludes dramatically but reassuringly: "These events will not come to pass for thousands of millions of years."[6] This reassuringly vague gesture at an inconceivably distant future is in strong contrast to the deliberately menacing quality of Lyotard's reiterated pseudo-precise "4.5." Fact, if it is fact, is being employed as rhetoric. And how should a "fact" of 4.5 billion years hence – or "thousands of millions" of years – influence our behavior?

Some recent fiction makes this kind of fact its subject – not surprisingly, perhaps, it is often labelled "science fiction," although this label is far too restrictive of its scope and still implicitly dismissive of its literary value. One of the best writers in this genre – Suvin classes his work as "speculative fiction" – is J.G. Ballard.[7] One of his most striking titles is the collection *Myths of the Near Future*. A number of his other short stories and novels could well have appeared under this collective title. Ballard projects "scientific" scenarios not 4.5 billion years hence but thirty years hence. The "factual" claim allied with their imminence gives them a chilling persuasive power. Typical Ballard scenarios: a genetic defect will cause living creatures to be born blind, beginning with cattle and moving on to humans. A new crop fertilizer will induce monstrous growth in birds who then prey upon farm cattle and humans (as in the story "Stormbird, Stormdreamer," in *The Disaster Area*). Oil supplies will run out and the great cities have to be abandoned (as in "The Ultimate City" in *Low-flying Aircraft*). The waters will rise and only a few northern outposts of human life will be left, soon to go under, as in his early novel The Drowned World (1961).

These scientific hypotheses or plausible extrapolations of them employed as facts by fiction writers and cultural commentators are perhaps the most significant fictions of the present day. Ballard himself has ventured to say that the literature from our time that will live on is "science fiction" in this extended sense, and that it will live on simply as the fiction of our time, while reworkings of more traditional literary material will sink without trace.

In the hands of a cultural critic like Lyotard or a cosmological commentator like Hawking it becomes evident that these fact-fictions are not adequately described by the anodyne (or dismissive) generic phrase "science fiction," or even the more nearly appropriate "speculative fiction." They lay claim to public attention and credence, and command it, in a way nothing clearly labelled "fiction" can.

Lyotard goes on in *The Inhuman* to produce his own scenario of life today based on the "fact" of the death of the Sun 4.5 billion years hence: we must prepare ourselves now, technologically and mentally, for "exodus from our solar system" – note the emotive Biblical word – and for the separation of thought from its vehicle the body.[8] Hawking, for his part, moves into the vacuum left by philosophy (he makes the school of linguistic analysis the guilty party) and talks freely of God (though His name is omitted from the index).[9]

Yet the similarities between Lyotard's "factual" scenario and one of Ballard's "fictional" ones are remarkable. In *Myths of the Near Future* (1982) Ballard develops a theme based on the sun and the relation of the future of humanity to it. In two stories in particular, the title story and "News from the Sun", he depicts the spread of a new disease closely linked with the apparently increasing heat of the sun. The "death of the sun", of course, in terms of current science, as the Encyclopaedia Britannica informed us (see note 6), could be expected to be preceded by a period of greatly increased heat, as the sun became a "red giant", before the final cooling. The story does not supply that information, but may derive plausibility from it; even without that information, the recent widespread publicity given to "global warming" and the "loss of the ozone layer" may be sufficient for the general public to accept the notion that there will be an effect of increased heat of the sun or increased exposure to it, which may have dangerous consequences. In the first story this is given local plausibility by being placed in the hot climate of Florida, as the abandoned space stations and dried-up swimming pools begin to return to wilderness; the second story shows the advance of the disease at a later stage, when Las Vegas had been abandoned, and the hot, arid deserts of Nevada surround the "Solar City", a utopian structure intended to run on solar power.

The disease itself is not sunstroke, blindness, or cancer (although unpleasant minor effects of over-exposure are recorded, such as "the blisters on his eyelids, lymph-filled sacs ...";[10] "the sunlight brought out a viral rash on my lips"[11]). It is a more complex condition in which human beings suffer "fugues" in which they go into a kind of stasis or paralysis for increasing amounts of time – at first, for a split second, later for nearly all their hours, so that they die by accident, or by starvation, or, in a more psychological twist, embrace their fate willingly. The sun is seen as inducing or advancing the "Time Disease", and is shunned in the early stages; but in the later stages it may be embraced. A number of different "visionary deaths" in which the victims embrace their ends gladly, even ecstatically are sketched: in the first story, we have the letters of a dying wife describing the beauty of the bird-life in the encroaching wilderness; in the second story, the mad jet-fighter pilot who had wished to be an astronaut kidnaps the last living astronaut and takes off with him in a light plane "into the sun" – both men are happy, for in life even the senior astronaut had reached only the moon; the main protagonist in the second story, a doctor, in whom the advance of the disease is shown from within his own mind, comes to believe that normal "clock-time" ("prissy point-to-point consciousness"[12]) is a mark of a more primitive state, and that the fugues indicate evolution is entering a new, more sophisticated state of consciousness in which all times are simultaneously present.

The parched, arid desert is perceived as a green, edenic landscape. He ends up crouching on the roofs of the runways, learning the language of the birds, and waiting for his lost wife to bring him "news from the sun".

The epidemic, and the shift in time-sense, which erases the distinctions of past-present-future, are viewed as the result of guilt – both the doctor's personal guilt ("as a member of the medical support team, he had helped to put the last astronauts into space, made possible the year-long flights that had set off the whole time-plague"[13]), and general human guilt incurred through the attempt to deny men's evolutionary position as denizens of earth by pretending to conquer space. It is also viewed as the possibility of a new phase of evolution: but if so, it will be a phase in which the human race is extinct and the monuments of human civilization crumble and return to nature. Finally, all these interpretations, testimony, and experiences are unreliable: they are those of a race stricken by a terminal plague.

If we set Lyotard's scenario next to Ballard's scenario they look uncannily similar. Both center on a diseased sun, and display the symptoms of human time-disease. Lyotard bears a resemblance to the crazed pilot who flies straight into his fate in a state of terminal ecstasy. Both are seeking a new version of time that will make it possible to stave off extinction – or at least consciousness of extinction. Lyotard promotes a new technological fantasy, the projection of incorporeal man into a space beyond the solar system, as Ballard's characters invent a myth of the overcoming of time (projected in machines which manipulate images) that enables them to ignore finality.

As we place these scenarios side by side it becomes evident that we are dealing not with theoretical systems (though often there is a putative theoretical matrix) nor with scientific facts (though some scientific facts are incorporated) but with a cluster of metaphors. That they are drawn from science does not make them the less metaphorical.

The rooted presence of metaphor in scientific as in other narratives has been traced by a number of scientists and philosophers of science, for example, John Ziman in *Reliable Knowledge* (1978) and Mary Hesse in *Models and Analogies* in *Science* (1963), as well as by the analysts of the "one culture" in which literature and science are asserted to be equally embedded.[14] Ziman, Hesse and others have carried out their analyses in all sobriety and rigor. But in our time these scientific fact-fictions are the stuff of cultural myth-makers drunk on their own residual metaphors. Their representations display the progression that Ricoeur has valuably analyzed as the attraction between different spheres of discourse expressed in or effected by the deceptive similarity of concepts, the overlapping of terms, analogy, or poetic metaphors.[15] They are more prone to erase the distinctions between discourses (between philosophical or scientific discourses on the one hand and poetic on the other, in Ricoeur's terms) than to observe them.[16]

Literary critics (such as myself) are still prepared to see fiction as a lifeline and to celebrate the power of the work of art to fictionalize fact and factualize fiction. Ballard's fiction, for example, gives genuine insight into the stuff of imaginative life in our times. This very professional vulnerability and responsiveness to fiction, however, should put us on our guard: these new scientific fact-fictions wielded by cultural critics not identified as fiction-writers need our closest critical scrutiny. This is of the utmost importance if only because scientists demand objectivity from the public, and castigate them for unnecessary fears and irrational judgements which may stand in the way of progress. This demand may itself be a remnant of one of the "grand narratives" of the Enlightenment. If the public is subjected to the rhetorical use of these scientific fact-fictions by pundits claiming scientific status for their diagnoses and nostrums, it can hardly be expected to make accurate distinctions and informed policy decisions.[17] Much has been made of the role of the media, and much blame has been heaped on them for misleading the public; but more fundamental in the molding of minds is the deployment of the scientific fact-fictions that dominate discourse of all kinds. This urgently needs further analysis.

Notes

1 Jean-François Lyotard, *The Postmodern Condition: a report on knowledge* [1979], trans. Geoff Bennington and Brian Massumi (Manchester University Press, 1984), p. xxiv.

2 Jean-François Lyotard, *L'Inhumain: Causeries sur le temps* (Editions Galile, 1988), The Inhuman. Reflections on Time, translated by Geoffrey Bennington and Rachel Bowlby (Stanford, California: Stanford University Press, 1991), p. 62.

3 Ibid., p. 23.

4 Ibid., p. 10.

5 Stephen Hawking, *A Brief History of Time* (London and New York: Bantam Press, 1988), p. 83.

6 The full paragraph is worth quoting: "Eventually, the sun will die as a white dwarf, but before that happens it will evolve as a giant star. The Earth will become uninhabitable and probably will be swallowed up in the vastly extended envelope of the red-giant-stage Sun. These events will not come to pass for thousands of millions of years." See "Stars and Star Clusters," *Encyclopaedia Britannica*, vol. 28, p. 217.

7 Darko Suvin, *Metamorphoses of Science Fiction* (Yale University Press, 1979), p. 67.

8 Lyotard, *The Inhuman*, pp. 12-14; and 64 (where he speaks of 'exodus').

9 Hawking, *A Brief History of Time*, pp. 174-5.

10 J.G. Ballard, 'News from the Sun', in *Myths of the Near Future* [1982] (London: Vintage, 1994), p. 107.

11 Ibid., p. 97.

12 Ibid., p. 102.

13 Ibid., p. 87.

14 E. S. Shaffer, "*The Sphinx and the Muses: the third culture*," Editor's introduction to *Comparative Criticism*, vol. 13, "Literature and Science" (Cambridge University Press, 1991), xiv-xxvii.

15 Paul Ricoeur, *The Rule of Metaphor* [1977] (London: Routledge, 1986), p. 267.

16 Ibid., p. 263.

17 Science and the Powers: a Colloquium sponsored by the Swedish Government, Department of Education and Science, Stockholm, Sweden, March 1994, in the (eds, Lars Gustafsson, Susan Howard, and Lars Niklasson).

Chapter 22

Comments
Rolf Hughes

Language is not just a system of signs operating according to certain rules. It is also an event, a coming-into-time and a coming-into-being of something new. This is invisible in the formalizable traits of the language. The words contain no marker for the reality. Their validity arises through the signature, through the reference to, or imprint of, a real body in the utterance.

Horace Engdahl[1]

When Bo Göranzon felt dissatisfied with his attempt to represent theories of knowledge in *The Practical Intellect*, he turned to the dialogue form in order to explore further the Turing-Wittgenstein confrontation. Dialogue is an inherently dramatic and dynamic form; it allows competing claims to be tested against each other, it invites participation in the play of unfolding meaning, and is the medium most suited to expressing *ideas in motion*. It is significant therefore that *Beyond All Certainty* should have initially not one, but two authors, each contributing different perspectives and priorities to the biographical, theoretical and theatrical material. For Anders Karlqvist, co-author of *Beyond All Certainty*, the play provided an opportunity to explore not only the two theories of knowledge represented by Turing and Wittgenstein, but also the relation of music in determining the 'algorithms of sayability'. As Hugh Whitemore's play, *Breaking the Code*,[2] stimulated Göranzon to adopt a dramatic mode of representation, so, for Karlqvist, music functioned both as a commentary on, and structuring principle for, the play. The genesis of *Beyond All Certainty* therefore occurred as part of a dialogue with existing texts, forms, dialogues.

'The dialogue provides a model for the reading of texts, even though we may not find a dialogue in the text. We can, however, always find something (yet) unsaid, before, in, and after the text.'

Bengt Molander[3]

The script of *Beyond All Certainty* was conceived at the outset as a process rather than a product – an open dialogue which set in motion an extended and widening collaboration, drawing in The Great Escape Theatre Company, postgraduate students and faculty from the University of East Anglia, the University of Cambridge, and the Royal Institute of Technology in Stockholm. In February 1993, after six weeks of rehearsals, the play was given its first full dramatic performance[4] at the Guildhall in Norwich as the

centrepiece of a weekend interdisciplinary seminar on Performance and
Text at the University of East Anglia. The seminar attempted to incorporate
dialogical principles into its structure by devoting the first day to discussions of the theoretical issues incorporated into the script, the evening to the
performance, and the following day to the practical considerations of staging, a format intended to foreground the interdependence of theory and
practice. Many participants felt that they had gained valuable insights into
their own research through talking to the cast about their preparations for
the performance, reinforcing the value of specific examples from working
life as an aid to the epistemology of reflection. This was also the month
Derek Jarman's film Wittgenstein was released, providing further evidence
of the enduring influence of and interest in the Austrian philosopher. The
cast attended the première at the Arts Cinema in Cambridge. In March
Beyond All Certainty was performed at the beginning of a workshop examining the legacies of Turing and Wittgenstein held at Clare Hall, Cambridge.
Once again, the play provided a focus for subsequent discussions, allowing
participants from a range of academic and working backgrounds to share a
common point of reference. Seeing the Turing-Wittgenstein confrontation
embodied enabled the audience to experience related theoretical issues. The
actors, similarly, had sought out biographical material – Ray Monk on
Wittgenstein, Derek Jarman's afore-mentioned Channel 4 film, Andrew
Hodges on Turing – in order to discover who is speaking before reflecting
on what is said, an illustration, perhaps, of Engdahl's observation that
words are validated through 'the signature, through the reference to, or
imprint of, a real body in the utterance'. Yet, as the cast remind us in their
transcribed discussions, biographical information per se is of limited value
in preparing a role. Too much research, as Jonathan Rea comments, may
restrict the actor's capacity to imagine or empathize with the character;

Some actors get so deep into their research, especially in the context of playing 'real' characters,
that they know too much to imagine and the performance suffers. [my emphasis]

Several months have passed between each run of performances and the
actors have been involved in other projects. Each time the company returns
to their production of Beyond All Certainty, they effectively enact a question
which interested Wittgenstein, namely, what does it mean to follow a rule? A
production is never complete but always evolving, and new additions,
developments or modifications will be made with reference to a shared
memory of previous performances. A model is created anew; it builds on
past experience, but is never simply resurrected in an unchanged form.

The play took on a different identity in each new venue according to the
size of the performance space, lighting, the position (and composition) of
the audience, entrance and exit points, the time available for a technical
rehearsal, amongst other factors. The actors, director, lighting designer and
stage manager had to adapt their roles at short notice. Flexibility – the
capacity to respond to changing circumstances and improvise as necessary
– was called for:

CG. [A] piece of theater is designed to work in certain ways according to the
     space around it.

JH.   It has to be responsive to the spaces around it.

RD.   Like engineering it uses space, space is fundamental, space is part of its material.

JR.   And like engineering, providing you know the conditions you are going to perform in, you can do theater anywhere, like building bridges. The important thing is to know the environment, the conditions and the earlier the better. But sometimes you just have to improvise. Especially when you're touring. Then its like a military campaign through unfamiliar terrain. You have to be able to throw up a bridge with whatever materials are at hand.

RD.   It's not only a matter of improvisation – it's about resourcefulness, preparation – and having thought out all the contingencies before setting out. That is the calculus; and where things go wrong is where the real situation throws up a contingency you had not imagined previously.

Chapter 15. Thoughts on Acting and
the Play *Beyond All Certainty*

An effective theatre company offers the student of skill valuable insights into the nature of teamwork, communication, problem formulation and resolution, and, by extension, into the limitations of so-called artificial intelligence. Computer software, as Karlqvist writes with reference to Turing's universal calculating machine, processes concepts mechanically in a sequence according to given instructions, and without external interference. A theatre company which attempted to devise a performance in this way would be demonstrating a similar level of *techne* to the innovative engineer who seeks to incorporate an ashtray into the design of a motorbike. We must respect the differences, as many of the contributors to the present volume have argued in different ways, yet also remain alert to the possibilities occasioned by the points of convergence between different practices.

In *The Paradox of the Actor* Diderot describes Voltaire's astonishment on hearing the actress La Clairon in one of his plays; *Did I write that?* he reputedly exclaimed. 'At that moment in the delivery at least', Diderot writes, 'her ideal model was far beyond the ideal model the poet had imagined when he was writing, but that ideal model was not her. Where did her talent lie, then? In imagining a great phantom and copying it brilliantly. She was imitating the movement, the actions, the gestures, the whole expression of a being far above herself.'[5] But how does an actor gain access or insight into this elusive 'ideal model'? A consideration of this question may have implications for our understanding of algorithmic complexity. Karlqvist notes Chaitin's use of a self-referential paradox to develop Gödel's results. Chaitin devised a computer programme with the following form; *Find a number that can be shown to have a complexity greater than the complexity of this programme.* 'The paradox', Karlqvist writes, 'lies in the programme thus being assumed to find a number that it can be proved to be incapable of finding. The conclusion from this contradiction is that no programme can produce a number more complicated than itself.' It is from a similar contradiction, metaphorically speaking, that the actor – or the 'creative' mind – draws so much imaginative energy.

Stephen Toulmin's chapter provides a context for the 20th century transition from foundationalism to pragmatism, a move from theory-based to practice-based philosophy. Alongside this redirection of attention from formal logic towards the rehabilitation of rhetoric, has been a transition from propositions to utterances (or 'language games', 'speech acts', 'illocutionary performances' etc.). Any appeal to 'theory', Toulmin argues, now has to be accepted as a kind of practice. The *meanings* that concepts, beliefs, judgements and utterances have in situations are embedded in the situations. They are *praxis* based, not *text* based. Language use, pragmatism, and narrative accordingly become central to any possible advances in philosophy today.

The end of 'grand narratives', famously proclaimed by Jean-François Lyotard in his influential œuvre *The Postmodern Condition*, is a theme picked up by Elinor Shaffer in her reflections on the claims to 'factual' status of the genre we conventionally label 'science fiction' and those of what we might provocatively term 'science *as* fiction'. In identifying the metaphorical basis of Lyotard's *The Inhuman*, a work of (so-called) critical theory, and J.G. Ballard's fiction, Shaffer argues that such contemporary 'scientific fact-fictions' are 'uncannily similar'; they both display 'the attraction between different spheres of discourse expressed in or effected by the deceptive similarity of concepts, the overlapping of terms, analogy, or poetic metaphors. They are more prone to erase the distinctions between discourses (between philosophical or scientific discourses on the one hand and poetic on the other, in Ricoeur's terms) than to observe them.'

The collapse of culturally-privileged codes of authority presents us with special challenges in attempting to establish values of competence or even *expertise*. Investigation of the situations in which concepts, discourses and practices are embedded leads us back to *Philosophical Investigations*, particularly Wittgenstein's reflections on the role of apprenticeship in teaching and learning. One may learn to discern differences, as Ingela Josefson indicates in her discussion of the place of theory and practice in nursing, by observing how more experienced people manage difficult situations. Universities may be good at teaching, for example, medical theoretical knowledge, an important basis for professional knowledge in nursing, but they provide no tradition for conveying the practical knowledge needed in clinical work. Josefson accordingly argues for a widening of the traditions of knowledge at universities in a way which incorporates the interdependence between practical and theoretical knowledge. Significantly, her own recent work includes the use of a dramatic text – Sophocles' *Antigone* – as a model for reflection upon different conflicts of values in medical practice. When the text was discussed with a group of research students, she reports, their disciplinary background seemed to determine what they saw in the play. We have, perhaps, a vivid example of Toulmin's comparison of a clinical, casuistical approach in medical ethics to the formal theories in Bioethics, a comparison which contrasts the practical basis of diagnosis and treatment with the dream of moral standards 'carved in stone'.

Josefson's example of *Antigone* reminds us that drama, like all dialogic forms, demands active participation or collaboration in the play of possible meanings. Our attention is engaged by conflicting forces and by the tension or energy of their drive towards resolution. By exchanging stories we learn that the conflicts contained in one story/discipline engender fresh perspectives on those contained in a parallel story/discipline. It requires an effort of creative will on the part of the spectator/listener to establish imaginative correspondences. A listener who listens *actively* – ordering information, reflecting on one's emotional responses, exercising the imagination in the available spaces – participates in a meaningful dialogue and is rewarded with a version of the 'story' relevant to his/her interests. The 'tacit' dimension of writing is thus *reading* – the ability of the imagination to transpose *and* extend resonant symbols – for it is in the nature of stories to generate further stories.

A writer, like an actor, is by nature and necessity an interdisciplinary person. The skills s/he acquires are transferable, combining as they do technical competence, flexibility of thought, and, arguably, what Knut Hamsun has sought to define as *uegennyttige Subjectivitet* ('unselfish inwardness'). Literature is an art of unspecified correspondences. Its values are ultimately measured against necessarily subjective notions of 'truth'. The separation between literary practice and theory at English universities is finally being undermined by, amongst other factors, the spread of courses in creative writing. Students who themselves grapple with the difficulties of literary expression are more likely to be sensitive to the achievements of writers they encounter on reading lists elsewhere. A writing workshop is an *open* narrative, a forum for the exchange of possible solutions to problems we define ourselves (and *by which* we define ourselves as writers). This is one of the few spaces in which contrary or contradictory beliefs may be held without fear of ridicule or recrimination. Ideas circulate freely, unhindered by the anxieties of ownership. Differences between theory and practice are not erased but measured against each other, and thereby held in a creative tension. Fiction, poetry, and drama provide a critique of the critique, if you like. In the absence of a transcendental system of belief such as 'God', and with the death knell of 'grand narratives' still ringing in our ears, narrative *per se* may be our only factor of 'truth'.

From 'beyond all certainty' emerges the need to resist the temptation to impale arbitrary solutions on the sharpened barb of our chosen jargon. Instead, we might endeavour to state a problem productively and explore the ensuing ripples of implication creatively.

The value of Diderot's dialogic principles and practice is demonstrated repeatedly in the section we have just encountered and that which follows. Georg Henrik von Wright's suggestion, for example, that we adopt, alongside Wittgenstein, both an 'intra-science' and an 'extra-science' perspective on discoveries which overturn previous theoretical assumptions, the former celebrating new advances as *scientific* advances, the latter viewing science as a 'conception of the world' and examining its 'paradigmatic' influence as a model for thinking, invites us to occupy a dual perspective in the manner of that advocated by Diderot's concept of *dédoublement*. Kate Startin's account of the difficulty experienced by technologists in finding the necessary distance or perspective between their own work and that of their users similarly refers us to 'the problem of *dédoublement*'. It is the problem, as Startin points out, faced by authors who are as yet too close to their material to be able to *represent* it effectively. Again Diderot has something to tell us on the subject:

I remember how I always trembled when I approached the one I loved; my heart was thump-
ing, my thoughts were confused, my words were mixed up, I made a mess of everything I said,
I answered no when I should have said yes, I made endless clumsy and awkward remarks, I
looked ridiculous from my head to my feet: I knew it and only looked more ridiculous. At the
same time, before my eyes, a cheerful, agreeable, relaxed rival, self-possessed, enjoying what
he was doing, missing no opportunity for flattery, and clever flattery at that, managed to be
amusing and pleasing, and successful; he asked for a hand which was abandoned to him, he
took it sometimes without asking, he kissed it, he kissed it again, and I, away in a corner, turning my eyes from a sight which angered me, stifling my sighs, clenching my fists so that the
joints of my fingers cracked, overcome with sadness, bathed in cold sweat, could neither show
nor hide my vexation.[6]

Diderot is here illustrating his view that the expressive skills of the man
of sensibility are inferior – or less persuasive than those of the emotionally
detached actor,[7] and the effectiveness of his 'cheerful, agreeable, relaxed
rival' exemplifies the importance of knowing an appropriate system of communication for a specific situation.

In discussing different ways in which the term 'application' is conceived
by developers, Startin identifies *communicability* as the concept which links
different aspects of understanding a problem before finding a technical
implementation. The role of communicability is taken up by Richard
Ennals, who reminds us that the typical graduate engineer today manufac-
tures not physical objects, but designs or reports – formulations in language
and symbols that are comprehended and used by the managers who constitute their audience:

This suggests that the engineer must develop expertise in a complex process of knowledge representation and mediation, maintaining dialogue with the client or commissioning manager
regarding the transformation of physical objects within the terms of an agreed specification,
and recording objectives and progress in a variety of media. [...] Engineers are actors in the
world of business, organizations and politics, and need access to insights both from acting and
the social sciences, much of which is best achieved through practice and reflection.

From Peter Brödner, meanwhile, we have the idea that the productivity of
manufacture largely depends on the usability and learnability of the (computer) artefacts used and the skills developed through work. The design
and use of artefacts and their effectiveness are in turn conditioned by how
we view humans and machines. Developing an adequate conception of the
human being therefore forms a necessary basis for the design of usable systems. A cognitive action or cognition emerges, he argues, if a human develops appropriate behaviour in a context; all primary experience that humans
gain from their cognitive actions is first of all implicit, internal (or embodied) knowledge private to the acting person ('tacit knowledge'). Intelligence
can thus be defined as a person's ability to actively appropriate parts of the
environment by producing a functional internal representation of his or her
actions through which the environment is restructured at the same time
('structural coupling'). Consequently, meaning must be realized in the acting itself.

Wittgenstein has taught us that concepts arise from the particular practical experience of their users, an observation which has implications for
engineers, as Albert Danielsson points out, whose different educational

backgrounds lead them into different jobs, involving different tasks and areas of responsibility, and thereby equipping them with different practical experience:

Where there is a lack of experience (including common experience) new ideas cannot be based on an existing common language; they cannot be *articulated*, they must be *demonstrated*. [...] If new scientific findings have to be *demonstrated* to be accepted, good teaching methods for a training course in this area must be based on *demonstrating* the content.

Dialogue, acting, communicability, representation, demonstration; we are encountering common concerns across supposedly very different disciplines. Ennals itemizes some of the 'critical characteristics' of actors which are pertinent to a consideration of professional development:

They have to present a public face to an audience, working from a script on commission, mediating complex issues for the non-specialist. They are subject to critical scrutiny, and their ongoing employment is contingent on successful performance. Though working from a script, the intervention of the actor is critical, and each performance constitutes a test of professional skill.

The skilled actor can manipulate his audience as an engineer can modify his system, and playing an active role in a real-time set of events, dispels views of the adequacy of prepackaged solutions. The actor has to engage in implicit dialogue with his audience as the engineer does with his client, often working with rough hewn and inadequate material.

Engineers write consultancy reports on the working of particular systems, or compare and contrast alternative solutions to specified problems; they are, Ennals argues, critics for part of their work. Engineers and critics may share many characteristics in regards the study and manipulation of their systems or cultural products, but, traditionally, they have had little social discourse. Extending the dialogue between the professions, he concludes, makes for change, mobility, and the revival of productive skill.

Theatre, as Chris Bigsby indicates, does not merely imitate the dialogue form, but *is* dialogic by its very nature and technology. The actor, who is simultaneously artist and instrument, is polyvocal, various, and thus a threat to monologic culture. How do we think about thinking, Karlqvist asks at the conclusion of his paper. How do we study our brain with anything other than our brain? For Diderot, acting is both a reminder of alternative possibilities and a powerful metaphor for the workings of the mind. If the mind, like the eye, is incapable of seeing itself, then acting becomes a valuable *exteriorization* of creative and critical processes:

What didn't he do? He wept, laughed, sighed, his gaze was tender, soft or furious: a woman swooning with grief, a poor wretch abandoned in the depth of his despair, a temple rising into view, birds falling silent at eventide, waters murmuring in a cool, solitary place or tumbling in torrents down the mountain side, a thunderstorm, a hurricane, the shrieks of the dying mingled with the howling of the tempest and the crash of thunder; night with its shadows, darkness and silence, for even silence itself can be depicted in sound. By now he was quite beside himself. Knocked up with fatigue, like a man coming out of a deep sleep or long trance, he stood there motionless, dazed, astonished, looking about him and trying to recognize his surroundings. Waiting for his strength and memory to come back, he mechanically wiped his face. Like a person waking up to see a large number of people gathered round his bed and totally oblivious or profoundly ignorant of what he had been doing, his first impulse was to cry out 'Well, gentlemen, what's up? What are you laughing at? Why are you so surprised? What's up?'[8]

Why this sedimentation of representative strategies? What can be achieved in performance which is beyond the reach of a written text? Is this an attempt to represent the unrepresentable, one which reverses the Text → Stage paradigm? How may we learn from these expressive skills? We return to the idea of *dédoublement*, a concept which perhaps best expresses the symbiosis between the foregoing and ensuing Sections. The *conception* of a project will inevitably influence its outcome. The implementation of *a priori* theoretical assumptions will invariably exclude other imaginative possibilities. Theatre, a *process* which need not take place in any existing 'theatrical' space, may well provide us with the most valuable model for developing and expressing complex epistemological concepts. A performance, that culmination of a long process of rehearsals, research and revisions, represents the anxious moment when the private becomes public, the 'product' is unveiled for critical evaluation, incidents are resolved by action, and, thankfully, a new dialogue begins.

Notes

1 "The Personal Signature", Chapter 27, *Artificial Intelligence, Culture and Language: On Education and Work* [Springer-Verlag, 1990], p. 249.

2 Whitemore was himself motivated to write *Breaking the Code* by reading Stephen Toulmin's review of Andrew Hodges' biography of Turing in The New York Review of Books (November 1983)

3 "Socratic Dialogue: On Dialogue and Discussion in the Formation of Knowledge", Chapter 25, *Artificial Intelligence, Culture and Language: On Education and Work* [Springer-Verlag, 1990], p. 230

4 A dramatized reading of the script had been given at the Royal Dramatic Theatre on 16 February 1992.

5 *The Paradox of the Actor*, trans. Geoffrey Bremner [Penguin Books, London, 1994], p. 130

6 op. cit. p. 124

7 "The great actor observes the phenomena around him; the man of sensibility is his model, which he reflects upon, and, thanks to this reflection, decides what is best to add or take away." *The Paradox of the Actor*, p. 125

8 Denis Diderot, *Rameau's Nephew*, translated by Leonard Tancock, [Penguin Books, London, 1986], p. 104

Education and the Information Society

Chapter 23

Some Enigma Variations
A Selection of Dialogues Prompted by Turing's Work
John Monk

I. The Essay

ME. I've got to write an essay on Turing.

MYSELF. There's plenty of material there.

ME. It reminds me of Pygmalion.

MYSELF. The sculptor who didn't like the way some of the local women carried on.[39]

ME. Put him off. Wouldn't share his couch with any woman.

MYSELF. But he made a statue of a beautiful woman and fell in love with it. Kissed it and caressed it; was afraid of bruising it.

ME. Deluded.

MYSELF. Not entirely. He asked Venus for a wife just like the statue and Venus made the statue come to life. They had a child who founded the city of Paphos.

ME. Quite romantic. But it all gets a bit muddled. There was more than one Pygmalion and in some accounts their stories get mixed up. His wife is unnamed in some accounts and is called Galatea in others. Then there seems to be more than one Galatea.

MYSELF. It's a story. It's a myth. The names of the characters are ... just the names of characters. They're not the point of the myth. You tell a story to make some point. The details just provide the fabric. Perhaps it's really about ... loving your own work.

ME. Exactly. That's what I mean about Turing. There's too much material. Too many accounts. It's impossible to disentangle it all. What is the point?

MYSELF. The point of Turing's life?

ME. No, asking the point of someone's life is, well, theological. No, what's the point of telling stories about Turing?

MYSELF. Turing has become a bit of a legend. He's mentioned with names like Einstein or Feynman. People bandy his name about and tell stories about him. It doesn't seem to matter much whether the stories are invented or not.

ME. Turing got involved in a public debate involving the newspapers about "wireless valves" thinking.[65] I bet the newspapers didn't get it right.

MYSELF. The Times made it sound as though the main preoccupation of the University of Manchester was to find the degree of intellectual activity that a machine was capable of and whether or not a machine could think for itself.[65]

ME. It probably got Turing to be well known. I've seen a sort of spoof story on the Internet. Turing, he's canonized – in the story.[10] It's a bit irreverent you see.

MYSELF. Irreverent to refer to St. Turing?

ME. Well I think it's meant to be irreverent. He buries these gold bars.

MYSELF. I'd expect them to be silver. Or are you making things up/

ME. How d' you know they're silver?

MYSELF. His mum wrote about him burying silver bars during the War.[59]

ME. Oh. Well, some silver bars are dug up and they're wrapped in an oily rag that bears the imprint of a machine.

MYSELF. The Turing machine I suppose.

ME. Well it's a hoax isn't it because the Turing machine wasn't built. Was it?

MYSELF. You know there's 'The Turing Option',[24] it's science fiction, but on one of the opening pages there's a quote from Turing without a detailed reference.

ME. So it wouldn't be clear to anyone who had not read Turing's work whether the quote was part of the fiction or not.

MYSELF. In 'Turing's Man'[4] there's a description of the Turing test, but it's not quite the same as in Turing's paper[58] and in the same book it says that faster transistors are mainly bigger transistors whereas it tends to be the other way round.[36]. So you don't know what's right and what's wrong.

ME. On the Internet there's a piece about the Turing tar-pit!

MYSELF. The connectionists sometimes want to talk about a code where everything happens at the same time. To explain the code they describe a piano. The note you get by pressing each key conveys something different.[52]

ME. Each note conveys something different.

MYSELF. Yes. Now you could play a chord and convey a number of different things together.

ME. And someone with a musical ear could disentangle it all. So what?

MYSELF. Well they call the piano 'Turing's piano'. They're just using the name.

ME. And it's only a fiction, an allegory. They want it to sound authoritative and use his name because of that?

MYSELF. So it's a bit difficult to know what's true about Turing and what's not.

ME. Some people think he was a brilliant logician[3] or a mathematical genius.[1]

MYSELF. On the other hand he lacked interest in administration[21] and saw no need to make concessions to those less well endowed.[66]

ME. There've been a number plays about Turing and you can expect the authors to have taken some license with his story.

MYSELF. In 'Beyond All Certainty'[22] Turing discusses the name for calculating machines with Churchill.

ME. You mean he didn't meet Churchill.

MYSELF. Yes he did. He was pretty nervous about it.[21] No. He didn't coin the word computer.

ME. Oh! Where did it come from?

MYSELF. Well I guess it came from the Latin. It was used by Turing himself in his famous paper,[56] not to talk about calculating machines, but about people doing a job. Being a computer was a job. It'd been a job for years, especially in astronomy. There was even a hierarchy. There were those that decided on the best mathematical methods and those who were able by following rules to do all the detailed calculations. Babbage tried to automate the job of this last lot.[64]

ME. And then you get the dialogues and conversations like the one in the coffeehouse where they say Turing is such a legendary figure[29] and the plays...

MYSELF. There's "Breaking the Code".[63]

ME. The trouble with dialogues and plays is that they often wrestle with an idea. They present contradictory views.

MYSELF. Perhaps in those sorts of plays that's the point. There is no conclusion, no rationale and writing a dialogue is a way of dealing with it.

ME. Just confusion and conflict.

MYSELF. Alan Hodges wrote about Turing's lively and popular writing,[28] but Newman said Turing was a difficult author to read.[61]

ME. Newman didn't like Turing then.

MYSELF. I think they got on. Newman was Turing's supervisor at Cambridge, got him the job at Bletchley and got him the job at Manchester. He spoke well of him at his trial.

ME. Trial for what?

MYSELF. Being a homosexual.

ME. Was that a crime?

MYSELF. It was at the time. He was given hormone treatment.

ME. To change his sexual preferences. I suppose then they thought it was all chemical. Funny, people talk about it being caused by genes now. It seems to change with the science of the time. Why do people want to find out causes?

MYSELF. So they can come up with explanations.

ME. To justify doing things. It is strange though that Turing was a kind of war hero and was a homosexual.

MYSELF. There's nothing odd about that.

ME. No. It's just that you wouldn't expect his story to have been passed on. Attitudes being what they were. What was the other play?

MYSELF. That was called the "Imitation Game".[34]

ME. About the rights of homosexuals?

MYSELF. No more about women's rights. The main character is a woman, Cathy, who is clearly intelligent but she's smothered by the attitudes of her family, and her work mates and the establishment, in the form of the army.

ME. What about Turing? I suppose he was rough on her. He used to call the women he worked with "his slaves".[60]

MYSELF. Turing, called Turner in the play, is intelligent too but has a job that you feel Cathy has the potential to do. There is an opportunity for them to begin an affair, but Turing proves impotent.

ME. That's a bit cruel.

MYSELF. Well, it isn't so much about Turing but the potential impotence of men. Still Cathy is defeated by the establishment. She's defiant and tries to explain it all by saying: "The men want the women to stay out of the fighting so they can give it meaning". You know, give the war some purpose.

ME. I've often thought of Alan Hodges biography of Turing[27] in that way.

MYSELF. What way?

ME. As a piece of low key politics.

MYSELF. What do you mean?

ME. Well, Alan Hodges has been active in homosexual politics[12] and his book gives us a sort of homosexual hero. A legend if you like about someone who served his country, met its leaders, made a contribution to knowledge and had a dramatic death.[12]

MYSELF. Actually Alan Hodges does not wave the banner as much as he could, but perhaps it's the careful scholarship that makes it effective.

ME. The biography came at a time when many people would see Turing's treatment as a persecution. Especially with its tragic outcome.

MYSELF. You can't help being sympathetic towards Turing and his ideas because of that.

II. Universal Machines

ME. Didn't Turing write about a Universal machine before the war?

MYSELF. He proposed a Universal version of his machine. You could put a description of a machine on the tape and the Universal machine would read it and behave like the description said it should.

ME. How can a machine read a description and make any sense of it? If it was Universal, why don't we make our computers like Turing machines?

MYSELF. There is not one unique Universal machine. It's partly a matter of how you choose to write down descriptions.

ME. So there are lots of possible Universal machines?

MYSELF. Yes. Apart from the infinite memory, our general purpose computers are Universal computers.

ME. Of course our computers don't have infinite memory. Saying it's infinite sounds a bit theoretical.

MYSELF. The main differences are to do with matters of economy and the preferences of the designer.

ME. So it depends on what it's going to be used for, or what the designer thinks it's going to be used for that affects its design. There's no fundamental sort of computer. What did Turing use his machine for?

MYSELF. To get some results in the theories of mathematics. It was about functions which would naturally be regarded as computable.[57]

ME. Naturally? Naturally computable? That isn't very mathematical. It isn't like a theorem. You couldn't show something's naturally computable except by asking people their opinion.

MYSELF. Getting Turing's machine to do things is what some people say is equivalent to being naturally computable. They say the evidence is impressive and that mathematicians are led to believe it's always true.[14]

ME. What? It's true that if people believe it's computable, it can be done by a Turing machine.

MYSELF. Some people talk about effective procedures or even rules of thumb instead of computability.

ME. That's not very precise. I mean they all sound like different things.

MYSELF. Some people say algorithms or effective procedures, or whatever you want to call them, don't need any ingenuity or even intelligence. You just follow instructions.

ME. You'd have to understand them.

MYSELF. Well it's been said that it can be done by a calculating machine, a computer, a schoolboy or even a very clever dog.[13]

ME. Are you serious? I think of computing and algorithms more in connection with business.

MYSELF. Certainly the development mechanical computation was connected with a general rise in business as early as 1850.[38]

ME. Before electronic computers, and before Turing's machine, mechanical and electromechanical tabulators helped establish and carry out, what they called, effective procedures.[38]

MYSELF. One Victorian wrote about the engines which can do all manner of sums more quickly and correctly than we can?" and remarked on their accuracy saying "Our sum-engines never drop a figure..."[9]

ME. Turing described his machine in his famous paper.[56]

MYSELF. But in his following big paper on logic he only mentions the machine very briefly a couple of times.[57] He preferred to use Church's lambda calculus.

ME. It's a pretty weird design for a computer. I suppose you could say it was original. Where did he get the idea from?

MYSELF. It is odd by today's standards. He draws on the analogy of the computer, the person doing calculations. But there's some evidence that other people were thinking along the same lines.

ME. The same lines! You mean someone else thought it was a good idea?

MYSELF. Emil Post, who worked around New York, wrote a paper[48] which is reminiscent of Turing's machine. Post writes about a worker amongst a collection of boxes.

ME. Turing's computer could write on the tape or erase things from the tape...

MYSELF. Post's worker could move to the box on his right or to the left and determine whether the box he is in, is or is not marked.

ME. ...and Turing's computer could move the tape one section to the right or one section to the left and could read what was in each section. Who published first? Perhaps he copied Turing's idea.

MYSELF. No. The Editor pointed out that Post's work was independent of Turing's.[11]

ME. How did the editor know?

MYSELF. The editor was Church who was especially involved in exactly this problem. The appendix in Turing's paper shows how Turing and Church tackle the same problem.[56]

ME. It was just an odd coincidence that Turing and Post had similar sounding ideas. With Turing at Cambridge and Post in New York?

MYSELF. Yes. It seems that way. Though soon after their papers were published, Turing visited Princeton.[27] Turing's paper was more extensive in its scope than Post's, but you'd find Post's machine easier to understand. It's more like one of today's machines.

ME. In what way?

MYSELF. He proposed a fixed set of unalterable instructions to direct operations and the order in which they should be performed.

ME. Sounds like an instruction set.

MYSELF. Yes. And there was the row of boxes that Post called a symbol space.

ME. That's the memory. Some computer scientists today might talk about symbol space.

MYSELF. He had one direction that would trigger different operations depending on the markings in a box.

ME. A conditional instruction.

MYSELF. I think the instructions were kept separate from the work.

ME. So Turing's contribution was to propose the Universal machine and that's important. You can look at Turing's tape as a place to hold an encoding of the algorithm, some starting values, the result as it builds up and the rough notes. But Post put a lot of this in a slightly more familiar form.

MYSELF. Emil Post published a critique of Turing's approach[49] and points out that Turing had particular ways of using the machine which weren't part of the definition of his machine. With his conventions he'd have difficulty tackling some problems. He says that Turing's preoccupation with computable numbers marred the entire development of the Turing machine.[49] And he reformulated the machine.

ME. But it seems impossible to pin it all down. Post says Turing's description isn't complete but even Post had to qualify words like 'prints' to say what is meant is printing on a blank square. You can go on and on adding more and more detail like this and never get it exactly right.

MYSELF. Yes. Post says Turing's definition of an arbitrary machine is not completely given in his paper[49] and people writing about Turing's machine choose to take what they might call 'unimportant liberties with Turing's original specification'.[42]

ME. I came across a book that describes a box on wheels in a chapter on the Turing machine. It suggests looking at it as a man in the box who has a list of instructions. It's more like Post's machine. The instructions include the stop instruction that was a part of the specification of Post's machine. The box moves along the tape like a railway wagon.[5]

MYSELF. Some people would say "One thing to bear in mind about a Turing "machine" will be that it is a piece of "abstract mathematics" and not a physical object."[40]

ME. A real machine may not follow our rules.

MYSELF. We might use the movement of actual machines as an analogy but we don't have to worry about all the detail.

MYSELF. But there's no reason why the physical world should behave like a Turing machine.[15] If it did we might say that the Universe was computable...

ME. And the notion of computability would be important to physics as well as maths.

MYSELF. There are some pretty weird results that say if you use the wave equation, that's an equation physicists use, you can show that some things can happen that couldn't be modelled on a Turing machine.[32]
ME. But again these are just theoretical ideas. I can't go and buy a Turing machine. Can I?
MYSELF. No.

III. Computability

MYSELF. Turing says that numbers like π, which goes on for ever, is a computable number.[56]
ME. But I thought, to be computable there had to be an end to it. So numbers like 0.5 are computable but the decimal expansion of ⅓ wasn't because you keep on writing down threes. You know: nought point three, three, three, three ... and so on.
MYSELF. Well Turing's machine printed two sorts of symbol on the tape.
ME. 0s and 1s.
MYSELF. Not quite. One sort of symbol was the 0s and 1s that stood for bits of the answer. The other sort of symbol were to make up the rough notes. You know the sort of thing you jot down while you're working things out.
ME. So he invented the binary notation, the 0s and 1s we use today.
MYSELF. No! Binary numbers have been traced back thousands of years.[47]
ME. So what did he do? What's computability got to do with symbols?
MYSELF. Ah! You wouldn't want your computer to keep on writing down rough notes. Would you?
ME. That's true.
MYSELF. Computability is about when a machine gets stuck and can't print any more new 1s or 0s.
ME. But it could go on for ever printing 0s and 1s along the tape, then it would be computable. That doesn't sound very useful.
MYSELF. In Turing's definition, if a computing machine never writes down more than a finite number of 1s and 0s then what it writes down is not a computable sequence.
ME. That's a funny way of putting it. Wouldn't it be better to say if the computing machine writes down more than a finite number of 0s and 1s then it is a computable sequence. No. That sounds funny too. Or at least it doesn't sound very useful.
MYSELF. That depends what you want to use it for.
ME. OK. It doesn't sound a very useful idea for people writing computer programs. It sounds as though you have to wait forever to find the result if something is computable. I think people using computers are more interested in the computer coming up with something in a reasonable time. Which you say is non-computable.
MYSELF. You're thinking about a computer calculating a function.
ME. Yeh! You put an input in and you get an output. Quickly.
MYSELF. Turing would map out the whole function for you.
ME. Give every output for every possible input – but you only want one.

MYSELF. Not if you're proving that the function is computable.

ME. A computable sequence is not a function.

MYSELF. Turing invented a way of encoding a function so it could be written down as a sequence so, in some cases, could be computed. This was a function from whole numbers to whole numbers. Now if a machine can work out the whole function then you know it can work out one small part.

ME. So if the whole function is encoded as a computable sequence eventually the machine will get round to working out the values that you want. Not very efficient.

MYSELF. A large part of his paper is showing how different kinds of mathematical entity can or cannot be encoded by a computable sequence.

ME. There's not a lot of detail about that in his paper and it's all quite remote from the engineering of any kind of machine or program.

MYSELF. Turing wrote it. Not me. And he didn't want to write computer programs. He was interested in Maths and Logic.

ME. Anyway you were talking about computable sequences. What about computable numbers which is what I thought his paper is about.

MYSELF. Oh. A computable number is to do with the decimal part, the part after the decimal point.

ME. What about the part before the decimal point? That's important too.

MYSELF. Well, I hesitate to say this: Turing's computable numbers only deal with the part after the decimal point. It's computable if there's some machine that can write it down.

ME. So it's computable if it's just the decimal part of a number, it's infinitely long and can be worked out by a machine. I think the machine will wear out before you get the number. Does that mean that numbers like 0.5 aren't computable?

MYSELF. Yes they can be. If you treat them as 0.5 followed by an infinity of 0s and if you can make a machine to work that out.

ME. A guarantee that you can make a machine to do the job – now that sounds more like a job for physics and engineering. All this talk about infinities makes Turing's machine seem to be part of a mathematician's game.

MYSELF. It's not all infinities. His point was that a computer with a finite number of states of mind can work out an infinitely long decimal.

ME. Now you're mixing up machines and states of mind. I suppose you'll be telling me about the psychology of computing machines next.

MYSELF. No! No! When Turing wrote about a computer he was writing about a person. He used what computers, people, might do as an analogy to what his machine would do. He does say some intriguing things about the computer though.

ME. Hmph. You are going to talk about psychology.

MYSELF. The computer can't have an infinity of states of mind because then the difference between states would be so small that the computer, the person, would be confused.

ME. Well I get confused. Does that mean I've got an infinity of states of mind? There's scope for a philosophical error here.[20] There's nothing unusual in people getting confused. They get confused reading Turing's paper.

MYSELF. Turing also wrote that the computer does things in really simple steps, so simple you couldn't imagine splitting them up.

ME. Like atoms?

MYSELF. And each step, each operation, brings about a physical change in the computer, the person, and the tape that he writes the results on.

ME. We're into the workings of the brain here. I thought it was about maths.

MYSELF. Turing is really exploring the notion of computability and trying to show that it's the same as we would expect a person to do if we said they were computing. He goes on to show it's like working your way through a mathematical theory.

ME. Like a state machine where you can work out what to do next on the basis of a rule and the current state of affairs.

MYSELF. He's proposing analogies between the way people do things, working with a mathematical theory and a state machine. He does this to justify his machine.

ME. Why? If he had just said I am doing some maths he wouldn't get into hot water by trying to justify it. By using analogies between people, mathematical theories and machines he must have got into a lot of trouble.

MYSELF. Not with his paper on computable numbers.

ME. I don't suppose many people understood it. I don't suppose many people understood the title. What was it? "On computable numbers with an application to the..." What is it...?

MYSELF. The "Entscheidungsproblem". The trick was recoding everything until statements in logic became numbers.

ME. You could then have a statement about numbers encoded as a number.

MYSELF. So you'd get some odd things like a whole statement about a particular number could be encoded by that number.

ME. The statement and what it's about are the same thing.

MYSELF. That's roughly right.

ME. I bet you get some funny results playing around with things like that. So Turing did all this?

MYSELF. He was involved, but the coding scheme, the idea of using numbers to recode things was used earlier by Gödel who upstaged the presentation of Wittgenstein's work at the Conference in Königsberg.[37]

ME. You said Turing encoded logic statements as numbers and used that in his proofs. Where do the machines come into it?

MYSELF. He also coded the descriptions of machines using numbers.

ME. A serial number?

MYSELF. Not really. Turing's universal machine could simulate machines. The number of a machine was treated by the Universal machine as a description.

ME. A description number? A coded description?

MYSELF. Turing said there is no way we can design a machine that can work out whether another machine can compute a computable number or not.

ME. Eh! I am not sure whether that is useful or not. It sounds a bit circular. Talking about machines seems to make it more complicated.

MYSELF. He argues by showing that you arrive at a contradiction if you assume you can do it.

ME. Pretty serious. You're done for if you get a contradiction in a theory. You might as well give up.

MYSELF. No. That's when things get interesting. That's when you need a new analogy for your mathematics.

ME. Analogies. Mathematics. Mathematics has got nothing to do with analogies.

MYSELF. What about the Turing machine?

ME. I suppose you're saying that it's an idealized machine.

MYSELF. Yes. It's really just a set of rules. After all Turing didn't build his machine. He used his analogy of a machine to help in using the rules.

ME. Using an analogy helps in following the rules.

MYSELF. The rules don't make any sense without an analogy.

ME. But when you get into trouble, when you get a contradiction...

MYSELF. Then think of another analogy.

ME. The machine analogy helps you to work out how things will develop.

MYSELF. If you've got your own theory of how machines behave. There's quite a step from seeing a picture of a machine, and Turing doesn't even provide us with a picture.

ME. Only a word picture.

MYSELF. The machine, or the phrase "Turing machine", doesn't help a lot. It's a sort of symbol, just as the picture of the machine is a sort of symbol. You have to learn how to use it. It's a symbol for a kind of sequence or series of pictures. You don't need the machine, a picture is enough.

ME. The machine, the idea of the machine is just a shorthand.

MYSELF. But with it, it brings a particular technique, which Turing uses in his paper.

ME. The machine is taken to be a symbol, a mathematical symbol, not only a symbol but a potential series of symbols.

MYSELF. It passes Wittgenstein's test that we can deal with a picture of the machine and we don't need the machine.[16]

ME. With no photographs or plans the Turing machine, we can only deal with our picture

MYSELF. In Turing's paper it was a picture painted in words, and funny tables of mathematical symbols.

ME. The picture of a machine is a special kind of picture.

MYSELF. A picture of the machine seems to have the potential for movement and suggests a development.[16]

ME. But this suggestion of movement is based on expectations.

MYSELF. The tape on the machine isn't allowed to stretch.

ME. It might stretch so that only half of each symbol fitted in the machine. Or the symbols changed shape and were interpreted differently. Or as in the Colossus the tape could splinter into pieces and then stick together.[19] What would happen then?

MYSELF. There are unstated rules about how these abstract machines work, and some of the rules divorce the whole idea from a world where batteries run down, bearings wear out, tapes get creased, stretch and break.

ME. Turing's discussion is a piece of mathematics.

MYSELF. Barthes says "There is a depth in the Encyclopaedic image, the very depth of time which transforms the image into myth."[2]

ME. What!

MYSELF. The image, the description of a machine given by Turing, is turned into an activity when you think about the machine operating – over time.

ME. Like Pinocchio coming to life.

MYSELF. But because the machine is idealized the activity can only be mythical.

ME. It's funny. I'd not thought of doing maths as drawing a succession of pictures of a myth. I suppose mathematician's call that a proof.

MYSELF. If one mathematician develops the pictures in the same way as another, it might be called a proof.

ME. It sounds as though doing maths is like making an inoffensive cartoon!

IV. The Test

MYSELF. He was a catalyst in a debate about artificial intelligence.

ME. Was there a fuss?

MYSELF. Yes. It's hard to imagine today. Some people thought it was impious even to attempt to build a computer.[65] Actually, in his writing Turing side-stepped all the controversies by refusing to debate them or by changing the subject.[58] He linked intelligence with the ability to play a particular kind of game.

ME. Why didn't he just define intelligence?

MYSELF. There's really no need to have a definition and, in fact, we don't really want one. You can't define things, but only words.[26]

ME. The only reason we consider other people to be intelligent is when they behave intellectually like human beings.[26]

MYSELF. His game involved the use of language.

ME. So he treated language as the sign of intelligence. That excludes things like skill as an athlete, or craftworker, or lover, or painter.

MYSELF. It excludes animals as well.

ME. Unless, you treat what they do as a kind of language.

MYSELF. You could say that even a potato in a dark cellar has a certain low cunning about it.

ME. And you could say the potato was intelligent as long as you suggested the potato used a language.

MYSELF. You might say "The potato says these things by doing them, which is the best of languages."[8]

ME. But on the whole we don't say plants are intelligent. I think I'd say intelligence is more than the use of language.

MYSELF. Well, Turing proposed a game with language.[58] A sort of language game.

ME. Yes, I suppose so. I've read about it but I'd not looked at it that way before.

MYSELF. It used teleprinters.

ME. This language game. There are three players: the woman telling the truth...

MYSELF. Typing the truth. Being helpful to a questioner.

ME. A man who can answer questions however he likes. He can also say – I
    mean type – nothing in a game and let the computer answer the ques-
    tions instead.

MYSELF. The third person?

ME. That's the one asking the questions and getting the responses. The one
    they're trying to convince, the questioner.

MYSELF. What about the people who made the computer? And are you
    going to take the questioner's word that he was or wasn't fooled?
    Shouldn't there be a jury? And how d'you know whether the computer
    or the man answered the questions? The man could lie about that!

ME. So we'd need some witnesses. Wow! That's quite a circus. They'd all
    need to work within the rules. The computer just seems to be a small
    part of all of this. I mean all the effort would go into writing the pro-
    gram. The computer just runs it. It seems to be a test for the program-
    mers. If it's a competition, who would be eligible for the prize?

MYSELF. The computer?

ME. No. The computer is just a medium between the programmers and the
    interrogator. It's pretty limited.

MYSELF. Compared to what?

ME. Compared with the 'phone for instance. People are quite happy to talk
    to the 'phone and listen to it as though it were a person.

MYSELF. Well, they are talking to a person.

ME. See. You're doing it too. People talk and listen to a machine but say
    they're talking to a person.

MYSELF. There's someone at the other end.

ME. Just like the programmers and the machine operators for the computer.
    The computer is just a medium. Who are the competitors in this game?

MYSELF. I suppose it's the man and the woman.

ME. And the computer and its design team.

MYSELF. You'd have to do a series of trials and see how often the interroga-
    tor got it wrong.

ME. What? Mistook the man for the woman?

MYSELF. Yes and compare that with the number of times the computer was
    mistaken for the woman.

ME. And how would you win? How would you know how long each trial
    should be?

MYSELF. You'd have to have some rules and some way of scoring.

ME. It sounds more like a sport, like a chess tournament. It doesn't sound
    like a serious scientific investigation. People would do it just for the
    prize money or national prestige.

MYSELF. Well it was only suggested as a game.

ME. I suppose if we always guessed wrong when the computer was
    involved...

MYSELF. Assumed the woman was a man?

ME. Well, it would undermine our confidence. It would mean that comput-
    ers could convince us that what people were saying wasn't to be trust-
    ed.

MYSELF. The computer as a kind of propaganda machine. What's new about
    propaganda machinery?

ME. The computer as a propaganda machine. That's worrying.

MYSELF. It's not so bad. You know, we're dealing with a machine really. They use teleprinters. You know that. You'd be able to see it and touch it. That's a machine.

ME. No, I mean the response is generated by a machine.

MYSELF. Well it might be, sort of, but wouldn't people have made the computer the way it is. That's why we call them machines – because people had a hand in making them. A computer is not just any old lump of stuff.

ME. By using the computer you're reading the minds of the people that made it.

MYSELF. D'you think that's what Turing meant by extrasensory perception?[58]

ME. It gives them a chance to influence you.

MYSELF. A computer is just a thing like a book or a picture and with books and things people are really keen to say things about the author or the artist. The text isn't threatening.

ME. Are you sure about that? Remember "Fahrenheit 451"?[6]

MYSELF. Where they burnt the books?

ME. There's always someone wanting to ban particular books, pictures, videos and computer games. But with Salman Rushdie it is almost as though we had forgotten about the book. It's the author that's threatened.

MYSELF. I don't feel threatened by the books around me. Though they I do admit that they can have an effect even when people haven't read them.

MYSELF. Suppose I said a brick was an optical computer, designed to blend in with its environment.

ME. You're joking.

MYSELF. The brick senses when it is light and when it is dark. When it senses the light it emits light and it works out, computes if you like, the amount of light to emit so it's in proportion to the light that it senses.

ME. When it's light the brick appears to be light too.

MYSELF. When it detects darkness...

ME. ...it turns off its emitter. It's funny that's almost convincing. It would make good advertising copy: "The Intelligent Brick".

MYSELF. The brick's cleverer than you think. It senses the weight on top of it and pushes up and down exactly the right amount to stop it getting squashed. It takes time to work out the reaction. If you suddenly put a load on it and use a high speed camera you can see it bouncing up and down a bit until it gets the calculation right.

ME. You're saying that we can describe things as intelligent if we choose to. But I think if it is intelligent then it should be able to adapt to the circumstances.

MYSELF. Isn't that what the brick does? In response to changes it senses in its environment, it adjusts its emission of light and the forces it exerts

ME. What you're looking for is feedback.

MYSELF. Well, feedback is just a form of explanation. You can choose to explain a phenomenon, as though there was feedback or not. It's up to you.

ME. You mean you don't discover feedback. You put it there. And statements about behaviour, feedback and tests for intelligence will never be definitive because the use of words like 'intelligence' is restricted. Out of habit.

MYSELF. And by the end of the century the use of words and general educated opinion will have altered so much that we'll be able to speak of machines thinking without expecting to be contradicted.[58]

ME. Changes in our language practices give us intelligent machines.

MYSELF. Not changes in technology.

ME. The Turing test is a test of the state of development of our language.

V. Learning

MYSELF. But some people consider not language, but the ability to learn as the sign of intelligence.

ME. It's difficult to know how you learn, yourself.

MYSELF. And you can't see how other people learn. All you can do is see that somehow they do. They change what they do. How they do things.

ME. If you could build a machine and it learnt, then you could use instruments to see how it does it.

MYSELF. How would you know it was learning?

ME. By the way it reacted to circumstances.

MYSELF. Not by what went on inside the machine?

ME. No. You'd have to say that it did something new, did something differently.

MYSELF. Sometimes when people do things differently you say they've made a mistake.

ME. If you're intelligent you have to explore and when you explore you sometimes go wrong.

MYSELF. So if a machine is infallible, it can't be intelligent as well.[55]

ME. Making mistakes is a sort of consequence of looking for entirely new ways of doing things.[54]

MYSELF. On the other hand, a machine can be relied on, if it doesn't 'breakdown', whereas people like mathematicians make a certain proportion of mistakes.[54]

ME. Why is a breakdown not making a mistake?

MYSELF. Because with a mistake you expect it to be corrected automatically.

ME. You'd wait and see.

MYSELF. And a breakdown wouldn't get corrected.

ME. If you learnt you would expect a change but you wouldn't expect that to be corrected.

MYSELF. A change in behaviour has to be somehow made legitimate if you say it's to do with learning. It has to be approved.

ME. We take some changes in behaviour as evidence of learning but some changes in behaviour will be seen by us as being errors.

MYSELF. And some as a breakdown, a failure.

ME. If the machine changes its behaviour and we find the new behaviour useful then we might say it has learnt something?

MYSELF. You'd begin to talk about it in a different way.

ME. We'd treat it differently.

MYSELF. Whether it learns or not depends on what you say about it.

ME. Wear and tear can change what a machine does. Exposure to people and things, experience leads to wear and tear.

MYSELF. If it becomes unusable then you say it's broken. There is a fault. It's failed.

ME. Yet the machine might be worn but usable. Changed but usable.

MYSELF. Then the change is insignificant.

ME. A machine might be one of a series that were made. Each one is treated differently by its users. Some machines will begin to behave differently from the others.

MYSELF. They'll be different right from the beginning and different from the designer's predictions which are never entirely accurate anyway.

ME. This could happen to any machine.

MYSELF. But the differences are insignificant. Until it wears out and fails.

ME. It may wear out, change its behaviour, but still be usable although we may have to bang the box first, then it hasn't failed but we'd say it was temperamental.

MYSELF. As though the machine had a personality.

ME. Personality changes are often tolerable. If they became intolerable then we'd say there'd been a breakdown.

MYSELF. How subtle does the change have to be to prevent us calling it a breakdown?

ME. If it is terribly complicated, which is another way of saying you don't quite understand it all, then you don't know what to expect.

MYSELF. With some machines, like computers and calculators, if you knew what to expect you wouldn't need the machine.

ME. You're right! That's why you use the machine, because you don't know what the answer is.

MYSELF. You won't be able to say that what the machine does is right ... or wrong. Whether it's working ... made a mistake or ... learnt.

ME. It's only useful because you can't or don't want to work things out yourself.

MYSELF. If the machine is doing something terribly complicated how d'you know if it's made a mistake?

ME. You'll know. Suppose a machine worked out the interest on your loan from the bank and the answer was a huge sum or even that the bank owed you money. You'd know it was wrong. Of course if it didn't go wildly wrong you might not notice.

MYSELF. You could say that some errors were insignificant.

ME. A mathematician mightn't be happy with that. If it was terribly complicated you'd just have to trust the machine.

MYSELF. How can you trust a machine! Doesn't trust mean being sure that someone will do the right thing although they have the freedom to do all sorts of things.

ME. Does a machine have freedom?

MYSELF. In a way. Machines don't always behave the way we expect, that's why we say they go wrong.

ME. People say machines go wrong, certainly, but I've not heard anyone say a machine was intelligent when it did something unexpected.

MYSELF. Well, Turing did in a way. He said he was often surprised by computers. You get a bit lazy and make assumptions rather than working things out in detail. Your expectations are built on these assumptions. When the machine works things out it may well get a different result to the ones you expected because your assumptions weren't valid.[58]

ME. Or maybe you don't know how to work things out. Some expert had made the machine and you'd trusted the expert.

MYSELF. And the machine. You shouldn't be surprised. You just don't understand what it's doing. You don't really understand how to use it.[16]

ME. Unless it really has gone wrong.

MYSELF. You'd have to get the expert's opinion on that.

ME. You mean if you don't understand...

MYSELF. You guess, and sometimes your guess is wrong.

ME. To say the machine had learnt we'd have to see some changes in behaviour and we'd have to see the new behaviour as useful.

MYSELF. It might not be useful to us.

ME. No we'd have to have a explanation. A sort of story that made it sound useful to someone.

MYSELF. Or useful to the machine. A story where it was useful to the machine. A story that gave the machine a purpose.

ME. Describing machines as being intelligent is just another way of describing a machine. The machine is just a lump of stuff doing whatever machines do.

MYSELF. Well, maybe even that is a kind of story. Other stories about machines might make them appear purposeful. New ways of describing machines can make you believe that the nature of the machines has changed.

ME. If we believed the stories about machines being purposeful, we'd say the new behaviour was a sign of learning.

MYSELF. Not a single change in behaviour, but continuing change. Not transient.

ME. No. A transient change might be a transient fault or a mistaken attempt to learn that gets corrected.

MYSELF. Or some part of behaviour that we'd not seen before.

ME. A gap in our understanding.

MYSELF. Changes in behaviour have to be consistent if we're to say it's to do with learning.

ME. But what's consistency? Changes in behaviour can be quite subtle. Not repeated in exactly the same way. Is it just a lack of contradiction?

MYSELF. If it's inconsistent you might say it doesn't make sense. It's paradoxical.

ME. It isn't useful any longer.

MYSELF. Like an inconsistency in a mathematical theory where a 'formula is neither provable nor disprovable'.

ME. A Turing machine trying to prove it would ... continue to work indefinitely without producing any result at all.[54]

MYSELF. Much like mathematicians seemed to be doing when they were working on Fermat's last theorem.[54]

ME. I can imagine a Turing machine working with that old paradox, a contradiction, continually discovering 'I am lying' 'Therefore I am not lying' 'Therefore I am lying' ...Going backwards and forwards. If a machine started doing that. I wouldn't find that very useful.

MYSELF. Think of a Turing machine where the mechanism is a bit sloppy so it makes a kind of a click when it begins to move.

ME. Click.

MYSELF. No. More like "Tick".

MYSELF. Continually, going backward and forward. By any use of the word computable, it wouldn't be computable.

ME. It doesn't stop and it doesn't print out a string of digits. It's stuck. No, it's no use. Futile.

MYSELF. What noise would it make?

ME. Tick, Tick, Tick, Tick...

MYSELF. Suppose each time it reversed, it printed new symbols on a short stretch of tape.

ME. Without giving it a boundless set of symbols, it would get round to repeating the sequence of symbols that it'd already printed. It would just cycle through the same old sequence of numbers.

MYSELF. Like a digital clock?

ME. A bit like that.

MYSELF. Clocks are useful. Aren't they?

ME. Mmm. How would you know that it would keep good time?

MYSELF. An interesting question. If you used it as a clock and it didn't keep good time then you'd throw it away. How d' you know that your digital watch will keep good time?

ME. I don't know how. It just does.

MYSELF. If the machine had some behaviour and you found a new use for it...

ME. That's like finding a metaphorical use for a word.

MYSELF. By accident, a nonsense word or an old word gets used in a new way, and if people find that useful then it catches on.

ME. So it is a matter of seeing a suitable metaphorical use for a new behaviour.

MYSELF. Unless, of course, we want to make jokes or create confusion.

ME. But in a way they're uses for a new behaviour.

MYSELF. You may not foresee the use for the new behaviour. It may just happen.

ME. The changed behaviour of the machine might suggest the new use. A new activity.

MYSELF. When that happens some people would want to say that the machine showed some intelligence.[55]

ME. We see the changed behaviour and whether it's learning or invention or it's failure depends on us.

MYSELF. What we call learning, failure, mistakes, utility or insignificance are part of our customary practices.

ME. Learning is partly about adopting practices that someone in the community has found useful.

MYSELF. Adopting the customs of a community.

ME. Or adopting the practices that the stories in the community say are useful.

MYSELF. And rejecting practices that the community says are faulty.

ME. And rejecting practices that don't make sense. That nobody says are useful ... or faulty.

MYSELF. Except as metaphors.

ME. That might catch on.

MYSELF. The discoveries.

ME. If a machine were to learn, it would have to have a way of finding out about our views on its practices.

MYSELF. Turing wrote that the machine must be allowed contact with people so it could adapt itself to their standards,[55] and that to get learning started we would need to represent the ideas of pleasure and pain.[54]

ME. You might reasonably hope to be able to make progress ... if you confined your investigations to some rather limited field such as chess.[55]

MYSELF. Are the mechanics who constructed the machine allowed to keep the machine in running order?

ME. I suppose so.

MYSELF. If they suspect that the machine has been operating incorrectly can they put it right?[54]

ME. Yes.

MYSELF. If the machine breaks their laws?

ME. Careful! People often turn their metaphors around. If you use people as a metaphor for machines, then someone will turn the metaphor around.

MYSELF. They use the same statements, interpreting the machines as a metaphor for people.

ME. So someone might ask what kind of levers someone is made of rather than what their temperament is?[8]

MYSELF. Or look upon ethical conduct as something to be interpreted in terms of the circuit action of ... Man in his environment – a Turing Machine with only two feedbacks determined, a desire to play and a desire to win.[33]

ME. And if the circuits appear to go wrong? ...Who decides whether there's a fault or not? ...and how it should be rectified?

VI. Logic

MYSELF. To explain things we often analyze them. Split them up into parts.

ME. Then you can have theories about the relationships between the parts.

MYSELF. People do this with machines and people.

ME. To explain how they learn.

MYSELF. Or to explain what seems to the mystical by showing that the purely spiritual is a sort of disturbance of equilibrium in an infinite series of levers.[7]

ME. But not the emotions.

MYSELF. The question, at least, has been asked: whether there's a molecular action of thought, from which a dynamical theory of passions could be deduced.[7]

ME. If we separate things it helps us to find the source of the fault, when things go wrong.

MYSELF. Of course as people we go about apportioning blame: the machine had a fault, it was poor design, the programmer made an error, it cannot be totally reliable, poor workmanship, poor materials, it's getting old, it's beginning to wear out.

ME. We say someone or something learns when its behaviour changes.

MYSELF. But we don't usually expect a totally new behaviour otherwise whatever has changed becomes unrecognizable.

ME. So we assume part has stayed the same and part has changed.

MYSELF. Turing suggest the same thing by talking about two kinds of mistakes: mechanical or electrical faults which cause the machine to behave otherwise than it was designed to do.[58]

ME. Are those the two ways?

MYSELF. No. The other kind of fault is a fault in an argument. He says: how do we recognize a failure of the mechanism against a failure of conclusion?[58]

ME. He is thinking about some logic built into the machine. Perhaps they're the thoughts?

MYSELF. "Thinking about the core of the machine as the exercise of logic leads people back to thinking of the computer as a mind."[62]

ME. The exercise of logic is at the core, that means there is another part. Perhaps that's the mechanism?

MYSELF. It's like the mind and body distinction. Only this time applied to machines. The mind is where the thinking goes on.

ME. Logic is seen as a model of thinking. Is that valid?

MYSELF. You mean is it useful?

ME. I wondered what the evidence was.

MYSELF. There was a study of practicing scientists – leading successful research careers...

ME. You'd expect them to be logical thinkers. Is that a fair test?

MYSELF. Actually a substantial proportion of them made gross errors of inference on a seemingly straightforward test of propositional inference.[31]

ME. So logic may not be a good model of the way we think.

MYSELF. The Turing machine was divided into two parts.

ME. But Turing's description of his machine is not always entirely clear.[49]

MYSELF. One way of referring to his division between the 'device' and the 'external' part would be in terms of hardware and software.[41]

ME. Some people would say that the software is the logic inside the machine. Computers are not made of wood, or water, or silicon. They're made of logic.[62]

MYSELF. When you open up a machine. You don't see logic.

ME. No. You see the hardware.

MYSELF. So where is the software?

ME. It's in the hardware. In the pattern of electrical charge or magnetic dipoles.

MYSELF. How can you tell?

ME. You can't directly.

MYSELF. Diderot wrote about a stocking machine and regarded it as "a single and unique reasoning of which the work's fabrication is the conclusion".[17] It sounds as though the whole machine is a logical statement.

ME. The machine is like an argument where the product is the proven conclusion.

MYSELF. And Barthes wrote about pictures of machines saying that "the image has a logical function as well".[2]

ME. Looking at it you see logic.

MYSELF. He also wrote that "substance is nothing ... but the progress of reason".[2]

ME. It sounds as though the hardware is really software. Or all the logic is in the hardware.

MYSELF. Perhaps they're different ways of looking at the same thing.

ME. How is the software different from writing on paper?

MYSELF. That's all hardware.

ME. And the software is the sense you make of the stored patterns. Just as the logic is the sense you make out of the writing. The structures you see in the writing.

MYSELF. You mean software is your view of some hardware?

ME. Not any hardware.

MYSELF. Which bit? You said that when you looked in the box there was hardware and software.

ME. Yes.

MYSELF. And when you look at the hardware with software written on it...

ME. Not literally written on it...

MYSELF. Written in it? No. If you look at something that you call hardware, with no software in it, well, does it make any sense? Don't you see patterns in the hardware?

ME. Yes. Perhaps, as a student of these things, I see more than other people.

MYSELF. What you see depends on you and your experience?

ME. Yes. And what other people have taught me.

MYSELF. So how do I tell the hardware from software?

ME. It's more to do with the way the computer is built. The hardware is fixed. Once it's designed it doesn't change. Whereas the software you can alter.

MYSELF. You're not telling me that some designer designs the hardware, a factory makes it, then we all say "No need to make any changes"? Don't you get new sorts of computer? Don't people make mistakes in the design of computers?

ME. No. It's more that making what I call hardware takes more time and effort than making software.

MYSELF. The designers and makers spend less time making the software than they do making the hardware?

ME. Less equipment, less investment in making the software. Design is another matter.

MYSELF. So the difference between hardware and software is in the way it's made and the investment in its manufacture?

ME. That's close, but now I start looking into it. It isn't all that clear cut. But there is one big difference.

MYSELF. What's that?

ME. Software. The software design is written in computer languages, but in hardware they use diagrams, circuit diagrams and block diagrams.

MYSELF. They don't use diagrams in designing software?

ME. They do, but they're a different style and they seem to have different concerns.

MYSELF. And in hardware design, they don't use computer languages?

ME. They didn't. But I must say that there are languages that look a lot like a programming language[46] that are now being used, sometimes, for designing hardware... You've got me all confused... Let me see what is the difference. I know. It's this business of logic. The software contains the logic of the machine.

MYSELF. I could take any artefact, cut it in half and say this half contains the logic. Then what?

ME. From the logic you could predict what the machine was going to do. But, hang on, I don't think you can cut in half anywhere.

MYSELF. Why not? You said that you saw patterns in the hardware and you saw patterns in the software, and now your saying the patterns you see in the software are logic. You're only able to read the patterns in the software as logic because you have been trained to do it. Why can't you be trained to see patterns of logic in the hardware? People talk about logic design when it comes to hardware. Don't they?

ME. It's the logic in the software that's important. The hardware is irrelevant. That's part of what Turing was saying. We can make a Universal machine and it can simulate any other machine. The simulation is in the software ... on the tape. The complexity of the machine is concentrated on the tape and doesn't appear in the universal machine proper in any way."[55]

MYSELF. And the tape isn't hardware?

ME. Well the tape might be but it's what's in the writing on the tape that matters.

MYSELF. In the writing! In the writing! This gets more and more mystical. You're telling me by taking half of something, looking at it, reading it as though it were logic, I can say what the whole artefact will do. That's a bit like a fortune teller reading a palm and making prophesies about someone's life. It may be effective but it doesn't sound mathematical or logical at all. I really think we are getting into trouble by trying to split things into hardware and software. It sounds like the pickle people get into when talking about the split between mind and body. It's not so much that they are different parts of one thing, but different ways of talking about the same thing. You said as much when you said that hardware and software designers seemed to use different notations. It is the genre that is different. Surely you don't just look at the tape, surely you assume something about the rest of the machine. For instance that it's like one of Turing's machines.

ME. I suppose I do assume something about the machine. It's a bit like having axioms. A framework in which you can draw conclusions about programs. But nobody really talks about the framework very much. It's sort of there, whenever anyone talks about a program or a Turing tape.

MYSELF. There are two communities. The software people use their genre and have their stories. And their stories imply things about the hardware that aren't explicitly mentioned.

ME. The hardware people certainly write and tell things in a different way. They emphasize different things. They seem to work at a finer level of detail so they can't really describe what a whole computer will do.

MYSELF. And the software people can tell you what the whole machine does, but not in any detail?

ME. Well, some worry more about the detail than others. It isn't so clear cut. There are many fussy little details ... which ... would require special circuits, but in many cases we are able to deal with it by pure paper work,[55] that is with software.

MYSELF. You could think of what is on the tape of a Turing machine as being divided into a description of a machine and some data on which the machine operates.

ME. Where we draw the line seems arbitrary so if data on the tape changes we can say the structure of the machine appears to change.

MYSELF. Or you can say the structure stays the same but there are intermediate results of the computation.

ME. If someone scribbles on the tape we can say they're affecting the intermediate results.

MYSELF. Or they're changing data.

ME. Or we might say they're changing the machine.

MYSELF. Or changing the logic.

ME. Does it really matter?

MYSELF. It does when people are looking for explanations.

ME. Or you're trying to pin the blame.

MYSELF. Is it the logic in the software or the machine that's gone wrong?

ME. Someone must have put the detailed rules into the machine.

MYSELF. Yes. But they don't always know how the computer will follow them.

ME. They haven't always worked out the consequences of following the rule.

MYSELF. Well, Turing got round this by saying he was talking about abstract machines, that is with mathematical fictions rather than physical objects to avoid problems of machine failures.[58]

ME. Not talking about machines at all, just thoughts about machines.

MYSELF. Dealing with machines is difficult because we can't always predict exactly how they will behave, so it's easier to work with maths, or algorithms.

ME. I thought we used machines because the maths was difficult! Can you separate the algorithm from the machine?

MYSELF. Some people seem to see a separate Universe. A Utopia reserved for mathematical ideas, especially the more profoundly beautiful and fundamental ones.[43]

ME. What sort of things are in this mathematical heaven?

MYSELF. You might say the idea of computability seems to have a kind of *Platonic reality* of its own.[43]

ME. What about Engineering or Art?

MYSELF. Some would say with mathematics, the case for believing in some kind of ethereal, eternal existence, at least for more profound mathematical concepts, is a good deal stronger than in those other cases.[44]

ME. It makes mathematics sound like a religion.

MYSELF. And rather humbles artists and engineers.

ME. Maths is the queen of the sciences, that sort of thing.

MYSELF. The idea is that when you perceive a mathematical idea, your mind makes contact with Plato's world of mathematical concepts.[45]

ME. So you could say that mathematicians communicate, by each one having a *direct route to the truth*.[45]

MYSELF. With access to Plato's world directly, they could communicate with
each other better than you would've expected.[45]

ME. That sounds like Turing's suspicions about extra-sensory perception.[58]

MYSELF. I suppose you could make some kind of sense out of it without the
need for ESP by saying that people have things in common.

ME. It's their humanity that makes them think of similar things.

MYSELF. Some said "Mathematics is buried deep in the mind, far from anything human".[23]

ME. It's nothing to do with humanity?

MYSELF. It might be their upbringing. After all we're talking about a special
community with quite a common background. They've read the same
books, been to the same lectures.

ME. They jolly well ought to be able to communicate well. I'd be more surprised if they'd got nothing to talk about.

VII. Failure

MYSELF. When things go wrong...

ME. There's the algorithm and the way in which you interpret it. The algorithm could be OK but the maths you're using could be defective.

MYSELF. In what way could the maths be defective?

ME. You could set up the axioms so that there was a contradiction.

MYSELF. You use the maths to model some situation. It either fits the situation sufficiently well or it doesn't.

ME. If you built a bridge and it fell down, that could be the result of a defect
in your maths. The strength and structure of some bridges depend on
mathematics.[35]

MYSELF. Well, that's a bit complicated because there are lots of things that
could have gone wrong. It could be the materials, the way it was put
together, a slip in the calculations, a mistake in a computer program, a
failure in the theory of bridges, freak weather conditions, poor surveying, too big a load, anything.

ME. It could be there's a contradiction in the maths.

MYSELF. That is only a problem if the contradiction arises in your calculations and you can't think of an interpretation of the contradiction. But if
you don't have an interpretation it's more a problem for physics.

ME. You are using the maths to help you make predictions. If you have
some results that you can't interpret...

MYSELF. They're not much help for predicting. But not wrong.

ME. I suppose the maths could be OK but the algorithm might not be.

MYSELF. Does that make it wrong? It could still be an algorithm even if there
was a slip in it.

ME. It might not be for the calculation you wanted done.

MYSELF. So it's not wrong but it isn't what you wanted.

ME. What happens if the program doesn't correspond to the algorithm?

MYSELF. The program's what's in the computer's memory and the algorithm... It gets tricky because the abstract machine and the algorithm aren't there. Or at least not in this world. They might be in some mathematical heaven.

ME. You could say that the algorithm is what is written down, before you transfer it to the computer's memory.

MYSELF. All you've got are marks on paper and they might change when you look away.

ME. You could say that the algorithm is what is written and, yes you know it's physical, but it doesn't go wrong as computer hardware goes wrong. It's a different kind of physical thing and I'd trust paper not to go wrong.

MYSELF. Well, that's your experience. Let me agree that paper is pretty reliable. Or if it goes wrong, you'd notice. Let's say paper is absolutely reliable. You work through an algorithm on paper and show it's what you wanted. Then what?

ME. Because you've done it on absolutely reliable paper. Then you know it can't go wrong in the machine.

MYSELF. So you're saying that if you don't get what you expect from a computer, it must be the machine that goes wrong because you know the algorithm is right. But the algorithm is not in the machine.

ME. Yes it is. It's in the computer's memory.

MYSELF. You said it was written on paper.

ME. It's been copied and what is in the memory corresponds to what is written on paper. There is a correspondence between what is in the computer memory and the symbols on the paper.[16]

MYSELF. Are you saying the copying, storing in the computer's memory and comparing are absolutely reliable? They had a lot of trouble with the early computer memories. They kept on losing pulses in the mercury delay lines.[30] Do you remember when they had all that trouble with alpha particles?

ME. Alpha particles?

MYSELF. The plastic they put around memory chips was slightly radioactive and as the technology of memories improved, the memory cells got smaller. People noticed that there seemed to be spurious changes in what was in the memory.

ME. Someone realized that alpha particles would have quite an impact on the small memory cells and would change the data in the memories.

MYSELF. They've cured it now.

ME. Are you sure?

MYSELF. I guess I don't have the information, and that's the point. You don't know whether what is in the computer memory is what you think is there so what is there cannot be the algorithm because you say the algorithm has been proven to be right and there's no uncertainty in that.

ME. If what is in the memory doesn't correspond to the algorithm, you would say the memory had gone wrong.

MYSELF. You wouldn't say, if the memory changed or if the comparison suddenly didn't work, that one algorithm has moved out and another one has moved in.

ME. I suppose you might not notice any change.

MYSELF. With a program you can never be sure if it will do what you expect because in the end a program is part of a physical system and you can't prove anything about it, absolutely.

ME. If you want to say anything then you need to do tests and make predictions but even that may turn out to be wrong. What do they say? "Inconclusive relative verifications."[18]

MYSELF. If we built a machine based on Turing's outline and the tape stretched and the results given by the machine deviated from those predicted we would be inclined to say the design of the machine was faulty.

ME. Or the machine had failed.

MYSELF. If the machine always produced the wrong result and the tape always stretched then it would be called a design failure.

ME. What has gone wrong?

MYSELF. You could say tape stretching was part of the design and you just misunderstood what the machine was supposed to be calculating.

ME. Either the designer used the wrong physical law or you misunderstood what the machine was for.

MYSELF. If it made mistakes a machine would give itself away by making the same mistake over and over again, and being quite unable to correct itself, or to be corrected by argument from outside.[54]

ME. With a systemic error, you would be inclined to say it was a design fault, or the permanent failure of a component. Anyway, how can a machine judge what is a mistake and what is an innovation?

ME. How subtle does the difference have to be to call it a different personality rather than a fault?

MYSELF. Extremely subtle, especially in something as complicated as a computer. Diderot said that in a stocking making machine "there reigns among its parts so great a dependence".[17]

ME. He's saying that what one part of the machine does depends on the other parts.

MYSELF. '...that were we to remove even a single one, or to alter the form of those regarded as least important, we should destroy the whole mechanism'.

ME. Same as a computer program any change to any part can wreck what the computer does.

MYSELF. The machine just follows the rule embodied in the program.

ME. Unless the machine goes wrong!

MYSELF. Of course, machines do go wrong, that is they fail to meet our expectations.

ME. From time the machine fails to follow the rule.

MYSELF. If we were doing mathematics how would we detect it?

ME. We'd compare it with other results derived in the same way and if they were different from the one we'd got, we'd say a mistake has been made. The mistake may be because someone had made a slip, a clerical error in which case they might repeat the calculation and get a different result. If the new result agreed with the earlier results – we're back on course.

MYSELF. Of course, in looking into things we may find that people, or machines, have been following the rule in different ways and up to now, in spite of this they had got the same results. We would then have an argument about who was doing it right and we might come to an agreement to call the procedures by different names.

ME. If we make a slip accidentally, as a joke or to create an effect, if we don't follow the rule as we were expected to, it may catch on. People may find the odd way of following the rule useful for some new purpose. Perhaps they want to surprise others. This is a kind of metaphorical use of the rule. The metaphorical use of a rule can't be said to be wrong.

MYSELF. If a machine changes its behaviour and we find the new behaviour useful then we wouldn't be inclined to say the machine learnt but it would be difficult to say it had gone wrong. We'd take the credit. We begin to talk about the machine in a different way. If we expected the machine to learn, we might legitimate the new behaviour.

ME. We wouldn't say it had gone wrong.

MYSELF. You might rely on it to continue making the same mistake.

ME. If it begins to wear out, like my bike: I know the chain falls off every 400 metres. Now I know that that is 20 turns of the pedals. So I stop after 19 turns, kick the chain and it's fine for another 19 turns.[59]

MYSELF. It sounds as though your bike has learnt to measure 400 metres and has a way of letting you know.

ME. The bike has changed and I have learnt to cope with it.

MYSELF. There are different stories to be told. You could simply say the bike is worn out and is broken.

ME. Or you could say that your bike has learnt to measure.

MYSELF. The bike has changed as a result of its experience of being ridden by you.

ME. And I've found an explanation for its new behaviour. I say it has learnt to measure. Which is another way of saying I've found an explanation that puts a worn out bicycle in a good light.

MYSELF. And you would use words like 'learn' and 'intelligence' that previously you'd applied only to people.

ME. A machine doesn't follow a rule, but it may appear to follow a rule.

MYSELF. If it constantly appears to follow a rule, we'd be inclined to say that it does follow the rule. Though the machine can know nothing about the rule.

ME. Unless you think of the rule being stored in a computer's memory. Then what you say is that what is stored is knowledge of the rule. It's an analogy. A metaphorical use of the word 'knowledge'.

MYSELF. You might say that. Especially if you changed what was in the memory and the computer appeared to follow another rule.

ME. In a way a machine does what it does in spite of us and any rules that we write down or talk about. As a machine, as an artefact, as a piece of technology, it is affected by people. That's what technology is – something used by people and produced by people.

MYSELF. We make sense of what a computer does because it matches our expectations. It matches our experience or the stories that other people told us about the technology.

ME. Either by accident or as a joke or as an attempt to disrupt, shock or surprise us, our expectations can be overturned. The computer may sometimes simply not behave as people had expected.

MYSELF. Their techniques of prediction had been inadequate.

ME. Then we try to find explanations and our explanation depends on what structures we see in the computer.

MYSELF. How we carve it up into things like hardware and software.

VIII. Mind

ME. You know Turing wrote that it's been shown that there are machines theoretically possible which will do something very close to thinking.

MYSELF. Turing reckoned that machines can be constructed which will simulate the behaviour of the human mind very closely.[54]

ME. On the other hand he wrote that with a digital computer we can't rely on common sense.[55]

MYSELF. The machine interprets whatever it is told in a quite definite manner without any sense of humour or sense of proportion.[55]

ME. But perhaps Turing had a narrow view of what is meant by thinking...

MYSELF. One of his examples was that computers will for instance, test the validity of a formal proof in the system of Principia Mathematica, or even tell whether a formula of that system is provable or disprovable.[54]

ME. He's referring to his paper on the Turing machine there. As a mathematician he would see proving theorems and things as thinking hard. He might not have thought that doing everyday things was to do with real thinking.

MYSELF. When he said that the ACE can be made to do any job that could be done by a human computer,[55] he must've been talking about doing calculations, or playing games like chess.

ME. I'm sure people think of the machine as though it were a mind, not that it is a mind. It pays them to think of it as a mind because that seems to help them predict what it's going to do.

MYSELF. Or at least to explain what machines do sometimes.

ME. But they're probably interested in the apparently irrational things that machines do. Their common sense or their sense of humour.

MYSELF. Whereas Turing's use of the analogy was more to do with the rational and the logical.

ME. What gets you worked up is when you turn the analogy around, so that if you say computers are like minds, computers can be programmed.

MYSELF. And you jump to the conclusion that people can be programmed.

ME. You know, I don't think people get so worked up about it these days.

MYSELF. As Higgins said "It was interesting at first, while we were on the phonetics; but after that I got deadly sick of it ... the whole thing has become a bore".[53]

ME. Who was Higgins?

MYSELF. You know. The character in Bernard Shaw's play – Pygmalion.

References

1 Arthur C (1994) Checkmate by Silicon Chip. Financial Times, Friday, May 6, p. 16

2 Barthes R (1980) The Plates of the Encyclopaedia. In: New Critical Essays. Translated by Richard Howard, Hill and Wang, New York. Reprinted in: Sontag S (ed) (1993) A Roland Barthes Reader. Vintage, London

3 Bolter JD (1984) Turing's Man. Duckworth, London, p. 12

4 Ibid. p. 12

5 Boolos GS and Jeffrey RC (1989 edition), Computability and Logic. Cambridge University Press, pp. 20-22

6 Bradbury R (1954) Fahrenheit 451. Hart-Davis, London

7 Butler S (1872) Erewhon. Penguin Books, Harmonsworth, UK, 1970, p. 7

8 Ibid. p. 201

9 Ibid. p. 205

10 Boyd C (1990) The Turing Shroud – Amazing Archaeological Discovery! Chris Boyd, Edinburgh.ac.uk

11 Church A (1965) Editorial footnote to [48] Reproduced in: Davis M (ed) Undecidable. Raven Press, New York, p. 289

12 Campbell-Kelly M (1984) Review of Alan Turing: The Enigma. Simon and Schuster, New York, 1983 In: Annals of the History of Computing, 6(2):176-178

13 Cutland N (1980) Computability. Cambridge University Press, p. 8

14 Ibid. p. 67

15 Deutsch D (1985) Quantum Theory, the Church-Turing Principle and the Universal Quantum Computer. Proceedings of the Royal Society, London, A(400): 97-117

16 Diamond C (Ed) (1976) Wittgenstein's Lectures on the Foundations of Mathematics. Harvester Press, Hassocks, Sussex

17 Diderot D and le Rond D'Alembert J (1865) Encyclopédie. Quoted in: Barthes R The Plates of the Encyclopaedia. In: New critical essays. Translated by Richard Howard, Hill and Wang, New York, 1980. Reprinted In: Sontag S (ed) (1993) A Roland Barthes Reader. Vintage, London

18 Fetzer JH (1988) Program Verification: The Very Idea. Communications of the ACM, 31(9):pp.1043-1063

19 Flowers TH (1983) Colossus Design. Annals of the History of Computing, 5(3): 239-252

20 Gödel K (1972) Some Remarks on the Undecidability Results. In: Feferman S (ed) (1990) Collected Works Vol II. OUP, Oxford p.306

21 Good IJ (1979) Early Work on Computers at Bletchley. Annals of the History of Computing, 1(1): 38-48

22 Göranzon B and Karlqvist A (1994) Beyond All Certainty. In: Skill, Technology and Enlightenment. Cook J and Göranzon B (eds), Springer, London

23 Hall AG (1993) What is Engineering? Putting Engineering on the Map. International Journal of Engineering Education, 30(2): 99-109

24 Harrison H and Minsky M (1992) The Turing Option. Penguin, London

25 Ibid. p. 94

26 Ibid. pp.221-222

27 Hodges A (1983) The Enigma of Intelligence. Unwin, London, 1985, first printing 1983

28 Hodges A (1987) Turing's Conception of Intelligence. In: Gregory R and Marstrand PK (eds) Creative Intelligences. Frances Pinter, London, pp.81-88

29 Hofstadter DR (1981) The Turing Test: A Coffeehouse Conversation. In: Hofstadter DR and Dennett DC (eds) The Mind's I. Harvester Press, Brighton, UK, pp.69-92

30 Huskey HD (1981) From ACE to the G-15 Annals of the History of Computing 3(2): 130-168

31 Kern LH Mirels HL and Hinshaw VG (1983) Scientists Understanding of Formal Logic: An Experimental Investigation. Social Studies of Science, 13(1)

32 Kreisel G Review of [50] and [51]. Journal of Symbolic Logic, 47(4): 900-902

33 McCulloch WS (1952) Towards Some Circuitry of Ethical Robots or an observational science of the genesis of social evaluation in the mind-like behaviour of artifacts. 13th conference on Science, Philosophy, and religion, New York, September. Reprinted In: McCulloch WS (ed) (1965) Embodiments of Mind. MIT, Cambridge, pp.194-202

34 McEwan I (1981) The Imitation Game: three plays for television. Cape, London pp.95-175 see also pp.16-20

35 McGettrick AD (1994) A Bridge. Editorial, High Integrity Systems 1(1): 2

36 Mavor J, Jack MA and Denyer PB (1983) MOS LSI Design. Addison Wesley, London, p. 83

37 Monk R (1991) Ludwig Wittgenstein: The Duty of Genius. Vintage, London, p. 295

38 Norberg AL (1990) Punched Card Machinery. In: Business and Government. Technology and Culture 31(4): 753-779

39 Ovid, Metamorphoses. Book X, lines 243-297

40 Penrose R (1989) The Emperor's New Mind. Oxford University Press, p34

41 Ibid. p. 36

42 Ibid. p. 37

43 Ibid. p. 70

44 Ibid. p. 97

45 Ibid. p. 428

46 Perry DL (1993) VHDL. McGraw Hill, New York, 2nd edition

47 Phillips EW (1936) Binary Calculation. Journal of the Institute of Actuaries, 67: 187-221. Reproduced in: Randell B (ed) (1973) The Origins of Digital Computers. Springer

48 Post EL (1936) Finite Combinatory Processes. Formulation I. Journal of Symbolic Logic, 1:

103-105. Reprinted in: Davis M (ed) Undecidable. Raven Press, New York, 1965, pp.289-291

49 Post EL (1947) Recursive Unsolvability of a Problem of Thue. Journal of Symbolic Logic, 12: 1-11. Reprinted in: Davis M (ed) Undecidable. Raven Press, New York, 1965, pp.293-337

50 Pour-El MB and Richards I (1979) A Computable Ordinary Differential Equation which Possesses no Computable Solution. Annals of mathematical logic 17: 61-90

51 Pour-El MB and Richards I (1981) The Wave Equation with Computable Initial Data such that its Unique Solution is not Computable. Advances In: Mathematics 39: 215-239

52 Haugeland J (1991) Representational Genrea. In: Ramsey W, Stich SP and Rumelhart (eds) Philosophy and Connectionist Theory. Lawrence Erlbaum, NJ, p. 67

53 Shaw GB (1913) Pygmalion. In: The Complete Plays of Bernard Shaw. Hamlyn, London, 1965 p.739

54 Turing AM (1947) Intelligent Machinery, A Heretical Theory. In: Turing S (1959) Alan M. Turing. Heffer, Cambridge, pp.128-134

55 Turing AM (1947) Lecture to the London Mathematical Society on 20th February 1947. In: A.M. Turing's ACE report of 1946 and other papers. Carpenter BE and Doran RW MIT Press, Cambridge, Mass., 1986, pp.106-124

56 Turing AM (1936) On Computable Numbers with an Application to the Entscheidungsproblem. Proceedings of the London Mathematical Society, Ser.2, Vol.42: 230-265.Reprinted in: Davis M (ed) Undecidable. Raven Press, New York, 1965, pp.116-151

57 Turing AM (1939) Systems of Logic Based on Ordinals. Proceedings of the London Mathematical Society, Ser. 2, Vol. 45:161-228, Reprinted in: Davis M (ed) Undecidable. Raven Press, New York, 1965, pp.155-222

58 Turing AM (1950) Computing Machinery and Intelligence. Mind LIX(236)1950. Reproduced in: Hofstadter DR and Dennett DC (eds) (1981) The Mind's I. Harvester Press, Brighton, UK, pp.53-68

59 Turing S (1959) Alan M. Turing. Heffer, Cambridge, pp.69-70

60 Ibid. p. 70

61 Ibid. p. 74

62 Turkle S (1984) The Second Self. Granada, London, p. 284

63 Whitemore H (1987) Breaking the Code. Amber Lane Press

64 Wilkes MV (1956) Automatic Digital Computers. Methuen, London, p. 3

65 Wilkes MV (1985) Memoirs of a Computer Pioneer. MIT Press, Cambridge, Mass., p196

66 Wilkes MV (1967) Computers Then and Now. 1967 lecture. In: ACM Turing Award Lectures. Addison Wesley, 1987

Chapter 24

The Two Cultures in Engineering
Peter Brödner

1 Introduction: Two Engineering Cultures in Conflict

Throughout almost all the long history of engineering endeavour, there has been a struggle between two lines with strictly incompatible basic assumptions on the nature of humans and the function of technology, on the way of seeing the world, and on the human's being in the world.

One position, which I refer to as the "closed world" paradigm, suggests that all real-world phenomena, the properties and relations of its objects, can ultimately, and at least in principle, be transformed by human cognition into objectified, explicitly stated, propositional knowledge. Human cognition and this kind of knowledge would then represent the real-world phenomena so completely that they could be modelled, explained and simulated in all its aspects, and, consequently, could be reproduced by smart machines.

The counterposition, which I call the "open development" paradigm, does not deny the fundamental human ability to form explicit, conceptual, and propositional knowledge, but it contests the completeness of this knowledge. In contrast, it assumes the primary existence of practical experience, a body of tacit knowledge grown with a person's acting in the world. This can be transformed into explicit theoretical knowledge under specific circumstances and to a principally limited extent only ("experts know more than they can put into words", Schon 1983). Human interaction with the environment, thus, unfolds a dialectic of form and process through which practical experience is partly formalized and objectified as language, tools or machines (i.e. form) the use of which, in turn, produces new experience (i.e. process) as basis for further objectification.

In history, both positions and in particular both kinds of knowledge (which Ryle also refers to as "knowing that" and "knowing how", Ryle 1987) experienced changing relevance and dominance. Both paradigms have brought about whole cultures with traditions, institutions, and philosophies. In the age of enlightenment, the "closed world" paradigm has, interwoven with the rise of science and technology, clearly become the predominant way of seeing the world (at least in the Western hemisphere).

Yet it has, in connection with huge productivity problems and the undeniable failures of "artificial intelligence" attempts, run into a crisis in recent years. This crisis calls for an enlightening of enlightenment.

Sometimes, these two paradigms even show up in the works of the same persons. The young Wittgenstein, for instance, most incisively formulated the credo of the closed world: "The totality of all true thoughts is an image of the world" (TL 3.01). Much of the writing in his later life can be interpreted, however, as an attempt to defeat this position by stating e.g.: "Practice gives the words their meaning", BüF 317). Two more examples may augment this aspect: Terry Winograd, who once created one of the most advanced computer programs to interpret natural language (being constrained to a closed microworld, though, Winograd 1973), later came up with the book "Understanding Computers and Cognition" (Winograd and Flores 1986) where he developed a fundamental critique of AI. Or take R. Ackoff, one of the leading figures of operation research, who summarized his experience: "The future of OR is past", since "managers are not confronted with problems that are independent of each other, but with dynamic situations that consist of complex systems of changing problems that interact with each other. I call such situations messes. Problems are abstractions extracted from messes by analysis .... Managers do not solve problems, they manage messes" (Ackoff 1979).

This paper reflects in some more detail on the two paradigms outlined, with specific focus on production engineering. What appears to be a rather philosophical struggle turns out to be of highest practical relevance. The productivity of manufacture to a large extent depends on the usability and learnability of the (computer) artifacts used and the skills developed through work. The design and use of artifacts and their effectiveness, in turn, relate back to the basic question of how humans and machines are viewed. Developing an adequate model of humans, therefore, forms a necessary basis for the design of usable systems. This general conclusion is finally exemplified by two software prototypes being developed at the Institute of Work and Technology to demonstrate the value of artifacts being designed as tools.

2 The Rationalistic Demon and Human Reason: The Mistakes of the Rationalistic Tradition

It belongs to the core of scientific management since Taylor's days "to collect all knowledge handed down that previously was the worker's sole property, to classify it in tables, to derive rules, laws and formulae from this knowledge, ... that replace the worker's own discretion." (Taylor 1919, 38, 40). This view is embedded into the long rationalistic tradition from Plato through Leibniz, Boole and Turing up to the creators of "artificial intelligence" in our days which subscribes to the basic, mostly implicit assumption that the human world of living, and hence human work, can be entirely modelled as logical propositions and mathematical relations.

In particular, with the advent of operations research, game theory, and utility theory shortly after World War II, with the development of computer systems and cognitive science, it became a common and taken-for-granted belief to see the real-world as a "system" that was considered as being controllable, analyzable, comprehensible, and formally describable. The structure and dynamics of this "system" were assumed to be subject to complete formal modelling. Completely formalized mathematical descriptions, or at least other explicit propositional knowledge, would thus allow for entirely rational acting, i.e. to achieve chosen objectives under given frame conditions in the best possible way. Moreover, this would allow to imitate human abilities and replace skills by machine artifacts.

In light of this assumption, it does seem consequent to view the human mind as a symbol processing machine. This machine is assumed as being a model to explain human intelligence, or at least to produce intelligent behaviour. Thus, the computer metaphor became the battle cry of the propagandists of "artificial intelligence" who now see the old dream that humans, who making mistakes and are unreliable, can be replaced by superior machine systems, fulfilled: "German craftsmanship and the well-known quality work of German skilled workers will no longer be needed in the future. They will be replaced by flexible systems and intelligent control" (Grossman, quoted in Landesreport 1987). "A new production structure is emerging that, ... as an artificial organism with programmed and stored intelligence, is capable of producing goods automatically .... At this higher stage of development, the factory will need machine intelligence" (Spur 1984, V). It is no wonder that, as a consequence of the "closed world" paradigm's basic assumptions and beliefs, the social and cognitive distance between engineers educated in this tradition and skilled workers has grown considerably and become an almost unbridgeable gap.

There is no doubt that the relative success with which the development of industrial production has been driven forward by formalizing and automating human work seems to justify its huge efforts as well as its triumphant claims and expectations. As long as working processes can be described formally and can be modelled (which is undoubtedly possible under specific circumstances and in parts), in particular as long as requirements for flexibility of processes and for complexity of products have been rather limited, the "closed world" paradigm and technology-centred production strategy found favorable conditions for development. Today, however, the profound changes in circumstances and market requirements that have taken place make its drawbacks clearly visible. Ironically, the principal weaknesses become all the more significant as more far-reaching attempts are undertaken to automate more complex production processes in a dynamic environment.

These difficulties start already, with the fact that when analyzing logical propositions, symbol-manipulating machines as formal systems do not recognize the context, and they cannot discriminate between different logical types such as propositions and propositions about propositions. Therefore, they get easily caught in antinomies. Moreover, the meaning of a proposition can normally only be drawn from the context, which, of course, must be stated explicitly to be analyzable through formal symbol manipulation. This explication of the context requires that its meaning be decoded which, in turn, makes it necessary to explicitly represent the context's context and so forth. This attempt immediately leads into an infinite regress (Hofstadter 1979).

With respect to these formal problems, the question arises how humans can overcome them when dealing with symbols, how they can understand context-dependent meaning, discriminate figures from ground, act in a goal-oriented fashion without following rules, in short, how they produce the achievements of common sense that so far have never been simulated by symbol-manipulating machines. The answer results from an adequate conception of the human being built on recent findings about biological and cultural evolution (Bateson 1980, Maturana and Varela 1987) as well as about human acting (Holzkamp 1978, Volpert 1984).

Humans are considered to be thinking and acting agents having bodies with developed sensitivity and motor activity. Driven by their needs, they consciously and purposefully act in and interfere with the environment that has been growing with them. Through their acting and interventions, they cause environmental changes and experience the effects through their senses. Thus they find the meaning of their actions in the effects produced. These experiences provide them with the meaningful context of past actions (with its intentions and effects) and deliver the scope and expectations for future actions. Since they experience their acting and the environmental changes as a coherent whole (that need not be fitted by rules), they know how to act in a goal-oriented fashion even in uncertainty or unstructured situations.

A cognitive action or cognition emerges if the internal structural changes and actions of a human agent caused by changes in the environment appear as an appropriate reaction to the environment in a given context, i.e., if he develops appropriate behaviour in a context. In accordance with this, all primary experience that humans gain from their cognitive actions is first of all implicit, internal (or embodied) knowledge private to the acting person ("tacit knowledge", Polanyi 1985). Intelligence can thus be defined as a person's ability to actively appropriate parts of the environment by producing a functional internal representation of his or her actions through which the environment is restructured at the same time ("structural coupling", Maturana and Varela 1987). Consequently, meaning can be localized neither inside nor outside, but must rather be realized in the acting itself. Humans cannot externalize this implicit knowledge unless there are specific circumstances such as repeated acting in comparable situations or making experiments that, due to their ability for abstraction, allow them to bring out the recurring in the diverse and the general in the specific.

By grasping objects in the environment, they have perceived, and by exploratively acting with them, they understand the effects and comprehend how they work. The conceptual understanding and theoretical knowledge that is thus developed by interfering with the surrounding world (as an operationally independent environment) and by symbolically interacting with their fellow creatures (constituting the social system) can then be objectified as tools or as concepts in language. Their use and understanding is handed down through the process of socialization. Therefore, like concepts, tools and machines are nothing else than "coagulated experience", they incorporate objectified, explicit knowledge – knowledge of how they work and knowledge of how to work with them that can only be gained by using them. In other words, they are "implemented theory". It is now obvious that the basic assumption of the rationalistic tradition – to be able to reproduce intelligent behaviour just by formal manipulation of symbols (the computer metaphor of the human mind) – is incompatible with these facts of life (Winograd and Flores 1986).

This line of argument leads back to the dialectics of form and process, due to which humans acquire new practical experience while they use existing artifacts (such as concepts or tools and machines). By objectifying and explicating parts of this experience, additional theoretical knowledge is created which, in turn, may lead to deeper insight, and improved or even new artifacts. In this never ending spiral of open development, it is the bodily experience and the embodied tacit knowledge that forms the core of human skill, expertise, and competence. Gathering experience through the use of artifacts, exploring their functions and meaning, and adapting to new situations or new ways of using them; this is what constitutes its abundance and ingenuity. Explicit theoretical knowledge, on the other hand, is in principle incomplete and limited in validity. It is therefore impossible to completely specify the functional requirements for a technical system ex ante. For the same reason, its usability cannot be tested without the users.

The expert system technology, for instance, seeks to take into account these circumstances in particular, since it was originally created to establish and steadily extend the knowledge base together with the experts. Apart from the difficulties of objectifying the largely implicit knowledge of the experts into facts and rules, this leads to the unsolved problem of testing the correctness, consistency and reliability of knowledge-based systems. Heuristic rules that have been derived from interviewing experts are usually rather inconsistent, unreliable and vague. But while humans, thanks to their implicit background knowledge, are able to deal with such vague conceptions, this leads to an immanent insufficiency of knowledge-based systems. New rules have to be added for any case the existing knowledge cannot cope with, a process that is likely to increase the inconsistency. The less the reactions of such a system can then be understood or foreseen, the less its results can be verified. Its maintenance becomes a nightmare (Parnas 1985), and as a result of the maintenance problems involved, many expert systems have already been given up (Coy and Bonsiepen 1990). Ironically, management is thus becoming dependent on incomprehensible and unreliable means of production, while trying to get rid of humans who are assumed to be making mistakes and causing trouble.

All in all, the approach of extensively replacing human expertise in production by the massive use of computers has run into severe difficulties. The ruins of numerous CIM operations point to the fact that the high expectations of short lead times with reliable due dates and of substantially increased productivity have, if at all, only met with very limited success. More of the same remedy only produces more of the same misery: a rapid increase in capital intensity with extremely high risks, increasing problems with the availability of the expensive systems, causing high maintenance costs, yet limited flexibility (since every change must first be programmed), the disappearance of existing skills, and the weakening of the innovative capacity.

There are, on the other hand, leading competitors emerging in several core industries that achieve true quantum leaps in economic performance. They operate with at least double productivity, with development time almost halved, with fractions of in-process inventory, to mention only the most important advantages that make them so superior to average producers. The exciting fact is that this superior performance is engendered through the comprehensive development and use of human expertise rather than technology. This has been achieved on the basis of a new object-oriented organizational scheme avoiding the division of labour, of a participatory management style, and of the use of technology as a means of production that makes people more productive rather than replacing them (Brödner 1993). The internal modes of operation of these new production systems exactly fit the basic assumptions of the open development paradigm. Thus it not only claims theoretical superiority to more adequately conceptualize the human-machine relationship, but it also underpins more efficient production practice.

3 Consequences: Guidelines for Human Design of Work and Technology

In light of these serious problems, the particular strengths of human reason become clearly visible. The design of effective, productive and flexible production systems requires sensible use to be made of the unique human abilities. Instead of merely imitating human abilities and widely replacing them by machine artifacts, they should be productively combined with the performance of appropriately designed machines.

Among the unique human abilities the sensory perception discriminating holistic patterns, distinguishing differences and similarities, learning and inferring from experience, making fine judgements, coping with unforeseen events and acting in a goal-oriented fashion without relying on rules are the most important. Work and technology must then be appropriately designed so that these abilities can be maintained and developed through work. The following guidelines for design aim to support this.

Technology is the result of social relations, interests and needs. They are what determine the requirements for the development and use of technical objects. Engineering, then, in accordance with the open development paradigm based on the dialectics of form and process, is basically an endeavor to identify problems in human practice, in this case in production practice, to model those problems in terms of explicit theoretical propositions (e.g. mathematical models of mechanical or electrical systems that meet given requirements), to use the existing body of theoretical knowledge and methods for deriving a formal solution to the problem, to create an artifact according to this solution, and to evaluate the use of this artefact in the changed practice (see Fig. 1). Eventually, the body of theoretical knowledge has to be expanded in order to find appropriate solutions. Thus theory develops, while practice improves.

Once they are in the world, machines and tools make demands on the human who tries to use them effectively. At the same time, they form the

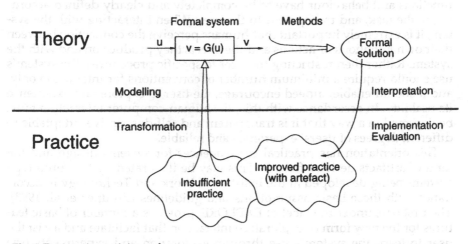

Fig. 1. Engineering activity cycle

basis for further technological developments. Thus, on the one hand one could design technology within certain limits, because it is the result of social relations, while on the other hand one must design technology according to social criteria, because it makes demands on human agents. In a given situation, the possible scope of design results from the social balances of power and the limits of objectifying knowledge.

The design process itself requires that the designer anticipates the expected demands on the human agent while he implements the functions of the technical system according to the design objectives. For these reasons, the development of technical systems must not be taken as a pure technical problem, but must be comprehended as a social relationship within which the system designers set the conditions under which the users have to act. Design is an effort to adapt form and social context, to bridge the gap between the technically feasible (what can be made) and the socially desirable (what is useful). Therefore, and due to the fact that there exists only limited theoretical knowledge, the design process should be organized in a way that iteratively produces improved versions of the system and that users can participate in, and jointly reflect on the artifact's use. Furthermore, system design has to be considered as being part of work design (Ehn 1988, Adler and Winograd 1992, Brödner 1994). Engineers who comprehend technology alone do not know much about engineering.

In order to combine the opposing attributes of humans and machines productively, some design principles have to be regarded that follow from these basic considerations on human acting. In the working situation a wide scope of action has to be allowed with respect to matters and time leaving initiative, evaluation, and decision making up to humans. Planning as well as executing tasks must be reintegrated. Furthermore, the working situation must allow for individual shaping of working conditions, provide sufficient and varied bodily activities (particularly calling for the use of sensory capacities), and encourage cooperation and direct interpersonal contacts (Volpert 1988). For the computer to be used as a tool in this situation, its functions and behaviour have to be completely and clearly defined according to the task, and transparent to the user. When interacting with the system, it is extremely important that humans perceive the connection between their own intentions or actions and the effects they produce on and with the system. Rather then restricting the user to specific procedures, the system's use should require a minimum number of conventions for interaction only, and it should enable, indeed encourage, the user to explore and experience its usability. In accordance with this, the human-computer interaction must be designed in a way that it is transparent and self-descriptive, adaptable to different degrees of users' experience and reliable.

This orientation has practical consequences for systems design and the kind of artifacts derived from it. This may be illustrated by two prototype systems being developed at the Institute of Work and Technology in accordance with these basic assumptions and guidelines (Brödner et al. 1993). The first one, under the label of EXPLORE, provides a number of basic features for the new form of explorative interaction that facilitate and assist the user to learn the system's use through exploration and experiments (see example 1). The second one, under the label of FABER, is a system implementation to assist designers in early phases of mechanical design. To this end, it combines an engineering knowledge base with conventional calculation procedures that can be interactively used as tools when the designer probes, evaluates and calculates functional design alternatives (see example 2). Comparisons with the use of conventional systems reveal considerable advantages.

Example 1 Explorative Acting with Interactive Systems

From what has been said about the basic features of human acting, it can be expected that the most effective way to learn about the purpose and functionality of a rather complex unknown tool is its practical use. Making experiments in the environment it has been designed for and exploring its functions is not only the fastest way to learn its handling but also to efficiently use it as a tool and to improve its use to a skill. So that a computer system can be used with such explorative interaction, it must of course have some specific properties allowing for this kind of use. No instructions or manual will then be needed, only conceptual knowledge about what it is made for. To this end the system should provide the following features:

Experimental interaction

- UNDO. This allows a completed interaction to be undone in a single step. This should be possible no matter when in the past it was carried out in the past, as long as it has been determined in advance by the user.
- Freezing points. These are frozen states, defined by the user. They provide a safe and direct return to a controlled and familiar situation. This feature allows the user to jump (back) across many interaction steps.
- Play Data. These data are objects of the application program. They are

necessary because most applications' functions require them as objects to deal with when exploring the function.

- Guided Exploration Cards. These are a deck of indexed cards ("Paperware"). Each of them helps to avoid intellectual deadlocks and gives task-oriented hints to productive experiments.
- Reducible systems. This feature is to reduce the complexity of an applications program in an individual and task oriented way. They cover both the system's functionality and the techniques of interaction (e.g commands, menus, graphical interaction, direct manipulation).

Exploring iteration

- Views. These are hierarchical, map- or net-like representations of the system's functional structure.
- Interaction graph. This is a visualization of the history of interaction, using the application program metaphor. This kind of history is not static but interactively editable via its visualization.
- Filters. These reduce the interaction graph according to criteria given by the user, e.g. by skipping steps which did not change any data of interest.
- Neutral Mode. This means a "conjunctive mode" which switches off all effects of applications functions. Instead of the triggering of functions the user finds a short description of what the application function in regular mode would have produced.
- Scenario Machines. These reduce the spectrum of interaction to a one-best-way of a pre-determined typical task and guide the user by simulated data all along the solution.

At the Institute of Work and Technology an address management system has been taken as an example of such an explorative interaction. The implemented prototype has been assessed by the EVADIS guideline of software-ergonomics (which is based on the criteria outlined above). The results approve the expectations that explorative features lead to more appropriate tools facilitating faster learning and more efficient use.

Example 2 FABER – Interactive Computer Aided Design of Mechanical Systems

The aim of the FABER project is to develop a tool supporting the designer in the early phases of mechanical engineering design. The prototype facilitates and enhances the efficient interactive use of appropriate calculation procedures and other objectified engineering knowledge by design engineers without replacing their competence. Thus computer support is provided for both solving numerical tasks (e.g. strength calculation) and in making decisions using engineering design rules (e.g. the selection of a certain material). Procedural (algorithmic) methods are used for numerical tasks and knowledge-based (logical) methods are used for the processing of design rules to help the design engineer in decision making. Knowledge based techniques

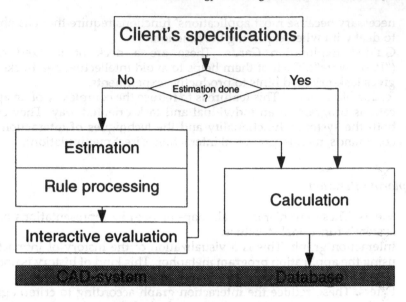

Fig. 2. The system's basic functionality

together with fuzzy logic methods facilitate the processing of incomplete information and of qualitative goals. Initiative, evaluation and decision making remain with the designer. The input, information and results are expressed in the terminology used by design engineers, so that inexperienced users of electronic data processing can use the system without specific training.

For the development and testing of interactive design methods, gear design was chosen as an example. Two stages of the conceptual design phase of the gear design process are supported: a rough estimation for main dimensions and an exact calculation of all relevant data for the gear design. If the most important data are known from the beginning (e.g. in case of design adaption and alteration) there is no need for an estimation (see Fig. 2). The rough estimation is done with the help of an integrated knowledge base containing objectified design knowledge.

The prototype is object-oriented; the design objects are grouped in classes together with their properties, design rules and constraints. This is a natural way to represent design objects and correspond to the design engineer's thinking. He can manipulate the design objects and the implemented design procedures directly, can complete the knowledge base and the set of procedures according to his design experience.

The results of calculations can be graphically represented, using the AUTOCAD CAD-system. The fuzzy logic based component of the system processes incomplete information and qualitative goals appearing during the design process. It offers advice on choosing design parameters (e.g. the number of teeth and a suitable gearing or the best types of bearings and shuft-shub connections).

References

Ackoff, R., 1979: The Future of Operational Research is Past, Journal of Operational Research Society 30, No. 2, 93-104

Adler, P.S.; Winograd, T.A. (Eds.), 1992: Usability: Turning Technologies into Tools, New York: Oxford University Press

Bateson, G., 1980: Mind and Nature. A Necessary Unity, Toronto: Bantam Books

Brödner, P., 1993: Anthropocentric Production Systems – A European Response to the Challenges of Global Markets, in: Smith, M. J.; Salvendy, G. (eds.): Human-Computer Interaction: Applications and Case Studies, Amsterdam: Elsevier, pp. 74-79

Brödner, P., 1994: Design of Work and Technology, in: Karwowski, W.; Salvendy, G. (eds.): Human Factors in Advanced Manufacturing, New York: Wiley (in print)

Brödner, P.; Hamburg, I.; Paul, H., 1993: Work-oriented Design of Computer Systems for Engineering Tasks, in: Müller, W.; Senghaas-Knobloch, E. (eds.): Arbeitsgerechte Softwaregestaltung, Münster: LIT; p. 107-138.

Coy, W. und Bonsiepen, L., 1990: Erfahrung und Berechnung, Berlin Heidelberg New York: Springer

Ehn, P., 1988: Work-Oriented Design of Computer Artifacts, Stockholm: The Institute for Worklife Research

Hofstadter, D.R., 1979: Gödel, Escher, Bach. An Eternal Golden Braid, New York: Vintage Books

Holzkamp, K., 1978: Sinnliche Erkenntnis. Historischer Ursprung und gesellschaftliche Funktion der Wahrnehmung, Königstein/Ts.: Athenaeum

Landesreport Baden-Württemberg Nr. 15, 1987: CIM in den USA. Evolution mit dem Ziel einer "arbeiterlosen Fabrik", Stuttgart

Maturana, H.R. und Varela, F.J., 1987: Der Baum der Erkenntnis. Die biologischen Wurzeln des Erkennens, Bern: Scherz

Parnas, D.L., 1985: Software Aspects of Strategic Defense Systems, Comm. ACM 28, 1326-1335

Polanyi, M., 1985: Implizites Wissen, Frankfurt: Suhrkamp

Ryle, G., 1987: Der Begriff des Geistes, Stuttgart: Reclam

Schon, D.A., 1983: The Reflective Practitioner: How Professionals Think in Action, New York: Basic Books

Spur, G., 1984: Über intelligente Maschinen und die Zukunft der Fabrik, Forschung – Mitteilungen der DFG, Nr. 3: I-VIII

Volpert, W., 1984: Maschinen-Handlungen und Handlungs-Modelle – ein Plädoyer gegen die Normierung des Handelns, Gestalt Theory 6: 70-100

Volpert, W., 1988: What Working and Learning Conditions Are Conducive to Human Development? IfHA-Berichte No 21, TU Berlin

Winograd, T., 1973: A Procedural Model of Language Understanding, in: Shank, R. and Colby, K. (eds.): Computer Models of Thought and Language, San Francisco: Freeman Press

Winograd, T. and Flores, F., 1986: Understanding Computers and Cognition. A New Foundation for Design, Norwood: Ablex Publ.

Wittgenstein, L., 1984: Tractatus logico-philosophicus. Logisch-philosophische Abhandlung (TL),Werkausgabe Bd. 1, Bemerkungen über die Farben (BüF), Werkausgabe Bd. 8, Frankfurt: Suhrkamp

Chapter 25

A Confrontation between Different Traditions of Knowledge
An Example from Working Life

Ingela Josefson

The confrontation I describe here takes place in the nursing profession. It is a conflict between nursing becoming more scientific than it was in earlier days on the one hand, and nursing taught and learnt on the foundation of practice on the other.

The main issue is this: what knowledge should constitute the core of the theoretical and practical training of nurses? Obviously, both theory and practice are needed but where should the main emphasis lie? Should we give priority to the general, or to the particularity of practice?

To put the issue into a context, let me quote two nurses with different opinions about theory and practice in nursing:

Karin:

We need theories in nursing in order to understand what we do as nurses. I must be able to theorize about why I treat a patient the way I do. Younger nurses with an extensive theoretical education are better at this than are the older ones. The following example serves to illustrate this.

"On our ward we had a patient who did not sleep at nights. She was also fairly senile. The older nurses wanted to call in an expert, a psychologist, to help, but two young nurses objected to that. They wanted to find out for themselves why this elderly woman was not sleeping. So they started to question her. It transpired that she had been married to a taxi driver who worked at night. He used to come home between trips and she stayed awake to keep him company. That was why she did not sleep at night. She was used to sleeping during the day instead." It was as simple as that, and the problem was solved without the aid of a psychologist. The nurse concluded: "It's interesting to see how theories can improve nurses' skill, so that young people can tackle problems like this". What this example has to do with theories is not immediately evident. Anyhow, it is an example which shows trust in scientific knowledge being able to solve almost every problem.

The second nurse, Ingrid, has a different attitude to nursing knowledge. She says:

"As a young nurse I was involved as an expert in a training course for child minders. They were middle-aged women who had several children of their own. They had extensive practical knowledge of taking care of children. But, now when they entered an educational situation, they seemed to lose all that they knew. On occasion we had endless discussions about how to change diapers. It seemed to me the course complicated what should have been obvious to them. They wanted to know what was the right way to change diapers or comfort a child. 'What do the experts say?' they asked. I realized it was time to put away the books. I started talking with them about their practical experiences instead. In fact, they were greater experts than I was. I am afraid that in matters like this, people's trust in expert knowledge robs them of their common sense."

With this example as a background, let me focus upon a striking feature in our culture: our high estimation of theoretical knowledge at the expense of practical knowledge. In recent years this conviction has become visible in educational policy where former practical education in, for example, nursing and nursery school teaching have been transferred to and subsumed with the universities and their traditions of knowledge.

One of the reasons for this shift is that university education adds status to low-status professions like nursing. There seems to be a taken for granted idea that theories may improve quality in nursing. The question which is rarely raised is: what are the problems in nursing are theories useful for and for what are not? It was also originally hoped that the incorporation of practical education in the universities would widen the knowledge tradition in the academies. This does not seem to be the case. In fact, education and training at universities has helped separate practice from theory in nursing.

The representatives of nursing science are fighting to have their subject acknowledged as a university discipline. Their way of doing it is to attempt to define what nursing knowledge is. It is the theory-minded nurses' way of proving the value of nursing. In practice, this means to define what – for example – 'loving care' is and to teach young students theories about what it is.

Correspondingly, in the university courses for handicraft teachers, you learn to define what a stitch is and have to teach the children at school the definition of it instead of starting by doing one.

I don't think that universities are the right places for courses of training such as nursing. They are probably good at teaching theoretical medical knowledge, which is an important basis for the professional knowledge needed in clinical work. This is true for both nurses and doctors.

Practical knowledge manifests itself in the ability to take care of a sick person according to her unique circumstances. Theoretical knowledge aims at teaching you to perceive similarities. In practical work you must learn to discern the differences, like the young nurses in the case of the taxi-driver's wife.

How do you learn this? Not by reading books, even if theories can serve as a guide to action – have a guiding significance. In considering the conditions for learning this knowledge we may cite Ludwig Wittgenstein, who touches upon this in a passage in Philosophical Investigations:

—Is there such a thing as expert judgement about the genuineness of expressions of feeling?

Even here, there are those whose judgement is 'better' and those whose judgement is 'worse'. As a rule the more correct prognoses will issue from the judgements of those with a better knowledge of mankind.

Can one learn this knowledge? Yes, some can. Not, however, by taking a course in it, but through experience. Can someone else be one's teacher in this? Certainly. From time to time he gives one the right tip. This is what 'learning' and 'teaching' are like here...

What one acquires is not a technique; one learns correct judgements. There are also rules, but unlike calculating rules (p.227), they do not form a system and they can only be applied correctly through experience.

Wittgenstein's reflection on teaching and learning would, if transposed to nursing, focus attention on apprenticeship. You learn to discern by observing how more experienced people manage difficult situations.

There are nurses in Sweden who have been influenced by the spirit in Wittgenstein's later philosophy. It gives them perspectives for reflection on the limits of science and the meeting between practice and theory in their work.

What is at stake here is the complicated relationship between general rules and the concrete perception of the unique case. The rules may work as guidelines but the priority should lie in considering the unique case. Reflection on the salient feature of every unique case creates the foundation for this development of the interdependence between practical and theoretical knowledge.

This draws attention to the role of examples in this kind of knowledge formation. The examples serve as a basis for reflection.

I started with two examples from conversations with nurses, examples which might be useful in reflective work. But the best examples for reflection are usually to be found in literature. I have been working with Antigone, the tragedy of Sophocles, in reflective work with doctors.

The tragedy shows us a deep human conflict between Creon, the king, and his niece, Antigone, king Oedipus' daughter. The prehistory of the tragedy is that Antigone's two brothers have killed each other in battle. The brother Poyneikos has attacked the city of Thebes in order to destroy it. The reason for his deed is that he has been cheated out of his right to rule as a king of Thebes every second year, alternating with his brother Eteokles. It is his brother who has deprived him of his rights. In the severe conflict that follows the two brothers are killed and Creon, their uncle, becomes the newly appointed king of Thebes.

His first action is to issue a decree that Polyneikos should not be buried. He, the traitor, should lie unburied outside the city gate, a prey for birds and wild dogs. This decree is terrifying in a culture where the citizens' foremost obligation is to bury their dead relatives so that they may be reunited with their family in the kingdom of the dead.

This decree breaks with the most basic assumptions about moral decency prevalent in this culture. Antigone refuses to obey. She buries her brother with her own hands. By doing this she refers to the voice of love and the law of nature which she has to obey.

Two different worlds of values come into conflict with each other.

Creon has created a law without roots in the ordinary citizens' conception of what is justice. He violates their conception of common decency. Antigone becomes an advocate of this practical humanism. The play portrays the conflict between the civic obligation to obey the ruler and the obligation of love towards the family.

In conversation with doctors, the tragedy serves as a model for reflection upon different conflicts of value in their practical medical work. The drama also contains passages on the conditions for reflection and deliberation which usually provoke them to lively discussions. A similar discussion in the spring of 1993 with research students at Cambridge developed in a different way. Their disciplinary background seemed to dictate what they saw in the play. The psychologist in the group saw the power conflict between Creon, the man, and Antigone, the woman, as the main point of the play. A student of creative arts criticized the structure of the play. It seems to me that practitioners are the most sensitive to moving tragedies of this kind. Among academics there is a risk that in analyzing the play it is dissected into small pieces.

Finally, I would like to raise two questions. What happens in a society when practical knowledge is made abstract? How should universities meet the demand for the scientification of, for example, the nursing profession? One way would be to reject education and training in these fields. Another would be to widen the traditions of knowledge at universities. There are traditions in philosophy and literature which might make substantial contributions to the development of practical knowledge.

Chapter 26

Engineering, Culture and Competence

Richard Ennals

1. Introduction

The future of a modern industrial economy depends to a significant extent on the strength of its manufacturing industry, and the skills of the workforce. Our focus of attention in this chapter is on engineering skills, their cultural context, and the extent to which they can be sustained and developed through an approach to education and training which is based on competence. It is argued that a broader approach is required, giving due attention to the tacit knowledge of the skilled worker and the culture of working life.

2. Government Policy

In the United Kingdom widespread dissatisfaction with industrial performance, especially in manufacturing industry, and disillusion with standards in education and training, has led government to develop a new approach. British government policy is ostensibly to expand Further and Higher Education, but to increase the emphasis on competence based qualifications as opposed to traditional academic modes of study and assessment. The National Council for Vocational Qualifications was established by government [Judd 1993] to construct a national system of qualifications covering the full breadth of industry and employment areas, and all levels up to and including postgraduate professional qualifications.

Working with Industry Lead Bodies comprising representatives of employers in different employment sectors, a process of Taylorist decomposition has been carried out on complex tasks, in order to identify the key competences which are necessary for efficient performance of standard tasks, set against agreed criteria. Occupations have been classified in a manner corresponding to the Registrar-General's long-established Classification of Social Class, and Vocational Qualifications are being developed and standardized for a growing proportion of lower-level occupations. Frequently the qualifications are to be awarded on the basis of a portfolio of Prior Experiential Learning, obviating the need for costly absence from work in order to study, but necessitating new and complex processes of verification.

To date the concentration has been at the lower levels of craft and technician qualifications, with a recent development of "General National Vocational Qualifications" to challenge the traditional academic GCSE and Advanced level courses, offered in schools and colleges. Vocational and academic qualifications, it has been declared, should be accorded parity of esteem.

At university level the Business and Management area was identified for early treatment, through the "Management Charter Initiative". Already tax benefits for students on courses in this area are being restricted to accredited National Vocational Qualifications, and universities are seeking to conform.

Industry and professional bodies have responded with some confusion. Government claims that standards for vocational qualifications are being set by industrial employers via Industry Lead Bodies, but employers remain distant and bemused, denying "ownership" and responsibility. Professional bodies (including lawyers, personnel managers and engineers) fear an assault on their status and power if their own qualifications are required to be accredited against externally imposed standards. Engineering Examination Boards remain attached to traditional qualifications, and are seeking to withhold recognition from university engineering courses which deviate from traditional entry requirements.

Government have recruited public relations advisers within the new Universities and Colleges Admissions System to persuade universities to accept General National Vocational Qualifications, or "Vocational Advanced Levels", as sufficient for university entry at a time when admissions are being further curtailed. Frustrated arts students may be in competition with those with the new vocational qualifications for places on low-budget engineering degree courses.

3. A Cultural Gap between Politicians and Engineers

In Britain very few politicians, or their senior civil servants, have a background in engineering, science or technology. An arts background has traditionally been the route to success in the professions (meaning accountancy and law), and in business and management. Even in manufacturing industry it has not been assumed that managers will have experience, or understanding, of the processes they are managing. This is replicated in the civil service, including civil servants responsible for vocational education and training.

The conventional assumption has been that engineers are concerned with making things, and that the age of manufacturing has passed, to be replaced by a new and more civilized age of service industries. This new age will require different skills, and "smokestack industries" must be closed.

To the extent that traditional industrial skills are still required, it has been assumed that they can be expressed in terms of specific competences, for which employees can receive specific on-the-job training, without requiring lengthy and expensive apprenticeship or formal education. Such employees would increasingly be contracted on a casual basis, rather than developing long-term expertise. Thus we have seen the growth of self-employment, and the reduction of trade union involvement in working life. Where public work is subjected to compulsory competitive tendering, there is pressure to accept the lowest bid, which involves the greatest degradation of wages and conditions, and reductions in standards of health and safety. Costs are reduced: that is enough for the accountants. Skill and Culture do not carry price labels.

4. Challenging Professionals

Just as trades unions were considered to pose a challenge to government power in the 1970s and 1980s, professionals are now being placed under pressure to conform. In a free market economy, where cutting costs is a primary objective, why should wasteful expenditure be devoted to education and training beyond the minimum required to secure competent performance of standard tasks? Why should the economy, and employers, be held hostage to the excessive and exorbitant demands of professionals and their professional bodies for protracted periods of study, and obliged to tolerate the arcane rituals of professional education and institutional practice? In the United Kingdom this question has been asked of teachers, doctors, nurses, firemen, police officers, ambulance men and prison officers: it is hardly surprising that the same challenges are being posed to engineers.

5. Engineering as a Form of Life

Engineering is a complex form of life, in which experienced practitioners have accumulated a mass of knowledge of different kinds [Cooley 1989; Rosenbrock 1989], including the modes of interaction with other professionals. Each artefact or tool embodies the skills of the maker: indeed the traditional craftsman would as a matter of course make his own tools. In so doing he would develop an awareness of strengths, tolerances, and variations from standard designs and constructions.

As Monk [1993] has pointed out, the typical graduate engineer is not directly engaged in the manufacturing process: his products tend to be designs and reports rather than physical objects. However, the designs and reports only derive their meaning from their relationship with the world of physical objects, and their formulations in language and symbols that are comprehended and used by the managers who constitute their audience. This suggests that the engineer must develop expertise in a complex process of knowledge representation and mediation, maintaining dialogue with the client or commissioning manager regarding the transformation of physical objects within the terms of an agreed specification, and recording objectives and progress in a variety of media.

In modern economic and industrial conditions it makes little sense to adhere to a traditional technocentric approach to engineering systems, where systems are regarded as complete and humans play a relatively subordinate role [Gill 1993]. Engineering efficiency and effectiveness will be enhanced if managers and workers can address technology in their own terms, recognising their role as active agents in systems which operate in a world of uncertainty and incomplete information. As Brödner [1990, 1993] has demonstrated in his work on anthropocentric systems in production engineering, the adoption of a new engineering culture has had a transforming affect on quality, the time taken to develop and bring to market new models, and levels of work satisfaction. Empowering workers at cell level on the factory floor, as Kaura and Ennals [1993] have shown, not only enhances manufacturing efficiency and effectiveness but changes working relationships and management structures across the company. In a context where human interaction and the shared interpretation of reports and designs are critical, it is somewhat anomalous if the emphasis of engineering education is overwhelmingly scientific, to the exclusion of insights from the humanities and philosophy. Engineers are actors in the world of business, organizations and politics [Corbett et al 1990], and need access to insights both from acting and the social sciences, much of which is best achieved through practice and reflection.

The philosopher Ludwig Wittgenstein was an aeronautical engineer by profession, and drew on a background of practical experience, skill and reflection when discussing examples of language games with a physical aspect. Language, he argued, acquires its meaning through the context of use. He took a similar view of the basic mathematics studied by young apprentices. As Professor of Philosophy at Cambridge he would spend evenings in the canteen at the local technical college, where he was known as John, helping engineering apprentices with their mathematics. Understanding a picture was, he wrote [Wittgenstein 1974], like making a move in a calculus, or in a language game. He thus brought together the different symbolic worlds between which the engineer has to translate and mediate.

Monk [1993] takes up this point when he argues:

Engineering communities have their own specialized cultures. Evidence of their cultures is in their languages, their mathematics, idealizations of components, theories and traditions. One way of looking at the education of an engineer is to see it as a cultural acclimatization for a branch of engineering; that is the development of a fluency in a specialized language and its specialized tradition.

Monk talks throughout about Education, while the prevailing mood of government is to talk of Training. He notes, after a brief survey of changing perceptions of engineering over recent decades, that:

It is unlikely that the engineers' narrow specialist education equipped them to understand and adapt to these cultural changes.

6. The Competence Approach

Monk [1993] has given illuminating insights into the work of the modern engineer. He writes:

Engineers do not deal with artefacts but denotations of objects; they produce blueprints, designs and reports. Their products are texts.

The distinction between work by hand and by brain has been falsely drawn, as Cooley has argued, and the present generation of computer technology permits us to end such arbitrary divisions of labour. The same engineer can both think and produce products.

In a society which makes no verbal distinction between the shopfloor mechanic and the graduate professional, calling both "engineers", the subtleties and rituals of the engineering culture are not recognized. The status of the British graduate engineer has suffered.

Instead, a Taylorist taxonomy of competences and standards has been offered, allowing the individual to claim competence in sub-tasks at any level on demand, and factoring out consideration of underlying knowledge and understanding, including craft and tacit knowledge. The competence approach offers cost savings, by declaring attendance at expensive courses superfluous as long as competence can be demonstrated in the performance of specified tasks.

The development of high power but low cost computing systems has further blurred understanding of skills. Increasingly manufacturing employees are required to mind machines, enabling unskilled staff to produce high technology products, but leaving them impotent if the machines malfunction.

Monk [1993] is right to note that although computers have changed the work of the engineer, they do not make the engineer redundant:

People are still needed to think about questions of reliability, safety and acceptability; people bring to bear experience, tradition, experiment and theory in answering these questions and making judgements about the contradictory evidence. How things are weighed up is affected by the culture in which the activity is taking place. This is not a task for computers.

Unfortunately executive decisions are often made at board level by managers who lack the necessary knowledge and understanding. Their use of the computer flows from their perception of the management task: the computer is merely the tool, a flawed management system is to blame.

7. Professional Education and the Third Culture

The work of the Swedish Institute for Worklife Research on the project "Education-Work-Technology" has demonstrated that there is a rich alternative tradition available, bringing insights from a humanistic tradition to the study of working life. Göranzon and Josefson [1988], Göranzon and

Florin [1990, 1991, 1992] and Göranzon [1992] have identified case studies and accounts of the "practical intellect" with which readers, particularly in a skeptical European context, can identify. The Springer "Artificial Intelligence and Society" series, in which the set of books appears, includes further titles dealing with Human-Centred Systems in engineering, by Brödner [1990], Corbett et al. [1990] and Rosenbrock [1989]. At Kingston University we have tried to rise to the challenge with "Managing with Information Technology" [Ennals and Molyneux 1993], to be followed by a new series of "Executive Guides" aimed at a management audience concerned with technology topics.

In what some have called the "Third Culture", we reject the over-rigid demarcation between arts and social sciences on the one hand, and natural sciences and technology on the other. We see science and technology as being conducted in a cultural context, and applied with the priority given to human need. While rejecting a narrow anthropocentric view of the world, which can have damaging implications for the environment and other species, we see humans, rather than technology, at the centre of systems. We regard technological systems as implementations of ideologies, and to be treated with similar caution: systems are based on models of reality, often with arbitrary approaches to quantification, and can never be relied on as substitutes for human judgement.

Engineers, including knowledge engineers, will need to play a central role in this "Third Culture", but this will require reforms in Engineering Education. In turn, this requires changes in the broader Educational and Political System.

If we wish to argue for the existence of a common culture, or a Third Culture which bridges the worlds of Arts on the one hand and Science and Technology on the other, then we must acknowledge the major implications for Education. Narrow vocationalism is destructive of a common culture, and serves only the interests of a ruling elite, typically drawn from a background in the Arts. Once professional skills have been destroyed, whether through automation or narrow vocationalism, it is not clear that they can be rebuilt: whole professions can vanish never to return.

We may identify common classes of concern across the professions, and see the case for new cross-disciplinary and international courses which may serve to enhance solidarity and mutual understanding.

Actors as Professionals

When considering professional development, actors are often excluded from the debate, yet they exemplify a number of critical characteristics of professionals. They have to present a public face to an audience, working from a script on commission, mediating complex issues for the non-specialist. They are subject to critical scrutiny, and their ongoing employment is contingent on successful performance. Though working from a script, the intervention of the actor is critical, and each performance constitutes a test of professional skill.

The skilled actor can manipulate his audience as an engineer can modify his system, and playing an active role in a real-time set of events, dispels views of the adequacy of prepackaged solutions. The actor has to engage in implicit dialogue with his audience as the engineer does with his client, often working with rough hewn and inadequate material.

Critics as Engineers

Engineers are frequently called upon to write consultancy reports on the working of particular systems, or to compare and contrast alternative solutions to specified problems. A professional vocabulary of critical language has developed, and a reference set of cases or systems which can be used as benchmarks or touchstones of quality. We can identify styles and traditions, techniques and devices, which may be more or less integrated, well-conceived and appropriate to the needs of the user.

We can thus see a sense in which engineers are critics for part of their work, but we may encounter more apparently principled resistance when we talk of critics as engineers. Many critics like to stand back from the phenomena they describe, reluctant to acknowledge their presence in the systems or cultural products under study. They point to their experience and technical expertise, but fail to notice the corresponding characteristics of engineers, with whom they may have little social discourse.

We do not claim to be able to create a world where all are multi-talented, able to work across the professions, but we need to open up and extend the dialogue which makes change and mobility possible. This approach makes for life and the revival of productive skill, in marked contrast to the policy of involuntary industrial euthanasia epitomized by National Vocational Qualifications.

References

Brödner P *The Shape of Future Technology: The Anthropocentric Alternative* Springer 1990

Brödner P *Two Traditions of Engineering Culture* presented at "Skill and Technology: Diderot, Education and the Third Culture", Stockholm, September 1993.

Cooley M *European Competitiveness in the 21st Century* EC FAST Programme 1989

Corbett M, Rasmussen L and Rauner F *Crossing the Border: The Social and Engineering Design of Computer Integrated Manufacturing Systems* Springer 1990

Ennals R *Can Skills be Transferable?* in eds Göranzon B and Josefson I 1988

Ennals R *Artificial Intelligence and Human Institutions* Springer 1991

Ennals R and Gardin J-C (eds) *Interpretation in the Humanities: Perspectives from Artificial Intelligence* British Library 1990

Ennals R and Molyneux P (eds) *Managing with Information Technology* Springer 1993

Gill K Human Centred Systems: *Foundational Concepts and Traditions* in eds Ennals R and Molyneux P 1993

Göranzon B *The Practical Intellect* UNESCO and Springer 1992

Göranzon B and Cook J (eds) *Skill, Technology and Enlightenment* Springer 1994

Göranzon B and Florin M (eds) *Artificial Intelligence, Culture and Language* Springer 1990

Göranzon B and Florin M (eds) *Dialogue and Technology: Art and Knowledge* Springer 1991

Göranzon B and Florin M (eds) *Skill and Education: Reflection and Experience* Springer 1992

Göranzon B and Josefson I (eds) *Knowledge, Skill and Artificial Intelligence* Springer 1988

Judd S *Hybrid Managers in Information Technology* in eds Ennals R and Molyneux P 1993

Kaura R and Ennals R *Human Centred Systems: The 21st Century Paradigm?* Working Paper, Kingston Business School 1993

Monk J *The Politics of Engineering and the Rituals of Engineering Education* presented at "Skill and Technology: Diderot, Education and the Third Culture", Stockholm, September 1993.

Rosenbrock H (ed) *Designing Human Centred Technology: A Cross Disciplinary Project in Computer Aided Manufacture* Springer 1989

Wittgenstein L *Philosophical Grammar* Blackwell 1974

Chapter 27

Engineering Training with a Human Face
The I-Program at the Royal Institute of Technology, Stockholm
Albert Danielsson

Lennart Mörk, the artist, has given the engineering technologists at the Royal Institute of Technology, Stockholm (KTH) a logo. It is an i with a "human face" – a logo which faithfully represents the ideas that lie behind the design of the engineering masters program.

***

Industry and other "users" of engineers often stress that engineers must possess not only purely technical competence and qualities of leadership, they also need to be competent in the field of economics. It is therefore important for us to identify the central aspects and the nature of these kinds of skills. One aspect of economics skills is, of course, knowledge of what we may call "business administration techniques"; knowledge of both external and internal accounting and computations for various purposes, including price-setting and investment. Yet the core of this competence should be the insight and judgement needed for both the development and application of technology based on criteria other than purely technical, economic, social, marketing, organizational, human and ethical considerations. If engineers are to participate successfully in managing both the design and implementation of technical applications, they will need the ability to make integrated assessments. At the same time, it is at least as important to emphasize that skills in the technical and natural sciences are essential if these integrated assessments are to be made at all. Without these skills as a basis there is a risk that the assessments will still miss the point and be as one-sided as a simple economic calculation, devoid of any real content – the emphasis being on form rather than on content. Moreover, it is essential that technical competence extends from basic technology right up to technical applications.

***

Technical applications must be designed and implemented in several stages, and one must often consider alternative technological designs at a number of these stages, not only in the introduction and use of the technology in question. The problems that occur in this work are many and varied. Adapting the final technological solution may sometimes require input at all the stages from basic natural science to direct application. While this opens up possibilities for alternative designs at each stage, it also generates a need for links between the different stages. Each stage should, as a general rule, be dealt with by people who are well-qualified in, and have a profound understanding of, their field. But an assessment of the entire chain requires an overall view of its component parts and, above all, an understanding of the whole and of the ultimate use. Therefore the task of leading and managing the development and applications of technology in its turn presupposes the ability to communicate one's viewpoints over the whole chain. The skills brought to bear must cover natural sciences-technology-economics both as links in a chain and as a whole.

* * *

A growing amount of attention is being given to the problem of engineers with different specializations, for example, design engineers and production engineers, failing to communicate with each other on complex or profound professional issues. Not least modern Japanese production philosophy has emphasized the need for this kind of communication, which is expressed in the term "concurrent engineering". To the superficial eye, social measures could perhaps be introduced to alleviate these difficulties, measures such as meetings, projects and shared coffee breaks. This is also the prevailing view of the problem and of the way to solve it. But without ignoring the fact that social contacts are an absolute prerequisite, and without minimizing the problems involved in achieving them – partly because people in these different occupational categories often work in different geographical locations – I must emphasize that the core of the problem is substantially deeper. Engineers who have majored in different specializations often get different kinds of job and therefore have different practical experience. They also have different tasks and areas of responsibility. The design engineer has to focus on the design of the product and its use, while a production engineer not only concentrates on the manufacture of the product, he is also responsible for the people who carry out the production.

The even greater differences in views, skills, work tasks etc. between engineers on the one hand and business managers on the other are a constant source of misunderstandings and poor co-operation.

Wittgenstein's philosophy tells us that concepts, above all their content, sense and meaning, spring from the concrete practical experience of their users. Language, concepts and thus the entire professional competency as such, are thereby also related to occupational training and experience. To achieve a deep level of communication one must therefore become familiar with the conditions that obtain in several parts of the whole. One way to acquire this knowledge is to study the formation of knowledge and the ways that knowledge is formed in these different areas of competency.

* * *

Let us take a closer look at the problem that the application of technology in a given situation raises its own, very complex skill problems. Everyone agrees that it is essential to have some basic technical knowledge, and an understanding of those parts of the natural and social sciences that are relevant to the technology to be used. In addition to this, however, we need to know about the situation in which the technology is to be applied, and also about the way the situation has developed. The best analogy here may be one taken from the field of medical care: before a physician can use his bio-medical, medical and physiological knowledge he must familiarize himself with his patient's situation and history.

* * *

We know from experience that an understanding that technology must be applied and the ability to apply technology are just as fundamental as a knowledge of mathematics. It follows that a program of education in which this knowledge and ability is of central importance must take great pains to ensure that this result is obtained. How is this done? How can one pass on the understanding that it is the application of technology that gives it its value? How can one instil the ability to apply technology? Here, if not before, the considerations we mentioned above (of economics, marketing etc.), have a part to play – in short, here is where man enters into perceived reality. It appears that the simplest response is the only response: the program of education must contain examples of technical applications. But the choice of applications and the number of applications to be included must be made in the light of practical considerations – the number of students, the resources available etc.

Together with the skills requirements mentioned above, the need for technical application produces a program of higher education that is made up of a large number of subjects which are in many respects disparate. If we are to understand and direct a complex operation we must not only consider both the parts and the whole, we must also consider the environment and context in which this whole is set. The environment and context may be purely spatial – the corporation and the markets for a division of a company, for example – or they may involve broader aspects and viewpoints such as a company's results and its economic position compared with its cost development. We sometimes use the term integration to describe the melding of the parts to form a whole. It is important that our efforts at integration are combined with a holistic approach.

The objective of this program of higher education was defined as the provision of knowledge and understanding of Technology-Economics-Leadership. It encompasses both the parts and the whole.

The ways that knowledge is formed in the different subject areas must become a central area of study in a program of higher education that encompasses such wide differences in perceptions of reality, scientific ideals and the formation of knowledge as the I-Program. An understanding of these differences appears to be an essential prerequisite for communication between the different parts of the program. At the same time, we have very limited knowledge and understanding of the components that we do not ourselves represent. Therefore, if we are to act as a bridge between the different areas involved, we need to begin by forming knowledge and understanding in these different areas.

* * *

The design of a program of education is not confined to planning the component subjects. A good syllabus is not enough; the content must also be of good quality. The other factors that have a decisive influence on the content and outcome of a course must be considered as well. These include the students, researchers and teachers, the "users" of the program, and the directors of the program.

In a program of education, content and form are related to each other in a number of fairly intricate ways. It is, of course, obvious that some subjects need laboratory work to be understood and learnt, while others (for example co-operation with and the management of other people) requires some experience if they are to be at all meaningful.

The form of the program is often addressed as pedagogics, as a distinct area, separate from the course content. Let me say that, at least when it comes to training of the nature of the I-Program, this kind of separation is quite impossible, not least because the form – the pedagogics – must follow the scientific view, i.e. the perception of what knowledge is and consists of, how it is formed etc.

Where there is a lack of experience (particularly common experience) new ideas cannot be based on an existing common language. Things cannot be said; they must be shown. One way of showing is to present examples, cases, reference facilities etc.

When it comes to the content and form of the program of education, it is not so immediately apparent that if new knowledge, ideas etc. must be shown because they cannot be said, this must also be true when people have to learn something that is new to them. If new scientific findings must be shown before they are accepted, then good teaching methods for a course in this field must be based on showing the content. In its turn, the way the content is shown very much depends on what that content is. In economics, for example, much of the teaching must take the form of studies of examples and practical cases. This corresponds to the laboratory work mentioned above. In more general terms, this means that a large part of economics has to be studied as a problem-oriented subject and as a complement to the more common discipline-oriented course structure. Problem-orientation is also an advantageous way of approaching the whole.

* * *

Knowledge, which is the result of education that is most frequently discussed, also appears to be the least permanent of all the things we acquire through education. At the same time, we often refrain from discussing the application of knowledge. Here I am referring mainly to two results of education that are related to the design of a program of higher education:

- The ability to solve problems – even very difficult problems.
- The ability to formulate problems.

That knowledge should be use both to solve problems and to posit problems is something that can hardly be said, it must be shown. But what happens when, as is often the case, the program of education focuses entirely on problem-solving? This is an example of one of the most profound aspects of every course of education, and which is naturally linked to the problem of showing what cannot be said that is discussed above.

A program of education always imparts what it shows

Another example of showing something is that the choice of what is and is not included in a program of education will create an impression of what is more important and what is less important. Thus, the very choice of mathematical methods to solve problems shapes our perception of what is a problem, and how problems should be defined. What is sometimes referred to as the right to formulate problems is one of the most important ways of exercising influence.

The most important aspect to emerge from a program of education is the way the student learns to relate to the world. Do (even ready-made) solutions exist for all the situations that a qualified engineer may face? Or – at the other extreme – is prompt action the most important factor, because, after all, one cannot foresee the effects of one's actions?

The attitude that one must strike a reasonable balance between these two extremes based on a thoroughly-prepared and well-informed assessment is implanted already at the training stage in a young person's life. That is to say, it is inculcated through the way in which the different parts of an activity are dealt with and presented, and the sequence in which they are introduced. It follows that the question: "What is a problem?" must be constantly present throughout this training stage.

The most enduring result of a program of education is the attitude that the form of the program helps to develop in the student. I myself have long since forgotten most of what I learned at the Stockholm School of Economics in the 1950s. But the spirit of enquiry that my teachers, Bertil Ohlin and Gerhard Thörnqvist, instilled in me by the way they questioned things and penetrated problems in their teaching – "reaching behind the apparent" – has stayed with me throughout my life.

* * *

The ability to be able to formulate your own opinions and define your own objectives is one of the unique and most distinctive qualities of man.

Chapter 28

The Systems Analysis Skill

Kate Startin

Introduction

The starting point of this study was an observation, made over a number of years in IT, that two communities of software developers approach their work in very different ways and rely on different types of knowledge. Further, it was noticed that the differences were systematic, in that one of the communities valued the technical skill, while other valued the communication skill.

It was realized that while the technical community enjoyed a higher reputation among computer people, it was often the non-technical one which displayed greater competence in the area of systems analysis. However, there seemed to be little theory underpinning this competence, and the skill appeared to be largely unspoken or 'tacit'. Further, there was little movement of staff between the two communities, and the more technical group seemed unable or unwilling to recognize the other's competence, let alone to learn from it.

This report is a first step towards exploring these issues. In the longer term, the research has the following aims:

(a) to describe the two communities in terms of their different histories, different knowledge, and the consequences of this in their different practices

(b) to name and better understand the tacit (unspoken) knowledge of systems analysis

(c) to understand why some of this knowledge is unique to the one community

(d) to consider how the competence might be shared with the other community.

Here, the attempt is made to describe the two groups, to sketch out some of the knowledge involved in systems analysis, to provide some insights into why it is localized in the one group, and to suggest some practical ways in which the competence might be shared.

Method

The work draws on the author's experience of working in the software industry for many years. It is not based on a systematic survey, but is the result of observation and reflection.

It is informed by the following theoretical positions:

i) a constructionist rather than an objectivist view of knowledge. According to this view, knowledge is socially constructed rather than always already 'there'. It therefore becomes important to look at the history of a group of skilled practitioners, in order to understand how their knowledge was constructed.

ii) the understanding that much knowledge is tacit or unspoken, and that some of it can possibly never be articulated for logical reasons. However, this does not mean that this tacit knowledge cannot be named. Nor does it mean that all knowledge which is currently tacit can never be articulated.

iii) the recognition that examples can help to convey knowledge which might otherwise be tacit, and further, that creative narratives may have greater potential in this regard than flat texts.

Historical Construction of Knowledge

A constructionist view of knowledge guides the description of the different software communities under consideration. It prompts consideration of the background of those involved. Their skills need to be understood in terms of their personal histories.

It is assumed that some of the relevant knowledge is tacit: the histories of the practitioners provide some pointers about what this knowledge might be. Where these histories are very different, the skill profiles also vary. This explains why some relevant skills are completely missing from one of the communities. The descriptions also prepare the ground for an understanding of why the exchange of knowledge between the two communities is so limited.

Tacit Knowledge

The notion of tacit knowledge underpins the investigation into the knowledge involved in the systems analysis task. There is obviously a problem in trying to identify tacit knowledge, and the personal histories of the practitioners give some indication of what knowledge is being used. It is also possible to analyze the social scene for symptoms that tacit knowledge is involved. These include the way in which the participants organize themselves and communicate with each other, as well as an assessment of their relative success in performing the work. Finally, reflections on the author's own practice as an analyst are used to speculate about how the work is done.

The aim is to look at what practitioners actually do and the way they reflect on it, rather than what theorists say they do. It is assumed that the relationship between theory and practice is problematic. The methodologies, techniques and tools taught on Systems Analysis courses are therefore of less interest.

Use of Examples

Specific examples of the two communities of software developers are given below. They are presented in a series of comparisons, of differences and of similarities, to highlight what identifies and distinguishes each community.

The differences and similarities are listed under four headings – Staffing, Organization, Communication and Concept of Knowledge. Together these help to point to the tacit knowledge being used, either in terms of personal histories or symptoms of knowing practice.

Subsequently, a key concept in the field of software development is explored, that of an 'application'. This illustrates some of the consequences of the differing concepts of knowledge, in the diverse practices of the developers concerned. It also provides some clues about what knowledge is involved in the systems analysis task, and how it is seen by practitioners.

Lastly, the author's personal experience as an analyst is presented as an example of the sort of background that systems analysts may have.

Perhaps later in the research, when the details of the systems analysis task have been further explored, it may be appropriate to further use the insight about examples and creative texts to present and share some more detailed aspects of the knowledge.

This whole study is the result of reflection on the author's long experience in the software industry. The attempt is being made to make sense of a significant anomaly – that familiarity with the accepted theory does not coincide with the best practice.

Three Examples, Two Communities

Three examples of software development groups are described below. Two of them are believed to be fairly common in the IT industry, and representative of different approaches to development. The third is not thought to be an example of a common occurrence, but it is included because it helps to sharpen the distinction between the other two.

The first was the group of developers which serviced the systems needs of users in an insurance company. The company's line of business was not concerned with technology. Examples of other companies which are known to tackle their development work in the same way are the banks and other financial institutions.

The second group worked as part of a telecommunications company, where the main line of business was new technology. They developed business software for the operating staff in the company. Other software groups which are believed to organize themselves in similar ways are those which service the engineering and defence industries.

The last group worked on Knowledge Based Systems (KBS) in the Research and Development branch of a leading software house. They undertook development projects using this technology in order to show other developers how to apply it. Their job was to transfer the new technologies to the more traditional development teams. The author has only encountered a similar approach to development once before, over twenty years earlier, in the R&D department of a major computer manufacturer.

These groups are compared below: firstly the R&D with the telecomms developers, and then the telecomms with the insurance developers. The R&D and the telecomms developers are found to be fairly similar, and are believed to belong to the technical community of software developers. The telecomms and insurance groups are very different and seem to come from different communities. The insurance group can be said to belong to the non-technical community of developers.

Comparison between R&D and Telecomms Developers

Similarities

Staffing:
Both recruited heavily from graduates in the scientific disciplines, especially Computing and Engineering, and both had a high percentage of staff with post-graduate qualifications. They expected their staff to be able to learn about new technology very quickly and to be competent programmers.

Organization:
A particular development team did not employ different types of specialists, but all members were expected to be good programmers and technicians for the hardware and software being used. Different projects recruited different technical experts: for example, one project might look for 'C' programmers under Unix, and another would look for Smalltalk programmers on Sun workstations. There were different types of technical expertise in the company, but there was very little variety on any one development team.

In each company, there was a separate group of Human Computer Interface (HCI) specialists who could be called in as consultants by a development team. Such expertise in the ergonomic and psychological aspects of systems was little valued by the development teams, who seldom consulted the HCI people.

Technical knowledge about the operating systems and the databases was diffused throughout the teams and was not centralized. There would be members on every team who were particularly interested in this deeper technical knowledge, and had taken the trouble to educate themselves in these areas. At the same time they would be expected to develop application programs, and their job titles would not differ from those who only wrote application code.

In neither group did the project managers have direct software development experience. The managers of the telecomms group came from the business areas, while those of the R&D group came from Sales or academic research.

Communication:
Communication about technical matters was informal and generally effective. Programmers would share their knowledge, give advice, and swap handy hints as they sat at their screens. They only read manuals as a last resort.

There was a great reluctance to document anything they had developed, and such documentation was felt to be at least a chore, and even a waste of time. They did not find writing the documents a helpful process, and others often complained that reading them was also unhelpful.

They were very keen to develop prototypes (i.e. quick mock-up programs which show the users what the screen layouts will be, what the system will do, etc.) to communicate with their users, because they were more comfortable writing code than text. They found prototypes more effective than documents for communication purposes.

They often had problems in distinguishing between what the system must do with how it should do it. They wanted to talk about how it would work, so that they could describe it in technical terms.

Communication with outsiders was often typified by an excessive use of jargon which effectively shut other people out from discussions and decisions.

Concept of Knowledge:
Both groups valued theories, and these were drawn from engineering and mathematics. Science was seen as the highest form of knowledge. The staff were generally keen on any new technology, and worked hard to keep themselves up-to-date. They envied those colleagues who worked on the most advanced technologies. They were not interested in the human aspects of computing or in the users' business problems. Their interpersonal skills were often poor.

Differences

Staffing:
There was one major resourcing difference. The telecomms developers had sometimes worked as engineers out in the business areas, where their users worked. Every project team seemed to have three or four people who had this experience. All of the project managers were very experienced, either in telecomms engineering or in business operations.

The R&D developers were generally much younger. Their systems knowledge was mostly theoretical, although they had gained practical experience in programming at the Universities. They had no background knowledge of their user areas, and little feel for what their customers would find usable or useful.

Communication:
The R&D groups sometimes had no idea who needed to know what, either within or beyond the development team. They were also unaware that their users' attitude to technology may be very different from their own, and were ignorant about the users' business problems. They had difficulties in managing the users' expectations about the new systems. In fact, this is obviously more difficult for a new technology than for an established one.

The telecomms developers communicated about the application among themselves: informal discussions were held at whiteboards, and any changes immediately and effectively communicated to those programmers whose work was affected. However, the lack of simple, formal documentation meant that many junior programmers did not know how their work fitted into the whole system. In addition, the managers did not know exactly what the system was going to do or how it was going to do it. They could only react to problems, rather than forestall them.

There were problems in establishing the requirements of the telecomms users, because the systems were intended for use in many very different business areas whose requirements varied. User Committees, consisting of senior staff, were set up to coordinate requirements. These were very political groups. This made it rather difficult to contact any ordinary users directly. However those developers who had previously worked in the business areas themselves were often able to steer a systems project in the right direction in spite of the problem.

The users' (i.e. the telecomms engineers') attitude to technology was similar to that of the developers, and so there was no great gap to be bridged here. Again, the experienced people from the business areas could advise the other developers in this matter.

Organization:
The organization of the telecomms company was deeply hierarchical. There was some evidence that this caused problems when the senior people on the User Committee had to be interviewed by the developers: they could not be interviewed by someone at a much lower level in the hierarchy, but the development manager might not be sufficiently familiar with the details to be able to conduct a useful interview.

The R&D people had a much flatter hierarchy and so this was not such a problem, although some experts did not appreciate being interviewed by very young staff.

Concept of Knowledge:
Industry knowledge was very highly valued by the telecomms group, and this often involved experience rather than qualifications. It was realized that it took considerable time to acquire this relevant background knowledge. Developers who came in from other industries had to start at the bottom, almost irrespective of their systems experience.

On the other hand, the R&D developers had little respect for the knowledge of the experts whom they interviewed, and were generally exasperated at their ignorance. They reified knowledge, regarding it as thing which could be captured or 'bottled' for future use. They did not anticipate any problems in specifying all of the preconditions on the rules in their expert systems. This attitude to the knowledge of their users was reflected in the way they saw the knowledge in the IT industry itself.

Summary of Comparison between R&D and Telecomms Developers

What stands out in these comparisons is the marked similarities between the R&D and the telecomms people. They seem to come from the same tradition of systems knowledge. They value the same types of knowledge, see problems in the same way, have the same sort of personal histories. This tradition is academic and theoretical. It owes a clear debt to both mathematical and engineering knowledge.

Perhaps it is seduced by new technology. Technology is not seen so much as a means but as an end in itself. We could call this the 'high-tech' tradition in IT. The application areas are themselves technical. The company is in the technology business, and all of the users see themselves as technologists.

Comparison between Telecomms and Insurance Developers

Differences

Staffing:
The insurance developers did not recruit from science graduates. In fact, there was some evidence that they actively avoided such staff, because their communication skills were thought to be so poor. The communication skill was very highly valued among these developers. If graduates were recruited at all, they would mostly be from the Humanities and would be very unlikely to have any post-graduate qualification.

However, young people were also brought in straight from school and trained on the job.

Some experienced insurance staff were brought into the development teams from the user areas, but they were not expected to work in any technical capacity. On the bigger projects, they would advise on requirements and usability.

Historically, the systems development teams in insurance and other similar companies grew out of the Accounting departments. This was because the first systems developed in such companies twenty-five years ago would have been accounting systems. It is still the case that the senior directors of systems departments are sometimes accountants rather than systems professionals.

Organization:
The insurance developers organized themselves into teams consisting of systems analysts and programmers. The analysts talked to the insurance staff about their requirements, and then defined them for the application programmers.

The more technical jobs, on the other hand, were centralized. For example, the systems programmers worked in a single team, specializing in knowledge of the computers' operating systems. This team of specialists supported the application programmers who worked on the many development teams. Similarly, the data administrators worked in a team specializing in database knowledge. The developers consulted them when necessary.

This centralization of the more technical jobs reflects in part the history of these developers in working on a large mainframe computer, rather than on distributed mini-computers. But it is mentioned here because it may reflect something else as well: it may be that communities group specialists together into homogeneous teams when they feel the need to formally manage the communication between that group and others. It could also be a symptom that the skill of the homogeneous group is scarce in the community, or perhaps that it is recognized that others have problems communicating with these specialists.

The telecomms teams were often larger and less structured than those in the insurance groups. They would contain a few good communicators who would be struggling with their programming work: however, their communications skills were not allowed any scope unless they also displayed technical expertise. The fact is that good communicators tend to gain access to knowledge associated with power. This was encouraged in the insurance teams, but it was not allowed to happen in the telecomms groups unless the communicator was also respected as a technician.

Communication:
The members of the insurance teams were usually experienced in working with the other specialists and there was a fairly clear understanding about who needed to know what.

Communication was typically via simple specification documents at different levels of detail. The systems analysts interviewed the users directly and specified the requirements before any programmers were involved on the projects.

There were sometimes misunderstandings: the analyst may have thought that something was technically viable when it was not. The programmer may decide to make a minor change for some technical reason, without appreciating its impact on the user. Basically, there was some tension between the analysts and the programmers, and some incredulity at each others' ignorance. It was the manager's job to minimize these problems.

Prototyping was little used except to show screen layouts, sequences, etc.

Concept of Knowledge:
The insurance developers did not value academic or theoretical knowledge in their staff, but experience was important.

They saw the systems analysis and programming tasks as being very different, requiring different types of people. The analysts needed to be good communicators, and the programmers needed to be good technicians.

The technical skill was not valued in the company as a whole, and technicians were unlikely to be promoted to the same level as the analysts. Systems managers tended to be recruited from among the analysts rather than the programmers.

Systems analysts were expected to be able to work on any application in the company, or indeed, on any application in the finance sector. It was thus assumed that the analyst could learn enough about the work in any department of the company, to be able to specify and design an effective computer system.

There was little interest in the latest technology for its own sake except among some of the programmers, and there was also little interest in software engineering theory.

The experienced managers all had their own pet theories about what worked and what did not. Basically, software was developed as it had always been, and change was resisted.

Similarities

Staffing:

Both communities brought people into the development teams from the user areas, in an attempt to bridge the communication gap. It was more difficult to spot this in the telecomms teams, because their ex-users became fully-competent developers. In the insurance groups, the users stood out more as they were unable to perform many of the technical development tasks.

Communication:

Both sets of developers were still criticized by their users for failing to understand what the business problems were. They were thought to be too remote from the business.

Concept of Knowledge:

Both groups saw the knowledge of the business area as very important, and difficult to acquire. Both recognized that it took time to gain familiarity with the way in which the industry operated, and prized the experience.

Summary of Comparison between Telecomms and Insurance Developers

Both the telecomms and the insurance developers 'kidnap' users to work on the development teams, and both acknowledge the need for developers to work in the industry sector for a number of years in order to get a 'feel' for the business.

One can see why it may be very difficult for those performing the systems analysis work to move freely between the different industry sectors of their users. This aspect of the profession is little mentioned in the literature.

However, there is no evidence that the two development groups arrived at the same point by sharing a common history. They seem to come from very different traditions of systems knowledge. They recruit different types of people, value different skills, use a different language.

The insurance developers come from a tradition which is not academic or theoretical. It is suspicious of new technology. Technology is seen as a means rather than an end in itself. This could be regarded as the 'low-tech' tradition in IT. The applications are not technical but relate to insurance. The company is not in the technology business.

The fact that the low-tech teams are multidisciplinary, whereas the high-tech teams are more homogeneous in their skill profile is interesting. Perhaps those with a scientific training are happier working in groups with a single perspective, along the lines that Kuhn suggests. The multidisciplinary groups may be more typical of the way industrialists organize themselves: different types of people work together on a production line of specialized functions.

The Concept of an 'Application'

The term 'application' in software development is used to refer to 'what we are going to automate'. Examples of applications are the general ledger, a personnel database, payroll, project planning, point-of-sale in supermarkets, medical records, diagnosing faults in computer networks, and credit assessment for loan applications.

'Application' is a key concept in the IT industry and it directs the actions of developers. The different concepts of knowledge used by the two communities of developers have clear ramifications on how they conceive of an application, and therefore how they conduct themselves in their practice.

It is apparent that the high-tech and low-tech developers think of applications very differently. Four ways of approaching this difference are presented below:

- objective *versus* constructive

- familiarity *versus* novelty

- implicit decision making

- distance *versus* entanglement

Objective *versus* Constructive

The high-technology people were proud of the fact that their applications were very complex. This betrayed a view that to them, the application was simply 'there', that it was in the nature of things. These developers did not believe that they could influence the complexity of an application. In this view, an application was a thing that a developer 'found'.

It was evident that when they interviewed their users about their requirements, the high-tech developers took all the requests at face value.

They did not seem to question or explore their relative importance, or to relate the stated needs to the business and administrative problems experienced by the users. In fact, they spent very little time with their users. They did not attempt to simplify the requirements. They saw it as part of their job to be able to handle whatever complexity they may encounter in the user areas. Such an 'objective' approach may well have its roots in the scientific training of the developers concerned.

In certain circumstances, such a strategy towards problem-solving may be crucial for applied scientists tackling practical problems in the natural world. Perhaps they cannot afford to shy away from perceived complexity.

This is in contrast to the attitude of the low-technology developers, who tried to make an application as simple as possible. It was an artefact to be fabricated by the developers. Different developers might define different requirements in response to the same situation. It was a question of judgement.

The users made an initial statement about their requirements. Repeated and frequent interviews placed these in the context of the users' business problems. The analyst became increasingly familiar with their day-to-day work, with the relative importance of solving the various problems. At the same time, various patterns were overlaid on the stated needs.

Different logical designs were tried against the mess of initial requirements. Above all else, a simple design or pattern was sought. The analyst 'rehearsed' the interview notes repeatedly until they were almost known by heart, and could be streamlined. This was tedious and exhausting, but it meant that a simple story could be told about the users' requirements.

On the one hand a dialogue was set up with the users to identify the crucial needs, and on the other a simple 'shape' had to be found. Some of the original requirements would be dropped from the application, and perhaps new ones added. Other management solutions had to be found for the problems not covered by the application. The analyst negotiated between the needs of the users and the need to keep the system simple or communicable. The simplicity was 'made'. Communicability was a necessary characteristic of any acceptable solution.

There are two crucial issues involved in the objective vs constructive viewpoints. The first view sees an application as 'found' and probably complex. The second sees it as 'made', and makes it as simple as possible.

Familiarity *versus* Novelty

The low-technology developers tended to recognize applications on a copy-cat basis which was largely unconscious. They assessed what was practical and likely to be successful on the basis of systems which they or others had already implemented. They tried to draw parallels between the business problems of their current users, and the users of systems developed in the past.

They looked always for the continuity with what had gone before. This hunt for familiarity ties back to the idea of the communicability of systems. If it is familiar, it will be easier to communicate.

The high-technology developers were less likely to recognize such similarities for a number of reasons. Firstly, they were looking for an exact fit with the users' stated requirements, and would be unlikely to consider anything which they regarded as a compromise. Secondly, they enjoyed technical novelty. New technology tends to deny its history, and to emphasize the discontinuity with all that has gone before.

Implicit Decision Making

The copycat recognition of applications by the low-tech developers seemed to be mostly unconscious, which is rather worrying. It may be useful to try to deconstruct how this instantaneous recognition of applications occurs. Among other things, it may help us to understand what social and ethical assumptions are implied in the development of computer systems. If we understand them, then we can challenge them.

It seems to be the case that recognition of when to use a new technology is initially conscious and laboured, but later it becomes unconscious and automatic. If the wider social issues are consciously considered when a technology is new, then perhaps later they may also be included when the recognition of applications becomes more automatic.

It is interesting to reflect that twenty years ago, software development was conducted only after an Organization & Methods (O&M) study had been completed. This study would consider various options for solving what was seen as a business problem, and might recommend automation.

Two things about O&M studies are interesting – they seriously considered alternatives other than automation, and they embodied principles about human work which were fairly obvious (usually Taylorism). Such principles have been much criticized for many years. However there is no reason why other studies should not be undertaken as a precursor to implementing new technologies, and they could embody different work ethics.

Nowadays O&M studies are seldom undertaken. Systems analysts now 'know' what should be automated with the more traditional technologies. The question is how did the change, from explicit assessment to automatic recognition of applications, come about? Is it the case that any new technology needs the equivalent of O&M studies when it is first launched, but that this need evaporates as the technology establishes itself? Would consideration of the wider issues in the initial studies, influence the later instantaneous recognition of what to implement?

Developers exploring new technologies could explicitly consider the possibility of not automating anything in some situations. Unfortunately those working on the newest technologies are the least likely to consider such an option because they are under pressure to 'sell', and because they personally want to explore any opportunity for the latest technology. Also, perhaps no new technology would ever get off the ground without the enthusiasm and drive of the technologists.

Distance *versus* Entanglement

There is another aspect to the 'application' issue. For the insurance developers, there was a clear distinction between their technical systems knowledge and their knowledge of the application area (the insurance industry).

It was rather different for the telecomms groups. Their users worked in a field which was very similar to the developers' own. Knowledge of the application area and knowledge of development technology were part of a seamless whole. They and their users were engaged in very similar work. Engineers could be users and developers at different times in their careers.

This may have contributed to the problems which they clearly had in writing functional specifications. These documents define what a proposed computer system is going to do, but should not mention how it is going to do it. The telecomms developers simply could not see any sensible distinction between the what and the how.

When an insurance developer talked about what a system did, she was talking about insurance: when she talked about how it did it, she was talking about technology. A telecomms developer only ever talked about technology – either telecomms technology or development technology.

The technologists were unable to get enough distance between their own work and that of their users to be able to 'see' it. This is sometimes referred to as the problem of dédoublement. It is experienced by authors who try to write about something they are deeply involved in: they find it difficult to get the necessary distance or perspective.

It is almost as if the high-tech developers understood the business problem only in terms of the technical solution. To the low-tech analysts, the telling of a simple story was what constituted understanding in the first instance: the technical implementation would come later and was not a prerequisite for an understanding of the problem.

Summary of the Concept 'Application'

The development practices of the two communities are different, largely because their ideas about knowing and their experience of knowing are different.

In the above presentation about the different ways in which the term 'application' is conceived by developers, the role of communicability stands out. It links all of the items listed above – 'making' as opposed to 'finding', simplicity against complexity, familiarity vs. novelty, implicit decision making, and distance against entanglement.

The systems analysts in the low-tech communities are preoccupied with making their systems communicable, whereas it does not seem to be a major issue for the high-tech developers.

In fact, there is some reason to suppose that the latter may have an ambiguous attitude to communicability: they want to be thought of as good communicators, as most people do. However, when they are not understood by others, it merely confirms their opinion that it is only intelligent people like themselves who can grasp the complex technology. The lack of communicability is necessary to maintain their high-priest status. They are in something of a communication 'bind', which is probably largely unconscious. The programmers in the low-tech community had the same problem: it seems to go hand-in-hand with technical competence.

A Preliminary Investigation of the Systems Analysis Task

Greater Competence in Low-Tech Requirements Specification

One of the starting points of this study was the observation that in one particular area, there was greater competence in the low-tech community than in its high-tech counterpart. This area was systems analysis.

The systems analysts in the low-tech community were better able to understand and specify the requirements of their users than were the developers in the high-tech tradition. It was far more likely that there would be simple documentation outlining what the proposed system would do, the system itself would be simpler and require less maintenance, and there were fewer surprises for the users when the system was installed in their work area. The requirements specification was quite simply better in the low-tech communities.

It is not obvious where the roots of the systems analysis work in the low-tech tradition lie. It may have grown out of the Accounting departments in large companies, or out of O&M studies. It may be unique to the Finance sector. It may come from the Humanities tradition in academia, except that some of its adherents clearly have very little academic background. Part of it certainly seems to be based on experience. This needs further investigation.

Some Personal Experience

It is part of the method of this research to reflect on my own practice as a systems analyst.

The first time I worked in this capacity on a development project, I failed abysmally. There were management problems: the work estimates were unrealistic, and the programmers had been allowed to start coding before I had a clear understanding of what system was required. The second time I got it right, and went on getting it right, with a few minor hiccups. The criteria for the successfulness of these subsequent systems was that the users were always pleased with them, and that few (if indeed any) bugs were ever reported on them.

I never worked closely with any experienced analysts, and I was only once given advice by anyone who had done the job in the past. I have never attended any course on the subject. (I later studied the theory of systems analysis, and it made little difference to my practice.)

However, I was not allowed to attempt the work until I had been in the industry for about ten years, and had undertaken numerous related tasks. I wanted to be a systems analyst for a long time before I was suddenly thrown in the deep end.

The related tasks which I performed in the meantime were either parts of the systems analysis job, or threw some light on it. They included development programming, maintenance programming, installation of word processing systems, designing parts of bigger systems, report writing, technical feasibility studies, interviewing people about their business problems, working for long periods in the user areas, and supporting the users in their day-to-day systems problems. Put together, these go a fair way towards covering the various skills required for systems analysis.

Reflecting on the Role of Experience

The following aspects of experience seem to be directly related to competence at systems analysis:

i)   Years of working with the users in the appropriate industry sector. This gives one a 'feel' for what they will regard as a usable system, and also what sort of system they will find useful. It has a direct bearing on one's judgement about what to implement. It does not seem to be necessary to gain this familiarity with the actual users of a given system, but just of the type of users who are typical of an industry sector (e.g. finance, manufacturing). Research by Human Computer Interaction theorists now addresses this as User Modelling.

ii) Experience in seeing what computer systems have been found to work. This involves some contact with working systems developed by other people, familiarity with the literature, and a track record of working on one's own successful projects. Experience of systems which do not work can also be very useful, under certain circumstances. One needs to learn what is practically feasible and what features of a situation increase the risks.

iii) Newcomers to the IT industry sometimes work on a team with a mix of experts, and learn what communication is necessary between these individuals. They learn who needs to know what by example, not by any explicit theory. They also learn roughly what work is involved in each specialism.

iv) Interview technique requires maturity as well as an analytical mind. It may not be necessary to watch an experienced interviewer in order to be good at it. It is important to understand the pressures the users (interviewees) are under in their work, and also to respect their practical knowledge. It is partly dependent on experiential knowledge of the users, mentioned in i) above. It takes some maturity to avoid competing with the interviewees, and to handle inconsistencies in their answers to questions.

v)   The definition of the users' requirements was described earlier in terms of making a simple story. People from the Humanities tend to be rather good at this, as do some people with very little academic training. However, no-one seems to need any lengthy systems experience to acquire the skill. It seems to be something to do with the type of person they are. It also seems to be an 'all or nothing' skill. People are either good at it or bad at it, but seldom anything in between. They either treat it as part of the job or they do not.

vi) The ability to recognize what aspects of a total, complex, messy, business situation are relevant to the systems task, appears to depend on experience. A competent analyst must know what to ignore and what attend to, and it varies from one project to another. It is a matter of judgement.

It may be that there are some transferable skills involved in the last three of the above items, and further reflection on these is necessary. Perhaps they can be acquired on Humanities courses, or perhaps such courses attract people who already have them. However, an academic background is obviously not necessary for acquiring the skills.

Knowledge Localized in one Development Community

It was claimed earlier that the requirements specification was better in the low-tech communities. This is surprising. It is generally held within the world of software development that the high-tech developers are better in every respect. It is heresy to suggest that low-tech developers could teach anything to their high-tech colleagues. There is no transfer of knowledge from the low-tech to the high-tech communities.

This is an important cultural issue. The high-tech communities regard themselves as high priests of systems knowledge: to suggest that they may learn from their 'inferior' colleagues is not just unmentionable, it is unthinkable.

There are a couple of reasons for this failure to transfer the skill of the systems analysts. The high-tech developers would not admit that the greater simplicity of the low-tech systems is 'made'. They believe that it is in the nature of the applications in low-tech industries that they are simpler: they take great pride in the fact that they are called upon to tackle more difficult problems. Therefore they fail to recognize any greater skill in the low-tech communities.

It is also most unlikely that they would ever have worked together with low-tech developers, allowing them the scope to make the simplicity. They will never have been close enough to the skill in action to believe in it.

Basically the problems are their different concepts of knowledge and their different experiences. These are not entirely independent.

There are a number of ways in which this problem might be addressed.

Firstly, it must worth trying to share with the high-tech developers insights about the limitations of the objectivist view. This must involve suggesting a viable alternative. It is important that the high-tech developers should understand that knowledge can be conceived differently, otherwise they are unlikely to appreciate what the systems analysts are doing.

Secondly, opportunities for seeing competent systems analysts in action might be provided, preferably on applications which come from the high-tech domain.

Thirdly, examples or even creative texts might be used to help to convey the knowledge which the analysts use. However, people with a scientific background may be suspicious of creative texts, and plain examples may be more immediately effective.

Finally, experienced systems analysts might be prompted to jointly reflect on their practice, in order to provide more insights into their work.

Summary and Directions for Further Research

This report provides some examples of different types of software development communities. They are described in terms of the personal histories of those involved, how they organize themselves and communicate with each other, and how they conceive of knowledge. The key concept 'application' is described for each community, and the consequences in their differing development practice. The claim is made for the greater competence in the systems analysis work of the low-tech community.

A preliminary study of the work involved in systems analysis is presented, and an attempt made to begin to name some of the tacit knowledge being used. Some reasons are given about why the knowledge seems to be localized in one of the communities described, and suggestions made as to how it might be shared with the other one.

Some suggestions are made about the possibility of deconstructing the process by which suitable computer applications are unconsciously recognized by systems analysts.

The following areas look promising for further work:

i)   more investigation of the systems analysis task, drawing on further theories from Kjell S. Johannessen, Allan Janik, Donald Schon, Betty Edwards and Martha Nussbaum

ii)   discussions with other practicing analysts, and their reflection on their work

iii)   meetings with more high-tech developers to establish the extent of the differences, and further reflection on the possible advantages of their problem solving strategy

iv)   deeper study of the official theory of Systems Analysis

v)   exploration of the use of examples and of creative texts in communicating tacit knowledge

Initially items i) and ii) above are of greatest interest and will be explored to identify more thoroughly the different types of knowledge involved in the systems analysis task.

Chapter 29

Comments
Jon Cook

The different pieces in this section all converge on a single question about the education of engineers. What they separately offer is a sense of the scope and dimensions of that question, the sense of what is at stake in posing it in the first place. Peter Brödner's paper identifies the problem in terms of two different traditions of belief about knowledge and practice. This finds an echo in the contrast Kate Startin discovers between 'high-tech' and 'low-tech' professionals in the software industry. Richard Ennals approaches the same problem from the perspective of national educational policy. Albert Danielsson provides a case study of what it means in practice to change the way engineers are educated by linking a technical and scientific education to an understanding of the cultural and practical forces at work in knowledge formation. Jon Monk's "Enigma Variations" builds on the immediately preceding section of this volume in its unfolding of the myth of Turing, in a way that draws out how easily discomforted our assumptions are not simply about Turing but about what it means to learn, or identify a machine as intelligent, or establish firm distinctions between hardware and software. Our knowledge of these things is finely implicated in the languages and cultures we inherit and in a manner that resists all attempts to break out into an unshadowed world of objective knowledge and transparent procedure. Ingela Josefson's account of conflicting traditions in the education of nurses shows that the problems addressed in this section are by no means confined to the education of engineers. The example she draws on from Sophocles's Antigone reminds us that the recurring tension between theoretical and practical traditions of knowledge, between the implementation of abstract law and the knowledge of the heart, is not subject to some dialectical reconciliation. An educational ethos based upon a confidence in the progress of knowledge through ever increasing forms of systematic explicitness is likely to avoid and then be haunted by the stubborn repetitions of tragedy, the form which addresses the limits of our knowledge and the sheer unavailability of the world to systematic understanding.

The purpose of these comments is not to offer a resumé of the various arguments and analyses put forward in this section. Taken together they all make a plea for the value of a subordinated and neglected tradition which values embodied knowledge, the skills that can only be developed fully through long experience, and the diversity of ways that knowledge can be represented and communicated. They all also raise a series of questions which are of crucial importance in thinking about the future of professional education.

The first of these has to do with the question of the national context. We are deeply accustomed to think of educational policy as the prerogative of sovereign nation states. At a time of intensifying economic competition it is not surprising that education policy should stress the cost-effectiveness of education and its relevance to increasing economic efficiency. The paper by Richard Ennals provides an example of how economic imperatives have driven education policy in the United Kingdom. One key phrase, "Taylorist decomposition', is important here and it is helpfully glossed by some sentences in Ennals's paper:

To the extent that traditional industrial skills are still required, it has been assumed that they can be expressed in terms of specific competencies, for which employees can receive specific on-the-job training, without requiring lengthy and expensive apprenticeships or formal education. Such employees would increasingly be contracted on a casual basis, rather than developing long-term expertise.

This process is already well under way in the United Kingdom. When educational objectives are reformed by economic imperatives in this way, it is unlikely that much attention will be paid, other than at the level of lip-service, to the development of a culture of deeply embedded skills and expertise. This is to put the worst case, at least if one of the objectives of the argument about tacit knowledge and skill is to change educational policy at national level. It may of course be in the long-term economic interests of nation states to give priority to tacit knowledge and skill in this way, but one question that hangs over nation states at the moment is whether they are able to act in relation to any long-term interest, whatever their aspirations.

But it may be that it is simply not an appropriate objective to seek to influence the formulation of national educational policy in this way. Should the education of engineers and other skilled practitioners be linked to and legitimated by a conception of national economic interest? Or is some other relation between knowledge, work, and economy emerging in the papers in this section, and indeed elsewhere in this book and the related books in this series? These questions cannot be answered here, but it is worth noting how closely in the past the education of engineers has been linked to projects of national construction and aggrandizement; how uneasily figures like Turing and Wittgenstein fit with ideas of national identity and interest (a point dramatized in the play Beyond All Certainty); and how important the issue of the location of ideas and practice is to the pieces collected in this section.

This last point can be illustrated in a number of ways. One has to do with a (further) question about the relation between the place of learning and the place of work. Again there is a familiar assumption: what is learnt in one place, the site of education, is applied in another, the site of work. In the case of professional education there is of course an interaction between these two sites while the qualifications to enter a profession are gained or ratified. But there is a kind of inertia built into this assumption which is at odds with the approach to professional education advocated here. What this assumption overlooks, or is in danger of overlooking, is the fact that the place of work is also the place of learning, and, as Ingela Josefson's essay suggests, this kind of learning may be actively threatened by procedures which link professional status to theoretical knowledge. Professional education needs to accommodate a kind of learning and knowledge which cannot be subject to formal testing, or, indeed, to Taylorist decomposition. This is so because it is a kind of knowledge which is inseparable from its application in practice. It exists in the act of its demonstration or performance. There are no simple rules or guidelines which can ensure its transmission or acquisition. But it does seem that working with but not imitating someone who is knowledgeable in this way is one necessary condition for its transmission. The process can be usefully compared to what happens when we catch a cold.

A familiar piety now haunts the argument: that professional education, whether of engineers or nurses, architects or teachers, poets or playwrights, is an education without end. It seems best put this way if only to distinguish it from the idea of 'education for life' which carries the resonance of long jail sentence. What is at issue here is a matter of perspective and practice, of working cultures attuned to the fact that people are always learning how to do their work, but (again) in ways that cannot be obviously formalized into a pedagogy which distinguishes teachers from taught. It may be that an effective working culture, and therefore an effective professional education, has to sustain both formal and informal modes of education, each with quite different and possibly incompatible assumptions. The danger of 'rationalization' of drives for 'more efficient use of resources' is that they will eliminate the informal cultures of learning and, in so doing, defeat their own objectives.

Albert Danielsson's essay raises another important question about the location of the education of engineers. Here the term 'location' has to do as much with metaphorical as literal places. What is the location of the concept of an education for engineers in relation to the diversity of activities and specialisms which go to make up engineering? The answer to this question does not come through the definition of some single abstract property which all these different activities share. It is more likely to come from an acknowledgement of that diversity and of the different working cultures that accompany it. And the diversity within engineering extends to the relation between engineering and other professions. One implication of this for the education of engineers as well as other professionals is that it is not only an education into a profession but into what lies beyond it.

But what appears to be beyond or outside a profession can in practice turn out to be at its centre. Ethical skill, for example is not some gratuitous extra for doctors or engineers but at the heart of what it means to be good at either activity. Or a training in knowledge formation encourages that sensitivity to differences, that art of discernment, which enables communication across professional boundaries. The contributors to this section provide different ways of thinking about how to go beyond what are commonly taken to be the limits of a profession and the education appropriate to it. It might involve a computing engineer writing a dialogue about Turing; or thinking about an engineer as an actor and writer as well as a technician and scientist; or reflecting on Sophocles's Antigone as part of a doctor's education; or understanding the implication of knowledge in practice. This in turn raises another question about location. How does professional education map on to the current academic disciplines? Are there important senses in which the deep division between the arts and sciences in the academic disciplines is at best irrelevant, at worst actively damaging to the education of skilled professionals?

The next section of the book, On Diderot, Analogy and Mathematics, is not intended as a direct or comprehensive answer to these questions. But that is because it may be more helpful to think about them indirectly. Thus Marian Hobson's commentary on the importance of analogy in Diderot's thinking extends Albert Danielsson's discussion of 'integrative assessments'. Paul Henry's essay on mathematics in the eighteenth century shows how a subject which is vital to the education of engineers can be thought about in the humanist perspective of history. It is a case study in knowledge formation as is Fedor Valach's discussion of Diderot's criticism of mathematics. Jan Unenge's essay turns more directly to the question of professional education in his discussion of new modes of teaching and, indeed, conceiving of mathematics in ways that stress the importance of judgement as well as rule following.

On Diderot, Analogy and Mathematics

Chapter 30

Diderot, Implicit Knowledge and Architecture
The Experience of Analogy[1]
Marian Hobson

Diderot was famous for his digressions: one commentator claims to have sat and listened to an uncontrollable stream which he satirizes in a manner not entirely unconvincing.[2] This paper is going to end by suggesting that Diderot's digressive practice is deeply related to his notion of analogy, as found in his art criticism, that he is developing a notion of analogy which will become precisely what links experience in a synthesis (and which is perhaps a preparation of Kant and 'die Analogien der Erfahrung' in *The Critique of Pure Reason*). Such analogy will both regulate the artist's treatment of the beautiful and anchor it to notions of the functionally dynamic. But – like Diderot – this paper will first move through what seems a digression about Diderot's digressions on architecture, asking what the relation between the ideas he is chasing is, and why he harps on about the great church of Saint Peter's in Rome.

At the end of the *Essays on Painting*, 1766, there are two last chapters, jokily called *My piece on architecture* and *A little corollary of the preceding* – which seem to be a set of digressions. In them, Diderot proposes the problem of the size of Saint Peter's in Rome, which is said to be so perfectly proportioned that it does not seem as big as it is. And he goes on to recount a discussion of illusion in proportions in architecture: some say it is better to make the building seem bigger than it is. This procedure may lead to disillusion – you may be disappointed when you realize that the building is actually smaller than your perceptions. Some on the other hand argue that it is perhaps better to let the proportions work harmoniously together and then to allow the comparison, which the spectator will infallibly make with his own size, to cause a gradual realization of the true vastness of the building. Diderot himself points to the social source of his discussion: There's the quarrel between gothic and Greek architecture put forward in all its force, he says. And contemporary with his piece on architecture is of course the re-entry of the gothic into the realm of publicly acceptable taste.

Now Diderot got into this question, into this digression, because he had started his chapter by claiming that if architecture was the founding structure for painting and sculpture, in return it was to these arts that architecture owed its perfection, because the sense of proportion could only be formed by the practice of drawing, that is how an artist forms his eye – and claimed the example of Michael Angelo and the dome of Saint Peter's. And after the digression on illusion of size in architecture he goes back to the question of proportion, in figure painting particularly. I remind you that *analogon* is the Greek for proportion. To finish, Diderot argues that architecture has been impoverished by a concern for modules, for perfect ratios, when it should only recognize "the variety of social conventions", that is social function.

But the next chapter in the *Essays* shows the problem: is not such a view of art relative? Does not Diderot's phrase, "variety of social conventions"[3] give away that there would be no common rule to such an art except a fitting to circumstance, it would be completely relative to its society. "Apage Sophista" he cries, and insists as he does so many times elsewhere: "The good the true and the beautiful hang together very closely." "What is taste then?" he asks. "It is a facility acquired by reiterated experiences to seize the true or the good with the circumstance that makes it beautiful, and to be promptly and strongly touched by it"(738). And this facility, when it is unconscious, so that the experiences which enabled the judgment are forgotten, is instinct. The example given is once more Saint Peter's in Rome. Michael Angelo creates the most beautiful possible form for the dome; when the French mathematician La Hire measures it, he finds that its outline is the curve of greatest resistance – the line of thrust. Michael Angelo was inspired by the experience of the play of dynamic forces in everyday life, says Diderot: the master carpenter will find the right angle to prop a crumbling wall up as well as the greatest living mathematician Euler. Likewise, experience will inspire him to find the optimum angle for the sail of the windmill. One can recognize here Diderot the editor of the *Dictionary of Arts* – one of the names of his great *Encyclopaedia*, edited with the mathematician d'Alembert.

Now Diderot had exercised these ideas before, in a letter written in 1762, and here, like the *Essays on Painting*, it is not at first sight clear what is linking the ideas together for him. But here too, it is a question of instinct. Instinct is the result of: "An infinity of small experiences which had begun from the moment we opened our eyes to the light, right up to the one where, guided secretly by those assays, trials, which we no longer recollect, we pronounce that something in particular is good or bad, beautiful or ugly."[4] And in apparently the same higgledy piggledy manner, Diderot trots out the example of St. Peter's, the strut for the wall, and the angle of the sail of the windmill. It is the notion of function, which seems to enable Diderot to link the beautiful (the shape of the dome) to the true and the good. The form which is the most economical and strong for a certain purpose will be the one instinctively felt as "right" in both moral and aesthetic senses. But if we want to try to go beyond this slightly unsurprising answer (Diderot speaks of "beauty whose base is always utility" (731)), and the simple equation of function and utility which is overtly performed in Diderot's Essays on Painting, then we need to tackle the problem of his digressions, of the interconnections in his argument. We need to ask: how are we to connect these themes, connected in Diderot's mind since they turn up twice together: tiny experiences, in the case of architecture physio-dynamic experiences; the problem of taste, and its relation to factors like social organization which may seem to make it dependent on human convention; the question of proportion, and whether it is numerical and stable, or whether it varies according to the same factors as taste.

The answer must start, as did the section of the *Essays on Painting*, with Saint Peter's.

Michael Angelo's architecture of Saint Peter's was thought to be perfect. And French travellers since the seventeenth century traditionally commented on the perfect proportions of the basilica, and the paradoxical impression it this produced in the visitor, given its huge size.[5] Montesquieu in his notebooks of his journey to Italy compares the impression made by Saint Peter's to pleasure in mountains, of the continuous sense of failure to measure exactly what one is seeing.[6] This is not the 'sublime avant la lettre', for the surprise created by the failure to measure does not go so far as to be a feeling of incommensurability; rather it remains a kind of suspension, continually restarted by changes in perception. It is surely connected with eighteenth century love of walks and with the subtle consciousness of dynamic physiological changes not just in visual sensation but in the sense of internal body space. Kant however, in 1790, referring to such reports, will in the *Analytic of the sublime* of the *Critique of Judgement* argue that this IS the sublime. It is interesting that he is no longer using the question of the proportions of the church, but the impossibility of taking in the whole.[7]

De Brosses – a friend of Buffon, lawyer, intellectual, one of the first writers who could be called an anthropologist, brings in a factor which pushes this enquiry on one step: he speaks of the admirable proportion which means that at first sight the basilica is not striking, because everything is in place, and admirably proportioned: unlike he says "a pointed vault in gothic style, or bold arches taken in an oval diameter."[8] The comparison with gothic architecture is in Diderot's mind, we have seen.

That Diderot had sustained contact with architects in the 1760s, can be proved via his letters, as well as via the remarks in the *Essays on Painting*. It is this implicit knowledge, developed by the contact with both practical technology and architectural theory which gives a depth and a richness to his thinking here. Reflecting about proportion, about analogy as a mode of thought and its relation to proportion, and relating it to these practices enables him to escape from the static formal idea of proportion common at the time, to link it with epistemology, with our organization of experience. His work does indeed point towards Kant's analogies of experience, though whether there is actual influence is unproven.[9] Unsurprising perhaps, when it is a question of implicit or tacit knowledge. Now the second anecdote connected with Saint Peter's that Diderot gives is not found in other writers on the basilica. The anecdote about the geometer La Hire and his assimilation of the profile of the dome of Saint Peter's to the curve of greatest resistance does not for example appear in the great work by Carlo Fontana on the basilica, though he does compare very carefully the inside and outside profiles of the dome.[10] In fact, the dome was actually constructed by della Porta, who it is now believed modified the Michael Angelo models. It is interesting for the argument I am developing that he is said to have eliminated certain features in which Michael Angelo seemed to have been moving towards a fusion of classical and medieval forms – that is the opinion of James Ackerman, who points out that della Porta took out from Michael

Angelo's designs the distinction between horizontal accents and vertical ones.[11] But however that may be, it does seem as if Diderot, or his informant, had understood the fundamental sense of dynamism, where according to Ackerman, there was a deliberate suggestion of muscular power. In fact it seems likely that his informant was an engineer familiar with La Hire's memoir on the construction of vaults in buildings.

La Hire was a son of a painter; he was also an engineer and an important mathematician.[12] He was interested in the practical application of his maths to machines – the theory of epicycloids for instance to cog machines. He worked on the shape of windmill sails and his published articles show that he was interested in the kind of practical knowledge of dynamics that construction workers had. Here of course Diderot would have recognized a precursor (he died in 1718, and had a series of important engineering pupils some of whom collaborated, or their pupils collaborated, on the engineering articles in the *Encyclopaedia*). The three examples Diderot gives, dome, buttress, and windmill, are all for the century examples of what the eighteenth century mathematicians called "the composition of movements" – resultants in present day maths, that is, the calculation of what happens when forces are not simple, but are operating in different directions to different degrees.

Now it is clear from his letters that Diderot in the first half of the 1760s was dining weekly with people whose importance has not always been appreciated by readers of his correspondence. Soufflot the architect of the new church of Sainte Geneviève, now called the Panthéon, which was in the very early stages of being built, is of course recognized. But Trouard and Blondel were also considerable architects and are also named as guests of Monsieur and Madame Le Gendre, brother-in-law and sister of Sophie Volland, Diderot's friend and probable mistress. Above all in importance there is the name of a man who cuts a slightly ridiculous figure in Diderot's correspondence, as an unwelcome perturber of Diderot's probably too familiar relationship with his mistress's sister: Perronet. Perronet was in love with Madame Le Gendre. He was also on the road to becoming an internationally famous engineer, one who radically changed the possibilities open to the constructors of bridges, in a way, we shall see, that affected Diderot. It is at this point that we rejoin the quarrel announced by Diderot between classic and gothic architecture.

Soufflot, with the aid of Perronet among others, was working on the structure of vaults, and attempting to find methods of construction of domes that would be lighter and less costly. He studied gothic architecture for this purpose: a civil servant points out that in his work for Sainte Geneviève the great Paris church now called the Panthéon, "his principal object as been to unite, in one of the most beautiful forms, the lightness of construction of gothic edifices with the magnificence and purity of Greek architecture".[13] The name of Sainte Geneviève in the present day, the Panthéon, takes on more meaning when one knows that Saint Peter's was itself supposed to be the modern and improved version of the Roman building and was designed in part to rival the great antique feat of engineering. But for the givers of the commission in Paris in the mid-1750s – building starts in 1756 – Sainte Geneviève is designed to bring together the magnificence of classic references and the great days of French Christianity, the gothic days of the saint herself, of King Clovis – and the public are said to have wanted a subterranean chapel like a Merovingian basilica. A commentator in 1778 promises for instance that "the view from the portico will give the illusion of the Roman Pantheon".[14] This was to be done using not the practices of classical architecture and contemporary French architects, but by an entirely new method of support for the dome, a method based on gothic architecture. Indeed, it is clear from other architects, or writers on architecture, that the motives behind this were in part economic – the royal treasury was in a parlous state, and if the church took so long to be completed it was because of the slow arrival of funds. Yet there were also aesthetic reasons: gothic architecture pleases because of the illusive effect of its loading, of the sense of thrust and dynamism created by the relation between the height and the fragility and complexity of the supporting pillars and buttresses. In that, it was obviously felt to be quite different from the static effect given by classical proportion in the Greek manner.

How had the gothic architects done this, creating buildings which were still standing? How had they got their building to stay up? Soufflot from early on in his career, in a memoir from 1741, shows interest in the technical questions of how the gothic cathedral supported its mass and admiration of the daring of the building skills it showed. In the 1741 memoir he wheels on the comparison between the gothic cathedral where our eyes are deceived by the proportions into believing them much bigger than they are, and Saint Peter's, where we believe it much smaller. And one can show that Diderot had this unpublished memoir in front of him when he wrote the *Essays on painting*.

There seems to have been round Soufflot, after the attribution of the commission for Sainte Geneviève, in the early 1760s "a concerted campaign to convince members of the Academy [of Architecture] of the practicability of [carrying a complex system of vaults and domes on elegant columns and light piers]". This campaign was conducted by the men with whom Diderot was regularly dining – Soufflot, Cochin, and Perronet.[15] It is precisely on this point, the loading of the dome, that Soufflot is attacked in 1769, after the commission for Sainte Geneviève was underway, by an old enemy of Diderot's, Pierre Patte. Patte claims that the building will not be able to bear the dome. (In fact the pillars did crack, but not for the reasons given by Patte).[16] The proponents of gothic construction say that studying gothic buildings could be of the greatest utility in order to prove:

...to what an extent we have abused the use of materials in the churches built in Paris in the last two centuries and to make us drop the prejudice which most architects had and seem to have that one can only build churches with huge square pillars and arcades, with thick walls and considerable side walls, for lack probably of having sufficiently examined Notre Dame and other churches of that type.[17]

In the struggle for power which followed, Perronet wrote two remarkable letters in defence of Soufflot, letters which throw a great deal of light on the context in which Diderot was working on his own aesthetics: Perronet points out that the weight of Soufflot's dome is not resting on the pillars, but is carried by a system of side buttressing, and says he has chosen an elegant and economical mean between gothic and classic construction.

The solidity of an edifice must depend more on the relation of active forces to those that are to resist them than on the size of the pillars or the walls and the disproportionate thickness of the vaults which in fact tends to make them collapse.[18]

So far he has pointed out that successful architecture is not just proportion, but a relation between active forces of strain and push. But he develops a remarkable comparison, that Diderot must have loved:

The magic of these edifices consists principally in having constructed them so to say in imitation of the structure of animals, the high weak columns, the nerves, the double arches, the ogives and tiercerons can be compared to animals' bones, and the little stones and voussoirs which are only four or five feet in thickness of cut to the flesh of these same animals. These edifices can subsist like a skeleton, or the carcass of ships which seem to be constructed according to similar models. In imitating nature thus in our constructions, we can with far less material make very lasting buildings; columns or ribbing weak in appearance, but fortified by abutting pillars of the same kind, easily hold up light vaults and domes which are in porte faux, which are not harmful here.[19]

Perronet points out that he is using the same principles to construct bridges, in particular the famous Pont de Neuilly (which alas was destroyed in 1958). Diderot gets himself invited in 1769 to see the bridge built on these new principles, and which was designed to close the perspective from the Champs Elysées which Soufflot had laid out.[20]

This remarkable analogy makes of the gothic cathedral a dynamic complex of thrusts and counter thrusts, and suggests that Perronet has been applying such principles to understanding the distribution of weight in living animals. Put with Diderot's remarks, engineering and architecture become linked to human perception of space. They make not an objective and static proportion, but a dynamic counterpoise derived from the eyes exploring what they see and translating this into complex structures of thrust and counter – thrust which correspond to internal sensation. This must be linked not just with the rediscovery of gothic architecture, but with Diderot's aesthetic as developed in his great art criticism. In the *préface* to the *Salon* of 1767, he describes how the artist develops a view of his subject which goes beyond what he sees, beyond the particular deformations which conditions, needs and functions have imprinted on it. This is not the work of one artist, in fact, but that of a whole tradition of artists. The work of this tradition was to separate individual deformation from functional structure. This was done "by long observation, by consummate experience, by exquisite tact, by taste, instinct, a sort of inspiration given to a few rare geniuses". This continued "with time, with a long and cautious development, with a long and painful testing [tâtonnement] with a submerged secret notion of analogy, acquire by an infinity of successive observations whose memory has been lost though the effect is still with us".[21] Such knowledge is doubly implicit: elaborated through inherited tradition, it is also developed unconsciously from experience, as Diderot had described the young Michael Angelo doing. It is this which develops the idea of proportion into a dynamic congruence of internal sensation, confirming function, and visual harmony. The "ideal model" is not in the antique sculptures, copying them will merely result in stylistic regression.[22] It is in the future, linked at each stage with specific social conditions,[23] but developed by an unconscious process which involves slow understanding of unexpressed relations.

That unexpressed relation is analogy. If these texts are related to the discussion of poetry in D'Alembert's Dream, analogy becomes not just a "rule of three"[24] but a complex and individual harmony based like a musical scale on rule-governed projection of intervals between notes.[25] Kant's conception of the analogies of experience is that we link our perceptions dynamically in relation to time and to temporal determination. Kant distinguishes the mathematical rule of three from philosophical analogy. The latter, unlike maths, does not give us the fourth member of the analogy, but the relation to it. This relation however, enables us to know where to look, so to speak. It doesn't constitute that fourth member by analogy, but regulates its detection. "An analogy of experience is, therefore, only a rule according to which a unity of experience may arise from perception".[26] "By these principles, then, we are justified in combining appearances only according to what is no more than an analogy with the logical and universal unity of concepts".[27] Analogies in both Diderot and Kant become part of the way we link together what we perceive, a way deep and mysterious. And Diderot's reader must reapply this theme to a reading of his work. The apparent swerves in his argument, the ceaseless digressions, force one to seek for the rule linking them, to pull them together into a dynamic and developing synthesis.

Notes

1 This paper is a version both shortened and developed of one being published in *Reflecting Senses: Appearance and Illusion in Cultural Representation*, ed. Walter Paper and Frederick Burwick, de Gruyter, Berlin, to appear autumn 1994.

2 *Mercure de France*, 1779, p. 172–174.

3 Diderot, *Oeuvres esthétiques*, ed. Paul Vernire, Paris, Garnier, 1959, p. 734. Pages hereafter in the text.

4 Diderot, *Correspondance 1713–1784*, ed. G. Roth, vol. 4, p. 125.

5 Cf. Misson, *Nouveau voyage d'Italie*, 1687. vol. II, p. 49.

6 Montesquieu, *Journal du voyage de Gratz à La Haye*, in *Oeuvres complètes*, collection l'Intégrale, Paris, 1964, p. 850. He reused the notes for his article *Taste* which he wrote for the *Encyclopaedia*, p. 267.

7 Kant, Immanuel, *Critique of Judgement*, 1790, § 26 (translated JH Bernard, New York and London, 1966, p. 91): "There is here a feeling of the inadequacy of his imagination for presenting the ideas of a whole, wherein the imagination reaches its maximum, and, in striving to surpass it, sinks back into itself, by which however, a kind of emotional satisfaction is produced".

8 de Brosses, Charles, *Lettres familières sur l'Italie*, ed. Yvonne Brizard, Paris, 1931, vol. ii, p. 159.

9 Kant was a voracious reader. But I have not been able to establish whether he might have had access to a copy of the *Correspondance littéraire*, the manuscript journal in which the *Essays on Painting* appeared.

10 Carlo Fontana, *Templum Vaticanum et ipsius origo, cum œdificiis maxime conspicuis, Editum ab*

equite Carolo Fontana. Romæ, 1694.

11 Ackerman, James, *The Architecture of Michaelangelo*, London, 1961, pp. 98–101.

12 See Jacques Heyman, *Coulomb's Memoir on Statics: an Essay in the History of Civil Engineering*, Cambridge, 1972, pp. 82–84 for an account of La Hire.

13 Quoted in Monval, Jean, *Soufflot, sa vie, son oeuvre, son esthétique (1713–1780)*, p. 423.

14 Ibid. p. 441.

15 Middleton, Robin H., *Viollet le Duc and the Rational Gothic Tradition*, Cambridge, unpublished thesis, 1959, vol.II, p. 38. This extremely important study is central to any understanding of the developments in architecture in the second half of the Eighteenth Century.

16 Heyman, Jacques, "The crossing piers of the French Panthéon", *The Structural Engineer*, 63, 1985, pp. 230–234. Heyman shows that the cracking was actually caused by inadequate workmanship in the preparation of the bedding faces of the stones. Patte's real disagreement with Soufflot was over the problem of the allowance to be made in constructions for the illusion of overhang.

17 Monval, *Soufflot*, pp. 446–447.

18 Ibid. p. 454.

19 Ibid. p. 453.

20 Diderot, *Correspondance*, vol. ix, p. 125. Cf. Jacques Heyman, *The Masonry Arch*, Ellis Horwood Series in engineering Science, Chichester, Ellis Horwood and John Wiley, 1982, p. 62: "[...] the advance first taken fully by Perronet, in which the internal piers are drastically reduced in thickness. For a multi-span bridge with more or less equal spans, the internal piers carry little more than vertical forces, the horizontal thrusts from adjacent spans being roughly self-equilibrating".

21 Diderot, *Salon of 1767* ed. Jean Seznec and Jean Adhémar, Oxford, 1963, p. 60.

22 Ibid. p. 61.

23 Ibid. p. 61: "the true line, not a tradition, which almost vanishes with the man of taste, which for a while forms the mind, the character, the taste of the work of a people, of a century, of a school; ideal model of beauty, true line, of which the man of genius while have the most correct notion according to climate, government, laws and thecircumstances which produced him".

24 Diderot, *D'Alembert's Dream*, in *Oeuvres complètes*, ed. Roger Lewinter, Paris, 15 vols., 1971, vol. VIII, p. 72: "If a certain phenomenon known in nature is followed by a certain other phenomenon known in nature, what will be the fourth phenomenon consequent on a third, wither given by nature, or imagined in imitation of nature".

25 Ibid. pp. 146–147.

26 Kant, *Critique of Pure Reason*, translated Norman Kemp Smith, London, 1970, [1929] p. 211, A 180/B222.

27 Ibid. p. 212; A 180, B 224. I wonder about Kant's distinction of schema from image in B181/A 142, and to what degree there might not be an aesthetic/visual model underlying it, close to Diderot's distinction "ideal model" and actual attained image.

Chapter 31

On Mathematics at the Time of the Enlightenment, and Related Topics

Paul Henry

The end of the eighteenth century, the age of the Enlightenment, is a period of doubt and pessimism about the future of mathematics, a feeling shared by almost all the leading mathematicians of the time. On September 21st, 1781, Lagrange writes to d'Alembert:

I began to sense my 'force of inertia' growing little by little, and I am not sure that I will still be able to pursue Geometry ten years from now. It also seems that the mine is almost too deep already, and that unless new veins are discovered, it will have to be abandoned sooner or later. Physics and chemistry now offer riches that are more brilliant and easier to exploit, and the taste of our century also appears to be turned entirely in this direction; it is not impossible that the chairs of Geometry in the Academies will soon become what the chairs in Arabic now are in the universities." As early as 1699, Fontenelle made a similar prediction, saying that mathematics might well soon become complete, while physics, by its very nature, would be endless. In 1808, in his famous *Rapport historique sur le progrès des sciences mathématiques depuis 1789 et sur leur état actuel*, Delambre writes: "It would be difficult and perhaps rash to analyze the chance which the future offers to the advancement of mathematics; in almost all its branches one is blocked by insurmountable difficulties; perfection of details seems to be the only thing which remains to be done. (...) All these difficulties appear to announce that the power of our analysis is practically exhausted, as was that of ordinary algebra with respect to transcendental geometry at the time of Leibniz and Newton, and that we need combinations capable of opening up a new field to the calculus of the transcendents and to the solution of the equations which contain them.[1]

Almost all the philosophers of the Enlightenment fostered these doubts and this pessimism about the future of mathematics. They even exploited them for philosophical ends and insisted on them instead of trying to dissipate them. Even Condillac, the famous inventor of the *langue des calculs*, does not entirely escape this trend.[2] His *langue des calculs* is not the algebra of the mathematicians. According to Condillac, mathematicians do not acknowledge that their algebra is just a language and that this language does not yet have its grammar. Developing such a grammar for algebra would belong to the field of metaphysics. But not any metaphysics, not the metaphysics born of a misuse of language and of the usual misleading philosophy of language to which we are addicted. That metaphysics is nothing but a cloud put between ourselves and nature. The good metaphysics is the one which adjusts itself to the most natural metaphysics, the one which preceded all languages. For there was a natural metaphysics before languages, a metaphysics which was less a science than an instinct which governed men without their knowing it, before they had the power of speech. A metaphysics of this kind is lost because languages have introduced ambiguities and indeterminations. But Condillac keeps the idea that we have nothing but language for communicating our ideas, for expressing them even to ourselves. He does not call for a return to the pre-linguistic age. So there is only one way: to create an artificial language, a perfect one, devoid of the ambiguities and indeterminations of ordinary languages, a language in which the correspondence between words and simple facts would be retained. The *langue des calculs* must be entirely arbitrary, formal and conventional if we are to be able to rid ourselves of the bad metaphysics in which ordinary languages have entangled us. The *langue des calculs* is intended for the reconstitution of the natural and pre-linguistic ground of natural metaphysics by suiting its radical formalization to the necessities of the simple. So, if Condillac criticizes the 'mathematism' of some philosophers, he nevertheless takes the object and the method of mathematics as a model, but as a model of a perfect language and not as a model of knowledge: "algebra is a well-made language, and it is the only one: nothing in it looks arbitrary. (...) So, mathematics (...) are in this book a topic subordinated to a larger one. The aim is to show how it is possible to give to all the sciences the exactitude which we believe to be the exclusive lot of mathematics."[3] The necessity, the absence of arbitrariness, we found in algebra are those we have in nature. And that is what we need in all the sciences.

Here we find three fundamental ideas expressed by Condillac. First, that we need to go back to what there is independent of language. Second, that ordinary, usual languages, or at least the ordinary use of language, are misleading, are masking reality, facts and nature. Third, that there is a link between the misuses of languages and the misuses of mathematics, and even a link between the critique of metaphysics and that of mathematics. Condillac is not far from Leibniz; his *langue des calculs* is close to Leibniz's *caracteristica universalis*, that symbolic artificial language which will not permit chimeras to be created that are not even understood by the person who proposed them.

Of the many differences between Leibniz and Condillac, there are at least two important ones that we should note. Leibniz's *caracteristica* is first and foremost a method without which our thinking would not be able to get very far without getting lost. It is intended to provide thought with a *filum Ariadnes*, i.e. a tangible and rough means of guidance, as are the lines we draw in geometry, according to Leibniz. These drawn lines are not the geometrical lines, and it is well known that reasoning on the drawn figure is a capital sin in geometry. But we need those drawn figures to guide our thinking and to prompt it to the discovery of truths. The *caracteristica*, in Leibniz's own words, has a similar function, and we should not mistake its symbols for the things themselves. Leibniz's main concern is that thought can mislead itself and get lost. Condillac's main concern is that languages put a screen between us and nature, between us and facts. We find in Condillac the idea of a pre-linguistic, factual knowledge, or of a knowledge made independent from language even when it is expressed through the *langue des calculs*.[4] His philosophy tends towards a metaphysics of facts. The paradox is that the return to facts should go through the creation of a completely artificial, formal and conventional language. In other words, Condillac intends to lead us out of the erring ways of artificiality by pushing artificiality to its most extreme limit. Condillac thus attempts to reconcile Leibniz and Locke. The second important difference between Leibniz and Condillac which I note here is that Condillac's metaphysics is not a primary science or philosophy; his *metaphysics* cannot but be a second-order science. Just as you could not have good grammarians in the absence of good poets and authors, the *langue des calculs* can operate only when some knowledge has already been acquired. The *langue des calculs*, and the 'good' metaphysics as well, presuppose scientific facts. They bring order and foundation to what have already been established as scientific facts. They give those scientific facts back their foundation and their full significance. This holds for mathematics as well. Condillac does not repudiate the knowledge of the mathematicians of his time. This knowledge is, from his point of view, a raw material which has to be enlightened and brought back to its source, which is the senses. Otherwise, the *langue des calculs* would have no corn to mill. But we may note that the idea according to which formalization is a second order activity was one which was to be fruitful during the nineteenth century. Furthermore, from Condillac's standpoint, mathematics needs to be completely rebuilt. In a way, that is what the nineteenth century has done, even if it has not been done with the idea of founding a new metaphysics which would stick to the facts.

Diderot's critique of both mathematics and metaphysics is far more radical than Condillac's. Of the Enlightenment philosophers, he seems to have been the one who has gone the furthest in the questioning of mathematics. Clearly, Diderot does not believe in the possibility of constituting such a language as the *langue des calculs*. He does not even believe in the usefulness of such a language. That does not means that we cannot find in his critiques of mathematics many aspects of Condillac's own, as well as some of Condillac's philosophical ideas. For Diderot too, the philosopher must start with facts established by the scientists. We can see Diderot, in particular in his *Éléments de physiologie*, relying entirely upon the observations made by contemporary scientists. In some cases this has been misleading. For instance, we see Diderot following Harvey in the latter's claim that the semen does not penetrate in the uterus, a fact alleged from observations made of the Charles I's deer. That seems all the more remarkable when we consider that this argument was usually used by the supporters of the doctrine of preformation and of ovism, who claimed that the preformed germ is in the egg and that there is therefore only maternal heredity. Diderot, on the contrary, always strongly defended the principle of biparental heredity, but he does not contest Harvey's observation.[5] So we can say that Diderot, as a philosopher, depends upon ideas the precede him. He uses the observations of the scientists as raw material without discussing them. And he uses them very freely, unembarrassed by the fact that he disagrees with the general philosophical or theoretical orientations of those from whom he borrows. One striking instance of this is the use Diderot makes of the *Essay upon the vital movement* by Robert Whytt. He borrows from Whytt his description of the movement of breath and of blood circulation; he relies upon him for his observations of involuntary movements and of the effect of some sensitive substances which act upon specific parts of the body. But at the same time, Diderot rejects vigorously the optimistic finalism and the animism of this Scottish physician. He rejects the claim that matter cannot, of itself, by any modification of its parts, be rendered capable of sensation, or of generating motion, as well as the accompanying doctrine of the two substances. He even uses Whytt's observations to confute those opinions. In general, Diderot does not discuss scientific observations, but only the doctrine or the theory in which they might be embedded by those who made them. Diderot took a definite position in almost all the great scientific controversies of his time. His positions in those controversies are always linked to his struggles with his lifelong enemies: the supporters of the doctrines of the liberty of the soul imprisoned in the body, of the two substances, and of the final causes. These are his landmarks. They do not prevent him from accepting some finality in, for instance, physiology, when this finality can be conceived as remaining inherent to the organization and not as coming from some providential arbitrariness. For instance, he readily acknowledges that the difference in the articulation of the jaws in man and in the lizard have consequences for the shape of the human brain but he rejects the physiological differences as an explamnation of the distinctiveness of the human brain. From that point of view, Diderot is not very far from Darwin.

Diderot's *Éléments de physiologie* is a good example of his conception of the task of the philosopher, and also of what he calls 'experimental philosophy'. To take up experimental philosophy is not to engage in the practice of experiment and scientific observation, nor does it assume an empiricism like Locke's. To Diderot, experimental philosophy means relying upon the practice of professionals in any field. From Diderot's standpoint the philosopher's task does not consist of the elaboration of any kind of metaphysics or general system which could encompass the whole of knowledge, gather it into a systematic whole, and lay down its limits. The task of the philosopher, according to Diderot, starts with the work of scientists, but also with that of artists or even craftsmen, as born out of practical activities. Making scientific observations is as practical an activity as that of the actor performing on a stage or of the craftsman making an armchair.

These activities require professionalism.[6] Diderot, as a philosopher, does not substitute himself for the scientist, nor for the artist or the craftsman. He considers the results of their activities and what can be thought on the basis of them. But he does not assume that those results speak for themselves. The philosopher defends some very general issues, confronts them with the knowledge of the professional, in doing so refines his positions and thus validates them. When Diderot considers the work of a scientist, an artist, or a craftsmen, he always has in mind his lifelong struggle against superstition, prejudice, established authorities, morality, general ideas ....

All this has direct links with what Diderot wrote on mathematics. Nowhere do we see him discussing a demonstration or a mathematical theory, nor trying to establish a better one. He never attempts to put himself in the place of the mathematician. That does not mean that he was not well-acquainted with mathematics. Even those who radically disagree with what he has said about mathematics acknowledge that he was far from ignorant in that field. Diderot does not criticize mathematics from the inside but from the outside. He takes doing mathematics as a practical activity. This is the main meaning of his *Lettre sur les aveugles* in which he discusses the case of the blind English mathematician Saunderson. He does not criticize mathematics as such, but the importance given to mathematics in sciences and the significance attributed to it in philosophy. And his judgements are severe, radical.

It is in his *Lettre sur les aveugles* that Diderot develops his criticique. There he describes abstractions as a common source of errors, saying that geometrical truths are merely identical propositions and are not able to generate new facts. Later, in 1756, in *Pensées sur l'interprétation de la nature*, he writes: "One of the truths which has been announced recently with the greatest courage and force, and which will certainly have the most advantageous consequences, is that the field of mathematicians is an intellectual world where what are assumed to be rigorous truths completely lose this advantage when brought down to earth." And he adds: "We are arriving at the moment of a great revolution in the sciences. Considering the inclination that minds, it seems to me, have for ethics, literature, the history of nature and experimental physics, I dare say that in less than a century we shall not have three great geometers left in Europe. This science will very soon come to a standstill where the Bernoullis, Maupertuis, Clairaults, Fontaines, and d'Alemberts will have left it."[7] Still in *De l'interprétation*, Diderot claims that it is the task of experimental philosophy to correct the results of geometrical calculus, that even geometers would agree with this conclusion, that mathematics – in particular transcendental mathematics – leads to nothing precise without experiment, that it is just a kind of general metaphysics. And he asks: would it not be quicker to confine ourselves to the results of the experiment? In 1758, d'Alembert leaves the *Encyclopédie* and Diderot writes to Voltaire: "The reign of mathematics is over. Tastes have changed. Natural history and letters are now dominant. At his age, d'Alembert will throw himself into the study of natural history, and it will be difficult for him to write a literary work which will live up to the celebrity attached to his name." In *Le rêve de d'Alembert*, he seems to restate some of Condillac's ideas. "It is the signs of language which have given birth to the abstract sciences. (...) Someone said: one man, one horse, two animals; then we said one, two, three, and the science of numbers as a whole is born. We have no idea of an abstract word. We observed that all bodies have three dimensions, length, breadth and depth; we have kept ourselves busy with each of these dimensions, and from that comes all the mathematical sciences. An abstraction is nothing but a sign devoid of idea. Any abstract science is just a combination of signs. We have canceled out the idea by separating the sign from the physical object, and it is only by reuniting the sign with the physical object that science once again becomes a science of ideas."[8]

We see that for Diderot too mathematics is, if not a language, just a combination of signs, that these signs are by themselves devoid of any meaning. That may coincide with the idea that mathematics can be a purely formal, conventional and arbitrary language. We also note that Diderot urges mathematicians to go back to facts and sensations: "Whenever, after a long combination of signs, you ask for an example, you require from the speaker only that he gives some body, shape, reality or idea to the successive sounds of his words, by relating them to experienced sensations".[9] But as for mathematics, he seems to consider that they have either lost any relation to the objects of experience, or that it is a waste of time to take the roundabout route which goes from experience and sensations to their abstract symbols and the back again to experience and sensations. Diderot does not believe in what d'Alembert holds. In the *Discours préliminaire*,[10] d'Alembert explains that algebra, for him the most abstract science, originally came from the sensory perception of physical objects; by a continuous process of abstraction, mind is supposed to have stripped away, one by one, the physical properties of matter, leaving only its 'phantom'. This is the process of analysis which would be involved in the constitution of any knowledge, but there driven to its limits. Through synthesis, it would be possible to give back to this 'phantom', one by one, the physical properties stripped away by the process of abstraction: add the concept of extension to the theory of numbers and you get geometry; add the concept of impenetrability to geometry and you get mechanics. It is as if, for Diderot, a limit is passed in the process of abstraction from which there is no return, in the same way as it is impossible to rebuild objects starting only with their 'phantoms'.

The idea that abstraction could lead to some 'outer space' from which one might not be able to return was fairly widely accepted at the time. We find it as an explanation for some forms of madness. Michel Foucault[11] noticed it in the works of Tissot and Pressavin. For Tissot and Pressavin, a too excessive and exclusive involvement in purely abstract matters, especially mathematics, may drive one to madness because one loses one's immediate relationship to nature and reality. They suggest a therapy consisting of practical exercises intended to help one to rebuild one's world as close to reality and nature as possible. That therapy has been considered to have anticipated some modern psychotherapies. In *Le rêve de d'Alembert* we have this very colorful scene of the philosopher tormented by earache: he no longer feels the pain when he is upset by a question of metaphysics or of geometry. When he comes out of his reverie, as the concentration of the mind relaxes, the pain reappears more furiously than ever and he feels exhausted and weary. Mademoiselle de l'Espinasse says to Bordeu, who related the anecdote, that such an effort of the mind may well leave one exhausted and weary, as happened to that man there, lying asleep and dreaming (d'Alembert). Bordeu: "It is dangerous; he should take care." – Mademoiselle de l'Espinasse: "I am always telling him that but he pays no attention." – Bordeu: "He no longer controls it; it's his life; he must die from it."[12] Bordeu then explains why it is dangerous to be so intent on abstract matters and why it leaves one exhausted and weary. When that happens the whole system experiences a violent tension focussed on a single center. Then Mademoiselle de l'Espinasse asks Bordeu about what might happen if this tension lasts or becomes a habit. And Bordeu answers: "The animal becomes mad – incurably mad."[13] Here, of course, we need to register the humour of this exchange. But we can find other places were Diderot holds that abstraction, in particular mathematical abstraction, is not only the common source of errors but dangerous for the health of the mind. Second, we can retrace in this amusing story some of Diderot's main points, in particular his rejection of any idea of center or system, or of any attempt to link everything to a center within a system. This takes us towards the much deeper reasons for Diderot's criticism of mathematics.

I believe the main reason for Diderot's opposition to mathematics is that he contests a definite model of knowledge, the one which takes mathematics, more precisely geometry, and even more precisely Euclidean geometry, as a paradigm both for particular sciences and for knowledge in its entirety. Or, at least, what he opposes is that the only good method for acquiring knowledge is the geometric method, i.e. the idea that the whole of knowledge should and can be rebuilt starting with clear, distinct and unquestionable truths from which all the rest should be deduced. In fact it is the Cartesian method which he contests.

A comparison between Spinoza and Diderot on this point can be very enlightening. The relation of Diderot to Spinoza could not but be complex, given the latter's reputation as a radical critic of all religions, of morality and of established authorities; given, moreover, Spinoza's sharp attacks on the very roots of all prejudices and superstitions and his disparagement of the general ideas which he thought of as existing only in the imagination and not in reality. The comparison especially deserves to be made given that Spinoza has been charged with the sin of materialism and that there is a real proximity between the materialism of Diderot and of Spinoza, beyond all that separates them. We see that Spinoza's enthusiasm for the more geometric way of reasoning does not imply an equivalent reverence for mathematics, in particular for arithmetic. On the contrary, and this is a disconcerting aspect of Spinoza's philosophy, he is very critical of numbers. Spinoza regarded numbers as inadequate to any conception of the infinite. Those who pretend the contrary and wish to dismiss the infinite are mistaking the auxiliary representation born out of the imagination (number, time, quantity) with the clear ideas produced by understanding. They apply to the productive and indivisible infinity of the substance, which is the core of understanding, its locus, operations (counting, division, addition) which can only be performed and conceived in the domain of the imagination, i.e. a domain abstracted from perceptive data (which is the only domain in which we can isolate parts, define units and compound them according to rules). They are mistaking what pertains to the imagination and what depends from the understanding. And Spinoza has engaged himself in extended efforts to show that mathematics nevertheless depend from the understanding by showing how the infinity of the substance can be present in the finite modes without having to divide itself within them.[14] In a way, Diderot's conception of numbers is not far from that of Spinoza[15] except that he does not believe in the infinite and indivisible substance, cause of itself, that Spinoza names God. It is not just by chance that Diderot's first critics of mathematics appear in *La lettre sur les aveugles*, since it is also in this text that he starts openly contesting deism. But Diderot does not fight against deism purely on the basis of atheist convictions. In fact, it is the link between deism and a precise conception of knowledge and of understanding which he contests. The conception of knowledge that corresponds to the "classical understanding" (that of Spinoza for instance) is, from Diderot's standpoint, much too narrow. It is much too narrow and much too close. All the efforts of Diderot are directed towards (and this has to do with the Encyclopédie) imposing an open conception of knowledge. Diderot struggles for a less aristocratic, or at least less elitist, conception of knowledge and of understanding. Diderot wants knowledge accessible to almost anybody, we could say "democratic". And it should be useful, practically useful. Mathematics, on the contrary, because it is abstract, because it is not useful by itself, may simply keep people away from knowledge. Instead of making philosophy popular, it puts a screen between nature and people. Diderot does not contest that it might be only in mathematics that we can reach unquestionable truths, but those truths are, in his opinion, useless by themselves. And if unquestionable truths are useless, we should not confine ourselves to them, and attempt to build the whole of knowledge on them, or on the model of them. I want to stress here the modernity of Diderot's conception of knowledge. One striking aspect of this modernity is that for Diderot knowledge is not homogeneous but heterogeneous, and there is no legitimate hierarchy between the different types of knowledge. Each type of knowledge, that of craftsmen as much as that of artists or scientists, deserves consideration. More deeply, we find in Diderot the idea that there is no standpoint from which we could hope to gather, even in a purely formal way, the whole of knowledge. There is no instrument able to give way in a satisfactory manner to this dream which ever lasts. Beyond the dream of a perfect language, Diderot systematically tears up that of a possible totalization of knowledge which is always a temptation. For this reason Diderot's materialism deserves to be reconsidered today. Of course, that does not mean that we should follow him literally in his criticism of mathematics. We cannot but acknowledge that he has not been very fortunate in his predictions concerning the future of mathematics. But we should not forget the aim of his criticism, and also acknowledge that bringing some materialism back to mathematics remains a task to accomplish.

The nineteenth century was just a year old, the wave of doubts about the future of mathematics had not yet receded and Delambre was yet to make his pessimistic predictions, when the *Disquisitiones arithmeticæ* of Karl Friedrich Gauss were published. This shows that the fact that this book was the beginning of a complete revival of mathematics was not apparent at the time of its publication, even to the experts.[16] The words usually used to praise Gauss's *Disquisitiones* speak for themselves.[17] The 'gaussian' revolution appears to be a kind of miracle in the handbooks of the history of mathematics. No explanation is given of the reasons why, in less than fifteen years, Gauss and Cauchy succeeded in getting rid of the difficulties which had bedevilled their predecessors. It is quite easy to see how they solved those problems. What remains unclear is why mathematicians of such great ability as d'Alembert or Lagrange, who devoted themselves to that task, failed, while these newcomers seem to have succeeded almost effortlessly. An oft-quoted explanation is that Gauss and Cauchy brought rigor back to mathematics. This explanation has to be challenged once and for all. It is a fact that throughout his life, Gauss urged mathematicians to return to the *rigor antiquus*. But there is, as we will see, a complete misunderstanding about the precise nature of this *rigor antiquus* to which Gauss refers. It is also a matter of fact that Cauchy urged his fellow mathematicians to be more demanding about some fundamental notions with which they operate, such as that of limit. He is the first to give a rigorous definition, according to our standards, of what is a limit in mathematics. But it is a shame that people have been led to believe that d'Alembert or Lagrange did not insist on rigor as did Gauss or Cauchy. On the contrary, it can easily be shown that both d'Alembert and Lagrange were literally obsessed by the improvement of rigor in mathematics. We see d'Alembert trying to get rid of the 'vanishing quantities' of analysis, which raised so many problems, by redefining them on the basis of limit. We see Lagrange, taking into account the failure of d'Alembert's attempt, trying to entirely rebuild the whole of analysis on a purely algebraic basis, without any use of the notion of 'vanishing quantities' or of limit. We note that d'Alembert or Lagrange did occasionally violate what has subsequently been defined as required mathematical rigor.[18] But the problem was that no one had a clear idea of what rigor in mathematics should be and on what grounds it should be defined. The abstraction-synthesis theory of the nature of mathematical entities seems to have misled the mathematicians. They had, given that theory, such a reliance in the existence of those entities that they were not able to pose the relevant questions. Thus, the theory according to which the renewal of mathematics at the beginning of the nineteenth century has been the result of a return to rigor does not explain anything.

Another explanation of the renaissance of mathematics at the beginning of the nineteenth century is that with Gauss the mathematical structures appear, and with them new methods and new objects. This explanation is nonetheless very puzzling given it is argued at one and the same time that the structures abound in Gauss's works but, at the same time, that they remain implicit and veiled in them.[19] We have to choose between two things. Either we hold that the structures are the very objects of mathematics on the grounds of the developments of mathematics during the nineteenth and twentieth centuries. Then we must say that from the very beginnings, that is to say at least since the Greeks, the whole of mathematics depended upon the structures even if they were not identified and characterized. Or we do not hold this position. In both cases the novelty introduced by Gauss remains to be clearly defined. Furthermore, if we acknowledge that Gauss, much more systematically than his predecessors, worked with the structures even if he did not identify them, it remains to be understood what has allowed him to do it and not d'Alembert, or Lagrange, or Legendre, who were working in the same fields just before him. We need to look much more closely at what Gauss really achieved.

Gauss devoted his first researches to the foundations of geometry. It seems that he was not more than fifteen years old when he reached a conclusion concerning the so-called problem of the parallels which had puzzled mathematicians since the Greeks. This problem of the parallels concerns the last of the Euclidean postulates, usually called the fifth postulate, which states that if a straight line intersects two other straight lines and makes with them interior angles on the same side with a sum less than two right angles, then these two straight lines intersect on the side where the sum of the angles is less than two right angles. This postulate has raised questions since the Greeks for two main reasons. First, because it seemed much more complicated in its statement and much less self-evident than the other postulates. Second, because it looked like the converse of a theorem which can be demonstrated on the basis of the other postulates, namely the theorem which states that if a straight line intersects two parallels lines, the sum of the interior angles on the same side is equal to two right angles.

Thus, since the Greeks, we have had attempts either to replace the questioned postulate with another one, more simple and apparently more self-evident, or to demonstrate the postulate on the basis of the others so as to make it a theorem (instead of a postulate). The problem was of the first importance given that a very great part of geometry depended on the fifth postulate, in particular the famous theorem on the sum of the angles of the triangle. We need the fifth postulate to demonstrate that this sum is two right angles. As for finding a more simple statement for the fifth postulate, attempts have been quite successful. The Arabs managed to replace it by what is now called the Payfair postulate: two straight lines which intersect cannot both be parallel to a third one.[20] In fact, geometers have discovered a whole range of statements equivalent to the Euclidean fifth postulate. But only one part of the problem was so resolved and not in a completely satisfactory way. The idea that geometry should be developed starting with propositions which on the basis of experience appear as unquestionable truths was maintained. What is a self-evident proposition is always matter of debate. As for the second aspect of the problem leading to attempts to demonstrate the postulate, the failure was complete. More precisely, many have claimed over the centuries to have demonstrated the postulate, but Gauss has rejected all those 'demonstrations' for one very precise reason. Take, for instance, the demonstration proposed by Lambert, who before Gauss went the farthest in this matter. Lambert attempted to demonstrate the proposition by *reductio ad absurdum*. He tried to show that if we replace the postulate with another proposition in contradiction with it, we are driven to a contradiction. So it would have been shown that only the Euclidean postulate does not lead to contradictions and thus is the only one that can be kept. But in doing this, Lambert has not reached a contradiction properly speaking but a theorem which, from his standpoint, was impossible on the grounds of the whole of our experience: "If the third hypothesis was true, we would have an absolute unit of measure for the length of each lines, the area of each surface, the volume of each solid, in contradiction with a proposition that we can count among the principles of geometry and which no one has contested up to now, namely that such a measure does not exist."[21] Gauss showed that the existence of such an absolute measure was not at all impossible, that what seems absurd at first glance might, after a closer and more careful examination, appear not to be absurd at all. He even argued that it is impossible to show that such a unit does not exist, that such a demonstration might be beyond the reach of human reason and of human experience; finally that it might be only in another life that we might be able to reach a well-established conclusion on this point. Gauss has been the first to contemplate the possibility of our space being non-Euclidean. No one before him could do i,t mainly because of the abstraction-synthesis theory. Gauss says that, starting with the hypothesis that the sum of the angles of a triangle is less than two right angles, we arrive at a strange geometry, quite different from the Euclidean one, which he developed to his entire satisfaction and without encountering any contradiction. And Gauss concludes that it is impossible to demonstrate the fifth postulate. But that does not mean that this postulate is true or untrue as well. It depends on what you call true. If you consider that any proposition which does not lead to a contradiction is true, then the Euclidean postulate shall be, from this standpoint, considered to be true. But the third hypothesis, or the equivalent proposition say-ing that the sum of the angles of the triangle is less than two right angles is also true. However, if you consider that only what corresponds to the "true nature of space" to use Gauss's own words, is true, then only one of these two contradictory propositions should be taken as true, but we have no means of knowing which one is the good one. As for that "true nature of space", Gauss says that we know almost nothing about it despite the vain discourses of the metaphysicians. From this standpoint, many other obscu-rities can be discovered in our geometry.[22]

Here we have a very strange situation: two contradictory propositions which must either be taken at the same time as true, or between which we cannot decide which is right and which is false. What is worse, for centuries one of these propositions has been taken as an unquestionable truth on the grounds of which we can safely develop the whole of geometry, secure in the belief that we are adhering to the truth and achieving certitude. The problem of the parallel has alone ruined the paradigm of the classical knowledge. The strange thing is that Gauss was driven to his conclusion by his faithfulness to the *rigor antiquus*, the model of which was the *Elements* of Euclid. Taken in all rigor, the Euclidean postulates were not seen as unques-tionable truths but as demands, demands which anyone wishing to engage in the proposed discourse must admit. If one refuses those demands, then one should not try to follow the discourse. In the *Elements*, there is no men-tion of the fact that those demands should be self-evident. This is the reason why, from Gauss's standpoint, we have, discursively at least, two possible geometries; one Euclidean and another which he labels non-Euclidean.[23] But Gauss's *rigor antiquus* includes other aspects which deserve to be considered here in relation to the problem of the imaginary or complex numbers.

Among the problems which worried mathematicians at the end of the eighteenth century were the 'vanishing' quantities of analysis (I have already mentioned this problem),[24] the 'imaginary' quantities and even the negative quantities. They were in common use despite the fact that these notions appeared self-contradictory given the conception of numbers at that time. Whereas for the Greeks only integers were numbers because numbers were defined by reference to the unity,[25] at the end of the sixteenth century, with Stevin among others, there occurs a redefinition of the concept of num-ber. Numbers are no more defined in reference to the unity but to the intu-itive notion of quantity. "A number," said Stevin, "is a measure of quantity". On the basis of this intuitive redefinition of numbers, it became possible to consider not only ratios as numbers, but also anything which could be conceived as a quantity, the non-rationals, for instance the square roots.[26] The rationale for this extension of the concept of number is the fact that one can calculate algebraically with ratios and irrational "quantities" as with integers. This extension of the concept of number coincided with the development of mathematical physics as well as with that of the application of algebra. But it also raised problems, given that the algebraic calculus implied dealing with "negative numbers". The idea of a negative quantity was very difficult to accept, and has given rise to numerous debates. Similarly, we can say that the definition of numbers on the basis of the notion of quantity has helped the development of infinitesimal calculus and analysis, even if it implied that one has to consider quantities which, from one point of view could be taken as zero, and at the same time, but from another point of view, as not zero. Furthermore, the development of the theory of equations, which had undergone a decisive step with the resolution of the general third degree equation by Cardan at the end of the sixteenth century, also raised difficulties inasmuch as it implied the consideration of "imaginary quantities". The problems of negative, imaginary and vanishing quantities are among the main concerns of the mathematicians of the end of the eighteenth century. The abstraction-synthesis theory applied to numbers was of no help in solving those problems; quite the reverse.

In a very famous letter to Bessel, dated December 18th, 1811, Gauss explained that we cannot be satisfied with protesting against the usage of qualifying the imaginary quantities as 'impossible', or with acknowledging that their use has never resulted in any contradiction. He shows that in order to achieve the autonomy of the analysis it is necessary to extend the theory of functions to functions of imaginary quantities. And he legitimates this extension by introducing a geometrical analogy:[27] the real quantities are to the line what all the quantities, real or imaginary, are to the plane. And he introduces there the famous geometrical representation of complex numbers.[28] In doing so, he is still faithful to the *rigor antiquus* because he is faithful to the geometrical realism of the Greeks.

Gauss was never satisfied with non-contradiction; he never took non-contradiction as a sufficient proof of existence. Non-contradiction is a necessary condition. But it is not a sufficient condition. Gauss is not satisfied with the fact that the use of complex numbers has never introduced contradictions. That is, for instance, the basis of his criticism of the demonstrations of the fundamental theorem of algebra proposed by Euler, d'Alembert, Lagrange and others. Before concluding that an entity exists Gauss requires that we identify what he calls "an adequate substratum". As for complex numbers, he finds this substratum in the orientation of space.[29] Once you have chosen a conventional orientation on the axis of the real numbers, the left and the right within the plane, that is to say the conventional orientation on the axis of the purely imnaginary entities must be defined. Complex numbers are complex because they combine in a single entity those two orientations. Gauss praises Kant for having criticized Leibniz's attempt to reduce space to a pure phenomenal relation between substance. From Gauss's standpoint, Kant has the merit of having seen in the asymmetry the proof of the absolute character of spatial positions. But, and this should be stressed, he criticizes Kant for having said that the orientation of space is a form of our external intuition. For Gauss, the space has an absolute existence, an existence independent of our intuition. There we see Gauss breaking with Kant's idealism and adopting what we might call a materialist position. But such a materialist position is of a very strange kind. If Gauss needs geometry to provide a foundation for algebra and analysis, we have seen that from his standpoint we know almost nothing of the "true nature of space", which remains for him the object of geometry. Thus we see Gauss grounding the whole of mathematics on something we know almost nothing about. Worse, he grounds the whole of mathematics upon the knowledge of what he has said to be, for its most fundamental features, beyond the reach of human reason and experience. We have there a conception of knowledge which is very new, and which still deserves consideration.

As for the emergence of structures within Gauss's works, we can still relate it to his 'geometrical realism'. If, as all historians of mathematics acknowledge, Gauss was able to see relations between very distant and very different parts of mathematics (such as between the theory of functions and geometry); if that is what led to the identification of the structures (of group, of field and so on), then Gauss owes this kind of extra-lucid perception to his 'geometrical realism'. Geometry was for him, as for the Greeks, the platform of the whole of mathematics. And the question which should be raised today is: can space still hold some surprises for us? Can it, create surprises, as it did with the Greeks, with the discovery of incommensurabilities, or for Gauss with complex numbers?

It is difficult to summarize this brief survey. Let me just stress a few points. First, we cannot say that the Enlightenment philosophy has had a direct influence on mathematics. From this point of view, the philosophies of Descartes or of Leibniz seem to have had a much more clear and direct influence. Even if we consider the case of d'Alembert, who was a very great mathematician and one of the leading figures of the French Enlightenment, his philosophical view of mathematics is not original and specific; conversely, his mathematics does not appear to be obviously linked to his philosophical ideas. It is not exactly the same with d'Alembert's conception of science as a whole and with the way he considers the role of mathematics in experimental sciences. Much could be said on this point but I cannot develop it in this paper. What the historians have retained is first and foremost the criticisms made by some leading Enlightenment philosophers of mathematics, those of Diderot, for example. This was clearly a change after a long period during which mathematics had been taken as a model for knowledge as a whole. Even Locke, despite the fact that he developed a competing conception of knowledge based on experience, had not openly attacked mathematics. What the Enlightenment brought was a radical challenge to the classical conception of knowledge and understanding. It would be very difficult to explain how it was possible for Gauss to be bold enough to adopt, even if with reluctance, a conception of mathematical knowledge based on what we know almost nothing about, without taking into account the criticism of the classical conception of knowledge which was developed by the Enlightenment. And we need to understand that the criticism of mathematics is a constitutive part of this criticism of classical knowledge. Furthermore, Diderot's materialism, closely linked to his conception of knowledge, seems to have some connections with what Gauss put in practice. This is precisely what protected him from Kant's idealism and opened up new paths for mathematics.

Notes

1 Delambre JB (1810), pp. 125-126.

2 Derrida J (1973).

3 Condillac (1798), p. 420.

4 One might see here something which foreshadows what is called 'tacit knowledge'.

5 It should be noticed that many other scientists have done the same: Malpighi, Spallanzani, Haller, Bonnet .... Nevertheless, this should not be taken as meaning that Diderot's reliance in the scientist's observations was not complete. These observations, as observations, and not their interpretations, are always taken by Diderot as facts beyond discussion.

6 "We exercise our senses as nature has given them to us, and according to what the needs and the circumstances require. But we do not improve them, we do not learn to see, to scent, to feel, to listen unless our profession compels us." Diderot (1875), p. 225.

7 Diderot (1964), pp. 178-179.

8 Diderot (1964), p. 369.

9 Ibid.

10 The *Lettre sur les aveugles* is reply to that *Discours*.

11 Foucault M (1961), pp. 405-410 and 446-449.

12 Diderot (1964), p. 352.

13 Ibid.

14 Desanti JT (1975), pp. 12-17 and 273-274.

15 "So Saunderson was seeing with his skin". Diderot (1964), p. 117.

16 Delambre mentions Gauss's book in his *Rapport* and praises the importance and the originality of the work, but not to the point of recognizing that it was opening new ways in mathematics which would allow him to overcome the difficulties which he still believed insuperable.

17 We could multiply the quotations taken out of handbooks on history of mathematics as well as from scholarly papers saying that a new era in mathematics starts with the *Disquisitiones*. Here are two of them taken as example. "His *Disquisitiones arithmeticæ* (...) contains such an enriching that they mark the beginning of the modern theory of numbers." (Collette JP (1979), p. 171). "It is thus a true Renaissance which starts with Gauss in 1796; trained only by the reading of the works of his predecessors he will in fifteen year renew all the mathematics." (Dieudonné J (1978), p. 113) ....

18 As when they introduce in calculus infinite series without having previously checked their convergence.

19 Vuillemin J (1962).

20 Ibn al-Haytam (965-1039).

21 Lambert JH (1786), § 79.

22 For instance, in the definition of the plane as a surface in which there is a straight line joining any two points, a definition which, according to Gauss contains more than what is needed for determining the surface and implies a tacit theorem which we should first discover.

23 It is Gauss who has forged this expression instead of those of 'imaginary' geometry, or 'astral' geometry, or 'impossible' geometry used by his predecessors and by himself as well occasion ally).

24 See also Berkeley's pamphlet, *The analyst* or Carnot L (1799).

25 In Euclid's *Elements* numbers are defined as multitudes composed of units. This implies that the Greeks could not conceive the ratios as numbers (they have instead developed a theory of proportions, or more precisely two theories of proportions, one for numbers – i.e. integers –

and one for magnitudes. The first is the topic of book VIIth of the *Elements*, the other of book Vth.) but also the "irrationals", like the square root of two, despite of the fact that they have discovered the incommensurabilities between magnitudes, in particular that of the side of the square and its diagonal – which corresponds to the square root of two – or of the side of the regular pentagon and its diagonal – which corresponds to the "golden number" $(\sqrt{5} - 1)/2$ – also despite the fact that Archimedes has calculated the first decimals of the "number" π, i.e. of the proportion between the length of the circle and its diameter.

26 It is worth noting that still for Kepler the incommensurables, i.e. for instance the proportion of the diagonal of the square and of its side, could not be expressed by numbers even if they could be approached, as much as one wants, by numbers.

27 Given the importance attributed to analogy by Condillac (see once more Derrida (1973), it would be interesting to develop here a comparison.

28 Gauss is the one who has introduced the expression 'complex numbers' instead of that of 'imaginary' numbers or quantities. The geometrical representation of the complex numbers had already been proposed, some time earlier, by Argand.

29 See Vuillemin J (1962).

References

Carnot L (1799) *Réflexions sur la métaphysique du calcul infinitésimal*. This version from reprint Albert Blanchard, Paris, 1970.

Collette JP (1979) *Histoire des Mathématiques*. Éditions du Renouveau Pédagogique, Montréal.

Condillac (1798) La *langue des calculs*. This version from Condillac *Oeuvres philosophiques*, vol. 2. Presses Universitaires de France, Paris, 1948.

Delambre JB (1810) *Rapport sur les progrès des sciences mathématiquyes depuis 1789*. This version from reprint *Rapports à l'Empereur sur le progrès des sciences, des arts et des Lettres depuis 1789*, I. Sciences mathématiques. Belin, Paris, 1989.

Derrida J (1973) *L'archéologie du frivole*. Foreword to the reissue of Condillac, *Essai sur l'origine des connaissances humaines*. Éditions Galilée, Paris.

Desanti JT (1975) *La philosophie silencieuse*. Le Seuil, Paris.

Diderot D (1964) *Oeuvres philosophiques*. Garnier, Paris.

Diderot D (1875) *Éléments de physiologie*. This version from reprint Librairie Marcel Didier, Paris, 1964.

Dieudonné J (1978) *Pour l'honneur de l'esprit humain (Les mathématiques aujourd'hui)*. Hachette, Paris.

Foucault F (1961) *Histoire de la folie à l'âge classique*. Plon, Paris.

Gauss KF (1863-1933) *Werke*. Teubner, Leipzig-Berlin.

Lambert JH (1786) *"Theorie der Parallellinien"*, Magazin für reine und angewandte Mathematik, Lepzig. This version from Engel F (mit Stäckel P) *Die Theorie der Parellellinien von Euklid bis auf Gauss, eine Urkundsammlung zur Vorgeschichte der nichteuklidschen Geometrie*. Teubner, Leipzig, 1895.

Vuillemin J (1962) *La philosophie de l'algèbre*. Presses Universitaires de France, Paris.

Collège International de Philosophie and C.N.R.S., Paris.

Chapter 32

Interdisciplinary Scope
Fedor Valach

At the present stage of development in the natural sciences a trend towards predicting new facts has manifested itself. Such ambitions are most appropriate in the so-called theoretical disciplines. Usually, the main aim is to predict new phenomena or new properties of objects such as substances and chemical compounds, or new physical properties of matter, etc. The creation of a new "langue des calcules" and some kind of metaphysics is undoubtedly popular – although often hidden – among scientists. This is a viewpoint which makes the deep understanding of the philosophy of sciences in the age of enlightenment topical. What was the reason for Diderot's criticisms of mathematics? This is a current issue for some contemporary scientists, and one which generates deep skepticism. In Wittgenstein's philosophy, the role of language is limited by its grammar.[1,2,3,4] Although in the Age of Enlightenment such limitations were probably not known, Diderot's relations with the scientists and artists of his time gives no indication of his intention to construct such a language. It may have been his orientation towards the abstract sciences that led him to reach conclusions like "the reign of mathematics is over". Considering the circumstances, his pessimism was justified.

In 1900, the mathematician David Hilbert formulated 23 problems for the best mathematicians of the world. The sixth problem was the axiomatization of physics. What a wonderful idea! The tasks of physicists would be substantially simplified, i.e., all other statements could be developed through a finite number of axioms. Unfortunately any attempt at the axiomatization of physics has hitherto met with failure. Even the enormous development of relativistic and quantum physics which reflects non-causality in physics has shown no ability to create such a closed model. On the contrary, many new problems were opened up. In this context Diderot's struggle to create the definite model of knowledge which is proper to mathematics could be the main reason for his opposition to the mathematicians of his age. Diderot's perception of D'Alembert's understanding of algebra as the most abstract science supports the idea that he intended to create a definite model of knowledge.

The Gaussian revolution of the 19th century was more than a renaissance of mathematics and the creation of an exact mathematical analysis. Let us not underestimate the *physical thinking* of Gauss. It seems that the unarticulated knowledge embedded in his mind connected mathematics and physics. In my opinion, Gauss was the first truly *interdisciplinary* thinker. Contemporary developments in the natural sciences are typical of unifying trends between different disciplines. These interdisciplinary sciences are usually most creative in connection with new ideas and discoveries. On the other hand, a clear distinction should be made between a "discovery" in mathematics and a discovery in the natural sciences. The first type of discovery simply fills a certain gap in grammar. But a conclusion in any of the natural sciences is usually reached from a *hypothesis*, a process that takes its evidence from several sources. As interdisciplinary knowledge emerges from sources in a number of disciplines, the interdisciplinary method can be developed.

Several sources of evidence are used in the modern interdisciplinary sciences, for example physical chemistry, chemical physics, biophysics, biochemistry etc. Wittgenstein's criticism[1] of Russell's concept of implication challenges the practice of using several sources of evidence for every proposition in one of the natural sciences. The *verification* of such a proposition (which uses the concept of implication) is both a part of the interdisciplinary method and also a problem of *experience*. If experience could completely verify a statement in any of the natural sciences the concept of hypothesis would lose its meaning. It seems that the *postulative formulation* of any interdisciplinary science is adequate. This method made a substantial contribution to the solution of many problems at the time of the birth of quantum physics.

Experimental physics has proved the existence of rational numbers. Morphological crystallography, for example, has clearly shown that the orientations of crystal planes can be expressed by using rational numbers, and this has been proved by modern analytical methods as a general rule in crystallography.

Referring to the Gaussian revolution, it is worth mentioning the problem of the "vanishing" quantities of mathematical analysis that was solved by mathematicians long before Gauss. In physics, such quantities do not lose dimension. Did Gauss use this fact before the introduction of limit definition in mathematics? I believe that the problem Gauss formulated as the "true nature of space" (Euclidian and Non-Euclidian space), and other geometrical obscurities will be solved by experimental and theoretical physics. Experimental research into the structure of matter in the last two decades has shown the real existence of highly symmetrical and regular polyhedrons which are implied from the solution of the algebraic equations to the fifth degree. The fact that Gauss was not satisfied with the non-contradiction as a proof may have its roots in his highly developed physical thinking. This may possibly explain his criticism of demonstrations of the fundamental theorem of algebra. Recent physical research into the nature of bonding between atomic entities of the matter of chemical substances proved the existence of the real roots of algebraic polynoms to the fifth degree. This solution implies the geometrical polyhedron which was experimentally observed in the atomic structure of matter.

I can only express my full agreement with Paul Henry that pure mathematics is interesting only if it can be applied. On the other hand, a mathematical theory becomes scientifically proved if it can be used as a model in a natural science. In this context, Diderot's explanation of algebra (mentioned earlier) has partially lost its sense. Exactly elaborated algebraic theories like the theory of groups and grupoids are useful tools for describing and classifying the symmetry of crystals.

I believe that the discoveries that prove the existence of complex numbers will be realized as part of the research into the nature of the mutual interactions of particles of matter at the atom-atom level and within the atomic nucleus.

Diderot's contacts with architects and engineers, described in Marian Hobson's article bear witness to his fascination with geometrical proportions. It seems that such relations at least partially reflect his orientation towards abstract sciences. Is the problem of Saint Peter's basilica in Rome caused by the geometrical symmetry in space? A similar problem may be formulated in nature: why do growing crystals keep their symmetry class? On the other hand, the concept of symmetry is not limited by geometrical space. The concept of symmetry may be generalized towards the properties of matter. Symmetry plays an important role in art and engineering. It can normally be divided into translational symmetry and local symmetry. The first means repetition, for instance the periodical repetition of tones in music. Local symmetry is the equivalence of properties within finite space. Experience repeated many times can lead through deformations of material objects to the forms of various kinds of symmetries. The geometrical invariants in symmetrical objects, so called symmetry elements, have the properties of algebraic units (groups and subgroups). It seems that Diderot was fascinated by the connections between the proportions in the architecture of Saint Peter's basilica and abstract algebra.

References

1 Wittgenstein L. (1961) *Tractatus logico philosophicus*. Transl. Parls DF and McGuines BF. Routlege & Kegan Paul, London.

2 Wittgenstein L. (1972) *Philosophical Investigations*. Transl. Ascombe GEM. Basil Blackwell, Oxford.

3 Wittgenstein L. (1974) *On Certainty*. Transl. Paul D, Ascombe GEM. Basil Blackwell, Oxford.

4 *Wittgenstein's Lectures*. Cambridge, 1930-1932. From the Notes of John King and Desmond Lee. Edited by Desmond Lee. Basil Blackwell, Oxford.

Chapter 33

Mathematics, Professional Knowledge and Technology
The Role of Mathematics in Society
Jan Unenge

Mathematics was "born" of the need to be able to state numbers and carry out some arithmetical operations with these numbers. The ability to "count" then became part of man's essential basic knowledge. For thousands of years mathematics has developed along two lines. The first, and initially entirely dominant, was mathematics as a tool in economics and trade, in astronomy, to calculate areas and the like. The second was the science of mathematics, whose great names include Euclid, Pythagoras and Archimedes. With scientists like Descartes, Newton and Leibniz in the 1600s came the first great steps towards the modern science of mathematics. Descartes introduced the system of co-ordinates and replaced the universally known circle with the equation $x^2 + y^2 = 25$, and was then able to solve all manner of geometrical problems without needing to draw any figures. This mathematics became abstract, and accessible to only a few.

Gauss, Riemann and Lobatjevskij stood, independent of one another, for an even bolder escape from reality. It was openly stated that because over the centuries it had been impossible to prove Euclid's parallel axiom and, for natural reasons, it was impossible to check, being a matter of lines that did not meet "however long they were drawn" – then it simply did not exist. And as an "intellectual game" they created a non-Euclid geometry, a completely useless invention at the time, containing amazing statements such as the sum of the angles of a triangle was *not* 180°. But as Frans G Bengtsson, a Swedish author, wrote of his favourite pastime, chess: "playing chess is quite useless, but only the useless can have a value in itself." The fact that it was then discovered that these three gentlemen's useless intellectual game could be of great value in the natural sciences is another, and perhaps more difficult story, which does not make it any the worse.

In school, mathematics has always been a self-evident, compulsory and high status subject. The position of mathematics has never been questioned. It is not until recent times that the content of the mathematics taught at schools began to be discussed seriously – and questioned. What was questioned was how much abstract mathematics should be taught in schools.

Jan Thompson, a Swedish researcher in mathematics, has the following thoughts on this issue:

The art of story-telling should replace the art of symbols in mathematics lessons! Perhaps in the perspective of five centuries one might dare to say that the art of printing books and symbolic abstraction (which presupposes the former) are two important events which mark the beginnings of what one may call the decline of dialogue, while the advent of the computer and the demise of English pub life heralds its end.[1]

This thought was put on paper ten years ago, and we can now see that English pub life appears to have survived. Perhaps rhetoric has, in some sense, returned when the idea of "talking mathematics" – and talking about mathematics – with school pupils is almost a watchword.

However, there have been obstacles to the development of the role of mathematics in society in recent decades, and the term "knowledge of mathematics" has therefore taken on a new meaning.

This is related to some extent to the development of new tools like the computer and the pocket calculator. But there is a different reason for the change in the way mathematical knowledge and skills are generally viewed.

In recent decades, more and more people have begun to talk about "different kinds" of mathematics. There is talk, for example, of situation mathematics and ethno-mathematics, and it is generally agreed that we need a day-to-day mathematics, separate from the academic discipline. This "new" kind of mathematics must be rooted in the structure of everyday life instead of the internal structure of mathematics itself. It must be a part of public education, and be perceived as an important part of human knowledge and general cultural training. Thus it must in some sense return from what are to many people the specialized symbols of mathematics to a more everyday language.

For some years Denmark's Research Council for Humanistic Studies has been running an inter-Nordic research project under the heading of "Mathematics, Teaching and Democracy". One reason for this project is the increasingly important role of mathematics in society. A growing number of political and administrative decisions are based on mathematical and statistical material, the presentation of mathematical proofs and arguments that people with only "basic school mathematics" find it difficult to interpret and even more difficult to subject to critical analysis.

The Danish research council therefore thinks that this should be given attention in all education, both at school and in the world of work. It may be said that the role of mathematics as a humanistic subject has expanded. Mathematics is no longer just a tool "to describe the world" from the natural sciences viewpoint. This new "variety" of mathematics attempts to reconstitute mathematics as a part of public education.

One of the changed roles of mathematics in today's society is the more widespread use of mathematical models. A mathematical model may be nothing more than a simple formula, for example the relationship between highway, speed and time. But these models may be complicated even for fairly trivial activities, for example the formula which may be used to calculate the costs of using the telephone. In many occupations there are more complicated, complex and enigmatic mathematical models and formula. Mathematical algorithms have become an important aid. They may be described as the plans with whose help one can, by following certain stated rules, carry out different operations. This may involve setting up multiplication, which means for example, the sum 65 x 43 is transferred to four simpler multiplications of single units and an addition. In a broader sense, one could call the telephone directory's description of how to make an international call an algorithm. The directory gives us a rule to follow.

A number of research projects related to the teaching of mathematics have focused on algorithms as rule-following. In a study in the KOMVUX municipal adult education programme, it was noted that adults were worse at solving different percentage sums *after* completing a course in mathematics. The spontaneous and creative way they had tackled these problems before the course disappeared when they tried to apply a rule or an algorithm that had been taught during the course, but which they had not become sufficiently familiar with.

The study introduced the term "algorithmatization" as a serious risk in mathematics teaching. Pupils learn an algorithm which they then apply to 20-30 tasks in their text books. These tasks are designed as applications of this algorithm. However, when such a problem is encountered in a different context, the rule or algorithm may have been forgotten or the pupil may not associate to the right algorithm.[2]

The ability to solve the unsolvable

Put simply, solving a mathematical problem may be said to have three phases.

A Choosing a strategy
B Carrying out one or more calculations
C Reflecting on the result of the calculation[3]

In the first phase the problem is interpreted, the formula, mathematical model and algorithm are selected, as is the kind of mathematical calculation, an equation is set out, or the like.

In the second phase the calculations are done, the equation is solved etc. The calculation may be done in your head or on paper, usually by applying an algorithm. Nowadays a pocket calculator is a natural aid in these calculations.

In the third phase the result is assessed and an attempt may be made to verify it, for example by a feasibility assessment.

The availability of modern tools such as computers and pocket calculators have given us the tools we need to deal with the calculations in phase B. but this may in its turn require a different approach to that of phase A. To return to Descartes, one cannot "feed-in a circle" but one can feed-in an equation which describes a circle in symbols. Their use has also created problems, one view of which has been underscored in research. One of the problems tackled in research into professional knowledge and technology is the computerization of parts of a body of professional knowledge. Case studies have been taken from different occupations, including meteorologists, forest surveyors and social insurance office staff. A general result of this research which is of interest here may be summarized briefly as follows: one effect of computerization is that in some respects it has "worsened" the results of work. Some occupational knowledge seems to have disappeared.[4]

The metaphor of the "inner picture" comes from a case study of the professional knowledge of meteorologists when computerized aids were introduced for weather forecasting.[5] If meteorologists are to make good weather forecasts, they must be in constant touch with the weather picture. Computerization may be seen as dividing the knowledge they need into parts (building blocks) with "facts" as one block, for example, and this deprives the forecasters of the overall picture, the "inner weather picture", i.e., the gathering of the wide and diverse range of knowledge which is a characteristic of professional skill.

Thus computerization may also lower the level of professional skill because when it is not regularly practised, tacit knowledge disappears. This is a core issue in the proposed research into the way the "right" kind of mathematical knowledge may be maintained when people use pocket calculators and can use computers for their calculations.

But there is another aspect which has not been studied in any detail and which is related to the three phases listed above. We have noted this problem in our research project "Alternative Teaching Paths in Mathematics" (the ALM project). Extensive trials have been carried out with pupils being given the use of pocket calculators from their first year at school.[6]

Using this tool pupils can solve problems that they would not normally be given until they were much older. They can understand that a certain problem may be solved by, for example division, i.e., they can manage phase A, but they would not have been able to perform the purely technical calculation, phase B, on paper. But the pocket calculator now does this work, so pupils can now concentrate on phases A and C.

But the next stage is interesting, and as yet unresearched.

By using this tool pupils can also solve a problem they do not understand at all. This may be a mathematical formula when they "only have to key in the numbers and let the calculator do the work", as the pupils sometimes put it. Thus they can solve the problem by finding a method for phase B without having clearly understood phase A. Thus this tool allows people to solve problems they have not understood! This may result in – and evidently often does result in – a specific part of a body of knowledge being transferred to a person without making him or her familiar with the activity involved in any way. People don't need to understand phase A and therefore cannot reflect on the answer, i.e. complete phase C. With a computer or pocket calculator they have the necessary technical assistance to perform phase B.

This problem is not exclusive to any particular occupation or occupational group. It is a general problem – or a general risk. People who have gone into further or higher education without mastering this kind of mathematics and who therefore have limited knowledge and a scanty or far too superficial understanding of the concepts of mathematics can thus work – or be put to work beyond their level of skill in mathematics with the obvious con-comitant risks. Their task is to complete phase B, to "follow a rule", perhaps without knowing anything about phase A, and thus nothing of phase C. Here are some of the dangers that the Danish Research Council for Humanistic Studies have pointed to. Bearing in mind the call for a more general content in mathematics teaching, it may also be true that people have the "wrong" aspects of mathematics in their education. The concept of school mathematics has not undergone any notable changes in the reviews of the national curriculum. The present proposed new primary and sec-ondary school national curriculum in Sweden is the first sign of a real change in direction.

Many of the adults interviewed as part of our research on pocket calcula-tors have told us about the implicit faith they had in this tool and how because of that faith they did not reflect on the result of their calculations unless they contained the kind of obvious error that may occur when, for example, one forgets to enter a decimal point. These people confirm that they were able to work without mastering phase A, which had been replaced by an order, a rule or an algorithm. To give an example, one per-son had been told to work out new prices when the VAT rate changed. This he did, that is to say, he performed phase B, by using a pocket calculator, without any real chance of reflecting on the results he obtained. With the benefit of hindsight he now says that he only reacted when the result devi-ated significantly from the usual results. "But sometimes I might have entered 37 instead of 47, and I couldn't possibly have noticed that."

If this ability to "solve problems that one cannot solve" occurs in schools, the problem can be tackled – provided the teacher notices it. Of course, the pupils are "under constant supervision".

But how is the same "ability" to be dealt with if it occurs at work or in daily life?

Until as recently as half a century ago people could earn a living from being able to count. Occupations such as "counting assistant" and "count-ing master" describe this kind of work. When electrical counting machines became common, these specialists in "pen and paper" calculations were no longer needed.

Today the "counting master" has been replaced by the pocket calculator. It is easy to learn to use a simple pocket calculator, and it can be put to use without delay. Or should we say that people "believe" that they can begin to use it at once. Some of our interviews show that many people don't know, for example, that simple pocket calculators do not apply the rules of mathematical priorities. They give the answer 35 when $3 + 4 \times 5$ is entered, while if mathematical priority rules are followed the answer is 23, because, "first multiplication, then addition". The percentage function of pocket cal-culators is not standardized, posing another, similar problem for their users.

The example also shows some difference in the use of pocket calculators and computers. Every use of a pocket calculator is a unique event, while a computer programme can be tested many times before it is used.

Research is also in progress which shows that blindly following rules also produces errors in other contexts. One example is the interpretation of the ordinary table of postage charges when working out the cost of a letter weighing 120 gm. Many failed to "read" the word maximum and added the charge for a 20 gm letter to the charge for a 100 gm letter. Another example is "working out the period of time from March 24th to June 12th". The success rate in, for example, year 2 of the upper-secondary school, was only 21%, because a well-known algorithm was applied and the number of days in March was calculated by subtracting 24 from 31.

But what are the consequences of the fact that when using these tools one can evidently produce an answer to a problem that one de facto does not understand and cannot solve? Should professional knowledge not include the skill of assessing the feasibility of the answers we get from pocket calculators or computers?

What kind of training is needed at different levels of professional life to allow the use of the pocket calculators, computer and other aids like table to reflect professional knowledge?

Contextless mathematics

In 1991 a study was made of the mathematical knowledge and skills in a nursing course, with alarming results. The students were given a 65 question test in secondary school-level mathematics. The average results were that the students got only about half the answers right.[7]

These results were reported in the mass media as an example of the skill of an entire occupational group. Editorial writers claimed that this lack of knowledge in mathematics made it "deadly dangerous to fall ill", something which is indeed ultimately true for most of us. There is therefore good reason to examine more closely this attempt to assess professional knowledge.

To begin with one may note that testing other occupational groups or groups of students, except students studying subjects with a mathematical orientation, would give the same result, one reason being that people who have failed to grasp or have the chance to penetrate "symbolic mathematics", seem to see mathematics as a collection of unrelated rules and algorithms. if one or more of these rules is forgotten, the problem becomes unsolvable. Many of these student nurses had certainly not come across some of the problems in the test since their secondary school days. Problems like 0.192/0.8 or multiplying 2.8 by ¾ "and give your answer in decimal form" are not problems you meet in this form in daily life. These are purely arithmetical problems, that is to say phase B problems, and the mathematics is wholly contextless. Instead of trying to solve the problem, people begin to look for rules – "now what was it you did with the decimal in the denominator?" or, "how do you multiply fractions?" It may be added that the answers to problems put in this way are uninteresting.

But a purely "rule-following" person who is doing a job finds himself in the same situation as the student nurses taking the test. The result of a single arithmetical operation – with or without using a pocket calculator – is uninteresting. Thus errors in calculation will not be discovered, with possibly dangerous consequences.

What the student nurses could not do may be described as "certain arithmetical skills" which may be seen as a *part* of the ability to solve problems or deal with situations. The problem 0.192/0.8 can be quickly "worked out" with the help of a pocket calculator without having to think about "where to put the decimal point". A (contextless) item of mathematical knowledge must instead take the form of a discussion of why the answer is greater than 0.192, that is a discussion of phase A and phase C.

But can the result justify questioning the professional skills of nurses? If so, we should remember that colleges of nursing set a final exam in "medicine dispensing" and students are required to get full marks in this subject to qualify as nurses. That test is more relevant and contains more than mathematical "rule-following". The arithmetical task (phase B) is part of the problem, but it is not the whole problem – all three phases – that is being tested. This kind of test is thus a more correct way of assessing nurses' mathematical skills in their profession.

If better knowledge in (traditional) school mathematics would make it any easier for student nurses to pass this final exam in "medicine dispensing" is another interesting but as far as we know unresearched question. But it is an example of the very kind of research that must be included in studies of mathematical knowledge and professional knowledge and which is therefore an important part of the research project presented here.

Many researchers have pointed out that this is not a real problem for a pupil who gets the wrong answer to a mathematical problem at school, for example. The pupil will look at the key, see he has the wrong answer and try again and again until he has an answer that agrees with the textbook key. Phase B dominates here, perhaps because mathematics at school concentrates mainly on the answer to the problem. Phases A and C are definitely subordinate here.[8]

The situation is quite different in the world of work (and in daily life). There is often no – or only one – right answer, and the wrong answer may have financial and – if we return to the nurses, for example – other, dangerous repercussions. If your car breaks down you do not want a mechanic who has to test several different solutions, you want a professionally skilled mechanic who only "gets the wrong answer" in exceptional cases.

Introducing computers and pocket calculators in schools and at work is by no means free from problems. A political decision taken in Sweden in the early 1980s to introduce the subject of "computer studies" in the nine-year compulsory school is an example of the difficulties of introducing without reflection a new tool into school teaching. The evaluation showed that only a small proportion of the programme was implemented. One reason for this was that the teachers were badly trained and prepared, with another more general problem being the artificial world of our schools. From our viewpoint this particular issue may be taken up here.

The trial of computer studies as a subject was a mistake. Sweden's new curriculum for nine-year compulsory and upper-secondary education also noted that computers must be a self-evident aid in different contexts and in different subjects – they must be put to use in suitable contexts and not be isolated as a separate subjects such as "computer knowledge". Pocket calculators often appear to be introduced in a haphazard way. Many pupils in upper-secondary education seem to be frustrated by this new aid which quickly solves columns of problems which they had spent a great deal of time and effort in learning how to solve on paper. The ability to perform pen and paper calculations also appears to be disappearing. There are two probable reasons for this. One cannot immediately use the pocket calculator in a curriculum that has not been planned with this tool in mind, and there must be a clear and non-artificial way of justifying the use of this aid. Methodical attempts to introduce the pocket calculator illustrate how essential these theories are. There is a clear need to overhaul both the content and objectives of courses. By analogy the same kind of analysis is essential if these tools are introduced at work.

But the trials also implicitly demonstrate that *within the school* it is impossible to set clearly-defined goals for either simple or programmable pocket calculators. They may be a useful aid in phase B but may – as is indicated above – have negative effects on phases A and C if used in artificial ways. When the pocket calculator is introduced *outside* the school, it is introduced into a real world where phases A and C are embedded in professional knowledge and when the calculator may *sometimes* be a technical aid in performing phase B (the dual approach). In other words it is experience from the world of work that may provide the background to improved professional knowledge. This may also guide us in finding ways to describe what is meant by using the pocket calculator and computer *effectively and with judgement*, as it is put in the new primary and secondary school national curriculum. It may also indicate *what* mathematical knowledge is required.

To problematize this by studying working life is an important aim of the research into professional knowledge and technology. Basically, it is a question of the theory of knowledge, of reflection, which is broken down into two parts. The first part is interpreting a result and reflecting on this interpretation. The second is to have such a distance to the "tool" – the computer/pocket calculator – that one no longer blindly trusts the results it produces.

In conclusion, let us return to the wrongly-accused student nurses. The kind of test carried out with them cannot assess their professional knowledge – and even less improve it. It is far from certain that all the different components of traditional school mathematics form an important basis. What is needed is first an analysis of *what* mathematical knowledge this category needs in order to deal with the important, professional function of calculating dosages of medicine. The analysis contains studies of which ways and in which contexts the pocket calculator and computer can be effective aids in the calculation phase without having an adverse effect on the process of reflection in the assessment phase.

In the same way the mathematical knowledge requirements of many other professions need to be analyzed. There is probably a common core of mathematical requirements in several occupations. When we know what that core is we can provide the proper education in mathematics for occupational training and working life. It is to be hoped that this project will make some contribution towards finding a way to raise the level of professional knowledge.

This article is based on the programme for a new research project entitled "Mathematics, Professional Knowledge and Technology" (the MYT project), produced by Jan Unenge, assistant professor in mathematics and researcher in mathe-

matical didactics, and Anita Sandahl, assistant teacher in mathematical didactics, both at the Institute of Higher Education, Jönköping, which finances this project jointly with the Swedish Working Life Fund. Bo Göranzon is the project leader.

Notes

1 Thompson, J. (1986) Historiens roll i matematikundervisning eller retorikens återkomst. In: Marton, F (ed) *Fackdidaktik III*. Lund: Studentlitteratur.

2 Alexandersson, C. (1985) *Stabilitet och förändring. En empirisk studie av förhållandet mellan skolkunskap och vardagsvetande*. Göteborg Studies in Educational Sciences, 53.

3 Skovsmose, O. (1988). Mathematics as a Part of Technology. *Educational Studies in Mathematics*, no. 19, pp. 23-41.

4 Göranzon, B. 1990). *The Practical Intellect*. London, Springer-Verlag.

5 Perby, M-L. (1988). Den inre väderbilden. In: Göranzon, B. (ed) *Den inre bilden*. Stockholm: Carlssons förlag.

6 Sandahl, A & Unenge, J. (1990). *Med miniräknare från början. Erfarenheter från ett försök på lågstadiet*. ALM-rapport nr. 5. Högskolan i Jönköping.

7 Kapborg I. (1991). *Utvärdering av sjuksköterskestuderandes kunskaper i matematik*. UHÄ, FOU-rapport 1991:2.

8 Unenge, J. (1992) Jakten på svaret. *Dialoger* no. 22-23, pp. 61-63.

Chapter 34

Comments

Magnus Florin

There are two ways of rendering a circle, and they are radically different from each other. One is by drawing it (in the sand, on paper etc.) and the other is to express a circle as a mathematical formula. These two ways are poles apart.

We may discern here links with the traditional contest between "applied" and "pure" mathematics. We may discuss the matter in terms of a difference in modality – a difference in mathematics and mathematicians' relationship with, and dependency on, reality. We may also see here the successful and revolutionary aspects of the development in seventeenth century mathematics of a rational, exact and universal mathematical language, a language of calculation and far-reaching formalizations beyond conditionalities and relativities.

The great and remarkable paradox is that the purpose of this language, untarnished by the continuum of reality, was to correctly and properly interpret and represent the facts of reality. In other words, an escape from reality, as Jan Unenge put it in his essay on "Mathematics, Professional Knowledge and Technology" – but as a way of achieving a desirable return to reality!

The fascinating story Paul Henry tells in his article is rooted in the veritable crisis that took place in mathematics, to which many of the practicing mathematicians of the eighteenth century bore witness. It was the mathematics of Descartes and Leibnitz that came to be regarded as a cul-de-sac. But at that point there was no new, alternative mathematics in sight. Existing mathematics appeared to be virtually perfected but solipsist in its self-sufficiency and reminiscent of a metaphysical system. Its pure world could be seen as being closer to the empty spaces of madness than to human fellowship.

On the very threshold of this new century, the 1800s, Gauss appears and completely transforms mathematics. This could hardly have been predicted on the basis of the questions that the mathematicians of the previous two centuries had been addressing. As expressed in Paul Henry's remarkable thinking, the mathematical advances of Gauss could as well be seen from the view of the philosophers of the Enlightenment, and Diderot in particular, namely that knowledge is something material, hierarchical and heterogenous. There is a relationship between the "geometrical realism" of

Gauss and Diderot's view of knowledge as physical.

This is not to say that the internal problems of mathematics were suddenly resolved. Taken together, the message of the articles in the section "On Diderot, Analogy and Mathematics", by Marian Hobson, Fedor Valach, Paul Henry and Jan Unenge is that the contest continues between pure and applied, formalization and concretization, abstract and material.

It is quite evident that modern computer technology has been based on the advances made by Descartes and Leibnitz. The flights of fancy in pure mathematics resulted in comprehensive and thoroughgoing transformations of the tools we use to deal with reality. But exactly parallel with this development, Diderot's view of knowledge maintains its validity and, as Paul Henry points out, actually asserts its modernity.

Fedor Valach speaks of Diderot's "physical thinking", a phrase which emphasizes not least the mutual dependency between the development of human knowledge and the world of immediate human experience. It is a world of spatial and temporal position, of individual perspectives, of subjectivity and thinking in terms of proportions, syntheses and analogies rather than definitions analyses and logic. In particular the central place of *analogy* in Diderot's thinking, which Marian Hobson discusses in her essay, shows this philosopher's strong opposition to any kind of theoretical fundamentalism and epistemological idealism.

"I am only a mathematician" said Gauss persistently in his polemic against multiplicity. Yet for most of his life, in addition to mathematics, he devoted himself to extensive reading of modern European literature and the classics, to critical comments on international politics and to serious studies of foreign languages and new developments in the natural sciences. It appears that nobody will claim there is a connection between, for example, a study of the Russian language and non-Euclidean geometry! But Gauss indisputably had a mathematical intellect, with his sense of connections, proportions, analogies, practical experience and physical perceptions. If not the first, Diderot was by far the most persistent observer of the dynamic between the respective activities of the philosopher, the craftsman, the actor, the scientist and the mathematician. *Au fond*, his was a critical view of civilization, a view which is hardly less of a challenge and a summons now than it was then.

Section VII:
Epilogue

Chapter 35

Diderot and Dialogue:
Reflections on the Stockholm Conference
Nicholas Lash

Faced with the daunting task of offering summary reflections on a diet of dialogue as rich and varied as that on which we have been feasting, I shall make some brief remarks under the five headings: acting, the wisdom of grandparents, rules and reasoning, the end of Enlightenment, and the future of dialogue.

Acting

I begin with a question raised by Christopher Bigsby. "Is there no end to acting, then?", he asked, "Is it a matter of I perform, therefore I exist?". With this question, he came close to saying: "*Ago, ergo sum*"; "I act, therefore I am". This is clearly correct, but let me try to spell it out a little. According to Bigsby, "a principal meaning of the verb to act is 'to represent by action, especially on the stage'". That way of putting the matter could, however, be misleading because if by "principal" meaning one intends to indicate the meaning with the widest range and reach, then, surely, the principal meaning of the verb "to act" is simply "to do" – whatever or whoever it may be that anyone or anything is doing. There is a second, more restricted sense of what is means to act, and that is: to do as only humans do. And from there we might move to a third, no less important but, again, more restricted sense, closer to that mentioned by Chris Bigsby: namely, so to do as to represent by doing.

Notice, however, that, if this is how we put it, then this third and most particularly human mode of doing has built into its performance and description an element of what Diderot called *"dédoublement"*. It is this which generates, and generates ambivalently, the possibility of philosophy, and of hypocrisy, the possibility of wisdom and betrayal and cruelty. All the familiar characteristics of human action *bubble up* within this space indicated by the non-identity of acting (as doing) and acting (as representation). This, I think, is why Bigsby said that "the actor's role is to threaten" the "structured language, the form, the ordered context ... with his or her physical being, to suggest, by his or her very skills, how *insecure* are the categories, the systems, the social and psychological roles in which we otherwise place our faith".

Actors, we might say, perform something like the prophet's role as critic of idolatry: of our tendency to absolutize and, in desperation, *cling to*, set our hearts on, facts and things and objects in the world (especially the things that we have made, the fantasies and objects of our mind's construction). And some remarks made by Allan Janik, on Diderot as skeptic, made me think how close *ideologiekritik* is, or may be, to the critique of idolatry. And yet, how rarely, these days, is this connection noted, worked through, and its implications seriously explored.

Consideration of the role of irony and skepticism might, perhaps, go hand-in-hand with renewed attention to the question of how it is that (to use a phrase Jon Monk used in his presentation) we "learn how to learn". In all our discussions at this conference about education, the spotlight seems to have been on the problem of being a teacher, rather than on the problem of learning. This is, I think, symptomatic of a widespread and serious neglect of the enormously puzzling phenomenon which learning is; a neglect the sources of which can be traced back, historically, to a dissociation of memory from argument which lies at the root of some of the most influential projects of the early modern world.

According to Allan Janik, Diderot voiced "a very important complaint" against a certain style of philosophical performance and self-presentation to the effect that "knowledge has been severed from learning". This is well said, and yet (as one who is no expert *diderotien*) I would suggest that Diderot's performance, bearing this complaint, may have been in tension with his theory.

Recall the headings of the "Système Figuré des Connoissances [sic!] Humaines" which Diderot constructed for the 1750 Prospectus for the *Encyclopaedia*: Mémoire, Raison, Imagination.[5] "Thus it is clearly manifest that history, poetry, and philosophy flow from the three distinct fountains of the mind, viz., the memory, the imagination, and the reason" (hence the former appear as the "vertical" titles of the columns headed by the latter: history by memory, philosophy by reason, poetry by imagination); "For history and experience are one and the same thing; so are philosophy and the sciences".[6]

That was not, in fact, Diderot, but Bacon. I find it slightly disturbing, but most interesting, that, a hundred and fifty years after Bacon, Diderot was able to take over, apparently in tranquillity, the entire structure of the *Advancement of Learning* (with the exception of a somewhat unhelpful shift in the location of theology!) including that unfortunate feature which I have already mentioned: namely, the dissociation of memory from argument.

This dissociation is thus still built in, in the late eighteenth century – not, admittedly, into Diderot's own literary practice or interests, but into his theory and his account of how the *Encyclopaedia* was to be designed. Now, the general lesson that I would learn from this has to do with the extent to which thought-patterns, structures of imagination, continue to shape and influence our thinking even though, on the occasions that they are explicitly adverted to, we may reject them as evidently mistaken or outworn.

We have, I think, seen several instances of this during our conference, whenever we have played the game of "Count the Cultures". All of us have said, at one time or another, that *of course* any dualism of arts and sciences is superficial, crude, silly. And yet we have continued, to a surprising extent, to operate on the assumption that this is roughly how things are and can be talked about. Our behaviour has thus exhibited a curious affinity with Diderot's relationship to Bacon's scheme of things.

Not much more, I think, needs to be said about the counting the cultures than that one has only to observe the diversity of discourses and practices in which people are, *in fact*, engaged in any modern university to see how ludicrous it would be to suppose that they could appropriately be grouped under any one, two, three – or even four – significantly illuminating overarching categories. And yet, under combined pressure from the inherited shapings of the mind and the proclivities of the government funding agencies, we still talk as if universities were almost entirely populated by poets and particle physicists.

The Wisdom of Grandparents

Lash's postulate of the Wisdom of Grandparents goes like this: everybody knows that their parents were stupid; but we forget that our parents also knew this in their turn! An illustration, if I may. As a Christian theologian, I am used to being told that something called "Judaeochristianity" is responsible for the current despoliation of the planet because we have taught people that, in the beginning, God ordered human beings to "dominate" the earth.

This may have been a view of things popular amongst some of our "parents" in the early modern period but, as a matter of historical record, I know of no significant reading of the Book of Genesis, before the seventeenth century, which thus misread it. So, apply the postulate of the Wisdom of Grandparents, and we may again discover that, for most of Jewish and Christian history, the myth has been construed as requiring something more like gardening than rape. And gardening is still quite a good model for our relationship to the planet of which we form an interesting part.

The End of Enlightenment?

According to Alasdair MacIntyre, "No conviction ... is more central to the encyclopaedist's mind than that 'morality' names a distinct subject matter, to be studied and understood in its own terms as well as in its relationships to other areas of human experience, such as law and religion. This conviction had already informed the first great modern encyclopedia, *L'Encyclopédie* of Diderot and D'Alembert, more than a century before it exerted its influence on the Ninth Edition of the *Encyclopedia Britannica*".[7] And Diderot's own article, "Encyclopedia", "summarized the aim of the editors as to 'inspire a taste for science ... and a love of virtue' "; on which MacIntyre comments: "These two aims were thought to harmonize".[8] We might, I think, at this dark century's ending, now wonder whether that

conviction did not constitute an important limitation of the project
Enlightenment.

Rules and Reasoning

Allan Janik said that "General rules fail to catch the most essential feature of
our actions, namely *how* they are performed".[9] That remark reminded me of
Martha Nussbaum's observation that "a good rule is a good summary of
wise particular choices".[10] Alongside that admirable piece of Aristotelean
sagacity, I would like to set a famous passage from a sermon of John Henry
Newman's, on "Explicit and Implicit Reason" which, being preached in
Oxford in 1840, comes almost midway between Diderot and Polanyi.

Reason, according to the simplest view of it, is the faculty of gaining knowledge without direct
perception, or of ascertaining one thing by means of another. In this way it is able, from small
beginnings, to create to itself a world of ideas, which do or do not correspond to the things
themselves for which they stand, or are true or not, according as it is exercised soundly or otherwise. One fact may suffice for a whole theory; one principle may create and sustain a system;
one minute token is a clue to a discovery. The mind ranges to and fro, and spreads out, and
advances forward with a quickness which has become a proverb, and a subtlety and versatility
which baffle investigation. It passes on from point to point, gaining one by some indication;
another on a probability; then availing itself of an association; then falling back on some
received law; next seizing on testimony; then committing itself to some popular impression, or
some inward instinct, or some obscure memory; and thus it makes progress not unlike a clam-
berer on a steep cliff, who, by quick eye, prompt hand, and firm foot, ascends how he knows
not himself, by personal endowments and by practice, rather than by rule, leaving no track
behind him, and unable to teach another. It is not too much to say that the stepping by which
great geniuses scale mountains of truth is as unsafe and precarious to men in general, as the
ascent of a skilful mountaineer up a literal crag. It is a way which they alone can take and its
justification lies in their success. And such mainly is the way in which all men, gifted or not
gifted, reason, – not by rule, but by an inward faculty. Reasoning, then, or the exercise of
Reason, is a living spontaneous energy within us, not an art. But when the mind reflects upon
itself, it begins to be dissatisfied with the absence of order and method in the exercise, and
attempts to analyze the various processes which take place during it, to refer one to another,
and to discover the main principles on which they are conducted.[11]

The Future of Dialogue

In conclusion, let me say just two things, apart from expressing my deep
personal gratitude for the invitation to participate in this conference, from
which I have learnt a great deal and which I have enjoyed enormously.
First, I would like to endorse Stephen Toulmin's hope that, if this group
really is dedicated to the primacy of practice, then we might meet next time
in some context other than that of a room which, even though it is a theatre,
has functioned operationally like an academic seminar. Secondly, if this is
truly the "Dialogue" Seminar, then our beloved and overworked organizers
should be encouraged to find some way of fostering, a little more effectively, more dialogue and less monologues like this one.

Notes

1 Christopher Bigsby, "Skill of the actor: an understanding of human beings and their behaviour:, [p. 11].

2 Bigsby, "Skill of the actor", [p. 3].

3 Bigsby, "Skill of the actor", [p. 5].

4 Allan Janik, *"Rameau's Nephew*. Dialogue as *Gesamtkunstwerk* for Enlightenment (with constant reference to Plato)", [p. 25].

5 Reprinted in P.N.Furbank, *Diderot. A Critical Biography* (London, 1992), p. 77.

6 Francis Bacon, *First Part of the Great Instauration. The Dignity and Advancement of Learning*, in Nine Books (first published, 1605), Book II, Chapter II. Quoted from Joseph Devey, *The Physical and Metaphysical Works of Lord Bacon* (London, 1864), p. 78.

7 Alasdair MacIntyre, *Three Rival Versions of Moral Enquiry: Encyclopedia, Genealogy and Tradition* (London, 1990), p. 174.

8 MacIntyre, loc. cit.

9 Janik, *"Rameau's Nephew"*, [p. 67].

10 Martha Nussbaum, "Non-Relative Virtues: An Aristotelian Approach", *Midwest Studies in Philosophy 13: Ethical Theory: Character and Virtue*, ed. P. French, T. Uehling, H. Wettstein (Notre Dame, 1988), p. 44.

11 John Henry Newman, *Sermons, Chiefly on the Theory of Religious Belief, Preached before the University of Oxford* (London, 1843), pp. 252-253.

Chapter 36

Themes and Possibilities
Bo Göranzon

Skill and Technology

1. Introduction

The study of professional knowledge is – even if Aristotle might be said to be its originator – a young field of research. This makes it a difficult and demanding area. Lacking an adequate epistemology of practical knowledge in general, one has to conduct the investigations at the empirical and conceptual levels simultaneously, as these aspects are internally related. On the empirical side, its core is the study of how professional knowledge is developed and maintained, not only at the level of the individual, but also in the working group and the community. Research in this field normally takes the form of case studies.

In recent years the main bulk of research has concentrated on documenting and analyzing the effect of information technology on various forms of professional knowledge. Difficulties connected with eliciting relevant knowledge for the design of workable computer systems have been examined – often in active interplay with other alleged conditions for successfully introducing computers into a working place. In case studies of this kind the researchers are confronted with a mixture of empirical and conceptual questions that can only be properly handled in an interdisciplinary way. The study of professional knowledge thus requires close cooperation between researchers who have made case studies their speciality and philosophers who have concentrated on the epistemology of practical knowledge.

2. Systems development and professional knowledge

The introduction of computer technology in working life contains an element of knowledge transfer. A personally stewarded and handed down professional skill is "translated" in the process of computerization into a set of rules capable of building up a system. When such "systems" began to be produced in Sweden on a more extensive scale in the 1970s, major difficulties soon emerged. The new technology that was to take over working duties, simplify routine procedures, and provide support for complicated judgments and decisions, tended to make people's work restricted, without context, and insusceptible to overview. These difficulties could be explained in different ways. By one way of thinking, the obstacles to computerization had to be studied as separate "problems", each of which would in due course be solved by the mutual adjustment of the users and the technology. By another radical way of thinking, the difficulties had to be viewed from the perspective of the theory of knowledge: the confrontation between the rules laid down by the systems and the practical reality.

3. The use of computers in practice

The research project entitled Skill and Technology acquired at an early stage its definitive basis in a succession of in-depth case studies in which the current influence of the new technology on Swedish working life was investigated from the perspective of the users. These studies were designed to provide a picture of the long-term effects of computerization on knowledge – a perspective that had been almost entirely absent in discussions of the new technology in working life.

A number of important case studies were subsequently performed. Photographer Peter Gullers investigated the manufacture of surgical instruments, showing how the instrument maker's skills as craftsmen were in direct opposition to automation, as regards the preservation and passing on of their knowledge. His study further showed that the results obtained by the surgeons were in direct dependence of the professional skills of the craftsmen, particularly when it came to the development of new instruments. Maja-Lisa Perby, engineer in Technical Physics, watched the meteorologists at Sturup Airport, and showed how their specifically meteorological knowledge – in the form of a composite "inner weather picture" – failed to harmonize with the volume of new aids to information. Ingela Josefson, language researcher at the Swedish Institute for Worklife Research, has worked with studies of the knowledge characteristically acquired by nurses, with a view to finding possible relationships to the current rationalization and "scientification" of Swedish medical care.

In the case study of the computerization of the work of forest rangers it is noted that the ability to calculate and the ability to make judgements are two sides of the same coin. Calculation and judgement make a single whole. Computerization severed the link between calculation and judgement. No clear line can be drawn between purely routine and more advanced operations. This case study provided insight into the relationship between well-founded experience and calculation – the mathematical model; an insight which Denis Diderot expressed as follows. "It is a question of calculation on the one hand, and of experience on the other. If the one is well-founded, then it must agree with the other."

4. Masters and apprentices

Taken in aggregate, these case studies provide a whole succession of examples from widely differing fields of how the introduction of new technology in fact relates to the sort of knowledge and skills that are anchored in the activity itself. One factor that attracted particular attention in these studies was the long-term effect of the technical changes. When the man-borne knowledge is transferred to computer programs, difficulties can easily arise with the tradition, or passing on, of knowledge, since this is often achieved by the force of personal example: the novice watches, and follows the practice of the expert.

To use a terminology dating back to the old crafts, a master/apprentice relationship is central to the transference of knowledge in the occupations studied. When one fails, in introducing new technology, to ensure that this relationship between the young beginners and their older, more experienced colleagues is maintained, there are clear risks of a loss of knowledge that will lead to insecurity of judgement and an incapacity to see the general picture. These effects do not appear immediately, only after several years, by which time the lost process of tradition will be difficult to restore.

5. The epistemological perspective

The studies undertaken so far have brought to light a lack of understanding on the part of both management and researchers with regard to the role of experience in practical knowledge. The need for clarification and epistemological guidelines is making itself felt as the complexity of the tasks for research are steadily increasing. To stick to traditional models for concept formation and knowledge production lands both researchers and management in a blind alley. Such models are only appropriate for handling propositional knowledge. The Scandinavian approach presented here has tried to cope with this problem by anchoring its research activities in an epistemological perspective developed by the Bergen philosopher Kjell S. Johannessen on the basis of Ludwig Wittgenstein's later philosophy. Johannessen has elaborated on Wittgenstein's analysis of rule-following behaviour by making the concept of practice the focal point of interest in epistemology. This has enabled him to show that the establishment and maintenance of propositional knowledge is internally related to various sorts of tacit knowledge. Two aspects of this tacit dimension of acquiring and applying knowledge have been highlighted in particular – knowledge expressed in complex forms of skilled behaviour and knowledge expressed in behaviour requiring familiarity with the phenomena in question. This is known for short as "the practice interpretation" of Wittgenstein's later philosophy and it has been widely accepted by philosophers and researchers.

Allan Janik, the renowned Wittgenstein researcher, presently at the Brenner Archive in Innsbruck and Tore Nordenstam, well known for his contribution to aesthetics and moral philosophy, presently at the University of Bergen, have both elaborated on this practice perspective in ways that are highly relevant to the study of professional knowledge. Janik has not only expanded on the very idea of tacit knowledge in general, he has also made use of it in various specific studies, for instance when investigating the dynamics of creative milieus and exploring the epistemology of aesthetic knowledge. Nordenstam has made creative use of the practice perspective when studying foundational problems in the history or art, when succinctly criticizing members of the Frankfurt School in Philosophy, and when writing on the history of the humanities. All of these investigations contain points that are relevant to the study of professional knowledge since they pertain to applying concepts and exhibiting a reflective grasp of various sides of social reality.

Stephen Toulmin has been writing on epistemology and method since the late 1940s. At first – e.g. in his first book *Reason in Ethics* (1949) – he faced a widely-accepted contrast between Facts and Values, Science and Ethics. In the subsequent 40 years he has done much to bridge this division of Science from Art – e.g. biochemistry from clinical medicine – in historical as well as intellectual terms. Now in the 1990s, indeed, he would argue that the building and application of Theory are themselves particular modes or varieties of Practice and so need to be studied in pragmatic terms as much as in logical ones. In recent years as a result he has been specially interested in reviving the older traditions of practical philosophy, deriving from, for example, Aristotle's analysis of the difference between *episteme* (conceptual grasp) and *phronesis* (professional practice).

6. Case studies and training

It is important to emphasize that work on the case studies has not related solely to working life. It is, of course, natural that there should be feedback to the activities in which the case studies were performed. But these studies have also been of outstanding pedagogical importance in the context of training. In the continuous and intensive activity with courses and seminars for the universities and other institutes for higher education, this bank of practical case studies has provided concrete examples of relationships and contacts between work and the new technology.

This approach has been extremely rewarding, particularly in the long term, when the students themselves have entered their respective occupations and started acquiring their own experience.

7. Public discussion, international work

The project has always uttered itself in courses, seminars, exhibitions and publications of different kinds, and this striving towards a public discussion has become steadily more evident in recent years, with the setting up of the Dialogue Seminar (in collaboration with the Royal Dramatic Theatre and The Royal Institute of Technology) and the allied periodical *Dialoger*, which has rapidly attracted attention as an important cultural vehicle in Sweden.

At the same time, a process of internationalization has taken place. Above all during the past few years, a network of working relationships has been built up with research workers in Europe, the USA and Japan. A work by Bo Göranzon entitled *The Practical Intellect. Computers and Skill*, at the request of

UNESCO was published in 1992.

Such internationalization was marked, in complete and organized form, in the project "AI-based Systems and the Future of Language, Knowledge and Responsibility", financed by the European Commission through its research program COST-13. This was initiated by the Swedish Institute for Worklife Research and carried out together with a large number of European research workers and institutions.

The internationalization process was more broadly manifested with the conference "Culture, Language and Artificial Intelligence" held in June 1988, which attracted several hundred researchers from some fifteen countries to an auditorium of the Royal Dramatic Theatre, Stockholm. Technologists, system engineers and other practitioners of AI encountered philosophers, literary scholars and theatre people in lectures, panels, and working groups. The conference raised questions concerning creative environments, tacit knowledge, the value of work, human versus mechanical language, perception and experience, the concept of dialogue, rational language etc., and it was permeated by the perspectives of epistemology, technology and the history of ideas. The conference was also distinguished by its aesthetic approach. The artistic program, with the participating actors and musicians, made an essential contribution to the emphasis placed by the conference on the dimensions of human life that stand outside the mechanics of computer systems.

The conference is documented in four comprehensive books, each of which collects a highly qualified selection of original articles, written by a large number of the foremost delegates: *Knowledge, Skill and Artificial Intelligence* with contributions by Mike Cooley, Richard Ennals, Allan Janik, Ingela Josefson, Peter Gullers and others; *Artificial Intelligence, Culture and Language: On Education and Work*, with contributions by John R. Searle, Hubert Dreyfus, Kjell S Johannessen, Dag Prawitz, Yuiji Masuda and others; *Dialogue and Technology: Art and Knowledge*, with contributions by, among others, Stephen Toulmin, Agneta Pleijel, Iurii Lotman, Lars Gyllensten, Erland Josephson; *Skill and Education: Reflection and Experience*, including contributions by Herbert Josephs, Lars Kleberg, Michael Robinson and Jon Cook.

8. Diderot and dialogue

Work after this international manifestation has continued in the same many-faceted way as before. The Dialogue Seminar has been developed in form and content, as has the quarterly journal: the themes include Translation, Mathematics and Culture; Technology and our Senses, the Art of Memory; Beyond All Certainty: a dramatization of the meeting between Turing and Wittgenstein – their destinies and their views of knowledge; Acting Skill and Analogies.

The Diderot Project, which was started after the 1988 Stockholm Conference, provided an international forum for discussions on the themes of enlightenment, skill and education. The epistemology of work lies at the centre of this project. The aim is to raise the highly unorthodox question, 'what is it that professionals with skills in fact know?' The Diderot Project led to another international symposium in Stockholm in the autumn of 1993. The theme was: *Skill and Technology: On Diderot, Education and The Third Culture.*

9. The contours of a new research field

The aim of the six books published by Springer in 1988–1994 is to present the contours of this new research field on skill and technology, together with a multitude of issues that demand thorough explanation. A fruitful distinction in the research process is that between exploration and surveying. These six books are written more in the spirit of exploration than of surveying. It offers the reader, in the spirit of dialogue, more questions and reflections than answers. If what it indicates is true, then much more exploration will need to be done. The new discipline it implies will take some time to emerge.

It is an unavoidable fact that far more knowledge of the practical intellect is needed – and what is more, respect is needed too, because there is more to professional knowledge than one, as an outsider, is capable of understanding.

The need to strengthen the competence of research is a background to the establishing of the research program "Skill and Technology", at the Royal Institute of Technology and The Swedish Institute for Worklife Research, with the support of the Swedish Working Environment Fund.

Seven Categories Exploring the Research Field of Skill and Technology

The following are the categories of the contours of the explorative studies published in the five books within the research field Skill and Technology.

I.   The Automatization/Computerization of a Work Process:
     Case Studies of the Long-term Effects on Professional Skills.
II. Case Studies on Professional Skills and Education.
III. Studies on Intransitive Understanding, Rule Following and Tacit Knowledge in Relation to Case Studies on Professional Skills (I+II).
IV. Studies on The Third Culture: Literature and Science.
V.   Studies on Designing New Technology: Skill and Artificial Intelligence.
VI. Studies on Philosophy of Mind.
VII. Studies on Skill, Education and The Information Society.

Key

KS & AI   Knowledge, Skill and Artificial Intelligence
AIC & L   Artificial Intelligence, Culture and Language: On Education and
           Work
D & T   Dialogue and Technology: Art and Knowledge
S & E   Skill and Education: Reflection and Experience
PI   The Practical Intellect: Computers and Skill
ST & E   Skill, Technology and Enlightenment: on Practical Philosophy

I. The Automation/Computerization of a Work Process: Case Studies of the Long-term Effects on Professional Skills

Forest Valuation
Göranzon, Bo (KS & AI, PI)

Case Handling in the Public Sector: Social Insurance
Göranzon, Bo (KS & AI, PI)
Karlsen, T.K. & Oppen, Maria (KS & AI)
Schartum, Dag (KS & AI)

Local Weather Forecasting
Perby, Maja Lisa (KS & AI, AIC & L)

The Dream of the Automated Factory
Gullers, Peter (KS & AI)

Photography as a Historical Example
Gullers, Peter (AIC & L)

Craftsmanship
Tempte, Thomas (D & T, ST & E)

II. Case Studies on Professional Skills and Education

Nursing
Josefson, Ingela (KS & AI, AIC & L, ST & E)

Engineering
Brödner, Peter (ST & E)
Cross, Michael (KS & AI)
Ennals, Richard (ST & E)
Monk, Jon (ST & E)
Rosenbrock, Howard H (AIC & L)
Startin, Kate (ST & E)

Leadership
Danielsson, Albert (S & E)
Janik, Allan (S & E)

Acting
Bigsby, Christopher (ST & E)
Göranzon, Bo (ST & E)
Josephson, Erland (D & T, ST & E)
Robinbson, Michael (ST & E)

Performing art: Music
Sinding-Larsen, Henrik (D & T)

Performing art: Creative writing
Robinson, Michael (S & E)

Translating
Basnett, Susan (D & T)
Kleberg, Lars (S & E, ST & E)
Zilliacus, Clas (D & T)

III. Studies on Intransitive Understanding, Rule Following and Tacit Knowledge in Relation to Case Studies on Professional Skills (I + II)

Bergendal, Gunnar (AIC & L)
Florin, Magnus (D & T, S & E)
Hobson, Marian (ST & E)
Hughes, Rolf (ST & E)
Janik, Allan (1988, AIC & L, S & E)
Johannessen, Kjell (AIC & L, S & E)
Molander, Bengt (AIC & L, S & E)
Nordenstam, Tore (AIC & L)

IV. Studies on The Third Culture: Literature and Science

Bing, Jon (S & E)
Cook, Jon (S & E)
Davies, Richard (ST & E)
Engdahl, Horace (D & T)
Florin, Magnus (D & T)
Florin, Magnus & Göranzon, Bo & Sällström, Pehr (D & T)
Göranzon, Bo (D & T, S & E, ST & E)
Hilton, Julian (D & T)
Hyde, Jon (ST & E)
Janik, Allan (D & T, S & E, ST & E)
Josephs, Herbert (D & T, S & E)

Karlqvist, Anders (ST & E)
Kleberg, Lars (D & T, S & E)
Lotman, Jurij (D & T)
Molander, Bengt (AIC & L)
Monk, Jon (ST & E)
Pleijel, Agneta (D & T)
Printz-Påhlson, Göran (ST & E)
Sällström, Pehr (D & T)
Shaffer, Elinor(ST & E)
Toulmin, Stephen (S & E, ST & E)

V. Case Studies on Designing New Technology: Skill and Artificial Intelligence

Bolton, Malcolm (S & E)
Cannataci, Joseph A (S & E)
Cooley, Mike (KS & AI)
Ennals, Richard (KS & AI, AIC & L, S & E)
Gill, Karajmit S (KS & AI, AIC & L)
Hart, Anna (KS & AI)
Hilton, Julian (KS & AI, AIC & L)
Jameson, Gordon (AIC & L)
Nitsch, Ulrich (AIC & L)
Östberg, Gustaf (AIC & L)
Östberg, Olof (KS & AI)
Pritchard, Peter (KS & AI)
Sharples, Mike (S & E)
Whitaker, Randall & Östberg, Olov (S & E)

VI. Studies on Philosophy of Mind

Dreyfus, Hubert L (AIC & L)
Florin, Magnus (ST & E)
Gustafsson, Lars (ST & E)
Gyllensten, Lars (D & T)
Henry, Paul (ST & E)
Hertzberg, Lars (AIC & L)
Hobson, Marian (ST & E)
Janik, Allan (ST & E)
Karlqvist, Anders (ST & E)
Lash, Nicholas (ST & E)
Lerda, Franceso (S & E)
Naletov, Igor (ST & E)
Prawitz, Dag (AIC & L, ST & E)
Sällström, Pehr (D & T)
Searle, John R (AIC & L)
Tilghmann, Ben (AIC & L)

Toulmin, Stephen (ST & E)
Valach, Fedor (ST & E)
von Wright, Georg Henrik (ST & E)

VII. Studies on Skill, Education and The Information Society

Brödner, Peter (ST & E)
Cook, Jon (S & E, ST & E)
Cooley, Mike (AIC & L)
Danielsson, Albert (ST & E)
Deutsch, Steven (AIC & L)
Engdahl, Horace (AIC & L)
Ennals, Richard (S & E, ST & E)
Ford, Bill (AIC & L)
Gill, Karajmit S (KS & AI, AI & L)
Hilton, Julian (KS & AI, AIC & L, D & T)
Janik, Allan (D & T)
Masuda, Yuji (AIC & L)
Östberg, Olov (KS & AI)
Smith, David (S & E)
Sörbom, Pehr (S & E)
Stieg, Gerald (AIC & L)
Toulmin, Stephen (D & T)
Unenge, Jan (ST & E)

Articles Published in a Series of Six Volumes by Springer-Verlag

Numbers in brackets denote Categories I–VII

Basnett, Susan
D & T   The Translator's Knowledge (II)

Bergendal, Gunnar
AIC & L   Professional Skill and Traditions of Knowledge (III)

Bigsby, Christopher
ST & E   The Actor as Paradigm? (II)

Bing, Jon
S & E   The Image of the Intelligent Machine in Science Fiction (IV)

Bolton, Malcolm
S & E   The Introduction of Information Technology into the Workplace –
           Some Practical Considerations (V)

Name Index